Innovations in
Collaborative Modeling

Innovations in
Collaborative Modeling

Edited by Laura Schmitt Olabisi, Miles McNall,
William Porter, and Jinhua Zhao

Michigan State University Press | East Lansing

♾ The paper used in this publication meets the minimum requirements
of ANSI/NISO Z39.48-1992 (R 1997) (Permanence of Paper).

Michigan State University Press
East Lansing, Michigan 48823-5245

Library of Congress Cataloging-in-Publication Data
Names: Schmitt Olabisi, Laura, 1978– editor.
Title: Innovations in collaborative modeling / edited by Laura Schmitt
Olabisi, Miles McNall, William Porter, and Jinhua Zhao.
Description: East Lansing : Michigan State University Press, [2020] |
Series: Transformations in higher education : the scholarship of
engagement | Includes bibliographical references and index.
Identifiers: LCCN 2019028385 | ISBN 9781611863543 (paperback)
| ISBN 9781609176297 | ISBN 9781628953916 | ISBN 9781628963922
Subjects: LCSH: Environmental sciences—Methodology.
Classification: LCC GE40 .I56 2020 | DDC 304.201/1—dc23
LC record available at https://lccn.loc.gov/2019028385

Book design by Charlie Sharp, Sharp Designs, East Lansing, MI
Cover design by Shaun Allshouse, www.shaunallshouse.com
Cover art by Kelly Hansen

Michigan State University Press is a member of the Green Press Initiative and
is committed to developing and encouraging ecologically responsible publishing
practices. For more information about the Green Press Initiative and the use of
recycled paper in book publishing, please visit *www.greenpressinitiative.org*.

Visit Michigan State University Press at *www.msupress.org*

Transformations in Higher Education: Scholarship of Engagement

The Transformations in Higher Education: Scholarship of Engagement book series is designed to provide a forum where scholars can address the diverse issues provoked by community-campus partnerships that are directed toward creating innovative solutions to societal problems. Numerous social critics and key national commissions have drawn attention to the pervasive and burgeoning problems of individuals, families, communities, economies, health services, and education in American society. Such issues as child and youth development, economic competitiveness, environmental quality, and health and health care require creative research and the design, deployment, and evaluation of innovative public policies and intervention programs. Similar problems and initiatives have been articulated in many other countries, apart from the devastating consequences of poverty that burdens economic and social change. As a consequence, there has been increasing societal pressure on universities to partner with communities to design and deliver knowledge applications that address these issues, and to co-create novel approaches to effect system changes that can lead to sustainable and evidence-based solutions. Knowledge generation and knowledge application are critical parts of the engagement process, but so too are knowledge dissemination and preservation. The Transformations in Higher Education: Scholarship of Engagement series was designed to meet one aspect of the dissemination/preservation dyad.

This series is sponsored by the National Collaborative for the Study of University Engagement (NCSUE) and is published in partnership with the Michigan State University Press. An external board of editors supports the NCSUE editorial staff in order to insure that all volumes in the series are peer reviewed throughout the publication process. Manuscripts embracing campus-community partnerships are invited from authors regardless of discipline, geographic place, or type of transformational change accomplished. Similarly, the series embraces all methodological approaches from rigorous randomized trials to narrative and ethnographic studies. Analyses may span the qualitative to quantitative continuum, with particular emphasis on mixed-model approaches. However, all manuscripts must attend to detailing critical aspects of partnership development, community involvement, and evidence of program changes or impacts. Monographs and books provide ample space for authors to address all facets of engaged scholarship thereby building a compendium of praxis that will facilitate replication and generalization, two of the cornerstones of evidence-based programs, practices, and policies. We invite you to submit your work for publication review and to fully participate in our effort to assist higher education to renew its covenant with society through engaged scholarship.

HIRAM E. FITZGERALD
BURTON BARGERSTOCK
LAURIE VAN EGEREN

Contents

Part 1. Methods for Collaborative Modeling

Part 2. Applications in Collaborative Modeling

Foreword

Marjan van den Belt

The editors of this volume asked me to write the foreword for this book, like Thomas Dietz had done for my book on *Mediated Modeling: A System Dynamics Approach to Environmental Consensus Building* (2004). As I reread his foreword, I realize that the basic premise of the significance of collaborative modeling remains the same after fifteen years: science and democratic discourse have to co-evolve. This involves taking people from different walks of life along the path with us. In addition, across the various disciplines, we cannot expect everybody to understand the workings of each complex system at the same level of detail as disciplinary scientists do. Yet we have to find ways to bring data and knowledge together. Collaborative modeling and the bringing together of disciplinary detail and systemic integration across science, policy, and practice are essential. This process has the scope to strengthen the democratic discourse by combining stakeholder expertise with science expertise.

There are different roles in creating the outcomes that we collectively want. This requires collaboration and transdisciplinarity, two characteristics intrinsic to "collaborative modeling." While my personal emphasis has largely been on "environmental consensus building," the applications of collaborative model building, in principle, know no bounds. In fact, collaborative model building is a tool to explore boundaries of data and knowledge as well as provide the courage to lead systemic changes. As such, collaborative modeling is a mindset of *and* rather than *or*. It encourages the application of logic and wisdom to navigation of the paradoxes that invariably reveal themselves during a collaborative modeling process. While we may not always be in a position to determine risk or control uncertainty, we can recognize uncertainty and develop more resilience and resilient systems to absorb uncertainty.

Dietz's premise remains. However, the urgency—especially from a social-ecological sustainability lens—is increasing exponentially. As with any reinforcing feedback loop and exponential function, time is not on our side. As every system dynamicist knows, not only the feedback mechanisms but misjudgment of time lags often cause blind spots and unintended consequences. As of August 2019, the world had been put on high alert by the Intergovernmental Panel for

Climate Change as well as by the Intergovernmental Platform for Biodiversity and Ecosystem Services that we are in a climate and ecological crisis. We are watching in horror as wildfires rage in places that are not supposed to burn, such as the Amazon rainforest and Arctic areas. Has the tipping point been reached? From a system dynamics perspective, the writings of this impending acceleration have been on the wall for decades.

We live in a complex, highly interconnected and "full" world. These are easy words to rattle off, so let's unpack them a bit. A full world is one abundant in human artefacts, in which the human subsystem encroaches on the self-sustaining capacity of the natural system. Today's world is also interconnected, enabling the spread, for example, of information or disease across the globe in short timeframes. What we do at a local level can have global impacts; in turn, changing global systems, such as the climate, has impacts locally.

It is therefore imperative that we learn to deal with "complexity," which on its face means the many parts that interact with each other in multiple ways. But this is so complex, that there is no widely accepted definition for "complexity," although "complexity scientists" seem to unite under the study of the phenomena which emerge from a collection of interacting objects, thereby emphasizing linkages. Each individual or "stakeholder group" has their own interpretation of phenomena.

This book is absolutely critical and a source of hope. In many different realms, scientists and practitioners are getting better at looking beyond events and patterns to recognize the underlying structures that generate them. We are getting better at "putting the pieces together" and dealing with often-divergent worldviews. How we use technology and upgrade our institutions to deal with complex challenge requires bringing the public and institutional decision-makers with us. To quote E. O. Wilson, "The real problem of humanity is the following: we have paleolithic *emotions*; medieval *institutions*; and god-like *technology*. And it is terrifically dangerous, and it is now approaching a point of crisis overall."[1]

More than ever, is it important to develop transdisciplinary skills and the tools to curb a systemic breakdown across the ecological, social, and economic spectra. It is critical that we use model building to design systems we want within the carrying capacity of the life-sustaining ecosystems on which we depend.

Models are often used as a weapon: "my model against yours." Academic careers rest on this, which makes academia part of the problem as well as the solution. Often models are built to foregone conclusions or are limited to available data. This reinforces a narrow perspective. What if the available data are not available and we have to make decisions in the absence of data? Then it comes down to co-creating a vision and using available data on par with the knowledge of people. It comes down to how they collaborate to forge new pathways.

Sometimes, we know the truth because it really is a matter of (un)common sense, but there is a lack of political will to make the desirable changes. Collaborative modeling can help but, just like a surgeon chooses his or her tools carefully, a modeler has to know what modeling tool from the toolbox to use and when. It is a privilege to be an academic and have the opportunity to apply logic and the deep thought of analysis. It is also a duty of an academic to package insights in a way that has impact: interdisciplinary as well as transdisciplinary co-creation, synthesis beyond analysis. Our academic institutions, where arguably a host of ideas and skills are developed, need to reflect this and provide a breeding ground for inclusive leadership.

Looking back at my own *Mediated Modeling* work at scoping level, it is clear that many of the challenges that stakeholders agreed on either happened as anticipated (in Coastal Zone Management in Patagonia), persist as a structural problem (development taking place in a highly erodible areas in Ria Formosa), or became part of an emerging discourse (ecosystems services in Wisconsin). Various aha moments that occurred during the model building process led to solutions that were instantly implemented, for example in the cases of participatory electric planning for Vermont, where renewable energy credits were considered for generating more renewables. Looking for systemic improvements for the Tauranga Harbour in New Zealand led to the informal discovery that certain data collection could be coordinated across local governments, saving taxpayers money instantly. These follow-ups happen because an aha moment unlocks common sense of a solution as it occurred in a critical, influential group. More often than not, a collaborative modeling process signals and seeds a change. It may be difficult to establish the exact impact of collaborative modeling, but those who do engage with this family of tools know change does occur (e.g., Intergovernmental Platform on Biodiversity and Ecosystem services, Deliverable 3c on Modeling and Scenarios).

In conclusion, do not underestimate the power of the process of bringing people together. The potential for better decision support tools in the collaborative modeling family is unprecedented and crucial in evolving toward a world we want to live in and can survive in.

NOTE

1. Emphasis added. E. O. Wilson, quoted in "An Intellectual Entente," *Harvard Magazine*, September 10, 2009, https://harvardmagazine.com/breaking-news/james-watson-edward-o-wilson-intellectual-entente.

Preface

Collaborative applications of a variety of modeling methodologies have multiplied in recent decades, due to widespread recognition of the power of models to integrate information from multiple sources, test assumptions about policy and management choices, and forecast the future states of complex systems. However, information about these modeling efforts is often segregated by both discipline and modeling approach, preventing modelers from learning from one another across these divides. For example, researchers working on modeling food security in Detroit may not come across articles on modeling the dynamics of depression or substance abuse, although they might find insights from these studies useful. Similarly, system dynamics modelers may not appreciate the advances in modeling theory and practice achieved by agent-based modelers, social network modelers, or process-based modelers. This volume is an attempt to fill the need for cross-disciplinary and cross-methodological communication around collaborative modeling. It arose out of the first conference of the same name, "Innovations in Collaborative Modeling," held at Michigan State University in June 2015. Feedback from the conference attendees was almost uniformly positive, indicating the unique function of this gathering of academics and stakeholders for sharing insights from modeling work taking place in complex systems.

By the term "collaborative modeling," we mean modeling approaches that help modelers communicate with stakeholders and scientists communicate with one another. We argue that the tools needed to achieve communication across these different groups for enhanced understanding of systems problems are similar. Scientists from different disciplinary backgrounds working on a common project must learn to integrate information from their respective fields, deal with issues of scale and focus, and rigorously investigate assumptions in much the same way that scientists and stakeholders who are working together must do. The differences in terminology and communication styles between scientific disciplines can be just as great as the gaps between scientists and stakeholders! One further definition is needed to set the context for this volume: by "stakeholder," we mean any person who is not a modeler, but who has an important insight into, or interest in, a problem being investigated by modelers. We resist the common stakeholder–expert dichotomy because we argue that stakeholders *are* experts in their experience of the problem space.

Chapters in the first part of this volume explore modeling methodologies for enhanced collaboration, while chapters in the second part contain case studies of collaborative modeling across different complex systems problems. We intend this volume to be useful for experienced and beginner modelers, as well as scientists and stakeholders who work with modelers. In order to tackle the challenges of the twenty-first century, all of us will have to be more innovative and collaborative.

In "Principles of Participatory Ensemble Modeling to Study Complex Socioecological Systems," Arika Ligmann-Zielinska et al. discuss the merits of developing a single, integrated model to capture contemporary socioecological systems. While recognizing the computational challenges and confounding of uncertainties in such models, they argue that a more integrated approach can yield greater synthetic insights. This chapter discusses three guiding principles to such an integrated approach. First is model legitimacy, which addresses the need to include the perspectives of all stakeholders. Second is parsimony, which seeks to maintain simplicity of models that, because of their intention of capturing overlapping ideas, readily can become more complex than necessary. Third is practicality, which reflects a need to cope with significant uncertainty inherent to socioecological models.

In "Nova: A Novel Tool for Collaborative Agent-Based and Dynamic Systems Modeling," Nancy Darling et al. introduces open-access Nova software, a new tool for collaborative modeling that incorporates agent-based, system dynamics, and spatial modeling platforms. The software is written in an extension of JavaScript and is capable of integrating with other modeling and graphical programs. The authors demonstrate how Nova may be used in teaching and scientific collaboration through a case study example modeling student behavior. This chapter contributes to an ongoing discussion around how to best design tools that combine the power of quantitative simulation modeling with an accessible platform for modeling collaborations. Nova has already been used in multiple environmental science and epidemiology projects.

"Typologies and Trade-offs in FCM Studies: A Guide to Designing Participatory Research Using Fuzzy Cognitive Maps" is one of two chapters in this volume to discuss a relative newcomer to participatory modeling techniques—fuzzy cognitive mapping (FCM). In this chapter Alexander Metzger et al. review the literature on participatory FCM using the "four Ps" framework: purpose (why was the participatory modeling approach selected?), partnership (who participated and why?), process (how were stakeholders involved?), and product (what was produced?). Using this framework, Metzger and Gray identify trends in the use of participatory FCM and emerging norms and standards of practice. Their review also reveals the tradeoffs involved in selecting different participatory FCM approaches. The chapter culminates in a rich typology of participatory FCM approaches and their limitations, providing researchers and their collaborators with a convenient guide for making informed choices about the methods best-suited to their purposes.

In "Designing and Deploying Collaborative Models for Multifunctional Landscape Design: Geodesign in Practice," Bryan C. Runck et al. describe an innovative process of collaborative geodesign which took place in Southern Minnesota around multifunctional landscape design for biomass production. Stakeholders were involved in defining the goals and objectives of the design process, as well as the user interface features. The authors find that this codesign approach allowed for an iterative process that was successful in enabling diverse stakeholder groups to improve landscape multifunctionality. This chapter demonstrates that participatory computational modelers may have much to learn from planners, who have been successfully using collaborative design tools with communities for many years.

In "Collaborative Modeling Institute: A Conception, Paradigm and Protocol for Transdisciplinary Integrative Team Science" Stuart J. Whipple and Bernard C. Patten explore team-centered modeling within the framework of multigenerational investment in efforts to understand complex systems. The authors observe that gaining insight into complicated ecological processes can be limited in the absence of collaborative teams of diverse expertise. They extend this idea by addressing a second limitation, the traditional research approaches built on three- to five-year efforts. They propose building models with a specific intent to transcend generations of scientists through support of larger research institutes. The synergistic pairing of collaborative teams with long-term, iterative evolution of complex models offers an avenue to capturing ecosystem processes and gaining insight. The paper explores potential organizational structure of the modeling environment, dealing with needs for scientific credit and creating sufficient trust within teams to enable growth of new ideas.

In "Using Participatory System Dynamics Modeling of Agricultural-Environmental Systems in a Developing Country Context," Robert B. Richardson et al. examine the role of broad input by stakeholders in modeling the dynamics of managing for agriculture and forestry on a landscape scale in the developing world. The intent is to explore these dynamics on large landscape scales to better understand progressive deforestation and intensification of agriculture and the opportunity to create sustainable agricultural economies. Models depict the complicated nature of forest harvest to support energy needs of growing society through production of charcoal and loss of forest land to agriculture. Model simulations suggest that impacts of charcoal production are likely to diminish with advancing electrification, but that population growth will demand clearing forests for agriculture and will drive landscape change over the next fifty years.

French development agency CIRAD has been using collaborative modeling techniques (sometimes called "companion modeling") for decades to integrate stakeholder knowledge into the development process and foster social learning. A particularly innovative approach for which CIRAD is known internationally is its use of role-playing games either on their own as a data collection and social learning tool or to inform agent-based modeling efforts. In "Co-Designing a Role-Playing Game to Characterize and Parametrize an Agent-Based Model on Coexistence of Farming Activities and Wildlife Conservation in the Periphery of the Sikumi Forest, Zimbabwe" Arthur Perrotton et al. discuss the application of such a collaboratively constructed role-playing game to study the impacts of cattle herding practices on a protected area in Zimbabwe. The modelers describe their practice of living in the study area and entering into the "shoes" of the farmers and cattle herders by playing the game through their perspective. This chapter shines a light on how relationship-building between modelers and stakeholders supports and sustains collaborative research efforts.

"Participatory Complex Systems Modeling for Environmental Planning: Opportunities and

Barriers to Learning and Policy Innovation" by Moira Zellner et al. considers deeply the issue of how participatory modeling supports learning and innovation among diverse stakeholders in land and water-use planning. Describing their successes and challenges through the iterative development and refinement of a planning support system consisting of agent-based simulation models with user-friendly graphical interfaces, Zellner and colleagues show how their team progressively improved its ability to support stakeholders in challenging false assumptions, abandoning familiar strategies, embracing innovation, recognizing the competing value stances of other stakeholders, and adopting workable solutions.

In "Developing a Collaborative System Dynamics Model of College Drinking Events: Finding a Common Language," John D. Clapp et al. offer a captivating case study of how teams from disciplines that seldom interact can work together to achieve a deeper understanding of dynamic systems through collaborative modeling. Clapp and colleagues describe in detail how a team of social scientists and engineers worked together over three years to develop a dynamic model of alcohol drinking events using system dynamics modeling, with the social scientists contributing their deep expertise in alcohol research and the engineers contributing their proficiency in modeling dynamic feedback systems.

In "Using Systems Thinking to Promote Wellness Program Planning and Implementation in Urban High Schools," David W. Lounsbury et al. describe the use of systems thinking and causal loop diagrams to promote collaborative wellness programming in high school settings. They demonstrate how the use of systems thinking and the Theory of Triadic Influence helped stakeholders shift their mental models of adolescent obesity from individual-level risk factors and outcomes to complex systems of interrelated factors operating at three levels: intrapersonal, interpersonal, and sociocultural. Using a theory-driven causal loop diagram, Lounsbury and his team helped collaborators explore feedback processes, deepen their understanding of complex patterns of relationships within and across levels, and develop a comprehensive set of intervention components. In addition, Lounsbury and colleagues describe the evaluation plan they developed to assess change at each level, as well as preliminary evaluation findings that indicate that skills-based training was not only well-received by students, but effective.

"Participatory Modeling with Fuzzy Cognitive Maps: Studying Veterans' Perspectives on Access and Participation in Higher Education" is the second chapter to discuss FCM, this time as a compelling case study of how FCM was used to capture the individual mental models of access to and participation in higher education among sixty-nine post-9/11 military veterans suffering from disabilities and traumatic stress. These individual mental models were integrated into a single model of veterans' participation, learning, persistence and success in STEM (science, technology, engineering, and math) education to simulate the possible outcomes of different educational programs on veterans' success in STEM education. As this case study demonstrates, such simulation models can provide valuable insights to leaders of institutions of higher education and policy makers regarding how best to support the transition of military veterans to successful careers as civilians.

Acknowledgments

We gratefully acknowledge the generosity of the following individuals for offering their time and efforts to review chapter drafts:

Andrew Bradley	Ifigeneia Koutiva	Jose L. Salmeron
Deirdra Chester	Florian Labhart	Anthony Starfield
Emily Gates	David Lounsbury	Linda Thurston
Wayne M. Getz	Nicole Mason	Tabitha Underwood
Rebecca Jordan	William McConnell	Alexey Voinov
Birgit Kopainsky	Timothy Nyerges	Bob Williams
	Deborah E. Polk	

PART 1

Methods for
Collaborative Modeling

Principles of Participatory Ensemble Modeling to Study Complex Socioecological Systems

Arika Ligmann-Zielinska, Eric Jing Du, Louie Rivers III, Saweda Liverpool-Tasie, Riva C. H. Denny, Alexa L. Wood, Udita Sanga, Sandy Marquart-Pyatt, Victoria Breeze, Rajiv Paudel, and Laura Schmitt Olabisi

1. What Are Complex Socioecological Systems, and Why Can't Single Models Cope with Them?

In today's crowded world, where human activity permeates every aspect of the environment, conventional equilibrium approaches to managing human, economic, and natural resources are prone to failure (van den Belt, 2004) because they do not capture the dynamic interactions between humans and the constantly changing environment. Multiple disciplines have their unique perspectives on emulating Socioecological Systems (SES). SES models simulate the patterns and processes that link human and natural systems (Liu et al., 2007) and focus on modeling the flow of matter, energy, and information between social systems and ecosystems.

Understanding the complexity of interactions within SES does not come naturally to humans, who tend to think in a linear manner characterized by univariate and unidirectional causality and lack of feedback loops (Shoham, 1990; van den Belt, 2004; Weiner, 1985). By employing modeling, people can exchange their individual perceptions and expertise, synthesize knowledge from different disciplines, and ultimately achieve a certain level of consensus (McIntosh et al., 2007; Schmitt Olabisi et al., 2013; van den Belt, 2004). For modeling to be successful in addressing complex issues and providing proposals for improvement, multiple stakeholders should be involved in conceptualizing, developing, validating, and applying the models. This is the major purpose of participatory modeling. We argue that the success of participatory modeling requires a comprehensive representation of all relevant perspectives, which are clearly and concisely formalized and which are implemented in a manner that encourages reasoning about future scenarios under a wide range of assumptions and hypotheses.

To gain insight into natural and social systems, scientists and policymakers have used models developed by single disciplines. Such models focus on either natural or social systems, with the other component ("social" in natural systems models and "natural" in social systems models) represented by exogenous variables. For example, groundwater models may include farmer decision making on irrigation simply by introducing a numerical variable manipulated to simulate water withdrawals. Actions of all farmers are lumped into one aggregate variable as if irrigation was a top-down homogenous decision. Consequently, we lose the opportunity to represent diffusion of innovations like precision irrigation. On the opposite side, to forecast long-term energy consumption in a big country like Russia, econometric models may include climatic variability using only one aggregate scalar. This all-in-one variable does not include the complex, spatially heterogeneous interdependencies among temperature, cloud cover, defor-estation, or permafrost thaw. In this case, modelers lose the opportunity to explore a variety of policies under different climate change scenarios.

Single-discipline models often use one specific modeling approach, such as qualitative mental models, statistical regression, or agent-based simulation. We call it "one-method modeling"—a distinct way to represent selected aspects of the target system (Borshchev & Filippov, 2004). The shortcomings of one-method models can arguably be overcome by integrating them with other co-acting models. A number of examples of such integrated models can be seen in SES research: for example, Cellular Automata (CA) are highly popular in simulating urban growth. But as a bottom-up approach, they do not effectively capture the influence of macro scale political, eco-nomic, and cultural factors or act as an effective tool to simulate scenario based urban growth. To address this deficiency, He et al. (2006) combine CA with top-down System Dynamics (SD) to develop their Urban Expansion Scenario model. Their SD-based module explores scenarios of the regional land demand, while a land-use allocation module, simulated through CA, allocates urban land at the local level based on the established demand. Similarly, Bithell and Brasigton (2009) integrate social, hydrological, and ecological models to analyze the effect of population growth on forest structure and regional hydrology. Households, represented through an agent-based model, consume trees that are simulated through an individual-based forest model for fuel, fodder, and to obtain agricultural land.

Facing the challenge of incorporating knowledge from social and natural sciences, it is easy to see why recent trends in SES modeling have stressed the value of model integration, in which multiple disciplines contribute to building one comprehensive model that jointly emulates social and ecological systems (Bithell & Brasington, 2009; Couclelis, 2005; Letcher et al., 2006; Parker et al., 2008; Polhill & Gotts, 2009; Schaldach & Priess, 2008; Soboll et al., 2011; Swinerd & McNaught, 2012; Zellner, 2007). Although integrating multiple models reduces the shortfalls of single-discipline models, integrated models contain a number of potential limita-tions (Bankes, 1993; Lee, 1973; Lempert et al., 2002). For a start, the contributing disciplines have to make compromises in terms of structure and function of their models. As noted by Bitchell and Brasington (2009), establishing relationships and feedbacks between individual models can become too difficult to ascertain. As a result, the sub-models may not be used to their full potential. Another prominent issue is matching spatial and temporal scales across multiple models. In Bitchell and Brasington's model, all the sub-models consider the same spatial extents but differ in temporal scale. In addition, coupled models are prone to higher levels of uncertainty. Due to the multiplicity of simplifying assumptions associated with ac-commodating multiple one-method modeling, uncertainty becomes confounded. Different categories of uncertainty are mixed in such models (e.g., probabilistic with fuzzy, structural with parametric, or qualitative with quantitative) leading to hard-to-trace logical flaws (Beven,

2008). Due to the algorithmic complexity of coupled models, they are harder to understand and communicate. They are often perceived as "black boxes"—computational entities that take inputs and "magically" produce outputs, without providing any understanding of their inner mechanics. Integrated modeling adds programming as well as computational requirements (i.e., the model requires a long time to execute, which diminishes its potential for experimentation and discovery of surprising behavior).

A corollary of uncertainty is the confusion between system complexity and model complexity. Senge (1990) argues that understanding how a complex system operates (its dynamic complexity) is more important than getting all the details in order to predict the future (its detail complexity). Yet, during integrated model development, scientists often include more variables and mechanisms that are necessary to emulate the studied system, as most systems have only a few strongly significant drivers (Saltelli et al., 2004; Schmitt Olabisi et al., 2013). In addition, some variables may overlap, representing the same system characteristic multiple times. This redundancy further complicates the model and contributes to the "black-box" syndrome.

In this chapter, we propose multiple non-coupled models to study SES problems. We argue that simple and elegant one-method models can still capture dynamic complexity without compromising model cognitive tractability. Our approach is different from single discipline models in that we concurrently use multiple individual models to study the same problem from many different angles. We then synthesize the results using a scenario study tool that comprehensively probes the input-output space to find (groups of) distinct scenarios. As a result, we produce a small number of numerically rich narratives that cover many possible futures of a given system.

We put forward a new framework for studying complex SES systems that we call Participatory Ensemble Modeling (PEM). Ensemble modeling is a framework in which a large number of differing yet plausible models are evaluated against benchmark measures representing many value systems to select scenarios that would hold under variable future conditions (Schmitt Olabisi et al., 2013). To accurately incorporate many value systems, we extend the framework to include an explicit participatory component, in which many stakeholders are actively involved in multiple stages of the modeling process from conceptualization, through evaluation, to application and audit (Arnstein 1969, Saltelli & Funtowicz, 2014). Consequently, we define PEM as ensemble modeling with a participatory component, during which scientists and stakeholders collaboratively develop a large number of multivalued and simple representations of a given system, and synthesize them to generate robust future scenarios.

We develop our framework to represent and examine a food system process at various spatial, temporal, and human choice scales (Agarwal et al., 2002; Gibson et al., 2000). Our goal is to design and test these one-method models through discussions with stakeholders with on-the-ground knowledge of food systems in dryland West Africa. In this respect, this project builds, in a participatory and iterative manner, a large collection of small and independent models, encompassed by a scenario study tool that allows for synthetic thinking about food security from different perspectives. The scenarios become model-informed rich descriptions of the plausible futures of a given SES that are of interest to a particular group (Staley et al., 2009).

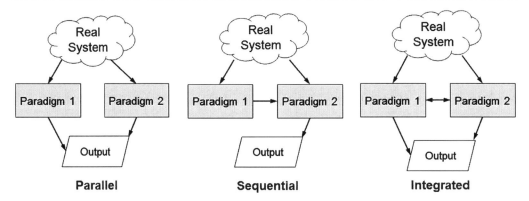

FIGURE 1. Different levels of model integration, adapted from Swinerd & McNaught (2012). For clarity, we only included two one-method models.

2. Integrated Modeling

Different one-method models have been used and refined in different disciplines because the problems these disciplines study vary in nature. For example, cognitive decision scientists, who study complex processes leading to human choices, make use of qualitative mental models (Hastie et al., 2010). Agricultural economists typically use agricultural household models to conceptualize and explain household behavior and these lead to various empirical specifications depending on the nature and distribution of the outcome of interest (Singh et al., 1986). Sociologists favor multilevel modeling to account for the interrelationships between societies and individuals (Blalock, 1984; Snijders & Bosker 2012). Hydrologists employ differential equations to rigorously represent the physics of the water cycle (Bodo et al., 1987); ecologists use system dynamics to model stocks and flows within the natural resource systems (Meadows & Wright, 2008); and urban planners, who want to simulate the evolution of a city, will rely on GIS and cellular automata (Batty, 2007). Integrated Modeling (IM) attempts to bring these different one-method models together as a series of sub-models. IM can have different levels of coupling: from concurrently executed, tightly coupled models embedded in one software to loosely coupled models that sequentially pass inputs and outputs among each other (Parker et al., 2008). A typical classification, given by Shanthikumar and Sargent (1983) and Swinerd and McNaught (2012), is illustrated in figure 1. In this classification, two or more modeling approaches emulate the same real system by adopting different ways of data transfer (intra- and inter-models). In the "parallel" IM, models simulate the real system separately and independently, and aggregate the results into a single interpretation. In the "sequential" IM, one model output constitutes the input to another model. According to Swinerd and McNaught, the highest level of IM is the so-called integrated model, where the interim simulation results of one-method models are dynamically fed into each other to update model contexts and parameters on a regular basis. This level of tight integration means that a variety of different one-method models are mixed in the same architecture.

Following Swinerd and McNaught (2012), we base our approach on parallel IM. The concurrent

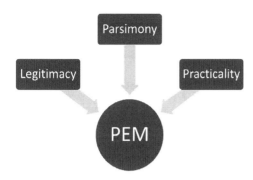

FIGURE 2. Three design principles of the participatory ensemble modeling (PEM) framework.

one-method models that we apply are decoupled when feasible. Not only do they run independently (as the parallel approach in figure 1), but they are also decoupled spatially (different geographic extents and resolution), temporally (days, months, years, decades), and thematically (political upheavals, household life cycles, crop markets). We employ this approach for three reasons. First, one-method models address the specificity of a given operational research question without compromising their unique analytical benefits, thus contributing to a richer understanding of the problem. Second, one-method models are more likely to be parsimonious because they are not part of one, complicated "macro-model." Third, they can be instrumental in generating an extensive and exhaustive set of future scenarios due to their different and distinct conventions for handling uncertainty. For such models to work, however, we need an environment that semi-automatically synthesizes the results into a comprehensive and exhaustive set of scenarios.

3. Design Principles of Participatory Ensemble Modeling

As stated from the outset, the PEM framework combines ensemble modeling (Lempert et al., 2003) with participatory research (Minkler et al., 2003). PEM involves a collaborative development of a large number of different representations of a given system, followed by a synthesis to generate scenarios that would hold under variable future conditions. Consequently, we propose that the practice of PEM be based on three design principles: legitimacy, parsimony, and practicality (see figure 2), which are described in the following sections.

3.1. Legitimacy

Model legitimacy aims at faithful representation of the perspectives of all involved stakeholders. Interaction with stakeholders is necessary to incorporate expert knowledge, thereby increasing the transparency and applicability of the model in real-world decision making (Cumming, 2011; Mavrommati et al., 2013; Pahl-Wostl, 2002). A key aspect of stakeholder engagement is removing preconceived notions of how a system operates or what drives change in a system. It is important that researchers allow people to tell their own story, and that the modeling efforts reflect stakeholders' current reality and provide insight into their potential future. Another benefit of the participatory approach is that it brings together a diverse pool of stakeholders leveraging their heterogeneous experience and perspectives on an issue which, perhaps surprisingly, provides the means for generalization. To reach legitimacy, researchers need to employ participatory modeling in which we validate the model at every step of development both quantitatively and qualitatively. In addition to conventional statistical approaches (J. Smith & Smith, 2007), and model-to-model comparison (Axtell et al., 1996; Hales et al., 2003; Rouchier et al., 2008), PEM requires validation by stakeholders. They are consulted at many stages of model development and application to assure that the formal model reflects their conceptual representation of the system, to explain why it differs from their conceptions (e.g. lack of knowledge about the hydrological processes), and to correct the model for any biases introduced by researchers during model formalization and implementation. Multiple sessions with stakeholders also provide opportunities for learning from each other. As a system changes and undergoes shocks, managing it requires continual learning about the system from a variety of perspectives and at multiple scales (Borrini-Feyerabend et al., 2007).

3.2. Parsimony

Achieving legitimacy through collaborative problem solving may lead to a myriad of overlapping representations of the system under study. Aggregation and generalization are necessary. The challenge is to end up with representations that have high fidelity to the system being modeled but do not contain unnecessary details (Beven, 2002; Casti, 1997). We call this design principle model "parsimony" (i.e., well-founded model simplification). Parsimony requires finding a delicate balance between simplicity, coherence, and comprehensibility.

Simplification is crucial in model development following the philosophical principle of Occam's razor (Zeigler, 1976; Innis & Rexstad, 1983; Eberlein, 1989; Brooks & Tobias, 1996; Edmonds & Moss, 2005; Cox et al., 2006; Collins et al., 2015). For a given set of competing representations of the target system, researchers should choose those that have the lowest number of assumptions, focusing on keeping only those mechanisms that are relevant for a given problem (Edmonds & Moss, 2005). A comprehensive review of model simplification methods can be found in Innis and Rexstad (1983). These methods include input optimization, parameter filtering, sensitivity analysis, structural tests, logic tests, spatial and temporal generalization, metamodeling, finding analytical solutions, and/or reducing parameter space by eliminating collinearities.

SES models are concerned with representing the interactions in a coupled system. Models cannot represent every single piece of the system. A modeler should only include what is relevant to the phenomena they are trying to model. How do you decide what is relevant, especially for models that draw on data across disciplines? Variables relevant to hydrologists might not be the variables that sociologists deem most important. Balancing model complexity with parsimony when dealing with mixed sources of data is a daunting task. In addition, the interdisciplinary nature of SES models almost guarantees that modelers will have to handle large quantities of data. Data inputs for SES models are diverse in the sense that the modeler must integrate a number of different data sources and types from across multiple disciplines. In the earliest stages of the model development process—conceptualization, planning, and data collection—the modeler must make practical choices. How does the modeler develop relevant, parsimonious variables from such diverse data? Practical choices can be made by addressing model uncertainty (section 3.4).

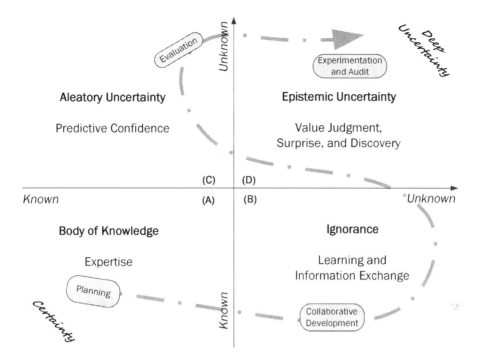

FIGURE 3. Relationship between the magnitude of model parameterization and model outcome space. Case [A]: lack of parameterization renders outputs that violate model assumptions and/or target system characteristics (i.e., are implausible; e.g., CO_2 in the simulated earth atmosphere varies from 0 to 100 percent of its composition). Case [B]: model parameters lead to results that comprise both observed and probable results (e.g., climate models that predict CO_2 values between 250 and 900 ppmv given different initial conditions). Case [C]: an over-parameterized model reproduces observed data, but provides little room for surprise, hypothesis building, or innovation in policy formulation (e.g., CO_2 values from 300 to 400 ppmv). Note: dots represent the simulated values (model output).

It is important to stress that simplification should be approached with caution. We should not limit ourselves to what is most probable and discard the outliers. Exploring a wide range of model outputs can be a method to think about systems in a formalized way rather than a crystal ball that provides predictions based on the prevailing past observations. The design principle of practicality serves exactly that purpose.

3.3. Practicality

Reaching parsimony should not be done in a way that compromises the exploratory power of models. How can we design models that are easy to use yet effective in locating the unexpected? We postulate that, in order to design robust policies, models should produce a variety of outputs that are later subjected to scrutiny through scenario analysis. Consequently, our principle of model practicality concentrates on leaving useful uncertainty in models (figure 3).

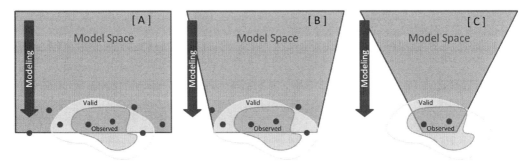

FIGURE 4. Exposing the four quadrants of (un)certainty during model development. The arrow shows the general path of development of participatory model ensembles. The boxes represent different model production stages.

3.4. Uncertainty in PEM

"Uncertainty" is an umbrella term to describe the problems that arise out of incomplete representations of the world (Longley et al., 2010; Messina et al., 2008). In modeling, uncertainty is exposed where disagreement exists on the appropriate models that describe the relationships among the key driving forces shaping the long-term future of a system. It is exposed where little is known on the probability distributions used to represent uncertainty about key variables in models. Finally, it is brought to light where diverse values produce conflicting outcomes. Lempert et al. (2002) calls the latter "deep uncertainty"—hard to recognize, hard to quantify, or simply denied and eliminated because it stands in conflict with our values and beliefs. In SES, deep uncertainty is encountered in ill-defined societal problems arising from individual needs, cultural values, economic stability, and ecological resilience, where a myriad of hard-to-quantify, interrelated factors are involved (Agusdinata, 2008; Kandlikar et al., 2005; Kasperson, 2008; Lempert et al., 2002).

Systems uncertainty has been studied by many disciplines and in many different contexts (Briggs 2016; Funtowicz & Ravetz 1990; Bammer & Smithson 2012; Renn 2008). We focus on how uncertainties are accounted for during various stages of model development and what variants of uncertainty are useful in PEM. We identify four quadrants representing the magnitude of (un)certainty (figure 3): known knowns (A), unknown knowns (B), known unknowns (C), and unknown unknowns (D). This idea was first proposed by Luft and Ingham (1961) and later adapted to define four levels of the conscious competence learning model (Burch, 1970). We extend this concept by looking at how different levels of (un)certainty are unmasked during PEM.

The known knowns are imbued with little to no uncertainty. They comprise all the disciplinary expertise of the research team that recognizes and formulates the SES problem and contributes to ensemble model planning (figure 3a). Because SES models require a transdisciplinary approach, the research team exchanges their disciplinary perspectives to reduce individual ignorance that stems from specialization. Such ignorance constitutes the unknown knowns for a given individual, that is, the competence that others bring to the table or the knowledge gained from literature (figure 4b).

SES problems usually concern a particular community affected by the environmental changes and the potential policies to be implemented and thus comprise another form of unknown knowns—the tacit and practical knowledge of the system, which is out of sight to the research team. For this reason, stakeholder participation is introduced to explicitly formulate the models, correct the perceptual models, and refine the conceptual models. Collaboration with stakeholders is also necessary during model development to uncover the potential biases introduced by researchers, to gain trust in the models, to ensure their transparency, and to establish their ownership by the community.

Collaboration may also safeguard against cherry picking or confirmation bias—searching for information that supports the team's position. It is important to note that the collaboration is reciprocal. The public may not always be correct in construing the system based on their experience and subjective observation. In this case, the research team has a responsibility to explain the modeled processes and clarify any misconceptions. In short, addressing unknown knowns (figure 3b) ensures PEM legitimacy.

SES problems are inherently stochastic—the system may undergo rapid changes caused by random, impossible-to-predict events. Such fundamental, irreducible uncertainty is referred to as "aleatoric" or "statistical" uncertainty (Oberkampf et al., 2004). It is often employed to establish our predictive confidence in the ensembles using both standalone statistical models or post-processing (evaluative) statistical tests (figure 3c). These tools also allow for model simplification. Specifically, aleatoric uncertainty can be reduced by employing comprehensive uncertainty and sensitivity analysis, the results of which allow modelers to leave out all inputs that do not significantly affect model outcomes for a given problem (Ligmann-Zielinska, 2013; Saltelli et al., 2008). Consequently, handling aleatoric uncertainty ensures PEM parsimony.

Achieving parsimony through simplification is a balancing act. SES modelers should aim to explore the interesting extremes hidden within the noise. They should not want to discount outliers, the chance to stumble on surprises. Not all uncertainty is redundant and not all should be avoided. To ensure PEM practicality, we need to embrace uncertainty as a positive—even desired—aspect of modeling. Smithson and Bammer (2008) argue that uncertainty can be constructive—it enables choices, provides opportunity for discovery, and provokes creativity. Parametric uncertainty, in the form of a probability distribution of a given variable, can be utilized in simulations to look for such combinations of inputs that lead to more desirable futures (Ligmann-Zielinska & Sun, 2010). Structural uncertainty, which indicates whether a particular model accurately represents its target system, is unavoidable when describing complex SES problems with multiple stakeholders (Brugnach et al., 2008; Sarewitz, 2004; Walker et al., 2003; Warmink et al., 2010). It may be a hindrance when forecasting is at stake, but it can also be a benefit when alternative scenarios are considered. For example, using multiple decision rules to represent different types of human decision making could allow models to serve as tools to evaluate more sustainable behaviors.

Note that models are as good as the knowledge base of their contributors, the assumptions made, the data collected and fed into the models, and the employed modeling approaches. Portions of the system remain hidden from model creators. This is called "epistemic" uncertainty (Oberkampf et al., 2004)—systematic ignorance of the investigated SES or unknown unknowns (figure 3d). These "missing pieces" often generate surprise in the system—an unanticipated event due to its nature, magnitude of effects, place and/or timing of occurrence (Lempert et al., 2002). Representation of these unknown elements is always absent in the model.

While surprises cannot be eliminated, experimenting with ensembles of models may shed light on epistemic uncertainty or protect us against the unforeseen consequences by promoting robust systems. As can be seen, addressing model uncertainty is not a trivial task, and yet it is required while designing legitimate, parsimonious, and practical models.

4. Framework in Action: Food Security in Sub-Saharan West Africa

The PEM framework has been used in a transdisciplinary research project on food security in sub-Saharan Africa. Despite consistent gains in global agricultural productivity over the past half-century, chronic malnutrition persists in the region. This recalcitrant problem is termed "lack of food security" (FAO, 2002; 2015; IFPRI, 2013) and comprises food availability (whether enough food is produced for a given population); food access (whether a population is able to purchase or obtain adequate food); food utilization (whether the food is prepared and consumed in optimal ways to ensure safety and proper nutrition); and food stability (whether a population is consistently able to obtain food over time; Barrett, 2010; FAO, 2009). West African cropping systems face dual challenges of food availability: increasing crop productivity in areas that historically suffer from relatively low yields compared to other African regions and enhancing the resilience of cropping systems to climate change (CGIAR, 2013; Gregory et al., 2005; Oluoko-Odingo, 2010). Limited nutrient availability, soil erosion, and water stress compound the challenges posed by climate change (CGIAR, 2012).

The multiple components of food security operate from the continental to the sub-household scales and involve environmental, economic, cultural, behavioral, political, social, and technological dynamics (Brown & Funk, 2008; Chung, 2012; Godfray et al., 2010; Lobell et al., 2008; Parry et al., 2005; Timmer, 2012). As such, the complexity of food security in the sub-Saharan region calls for multidisciplinary scenario analysis using ensemble of one-method models that focus on different aspects of the problem.

4.1. Model Development Protocol

Our project encompasses the following stages: (1) collect narratives from stakeholders; (2) generate mental models from these narratives; (3) build conceptual models (informed by the mental models and technical scientific knowledge) which are further validated by stakeholders; (4) implement and parameterize the validated models; (5) run simulations to obtain a pool of outputs that are integrated into disparate scenarios, which is then presented to stakeholders for evaluation and selection; (6) perform an assessment of the selected scenarios based on previously defined evaluative measures; (7) synthesize the selected scenarios back into narratives; and, (8) present them as final recommendations to stakeholders (figure 5). These tasks are exercised using a three-step modeling approach by Costanza and Ruth (1998): scoping (4.1.1), research modeling (4.1.2), and management modeling (4.1.3). We now describe how these three steps are driven by the three design principles of PEM: legitimacy, parsimony, and practicality.

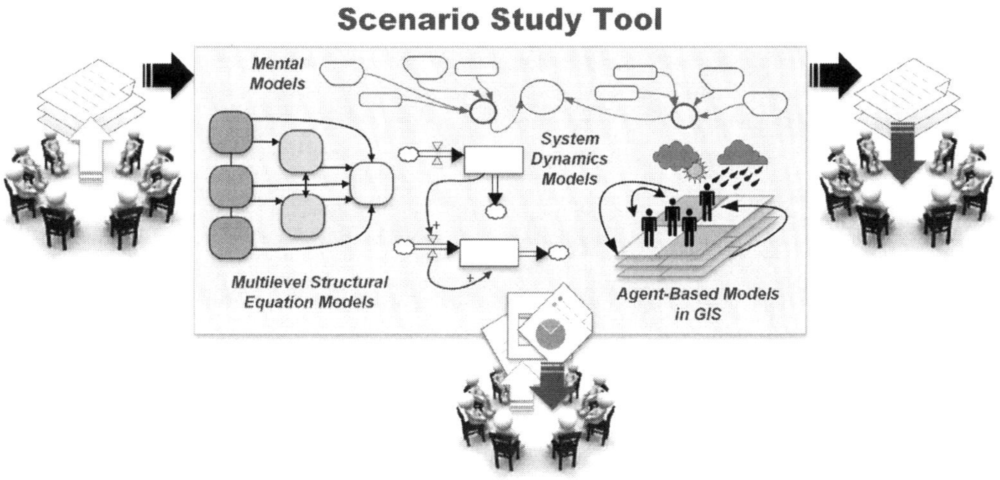

FIGURE 5. Model development protocol, where four standalone modeling approaches comprise an ensemble of models to study food security. The Scenario Study Tool (SST) provides a platform for simulation-assisted scenario analysis used to communicate and characterize deep uncertainty in modeling food security. SST is an interface that organizes both observed and simulated data, generates and evaluates scenarios, and provides means to extract important drivers of desirable futures (Godet, 2008; Lempert et al., 2003).

4.2. Scoping

Scoping reflects the legitimacy construct of the PEM framework. The goal of scoping is to formalize the research through consultation with stakeholders who share their perspectives and elicit their subjective conceptions of the problem (van den Belt, 2004). These consultations, coupled with team expertise, a literature review, and preliminary data collection result in a set of narratives about future food security in dryland West Africa and the causal mechanisms and "surprising" events that shape these futures. These narratives, in conjunction with secondary data, are used to build an ensemble of one-method models described in table 1, which also lists the different objectives of employing the distinct models.

An important aspect of PEM is to build consensus between researchers and stakeholders by using iterative research methods that are accessible to laypeople. For example, the development of mental models of food security at the producer level relies on open-ended individual interviews. These interviews are designed to encourage an open conversation between researcher and participant. It is critical that this conversation is driven by the participant's insights and concerns. In qualitative modeling, the element of "surprise" or "discovery" about the system in question lies in the unique insights provided by stakeholders. Open-ended, conversation-driven interviews provide the venue for this process to occur. The iterative nature of this interview methodology is also key. In our project, we have done multiple interviews with the same group of stakeholders. After the first visit, we updated our interview protocol with new topics that we were regularly encountering that required greater clarification. For example, in our interviews in multiple villages in Mali, we were told that rice was a special dish and a favorite of the children.

Table 1. Model ensembles built to study food security in Dryland West Africa

APPROACH	DEFINITION	PURPOSE
QUALITATIVE		
Mental Models (MM)	Graphical representations of how people know, perceive, make decisions, and construct behavior in a variety of complex environments (Craik, 1943; Gentner & Stevens, 1983).	To deconstruct and communicate stakeholder personal perspectives on food security.
QUANTITATIVE		
Multilevel Structural Equation Models (MSEM)	Statistical models that simultaneously examine nested relations and latent/unobserved variables, reciprocity, direct and indirect structural paths, and feedback loops (Preacher et al., 2010).	To explain how food availability results from individual attributes and structural factors.
Spatial Agent-Based Models (ABM)	Computational models, embedded in a geographic information system, composed of heterogeneous and autonomous entities that shape their common environment and act upon it, while simultaneously interacting among each other (Brown et al., 2005). Micro-scale agent interactions generate macro-scale dynamic characteristics.	To describe spatial and temporal variability of food access to explain how individual behaviors link with livelihood vulnerability.
System Dynamics Models (SDM)	Computational models characterized by interdependence, mutual causality, and feedback to examine stocks and flows within systems (Richardson, 2010).	To examine food stability by evaluating climate change, drought, hunger, and humanitarian relief over time.

However, we had little understanding of why that was the case. In order to address this information gap, we adjusted our interview protocol to specifically examine special dishes and rice in particular. It turned out that rice was not the beloved ingredient but the sauce served over the rice that featured fish or chicken. A meal featuring rice was much higher in protein and less common than the typical plant-based meals, making it special.

4.2.1. PRIMARY DATA: ESTABLISHING LEGITIMACY

Since July 2015, we have had multiple visits to collect interview data from villagers in Mali and Ghana. The interviews are in the form of extensive, open-ended narratives from individual household members (elder and younger men, elder and younger women). The aim of gathering the narratives is to gain insight into components of individual cognition and perceptions of agriculture, climate change, and food security as well as adaptation to climate risks and food insecurity in individual- and household-level decision making. Participant responses were audio recorded and captured with extensive note-taking. The interviews were then coded using qualitative analysis software NVivo according to classification rubrics based on the recurrent themes which emerged from the narratives as the coders reviewed each interview. To limit coding bias common in mental models (Chen, 2011; Sterman & Sweeney, 2007) multiple coders went through the coding texts individually and integrated their rubrics into the final classification nodes (Whitley et al., 2017).

The coding rubrics are used to develop qualitative mental models to build the foundation for PEM legitimacy. Qualitative mental modeling forces researchers to put system relationships and linkages before the data rather than retroactively trying to determine those interactions

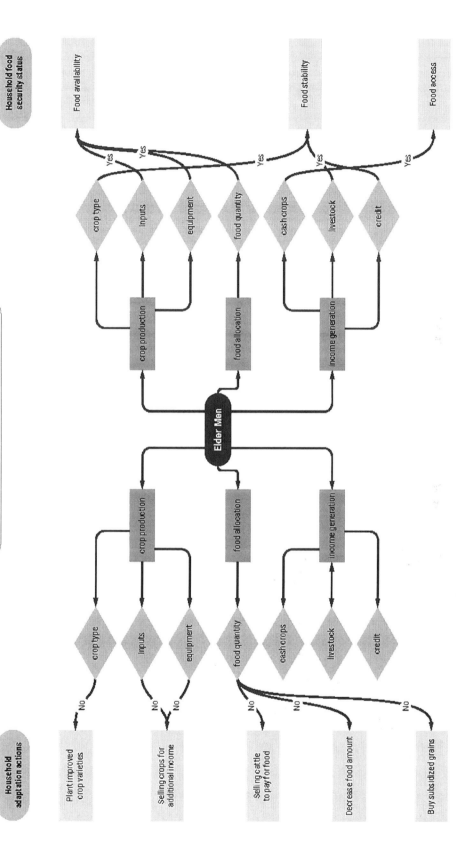

FIGURE 6. The decision tree of individual actors from our mental model building process. The shades of grey represent four different actors: young men, young women, elder men, and elder women. Black arrows are relationships between variables.

from the data. The question being asked is, what real outcomes and processes have we observed? Going a step further, mental models not only reveal additional variables emerging from stakeholders' different worldviews, backgrounds, and beliefs but also help build consensus among stakeholders and researchers alike. Finally, at the micro level, different mental models allow for representing the multiple ways in which household decisions are made to ensure individual food security.

In sum, our mental models are a graphical representation of how elder men and women and younger men and women within a household, understand, perceive, make decisions, and behave with respect to food production, utilization, and consumption and the impacts of and adaptation to climate change in their farming activities (figure 6). The decision structure and format of the mental models sets a platform for system dynamics, agent-based, and structural equation modeling.

Our mental models reveal interesting insights into the complex, intra-household dynamics in dryland West Africa with respect to food security. We discovered gender-based differences in the strategies implemented by households. Men (elder and young) mostly decide on strategies for food availability and various adaptation strategies to be undertaken by the household, while women (elder and young) decide on strategies for food utilization as well as availability. While older men prefer adaptation strategies which involve improved farming techniques—such as tolerant seed varieties, crop diversification—young men were more inclined to adapt to changing conditions by leaving farming activities (i.e., migrating and taking additional non-farming jobs). In other words, older men find it increasingly difficult to allocate adequate food to the sub-family units and, as a result, young men are choosing to branch out from their extended households to support their families. However, without support to fall back on during lean periods, these younger men are increasingly vulnerable to climate stressors. This separation, along with conflicts in allocation of food and resources to the family members, form the main source of a rise in intergenerational conflicts within households.

4.2.2. SECONDARY DATA: REINFORCING LEGITIMACY

National-level data provides a starting point for large-scale context and holds the potential to explain processes that may or may not be visible from the ground. We have compiled a dataset with over four hundred national-level variables from publicly available sources spanning 1960–2014 across all fifty-four independent African countries. Expanding the scope of the data beyond West Africa and across multiple years allows us to compare West Africa to other parts of the continent within and between regions as well as between nations, maximizing possible comparisons and providing sufficient observations to develop statistical models.

The majority of our variables are from the World Bank and the FAO, with additional variables coming from sources such as Freedom House, the International Disaster Database from the Centre for Research on the Epidemiology of Disasters (CRED), the CIA World Factbook, the Global Footprint Network, and the World Economic Forum. The variables fall into eleven general categories: agriculture, conflict and corruption, demographics, ecology and environment, ecological footprint, economics and trade, education, employment, geography, health and nutrition, and social programs and inequality.

Another important aspect is the collection and analysis of nationally representative data from household surveys, a source of information for several measures of food security that captures its multiple dimensions. One set of nationally representative data across eight countries in Sub-Saharan Africa is the household survey project called Living Standards Measurement Study—Integrated Surveys on Agriculture (LSMS-ISA). The LSMS-ISA project works with the national statistics offices of its partner countries to design and implement multitopic, nationally representative panel household surveys. The surveys cover multiple topics including socioeconomic status, non-farm activities, and agriculture and are very useful for understanding links among these dimensions.

Drawing from the conceptual models of UNICEF (1990) and Hammond and Dubé (2012) and guided by additional sources such as the FAO (2015), we have developed preliminary models of food security using national-level data. These models have been developed independently from our mental models. We use structural equation modeling with latent variables, which allows us to use multiple observed variables to measure a concept. This analytical approach is especially important for something as complex as hunger or food security where it would be very difficult to choose only one indicator and results could be very different depending on the indicator used (Barrett, 2010). Our preliminary models consider agricultural, ecological, political, economic, health, and social factors as drivers of undernutrition, related in a complex system that includes possible direct and indirect paths, interactions, and feedback. To date, we have tested this model for fifty-four countries in Africa over twelve years to determine general patterns in the effects of different sets of explanatory variables. We have also investigated this model for five West African countries (Burkina Faso, Ghana, Mali, Niger, and Nigeria) over fifty-five years. Our initial findings suggest the central importance of poverty as a concept connecting health and human-development factors with ecological, agricultural, and international trade factors in predicting undernutrition. We adopt an iterative approach to modeling where we build progressively more complexity into them either in terms of causal paths, sample composition, and the potential multiscale and cross-scale relations.

4.3. Research Modeling: Introducing Parsimony

PEM follows the conventional iterative model development procedure (Gilbert & Troitzsch, 2005; Jakeman et al., 2006). Based on the specifications, models are first implemented, then verified, validated, and used in the scenario generation phase. The uncertainties of quantifiable inputs are addressed by forming probability density functions. In a preliminary analysis of the field and secondary data, we notice a strong multicollinearity phenomenon—input variables are highly interdependent. This phenomenon is not new in data science; many natural and man-made systems consist of processes that link to each other. Multicollinearity, nonetheless, would distort the analysis findings, making the quantification of factor contributions vague and diminishing the PEM principle of parsimony. In our analysis, we propose to use high-dimensional statistics (such as Copula methods) to "replot" the probability density functions in a high-dimensional space. In this way, the interdependence among input variables is preserved. Depending on the character of inputs, probabilities are generated based on historical data or translated from interviews using a number of identified techniques (see Mallampalli et al., 2016). Our design principles guide us to tackle deep uncertainties and some of the data identified from our preliminary analyses (interviews, mental models, previous focus-group workshops) can hardly be quantified, or are impossible to fit to trends (e.g., the real decision-making processes of the farmers, the long-term environmental changes, or the economic conditions in the future). Consequently, our scenario study tool (figure 5) has been designed to be less sensitive to input probabilities.

4.4. Management Modeling: Seeking Practicality

Our practicality design principle dictates that during management modeling, which we call "critical driver identification," we focus on discovering combinations of uncertain inputs integral to the future of food security in our study area, identifying spatiotemporal points where policy interventions would result in decreasing vulnerability to food deficit and determining "safety zones" for the food insecurity indicators (ranges of values that guarantee food system stability).

Stakeholders are first asked to evaluate the quantitative future scenarios generated using our ensemble modeling (agent-based, system dynamics, and structural equation models). To maintain the principle of legitimacy, acceptable scenarios are selected through deliberation within the research team and with stakeholders who provide feedback on what should be expanded, simplified, or highlighted (van den Belt, 2004). Moreover, not all futures are equally important or likely. One of the tasks is to identify the "futures of interest." The quantitative, model-generated future scenarios are grouped into clusters using two criteria: likelihood and criticality. Due to input uncertainty, the number of futures contained in a given "future scenario" may vary from cluster to cluster. We use content density as an evaluative measure to show the likelihood of a future given reasonable inputs and policies. Another aspect of future scenarios is their magnitude of impact (Staley et al., 2009), quantified based on evaluative measures identified from the interviews. Upon occurrence, future food scenarios may have different effects on the social, economic, and environmental state of the dryland West Africa system. Some may be more critical than others even though they may be less likely to happen. Therefore, inductive and deductive processes are used to examine the less likely scenarios in addition to the more likely ones (Bradfield et al., 2005).

One way of discovering less likely futures is "counterfactual thinking" (Staley et al., 2009). When exercising counterfactual thinking, a group of participants is asked to develop a mental representation of reality, intentionally alter some basic facts, and think through the future so altered. Another way is "history analogies," where the group is encouraged to consider the structure, events, and concepts from the past and imagine what they might look like in the present situation (Staley et al., 2009). The more likely and/or more critical future scenarios constitute a candidate pool of solutions subjected to statistical and data mining analyses to identify the most influential drivers of the selected future scenarios. The candidate pool of solutions encompasses robust scenarios—scenarios that are good enough to succeed in both baseline and low-probability, high-consequence circumstances (Lempert et al., 2003; Schmitt Olabisi et al., 2013). The described methods of scenario deliberation are examples of how to use uncertainty in a constructive way (section 3.4).

4.5. Management Modeling: Practicing Parsimony

The principle of parsimony has guided us to develop a high-dimensional scenario analysis method based on statistical spatial analysis named the Robustness-Optimization-Efficiency (ROE) method. Classic scenario analysis methods usually treat simulation as an indivisible process—when model inputs are set, the simulation will be executed using a predefined procedure until all needed outputs are generated. The ROE method, in contrast, is interactive in a sense that interim analysis results are used to refine the models and simulation experiments, such as removing irrelevant factors or skipping unnecessary value ranges. Therefore, it can substantially reduce the computing load of PEM by removing irrelevant simulations. In addition, instead of analyzing each and every generated data point, the ROE method splits the future scenario space into zones that are definitely unfavorable, definitely favorable, and unclear (due to the possibly changing expectations of the future generations). Policies and actions of today are then grouped into different classes based on their contributions to different future scenario space zones. All of these characteristics of ROE can be seen as a direct realization of the principle of parsimony, balancing model simplicity, coherence, and comprehensibility.

So far, ROE has been tested in a simulation study to examine the land preservation policies in Michigan using a spatially explicit agent-based model (Ligmann-Zielinska et al., 2014). Based on limited empirical data, we have applied the Copula method (figure 7), a statistical sampling method that reproduces a high-dimensional probability density function and predicts the empirical probability distribution, which is used to generate millions of possible inputs for a very large number of simulations. To maintain the parsimony principle, we cluster the generated future scenarios into three larger groups: (1) "system collapse" (SC, or "must avoid") zones, (2) "bright future" (BF) target zones, and (3) "undefined" (UD) zones. The UD zones specify scenarios that may or may not be good in the eyes of future generations. The next step is to evaluate the relevance of the policies/actions of today to the zones in the future. First, we identify what policies/actions today could lead to the SC zones based on the preliminary simulation experiments (counted in thousands instead of millions). We remove these policies/actions immediately from our input, reducing the computational load and simplifying the follow-up analysis. Removing these policies/actions makes the input space look like a Swiss cheese, where the holes are the policies/actions removed from our input data.

The next step is to mark the policies and actions associated with the BF zones—these policies and actions became the policy target. There could be numerous paths from the current position to the policy target; hence, sensitivity analyses are performed at each time interval to decide the most economic and efficient path to the target. Meanwhile, the conceived paths are carefully selected to bypass the Swiss cheese holes (areas leading to SC zones) and the areas that may lead to the UD zones. Since we are unsure about the UD zones, we prefer to avoid them even though they may seem harmless today.

ROE is designed to heed the call of the parsimony principle of PEM. It strives to simplify the simulation and post-simulation analyses while maintaining the comprehensive knowledge of the modeled systems. This can be done by constraining ourselves only to the meaningful clusters rather than basing our analysis on thousands or even millions of simulation results. Also, policy

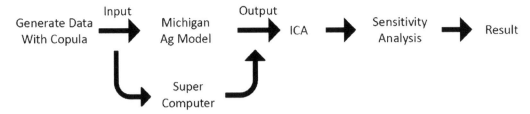

FIGURE 7. The "Robustness-Optimization-Efficiency" method used in a land preservation simulation study. ICA stands for Independent Component Analysis, a statistical technique for decomposing a complex dataset into independent subparts. The goal is to remove interdependence among input variables so the results of sensitivity analysis are more reasonable.

recommendations are not made for each and every action item, but only the combination of items that will have the biggest likelihood to achieve the "bright future." Lastly, since we adopt the "early abandon" strategy (removing most definite dangerous policies/actions from the analysis in the early phase of simulation), we reduce the computational load and leave resources for a more detailed analysis of the most promising policies/actions.

5. Summary

This chapter presents a methodological framework that outlines an extensive, stakeholder-guided, data-driven, and exploratory path to building, evaluating, and applying complex socioecological systems (SES) models. We call this framework "participatory ensemble modeling" (PEM): "participatory" because we rely heavily on stakeholder involvement throughout model development and evaluation, and "ensemble" because we run multiple independent models concurrently to emulate the system in many unique ways and combine the simulation findings into a robust policy discovery process based on a high-dimensional scenario analysis. PEM embodies three intertwined principles that constitute a new model validity framework:

1. LEGITIMACY: ensembles of models should incorporate the perspectives of all involved stakeholders;
2. PARSIMONY: legitimate models often result in a large number of overlapping system representations, which can be further simplified and grouped to minimize model complexity; and
3. PRACTICALITY: a certain level of uncertainty in models should be maintained to provide means of experimentation that can augment consensus building.

For non-modelers, constructive learning with modeling (model-based reasoning) can only be achieved through simple, transparent, across-the-board models (Saltelli & Funtowicz, 2014). We chose one-method models as the most appropriate way to achieve this goal. They are legitimate because they offer distinct techniques to build a richer understanding of the problem (Badham, 2010). For example, mental models are ideally suited for farmers' introspections about personal wellbeing during drought, whereas multilevel structural equation models are most effective when an NGO expert seeks a rigorous explanation of the reciprocal relationships between individual food deficit, long-term regional drought, and international humanitarian aid. Since one-method models are not part of one complicated "macro-model," they are more likely to be parsimonious. As they have different conventions for handling uncertainty, they can also be instrumental in generating an extensive and exhaustive set of future scenarios (practicality). SES models walk a fine line, navigating the "tension between the need . . . to convince decision makers of their ability to represent causal outcomes" and the "impossibility of accurately predicting future states of complex systems" (Schmidt et al., 2014). To address this challenge, we should strive to organize transdisciplinary research projects around well-defined principles and apply stringent criteria in model design, implementation, application, and audit (Saltelli & Funtowicz, 2014). We hope that our framework is a good step in this direction.

ACKNOWLEDGMENTS

This material is based upon work supported by the National Science Foundation under Grant No SMA 1416730. Any opinion, findings, and conclusions or recommendations expressed in this material are those of the authors(s) and do not necessarily reflect the views of the National Science Foundation. The authors would like to thank two anonymous reviewers for their constructive feedback on an earlier version of the manuscript.

REFERENCES

Agarwal, C., Green, G. M., Grove, J. M., Evans, T. P., & Schweik, C. M. (2002). *A review and assessment of land-use change models: Dynamics of space, time, and human choice* (General Technical Report NE-297). Newtown Square, PA: U.S. Department of Agriculture, Forest Service, Northeastern Research Station.

Agusdinata, B. (2008). *Exploratory modeling and analysis: A promising method to deal with deep uncertainty* (Doctoral dissertation, University of Delft). http://resolver.tudelft.nl/uuid:8a371ab4-3582-4506-bbd2-685e127f8bd7.

Arnstein, S. R. (1969). A ladder of citizen participation. *Journal of the American Institute of Planners, 35*(4), 216–224.

Axtell, R., Axelrod, R., Epstein, J. M., & Cohen, M. D. (1996). Aligning simulation models: A case study and results. *Computational & Mathematical Organization Theory, 1*(2), 123–141.

Badham, J. (2010). A compendium of modelling techniques. *Integration Insights, 12.*

Bammer, G., & Smithson, M. (Eds.). (2012). *Uncertainty and risk: Multidisciplinary perspectives.* London: Routledge.

Bankes, S. (1993). Exploratory modeling for policy analysis. *Operations Research, 41*(3), 435–449.

Barrett, C. B. (2010). Measuring food insecurity. *Science, 327*(5967), 825–828. doi: 10.1126/science.1182768.

Batty, M. (2007). *Cities and complexity: Understanding cities with cellular automata, agent-based models, and fractals.* Cambridge, MA: MIT press.

Beven, K. (2002). Towards a coherent philosophy for modelling the environment. *Proceedings of the Royal Society A, 458*(2026), 2465–2484. doi: 10.1098/rspa.2002.0986.

Beven, K. (2008). *Environmental modelling: An uncertain future?* New York: Routledge.

Bithell, M., & Brasington, J. (2009). Coupling agent-based models of subsistence farming with individual-based forest models and dynamic models of water distribution. *Environmental Modelling & Software, 24*(2), 173–190. doi:10.1016/j.envsoft.2008.06.016.

Blalock, H. (1984) Contextual-effects models: Theoretical and methodological issues. *Annual Review of Sociology* 10, 353–372.

Bodo, B. A., Thompson, M.E., & Unny, T. E. (1987) A review on stochastic differential equations for applications in hydrology. *Stochastic Hydrology and Hydraulics. 1*(2), 81–100. doi:10.1007/BF01543805.

Borrini-Feyerabend, Grazia, Farvar, M. Taghi, Nguinguiri, Jean Claude, & Ndangang, Vincent. (2007). *Co-management of natural resources: Organizing, negotiating, and learning-by-doing.* Heidelberg: Kasparek Verlag.

Borshchev, A., & Filippov, A. (2004). *From system dynamics and discrete event to practical agent-based modeling: Reasons, techniques, tools.* Paper presented at the 22nd International Conference of the System Dynamics Society, Oxford, UK.

Bradfield, R., Wright, G., Burt, G., Cairns, G., & Van Der Heijden, K. (2005). The origins and evolution of scenario techniques in long range business planning. *Futures, 37*(8), 795–812.

Briggs, W. (2016). *Uncertainty: The soul of modeling, probability & statistics.* New York: Springer.

Brooks, R. J., & Tobias, A. M. (1996). Choosing the best model: Level of detail, complexity, and model performance. *Mathematical and Computer Modelling, 24*(4), 1–14.

Brown, D. G., Riolo, R., Robinson, D. T., North, M., & Rand, W. (2005). Spatial process and data models: Toward integration of agent-based models and GIS. *Journal of Geographical Systems, 7*(1), 25–47.

Brown, M. E., & Funk, C. C. (2008). Climate-food security under climate change. *Science, 319*(5863), 580–581. doi: 10.1126/science.1154102.

Brugnach, M., Dewulf, A., Pahl-Wostl, C., & Taillieu, T. (2008). Toward a relational concept of uncertainty: About knowing too little, knowing too differently, and accepting not to know. *Ecology and Society, 13*(2), 1–16.

Burch, N. (1970). *The four stages for learning any new skill.* Solana Beach: Gordon Training International.

Casti, J. L. (1997). "Can you trust it?" *Complexity 2*(5), 8–11.

CGIAR. (2012). *Integrated agricultural production systems for improved food security and livelihoods in dry areas.* Addis Ababa, Ethiopia: CGIAR Research Program on Dryland Systems.

CGIAR. (2013). *New research approaches to improve drylands agriculture to deliver a more prosperous future.* Addis Ababa, Ethiopia: CGIAR Research Program on Dryland Agricultural Production Systems.

Chen, X. (2011). Why do people misunderstand climate change? Heuristics, mental models and ontological assumptions. *Climatic Change, 108*(1–2), 31–46. doi: 10.1007/s10584-010-0013-5.

Chung, K. (2012). *An introduction to nutrition-agriculture linkages* (MINAG/DE Research Report 72E). Maputo, Mozambique: Directorate of Economics, Ministry of Agriculture.

Collins, A., Petty, M., Vernon-Bido, D., & Sherfey, S. (2015). A call to arms: Standards for agent-based modeling and simulation. *Journal of Artificial Societies and Social Simulation 18*(3), 12.

Costanza, R., & Ruth, M. (1998). Using dynamic modeling to scope environmental problems and build consensus. *Environmental Management, 22*(2), 183–195.

Couclelis, H. (2005). "Where has the future gone?" Rethinking the role of integrated land-use models in spatial planning. *Environment and Planning A, 37*(8), 1353–1371.

Cox, G. M., Gibbons, J. M., Wood, A. T. A., Craigon, J., Ramsden, S. J., & Crout, N. M. J. (2006). Towards the systematic simplification of mechanistic models. *Ecological Modelling 198*(1–2), 240–246.

Craik, K. (1943). *The nature of explanation.* Cambridge: Cambridge University Press.

Cumming, G. (2011). *Spatial resilience in social-ecological systems.* London: Springer.

Eberlein, R. L. (1989). Simplification and understanding of models. *System Dynamics Review 5*(1), 51–68.

Edmonds, B., & Moss, S. (2005). From KISS to KIDS—An "anti-simplistic" modelling approach. In P. Davidsson, B. Logan and K. Takadama (Eds.), *Multi-agent and multi-agent-based simulation* (pp. 130–144). New York: Springer.

Food and Agriculture Organization (FAO). (2002). *The state of food insecurity in the world, 2001.* Rome: Food and Agriculture Organization of the United Nations.

Food and Agriculture Organization (FAO). (2009). *Declaration of the world summit on food security.* Rome: Food and Agriculture Organization of the United Nations.

Food and Agriculture Organization (FAO). (2015). *The State of Food Insecurity in the World 2015.* Rome: Food and Agriculture Organization of the United Nations.

Funtowicz, S. O., & Ravetz, J. R. (1990). *Uncertainty and quality in science for policy.* New York: Springer.

Gentner, D., & Stevens, A. L. (1983). *Mental models.* Hillsdale: Lawrence Erlbaum Associates.

Gibson, C. C., Ostrom, E., & Ahn, T. K. (2000). The concept of scale and the human dimensions of global change: A survey. *Ecological Economics, 32*(2), 217–239. doi: 10.1016/S0921-8009(99)00092-0.

Gilbert, N., & Troitzsch, K. G. (2005). *Simulation for the social scientist* (2nd ed.). Maidenhead: Open University Press.

Godet, M. (2008). *Strategic foresight la prospective.* Paris: Dunod.

Godfray, H. C., Beddington, J. R., Crute, I. R., Haddad, L., Lawrence, D., & Muir, J. F. (2010). Food security: the challenge of feeding 9 billion people. *Science, 327*(5967), 812–818. doi: science.1185383 [pii]10.1126/science.1185383.

Gregory, P. J., Ingram, J. S. I., & Brklacich, M. (2005). Climate change and food security. *Philosophical Transactions of the Royal Society B: Biological Sciences, 360*(1463), 2139–2148. doi: 10.1098/rstb.2005.1745.

Hales, D., Rouchier, J., & Edmonds, B. (2003). Model-to-model analysis. *Journal of Artificial Societies and Social Simulation, 6*(4).

Halbrendt, J., Gray, S. A., Crow, S., Radovich, T., Kimura, A. H., & Tamang, B. B. (2014). Differences in farmer and expert beliefs and the perceived impacts of conservation agriculture. *Global Environmental Change, 28,* 50–62.

Hammond, R. A., & Dubé, L. (2012). A systems science perspective and transdisciplinary models for food and nutrition security. *Proceedings of the National Academy of Sciences, 109*(31), 12356–12363.

Hastie, R., & Dawes, R. M. (Eds.). (2010). *Rational choice in an uncertain world: The psychology of judgment and decision making.* Thousand Oaks: Sage.

He, C., Okada, N., Zhang, Q., Shi, P., & Zhang, J. (2006). Modeling urban expansion scenarios by coupling cellular automata model and system dynamic model in Beijing, China. *Applied Geography, 26*(3),

323–345.

Innis, G., & Rexstad, E. (1983). Simulation model simplification techniques. *Simulation 41*(1), 7–15.

International Food Policy Research Institute (IFPRI). (2013). *2013 global hunger index map.* Washington, DC: International Food Policy Research Institute.

Jacobson, M. J., & Wilensky, U. (2006). Complex systems in education: Scientific and educational importance and implications for the learning sciences. *Journal of the Learning Sciences, 15*(1), 11–34. doi: 10.1207/s15327809jls1501_4.

Jakeman, A. J., Letcher, R. A., & Norton, J. P. (2006). Ten iterative steps in development and evaluation of environmental models. *Environmental Modelling & Software, 21*(5), 602–614.

Kandlikar, M., Risbey, J., & Dessai, S. (2005). Representing and communicating deep uncertainty in climate-change assessments. *Comptes Rendus Geoscience, 337*(4), 443–455.

Kasperson, R. E. (2008). Coping with deep uncertainty. *Integration Insights, 9.*

Kraemer, W. (2010). The cult of statistical significance. *CESifo Working Paper Series* (No. 3246).

Lee, D. B. (1973). Requiem for large-scale models. *Journal of the American Institute of Planners, 39*(3), 163–178.

Lempert, R., Popper, S., & Bankes, S. (2002). Confronting surprise. *Social Science Computer Review, 20*(4), 420–440. doi: 10.1177/089443902237320.

Lempert, R., Popper, S., & Bankes, S. (2003). *Shaping the next one hundred years: New methods for quantitative, long-term policy analysis.* Santa Monica, CA: RAND.

Letcher, R., Croke, B., Jakeman, A., & Merritt, W. (2006). An integrated modelling toolbox for water resources assessment and management in highland catchments: Model description. *Agricultural Systems, 89*(1), 106–131.

Ligmann-Zielinska, A. (2013). Spatially-explicit sensitivity analysis of an agent-based model of land use change. *International Journal of Geographical Information Science, 27*(9). doi: 10.1080/13658816.2013.782613.

Ligmann-Zielinska, A., Kramer, D., Spence Cheruvelil, K., & Soranno, P. (2014). Using uncertainty and sensitivity analyses in socioecological agent-based models to improve their analytical performance and policy relevance. *PLoS ONE 9*(10).

Ligmann-Zielinska, A., & Sun, L. (2010). Applying time dependent variance-based global sensitivity analysis to represent the dynamics of an agent-based model of land use change. *International Journal of Geographical Information Science, 24*(12), 1829–1850.

Liu, J. G., Dietz, T., Carpenter, S. R., Alberti, M., Folke, C., Moran, E., . . . Taylor, W. W. (2007). "Complexity of coupled human and natural systems." *Science 317*(5844): 1513–1516.

Lobell, D. B., Burke, M. B., Tebaldi, C., Mastrandrea, M. D., Falcon, W. P., & Naylor, R. L. (2008). Prioritizing climate change adaptation needs for food security in 2030. *Science, 319*(5863), 607–610. doi: 10.1126/science.1152339.

Longley, P. A., Goodchild, M. F., Maguire, D. J., Rhind, D. W. (2010). *Geographic Information Systems and Science.* Jefferson City: Wiley.

Luft, J., & Ingham, H. (1955). Luft, J., & Ingham, H. (1961) The Johari window, a graphic model of interpersonal awareness. *Human Relations Training News, 5*(1), 6–7.

Mallampalli, V. R., Mavrommati, G., Thompson, J., Duveneck, M., Meyer, S., Ligmann-Zielinska, A., Gottschalk Druschke, C., Hychka, K., Kenney, M. A., Kok, K., Borsuk, M. E. (2016). Methods for translating narrative scenarios into quantitative assessments of land use change. *Environmental Modelling & Software, 82,* 7–20.

Mavrommati, G., Baustian, M., & Dreelin, E. (2013). Coupling socioeconomic and lake systems for sustainability: A conceptual analysis using Lake St. Clair region as a case study. *Ambio, 43*(3), 275–287. doi: 10.1007/s13280-013-0432-4.

McIntosh, B. S., Seaton, R. A. F., & Jeffrey, P. (2007). Tools to think with? Towards understanding the use of computer-based support tools in policy relevant research. *Environmental Modelling & Software, 22,* 640–648. doi: 10.1016/j.envsoft.2005.12.015.

Meadows, D. H., & Wright, D. (2008). *Thinking in systems: A primer.* White River Junction: Chelsea Green.

Messina, J. P., Evans, T. P., Manson, S. M., Shortridge, A. M., Deadman, P. J., Verburg, P. H. . (2008). Complex systems models and the management of error and uncertainty. *Journal of Land Use Science, 3,* 11–25.

Minkler, M., & Wallerstein, N. (2003). Introduction to community based participatory research: New issues and emphases. In M. Minkler & N. Wallerstein *Community-based participatory research for health* (pp. 5–19). San Francisco: Wiley.

Oberkampf, W. L., Helton, J. C., Joslyn, C. A., Wojtkiewicz, S. F., & Ferson, S. (2004). Challenge problems: uncertainty in system response given uncertain parameters. *Reliability Engineering & System Safety, 85*(1), 11–19.

Oluoko-Odingo, A. A. (2010). Vulnerability and adaptation to food insecurity and poverty in Kenya. *Annals of the Association of American Geographers, 101*(1), 1–20. doi: 10.1080/00045608.2010.532739.

Pahl-Wostl, C. (2002). Towards sustainability in the water sector—The importance of human actors and processes of social learning. *Aquatic Sciences, 64*(4), 394–411. doi: 10.1007/pl00012594.

Parker, D. C., Hessl, A., & Davis, S. (2008). Complexity, land-use modeling, and the human dimension: Fundamental challenges for mapping unknown outcome spaces. *Geoforum, 39*(2), 789–804. doi: 10.1016/j.geoforum.2007.05.005.

Parry, M., Rosenzweig, C., & Livermore, M. (2005). Climate change, global food supply and risk of hunger. *Philosophical Transactions of the Royal Society B: Biological Sciences, 360*(1463), 2125–2138. doi: DOI 10.1098/rstb.2005.1751.

Polhill, J., & Gotts, N. (2009). Ontologies for transparent integrated human-natural system modelling. *Landscape Ecology, 24*(9), 1255–1267.

Preacher, K. J., Zyphur, M. J., & Zhang, Z. (2010). A general multilevel SEM framework for assessing multilevel mediation. *Psychological Methods, 15*(3), 209–233. doi: 10.1037/a0020141.

Raudenbush, S., & Bryk, A. (2002). *Hierarchical linear models.* Thousand Oaks: Sage.

Renn, O. (2008) *Risk governance: Coping with uncertainty in a complex world.* London: Earthscan.

Richardson, G. (2010). Reflections on the Foundations of System Dynamics and Systems Thinking. Paper presented at the System Dynamics Society Conference, Seoul.

Rouchier, J, Cioffi-Revilla, C., Polhill, J.G., Takadama, K. (2008) Progress in model-to-model analysis. *Journal of Artificial Societies and Social simulation, 11*(2), 8.

Saltelli, A. & Funtowicz, S. (2014). When all models are wrong. *Issues in Science and Technology, 30*(2), 79–85.

Saltelli, A., Ratto, M., Andres, T., Campolongo, F., Cariboni, J., & Gatelli, D. (2008). *Global sensitivity analysis: The primer.* Chichester, UK: Wiley-Interscience.

Saltelli, A., Tarantola, S., Campolongo, F., & Ratto, M. (2004). *Sensitivity analysis in practice: A guide to assessing scientific models.* Chichester, UK: Wiley.

Sarewitz, D. (2004). How science makes environmental controversies worse. *Environmental Science & Policy, 7*(5), 385–403. doi: 10.1016/j.envsci.2004.06.001.

Schaldach, R., & Priess, J. A. (2008). Integrated models of the land system: A review of modelling approaches on the regional to global scale. *Living Reviews in Landscape Research, 2,* 1–34 doi: 10.12942/lrlr-2008-1.

Schmitt Olabisi, L., Blythe, S., Ligmann-Zielinska, A., & Marquart-Pyatt, S. (2013). Modeling as a tool for cross-disciplinary communication in solving environmental problems. In M. O'Rourke, S. Crowley, S. Eigenbrode & J. Wulfhorst (Eds.), *Enhancing communication & collaboration in interdisciplinary research* (pp. 271–291). Thousand Oaks: Sage.

Schmitt Olabisi, L., Kapuscinski, A. R., Johnson, K. A., Reich, P. B., Stenquist, B., & Draeger, K. J. (2010). Using scenario visioning and participatory system dynamics modeling to investigate the future: Lessons from Minnesota 2050. *Sustainability, 2*(8), 2686–2706.

Schmitt Olabisi, L., Reich, P. B., Johnson, K. A., Kapuscinski, A. R., Suh, S., & Wilson, E. J. (2009). Reducing greenhouse gas emissions for climate stabilization: Framing regional options. *Environmental Science & Technology, 43*(6), 1696–1703. doi: 10.1021/es801171a.

Senge, P. M. (1990). *The fifth discipline.* New York: Century Business.

Shanthikumar, J. G., & Sargent, R. G. (1983). A unifying view of hybrid simulation/analytic models and modeling. *Operations research, 31*(6), 1030–1052.

Shoham, Y. (1990). Nonmonotonic reasoning and causation. *Cognitive Science, 14*(2), 213–252. doi: 10.1207/s15516709cog1402_2.

Singh, I., L. Squire, & J. Strauss. (1986) *Agricultural household models: extensions, applications, and policy.* Baltimore: Johns Hopkins University Press.

Smith, J., & Smith, P. (2007). *Introduction to environmental modelling.* New York: Oxford University Press.

Smithson, M., & Bammer, G. (2008). Uncertainty: Metaphor, motives and morals. *Integration Insights, 8.* https://i2s.anu.edu.au/wp-content/uploads/2009/10/integration-insight_8.pdf.

Snijders, T. A. B., & Bosker, R. (2012). *Multilevel analysis: An introduction to basic and advanced multilevel modeling* (2nd ed.). Thousand Oaks: Sage.

Soboll, A., Elbers, M., Barthel, R., Schmude, J., Ernst, A., & Ziller, R. (2011). Integrated regional modelling and scenario development to evaluate future water demand under global change conditions. *Mitigation and Adaptation Strategies for Global Change, 16*(4), 477–498. doi: 10.1007/s11027-010-9274-6.

Staley, D., Dias, M. P., Tzankova, V., Schiphorst, T., & Behar, K. E. (2009). Imagining possible futures with a scenario space. *Parsons Journal for Information Mapping, 1*(4), 1–8.

Sterman, J., & Sweeney, L. (2007). Understanding public complacency about climate change: adults' mental models of climate change violate conservation of matter. *Climatic Change, 80*(3–4), 213–238. doi: 10.1007/s10584-006-9107-5.

Swinerd, C., & McNaught, K. R. (2012). Design classes for hybrid simulations involving agent-based and system dynamics models. *Simulation Modelling Practice and Theory, 25,* 118–133. doi: 10.1016/j.simpat.2011.09.002.

Timmer, C. P. (2012). Behavioral dimensions of food security. *Proceedings of the National Academy of*

Sciences of the United States of America, 109(31), 12315–12320. doi: 10.1073/pnas.0913213107.

UNICEF. (1990). *A UNICEF policy review: Strategy for improved nutrition of children and women in developing countries.* New York: United Nations Children's Emergency Fund.

van den Belt, M. (2004). *Mediated modeling: A system dynamics approach to environmental consensus building.* Washington, DC: Island Press.

Walker, W. E., Harremoes, P., Rotmans, J., Van Der Sluijs, J. P., Van Asselt, M. B. A., Janssen, P. (2003). Defining uncertainty: A conceptual basis for uncertainty management in model-based decision support. *Integrated Assessment, 4*(1), 5–17.

Warmink, J. J., Janssen, J. A. E. B., Booij, M. J., & Krol, M. S. (2010). Identification and classification of uncertainties in the application of environmental models. *Environmental Modelling & Software, 25*(12), 1518–1527.

Weiner, B. (1985). "Spontaneous" causal thinking. *Psychological Bulletin, 97(1),* 74–84. doi: 10.1037/0033-2909.97.1.74.Whitley, C. T., Rivers L., Mattes, S., Marquart-Pyatt, S., Ligmann-Zielinska, A., Schmitt Olabisi, L., & Du, J. (2017). Climate-induced migration: Using mental models to explore aggregate and individual decision-making. *Journal of Risk Research, 21*(8), 1–17.

Zeigler, B. (1976). *Theory of modelling and simulation.* New York: Wiley.

Zellner, M. L. (2007). Generating policies for sustainable water use in complex scenarios: An integrated land-use and water-use model of Monroe County, Michigan. *Environment and Planning B: Planning and Design, 34*(4), 664–686.

Nova: A Novel Tool for Collaborative Agent-Based and Dynamic Systems Modeling

Nancy Darling, Richard Salter, and Ian Burns

olving complex problems requires teams of people who bring different skills and expertise to the table. Interdisciplinary collaboration requires its own skillset. Not only do people working in different disciplines often use different vocabularies, they may have different paradigms for understanding and producing knowledge and different priorities about what they believe is practical, important or necessary in attacking a problem. Finally, people in different fields may work at different levels of analysis. For instance, infant malnutrition can be approached as a cellular-level problem in terms of food consumption and composition, as a dyadic problem of feeding in the parent-infant relationship, or as a broader problem of family dynamics, education, shopping choices, or city-wide access to food. Understanding each level of a problem can be important, but it can be difficult for teams to communicate across levels and understand the complexities of how each set of processes feeds into the other.

Models and simulations can be useful for articulating the linkages among different levels of analysis and areas of expertise. By making assumptions explicit, they also help to facilitate communication among collaborators. Nicolson and colleagues (2002) point out that the specialization of knowledge in, for example, ecological and environmental science demands a problem-solving approach that is interdisciplinary and collaborative. Ecological and environmental science provides a particularly cogent example because the level of analysis used to approach different components of a problem may run from the genetic to the individual to the landscape. Almost by definition, generating solutions requires understanding how different systems interact over time. Simulation models are particularly effective for integrating disciplinary knowledge of stakeholders with different areas of expertise. When the diverse nature of the participants' knowledge is reflected in the model structure, both building and running models allows them to see how different systems work together (Nicolson et al., 2002). The ability to develop a series of models that can be tested and refined ("rapid prototyping"; Starfield & Salter, 2010) is facilitated by software and other tools that are easy to use and provide readily understood graphic output. Running live models that can be manipulated to simulate different assumptions allows stakeholders to have a better understanding of the dynamic processes under discussion. Looking at concrete results of a prototype model provides stakeholders with "real" data to discuss and facilitates productive exchanges and refinement of conceptual models. Success is more likely when the software system used facilitates easy editing, rapid prototyping, sensitivity analysis, and modular construction.

Having teams use software to turn conceptual models into computational models can provide additional benefits. In this chapter, we use the term "computational models" to refer to computer simulations that illustrate how different processes unfold over time. Teams can use computational models in different ways to achieve different ends. Collaborative teams can (1) manipulate pre-built models to gain insight into their problem, (2) develop progressively more specific understandings of a problem through moving from a "sketch" to a finished model, or (3) develop new models from scratch. The goal of this chapter is to describe a freely distributed software package, Nova (Getz et al., 2015; Starfield & Salter, 2010; Salter, 2013), that can be used to facilitate collaborative modeling of a wide range of problems.

Nova was developed as part of an NSF initiative for introducing dynamic systems thinking to novice modelers across disciplines. It is unique among computational modeling platforms in that it:

1. Naturally supports the creation of models in the system dynamics, spatial and agent-based modeling paradigms in a single desktop application.
2. Uses a visual toolbox to express model design, providing automatic conversion of such models to script form for execution.
3. Promotes hierarchical design, code reuse, and extensibility through the use of plug-ins.

This chapter uses an example drawn from the social sciences to illustrate how Nova works: student-teacher interactions in a classroom. This very simple set of nested deterministic models is used because it clearly operates at different levels of analysis and also because it illustrates how Nova models can be built up by different stakeholders with knowledge in different areas as well as the advantages of using dynamic system modeling to understand interactive processes that unfold over time. Although our example is drawn from the social sciences, Nova comes with an easily accessible library of models drawn from the biology, wildlife management, and physical science literatures.

Dynamic Systems Theory in Developmental Science: An Example

Like ecology and environmental science, the field of human developmental science has historically been interdisciplinary in nature and spanned research embracing biological, psychological, sociological, historical, and epidemiological approaches (e.g., Bronfenbrenner, 1979). The dynamic, interdisciplinary nature of the field is apparent in how the NICHD Child Health and Behavior Branch describes the developmental processes that underlie child health and behavior in its mission statement. They say child health and development is "best . . . studied as a variable process in which individual differences in cognitive, social, emotional, language, neurobiological and physical maturation, environment, life experiences, and genetics interact in complex ways" (NICHD CHBB, 2015). Despite this conceptual emphasis on multiple processes interacting over time, the techniques used to study these processes most often are linear, assume that within-person change can be inferred from between-person change (the problem of ergodicity; Gayles & Molenaar, 2013), and are not well-suited for studying multiple simultaneous processes that are reciprocal, recursive, or self-regulating over time (Kunnen, 2012; van Geert, 2012). In other words, they are most often approached using a statistical methodological framework rather than a systems dynamic one. Finally, it has become increasingly apparent that development and, particularly, medical and behavioral interventions, are best understood in terms of individual patterning of co-existing and self-reinforcing processes and behaviors (Darling & Cumsille, 2003; van Geert, 2012). It is exactly this type of relationship that dynamic systems techniques are useful for understanding (van Geert, 2012).

Despite this, computer-based dynamic systems modeling has rarely been used to study human development or related health-related behaviors. For example, only one of forty-one chapters in the *Handbook of Developmental Research Methods* (Laursen, Little, & Card, 2012) discusses dynamic systems methodology. A brief search yields only eleven articles using dynamic systems modeling published in *Child Development* and *Developmental Psychology* since 2000, and several of these papers focus on use of simultaneous differential equations for model development, rather than on the use of computational modeling per se (e.g., Howe & Lewis, 2005). Underutilization of dynamic systems modeling as a tool results from two major factors. First, sociology, psychology, and medicine have traditionally relied on sophisticated statistical models, with researchers receiving relatively little training in other methodologies such as modeling (cognitive science and epidemiology are exceptions). Second, software developed to serve the dynamic systems modeling community (e.g., Stella, Vensim, Netlogo) and the modeling libraries developed to teach this software have not reflected the research needs of most developmentalists, focusing on ecology, physics, and chemistry instead (e.g., http://www.iseesystems.com).

How can computational models help teams solve problems? Computational models focus on how things influence each other (processes) and how these processes change over time. For example, figure 1 is a simple conceptual model of our example. In this model, we have a focal dyad: a teacher and student$_t$. The teacher and student$_t$ influence each other reciprocally. As teacher discipline increases, student$_t$ mischief decreases. As student$_t$ mischief increases, teacher discipline increases. Importantly, this model is not static: it assumes that these reciprocal processes unfold over time. Because the influences of discipline on mischief and mischief on discipline are not mirror images of one another (the former is negative, the latter is positive), how these processes will unfold over time is not immediately clear. One possible scenario is illustrated in figure 2. This complex oscillating pattern that slowly amplifies over time was not immediately obvious from the initial conceptual relationship and depends on the exact assumptions of the model. This is where the collaborative team comes in and where computational models become useful. For example, three important parameters in determining how this system unfolds are (1) how big the influences of discipline and mischief are on each other (responsiveness), (2) how closely synchronized discipline and mischief are in time, and (3) the behavioral range or flexibility that teachers have in their discipline and students have in their mischief (k). Although

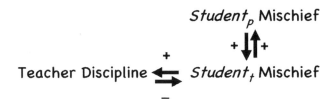

FIGURE 1. Conceptual model of teacher-student interactions. This model focuses on the target *teacher:student₁* dyad. In this model, teachers' discipline and *student* mischief are reciprocally related, as are students and peer mischief (*student_p*).

a group of collaborators might generally agree on the conceptual model, useful discussions of each of these parameters could result in a much clearer understanding of how this dyadic system works. Looking at the output of the model makes it much easier to talk about how the results of the model differ from collaborator expectations, why that might happen, and whether it results from a problem in the conceptual model or the way it is operationalized mathematically.

Models are based on rules about how things change over time. That's what collaborators need to hammer out. These rules are based on relationships that are articulated either mathematically or algorithmically. For example, in the model of student and teacher behavior illustrated in figure 2, changes in student behavior per unit of time get incrementally smaller as their behavior gets closer to maximum mischievousness.[1] In other words, we see a decelerating increase in mischief over time as they get more and more deviant. In some ways, that makes intuitive sense: as the student's behavior first begins to deviate from acceptable norms, changes may be relatively large. However, there may be only so far the student can go; thus their incremental increases in mischief become smaller and smaller as they get closer to that maximum level of deviance. Different stakeholders might disagree on exactly what those curves should look like. An alternative perspective might be that students start with small increases in mischief but increases in mischief accelerate as they become more deviant. As currently modeled, student change also decelerates as they get closer to expected normative behavior (low mischief). Teacher and student decelerate at the same rate. Are these assumptions correct? Discussion of such issues is exactly what the precision required by the modeling process facilitates. Mathematically, one can develop equations that express any of those behavioral patterns (and many more). We return to this model later to see how it can be further articulated.

Barriers to Modeling and the Advantages of Nova

Equation-based relationships can generally be referred to as a dynamic systems or stock and flow models. An alternative approach to modeling is algorithmic. You can write rules that say that if the people closest to you are more mischievous than you are, you will move away from them in virtual space. Or you can create a rule that says a tree has a 75 percent chance of burning if the one next to it is on fire. These are rule-based models where complex patterns derive from the behavior of individual agents (agent-based and spatial modeling). As can be seen in these examples, the development of a computational model requires very explicit articulation of

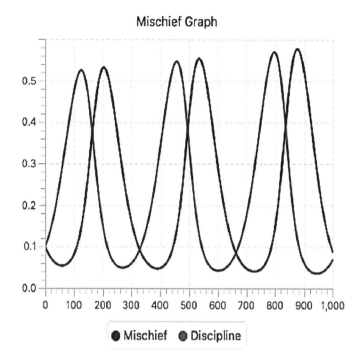

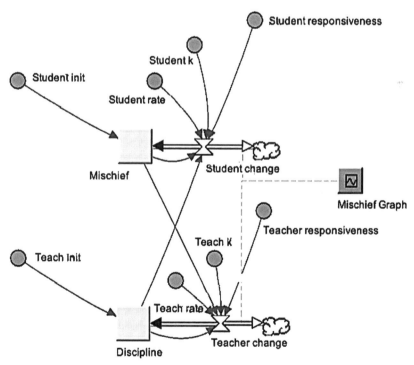

FIGURE 2. Student-teacher dyadic behavior over time. The top of this figure illustrates how student mischief declines in response to teach discipline. This output is derived from the Nova model in the bottom figure.

relationships. Useful discussions are often spurred when stakeholders make their assumptions and beliefs clear, revealing differences. Building computational models together helps to spark those conversations. Underlying assumptions need to be articulated and agreed upon. Broad statements of how one stock or process affects others need to be quantified (for linear effects) or articulated (for algorithmic ones).

Computational modeling has many advantages but requires software. Learning any software platform has costs. In addition, collaborators come to a project with their own preferences and requirements for hardware—they will typically already be working with hardware running Windows, Mac, Android, Linux, or iOS operating systems. Nova is versatile in that it runs custom models of various types on multiple platforms. Because it can run dynamic systems stock and flow models and agent-based, network, event-driven, and spatial models using the same interface, it minimizes learning time. Thus, rather than deciding whether to develop an agent-based or stock and flow model based on the available software, researchers can develop models to fit the problems they are studying. Importantly, as we illustrate below, different levels or aspects of a problem can use different types of models. For example, the interaction of a teacher and student can be modeled with a stock and flow model. This stock and flow interaction can then form the basis of a spatial model, with multiple students influencing each other, or an agent-based model in which students are attracted to others like themselves and reinforce each other's characteristics. This minimizes the learning time involved in mastering multiple platforms. In addition, because Nova models can be built on machines running Windows, Mac, and Linux operating systems and can be run and explored using smartphones or tablets, it increases accessibility to broader user communities.

Nova as a Modeling Platform: An Example

Stock and Flow Models

The following example illustrates key features of Nova and its use for a range of problems. Although the mathematical model on which this example is based is hypothetical, in a real-world application, it would be built upon theory and parameter estimates taken from the extant literature. Figure 2, which we examined earlier, shows a simple dyadic model in which *student mischief* and *teacher discipline* are reciprocally related. In other words, teacher discipline rises in response to student mischief, which declines in response to discipline. Both student and teacher *base rates* and *responsiveness to partner behavior* can be manipulated.

Several features of this model differentiate it from a traditional statistical model. First, the model illustrates how stable patterns of behavior can emerge from reciprocally related behaviors that change over time (the increasing oscillations to the right of the graph). In this model, all variables are reciprocally related and moderate one another. In addition, the changes in both student and teacher behaviors slow as they reach the top and bottom ranges of the measures, something not typically modeled using traditional statistics, which have difficulty making accurate predictions near the model floors and ceilings. There is another important paradigmatic distinction between traditional statistical models and computational models. While a statistical model parsimoniously summarizes observed data, a model such as this one would be used to generate data. It allows modelers to explore many different "what-if" scenarios. For example, collaborators could systematically vary teacher and student characteristics (mischief and discipline base rates and student and teacher responsiveness to each other's behavior) to see what patterns result. This can be done in Nova using batch processes running through researcher-specified permutations. Because it was designed to facilitate modeling of biological and social systems, different types of distributions for inputs (e.g., normal, Poisson) can be specified for each variable. Once this simulation data is generated, it can be analyzed and compared to predictions from theory or from empirical data to provide a stronger test of specific hypotheses.

Nested Models

Many important problems involve nested data. For example, cellular processes are nested within organs, conflict behaviors are nested within dyads (e.g., Darling, Cohan, Burns, & Thompson, 2008), and students are nested within classrooms (Raudenbush & Bryk, 2002). Nova facilitates modeling of nested processes because it is designed to save submodels as "capsules" and aggregate them at higher levels. Figure 3 shows the results of a model of a four-student classroom in which each student has a different initial mischief level. Their different trajectories in response to teacher discipline are seen in the graph. All students share a common teacher, whose store of patience is determined by recent mischief in the classroom as a whole. Models of individual teacher-student dyads were imported from the model discussed in figure 2, with dyads now nested in a classroom. Importantly, nested models can be used to examine individual trajectories under different conditions (for example, a well-behaved student in a classroom of mischievous peers). Using a team approach, classroom-level processes, such as patience, can be modeled by one group, while dyadic processes, such as student-teacher dyads, could be modeled by another.

Spatial Models

Spatial models are those in which individual agents are nested within groups and influenced by others near them. These can be literally "near," as when fire spreads from one tree to the next, or figuratively "near," as when memes spread through social networks. Spatial models can also be used to model neural nets. Some agent-based models allow individual agents to move, allowing modeling of, for example, social contagion, disease spread, or peer selection and reciprocal influence.

Figure 4 is the final result of a model of a twenty-eight-student classroom. Each student's mischief is modeled using the same capsules as in figures 2 and 3 and teacher patience is again modeled in response to the mischief aggregated across the classroom. What has been added to this model is that student mischief is now affected not only by the students' own base rates and by teacher discipline, but also by the mischief of the students' neighbors. We now have the full conceptual model sketched in figure 1. Different numeric and color values represent levels of mischief and teacher patience and discipline at the dyadic level at the model end point. This spatial model includes behavioral contagion of students seated next to one another. It was

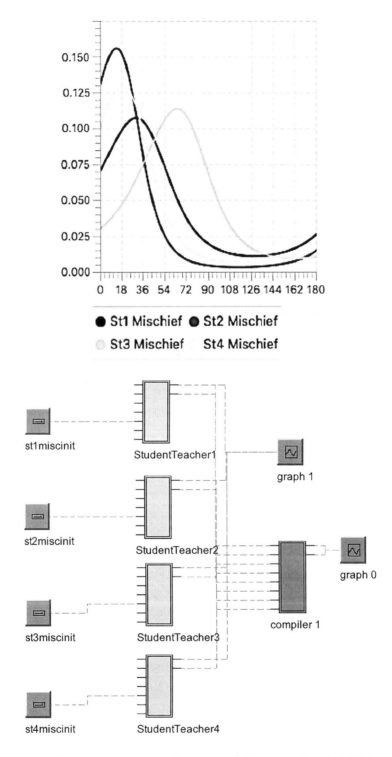

FIGURE 3. Four students in a shared classroom. The top graph illustrates the mischief of four students over time nested within a classroom with one teacher. It is the results from the model pictured at the bottom of the figure, in which teacher patience is depleted by all four students.

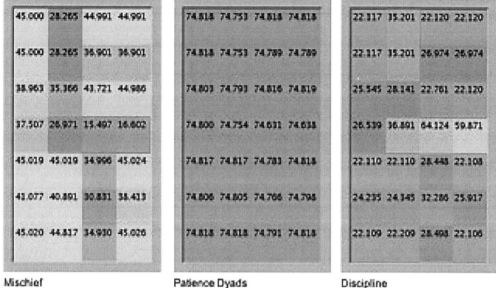

Mischief   Patience Dyads   Discipline

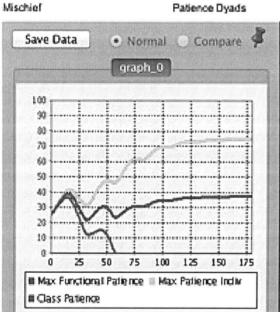

Patience Graph

FIGURE 4. A spatial model of 28 students in a classroom. Mischief of each student is represented in the first grid and the teacher's patience and disciplinary behavior with each child in the second two grids. Each cell in the grids enacts the full model shown in Figure 2 plus teacher patience.

initiated with a random normal distribution of student mischief levels. However, researchers could specify both initial levels and variability and create individual differences in, for example, students' susceptibility to peer behavior. In this way, researchers might model the behavior of a student with ADD in different types or classrooms and with different types of teachers. The bottom of figure 4 illustrates one consequence of allowing reciprocal processes to unfold at both the individual and classroom levels. The teacher's store of patience with the classroom as a whole falls precipitously as they spend more time disciplining the subset of students who engage in high levels of mischief. Figure 4 also shows the teacher's patience with the best behaving student in the classroom. Individual patience with this student rises over time because this student is seldom disciplined. However, the teacher's functional patience with this student is the patience that determines her discipline behavior. It is influenced by both their dyadic interaction with the student and their overall store of patience. In this classroom, the teacher acts with less patience with her best student than would be so in a less mischievous classroom. In addition, the functional patience of the teacher is not perfectly linked to the behavior of the individual student. As in real classrooms, each student is affected not just by their own characteristics and their own interactions with the teacher, but by how their neighbor behaves and by the discipline that other students experience. As with all models, Nova allows modelers to run through a series of theoretical or empirically derived values for each part of the process, output the results, and analyze them in an analysis package of their choice.

Agent-Based Spatial Models

Nova is capable of agent-based spatial modeling by layering models of "individuals" on top of models of their "ground." For example, the model of an individual student can accept input from models of nearby students. This information can then interact with the model of the student's corresponding ground to simulate movement within space. Grounds can be either two or three dimensional. The final model in this series shows the spatial model of the classroom above. In this model, students move towards others who are similar in mischief. This creates pockets of mischief in a classroom. Because mischief is contagious, difficult students become more mischievous over time and the least-mischievous students even less so.

Nova Nuts and Bolts: Understanding the Architecture

The previous series of examples illustrates some of Nova's potential for solving problems. How does it work? Nova is a Java-based modeling platform that naturally supports the creation of models in the system dynamics, spatial and agent-based modeling paradigms within a single desktop application that can be disseminated through browser-resident apps. Nova uses a visual, icon-based language to express model design and provides automatic conversion for such models to script form for execution. Nova's architecture promotes hierarchical design, code reuse, and extensibility through the use of plug-ins. Nova models can be built on computers running Apple, Windows, and Linux operating systems. Nova models can also be exported and run as in-browser applications on any device that the browser runs in, including smartphones and tablets.

As described in our teacher-student examples, Nova is fundamentally a dynamic modeling system that is extended through hierarchical design to express spatial and agent-based relationships. Stock and flow dynamic systems models are build describing processes, as in figure 2. Nova can easily multiply those individual models so they can be combined together at higher levels, as in the four-student classroom in figure 3. Those models can be used to populate a fixed matrix, as in the twenty-eight-student classroom (figure 4). Or an agent-based model can be developed in which dynamic systems models are used to control the interaction between individual agents and the ground on which they "move."

Stock and flow models are built using an icon-based visual language modeler to manipulate on a canvas by pointing and clicking. The functions that determine how these icons interact can be entered by clicking and entering equations. More-detailed editing and programming can be done directly through the equation editor. Users can use NovaScript—similar to JavaScript—to develop specialized functions. Nova also facilitates moving data into and out of other data analysis programs like R, SPSS, Excel, or SAS. Models, submodels, and scripts can be shared between models or between users.

Nova's Structure

The basic units for building Nova models are *capsules, chips,* and *aggregators* (figure 5). Nova focuses on the creation of a modular unit called a "capsule." Each capsule is a complete model that interacts with its environment through an interface consisting of input and output channels. The simplest capsule might contain a stock and flow model such as the teacher-student model in figure 2. When these complete models are introduced into a superordinate model of a classroom, they become chips. Figure 3 shows four student-teacher dyads. Each student-teacher dyad is represented as a chip and contains a full model of that interaction—the full functionality pictured in figure 2. In this case, we have a four-student classroom modeled in a capsule which contains four chips. Each of these chips has I/O channels that move data in and out of the dyadic, lower-level capsules and can communicate with one another or with other capsules or model elements. One of the most powerful features of Nova is that capsules (i.e., full models) can be introduced as chips into other larger and superordinate capsules, maintaining their full functionality. Capsules may also be exported and reused in other projects.

Looking at figure 3 in more detail, we see four student-teacher dyads represented as chips. The seven input pins on the left of each chip represent potential input parameters defined by the modeler in the student-teacher capsule the chip represents. They include, for instance, prior student mischief, prior teacher discipline, and teacher patience. Similarly, the two pins on the right side of each chip represent potential outputs from the student-teacher capsules, for example current discipline and mischief. In other words, the two outputs the student-teacher dyad produce are determined by seven inputs. There is an additional chip in the classroom model labeled "compiler 1." This chip takes information from each student-teacher model (chip) and combines it together to create classroom-level data. Note that there are two outputs from each student-teacher chip (eight total) and there are eight potential inputs to the classroom chip. The classroom chip compiler 1 has been configured to combine information from different inputs to produce two outputs: the maximum classroom Discipline and Mischief at each time point. These are output to a graph (the square labeled "graph 0" in figure 3). We have also taken the output of each individual student's mischief from their respective chips and output them to a second graphing chip (the square labeled "graph 1"). The output of this chip is shown at the top of figure 3. These functions are available in the Nova graphic palette and can be configured by the user. This nesting of models could continue, with the classroom

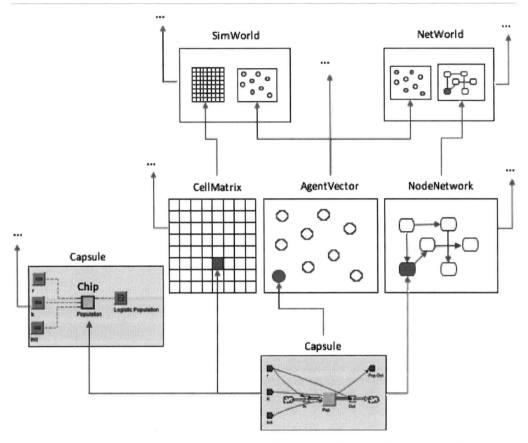

FIGURE 5. Combining Nova components. Capsules, which contain full models, can be easily integrated into different containers: as chips or within spatial grids (CellMatrices). They can also be integrated into AgentVectors or NodeNetworks that determine the state of different cells within a CellMatrix.

capsule in figure 3 becoming a chip that might be embedded in a higher capsule environment representing, for example, a school.

The chip is one type of *container*. It contains all the functions of a more complex submodel. Spatial and agent-based models are constructed using array-like containers called "aggregators." For example, the twenty-eight-student classroom in figure 4 is a 4×7 cell array, each of which contains a capsule containing the figure 2 model. The current implementation provides five types of aggregators that can be combined together to produce different model types (figure 5).

AgentVectors are how Nova represents agents moving through space. Technically, AgentVectors are one-dimensional arrays of agents. As described in figure 4, where students in a classroom moved through space and moved closer to other students with similar levels of mischief to themselves, each agent is a model (capsule). An AgentVector can be associated with an agent such that it includes a representation for location and movement within a two-dimensional space (the grid in which student agents move). AgentVectors also manage dynamic creation and destruction of agents. For example, AgentVectors can be used to represent bacteria and white blood cells, where bacteria die when they encounter white blood cells. In this model, an AgentVector would be used to describe changes in a series of cells representing the movement of the bacteria through a spatial grid. It would also determine that when the bacteria move to a cell occupied by a white blood cell, its state would go from alive to dead.

CellMatrices are two-dimensional arrays of capsules (e.g., the twenty-eight-student classroom). They provide a means for representing interacting capsules in a spatial array (cellular automata). CellMatrices can connect capsules using either a four-sided Cartesian or a hexagonal topology. CellMatrices represent the spatial structure within which information is exchanged between capsules. In agent-based models, they are spatial structures in which the agents of an AgentVector move. Figure 6 shows a simplified model of fire spreading through a forest. The forest is represented as a cellular automaton in a two-dimensional Cartesian array. Each cell represents either a tree or a firewall. If it is a firewall, it prevents transmission of fire. If it is a tree, it can catch fire from one of its neighbors, and subsequently ignite of its neighbors. Nova implements this by having each cell in the CellMatrix contain a Nova capsule with single state component ("tree") that has one of three states: unburnt, burning or burned. A 50×50 array of these capsules is contained in single CellMatrix, which facilitates the communication that allows a cell to detect the state of its neighbors.

NodeNetworks are another way of connecting agents. NodeNetworks are an array of graph nodes with weighted directed connections. These can be used to model diverse phenomena such neural networks, but also to model the relative likelihood of contagion under different conditions. Figure 7 shows a Susceptible-Infected-Resistance (SIR) model over a network of interconnected nodes. Such a model is useful in modeling the spread of a computer virus, for example. Like the CellMatrix, the NodeNetwork maintains the array of individual nodes (each a capsule) and facilitates communication. Note that, while this model limits connectivity to immediate neighbors in a cartesian grid, this is not an inherent limitation in the system.

SimWorlds combine Agentvectors with Cellmatrices, so that agent locations correspond to matrix coordinates. The result is a virtual space of interacting agents and cells. For example, disease vectors can be represented as moving agents that can interact with different types of tissues.

NetWorlds are analogous to SimWorlds substituting a NodeNetwork for a CellMatrix as the space in which the agents operate.

Nova Tools

In addition to assets that constitute the structure, Nova includes components used for visualization, data entry, advanced computations and the like. These are implemented as plug-ins; that is, Java-coded objects that are added to the base set of model components. Nova ships with a basic set of useful plug-ins, such as clocked chips; however, a user familiar with Java may write additional plug-ins. These may be specialized to very specific domains. For example, a neural net plug-in is available to model a feed-forward, back-propagating, multilayer perceptron-based neural network configurable to any desired topology). Specialized plug-ins would likely be an important part of any component kit built for specific problem domains.

Finally, it may be necessary to provide algorithms in code to define the relationships among

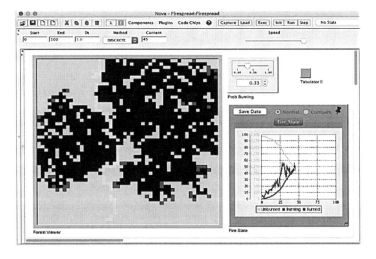

Treecell

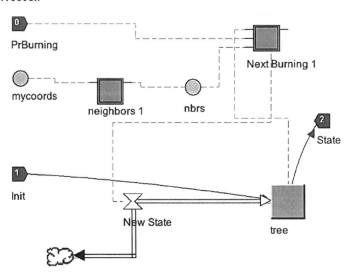

FIGURE 6. Fire spreading through a forest. The CellMatrix on the left is made up of a 50×50 grid of trees that are either not burnt (light gray), burning (dark gray) or burnt (black). A firebreak (white) is also represented within this model. The graph shows the current number of trees in each state at any point.

model components or to execute state-changing commands. Nova provides a component called a Codechip for this purpose. A Codechip is added to Nova's design canvas like any other component; unlike other components, a new Codechip is a blank slate. It has no built-in content. Any benefit must come from the programming that it includes. Like the Chip component, the Codechip presents input and output pins to connect with the rest of the model. They are represented by variables in the Codechip's program, which uses the NovaScript language, which is an extension of the familiar and well-documented JavaScript language. One example for a Codechip might be to compute the mean and variance of a set of data points. Once a Codechip has been created

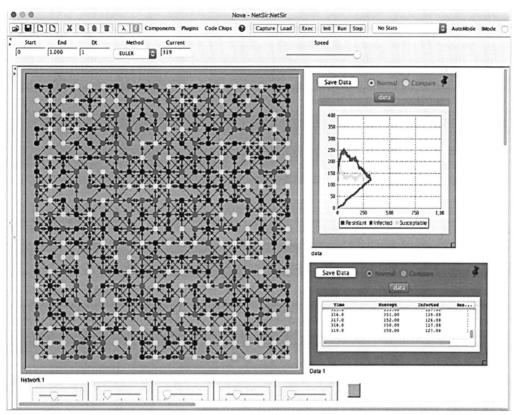

FIGURE 7. A NodeNetwork Susceptible-Infected-Resistance (SIR) model of the spread of a computer virus through a network. Each node in the matrix allows different likelihood of transmission to adjacent cells.

it enters the Codechip palette for the given model, and can be reused in multiple settings, or exported for reuse elsewhere.

At a deeper level, Nova's computational architecture comprises the semantics of NovaScript, a scripting language embedded in JavaScript. The NovaScript runtime environment is an extension of the ECMA 1.7 JavaScript standard. All Nova simulations are actually NovaScript programs executing on the NovaScript runtime interpreter. Nova has the flexibility that an experienced programmer can design many specialized components. These components can be saved, reused, and exported to other models and shared with other users.

Nova and Collaboration

Nova's flexibility and architecture make it particularly well-suited for collaborative efforts. We previously discussed how Nova's ability to export models to browser-resident apps allows stakeholders to manipulate, learn from, and refine models during collaborative work sessions. The graphic interface also facilitates experienced users working with teams to take sketch models and refine them through collaborative discussion of model outputs. The modular nature of capsules also allows collaborators with different expertise to work on different parts of a model. This is particularly easy because capsules can be exported, reused, and shared.

Summing up some of the advantages we have discussed through previous examples: Nova supports an eclectic set of modeling paradigms. Nova organically integrates system dynamics modeling with support for spatial geometries and mobile agents. Nova therefore provides a single platform for various models of different designs that may be produced by a single team. In other words, different team members can use Nova to develop stock and flow, spatial, agent-based, or neural net models without learning new software.

Nova's architecture promotes modular design. Nova's graphical design language encourages the creation of modular units (capsules) with well-defined interfaces. These submodels aid in model design by "factoring complexity" and promoting submodel reuse. They also permit simulations to be run at different levels. To use an analogy, one can build new models from previously developed capsules in the same way as one can build a new electronic device from previously developed chips or integrated circuits. This makes it easier to integrate contributions from multiple authors.

Nova is extensible. Nova's plug-in feature extends the expressiveness of the graphical language with new functionality. A plug-in API allows users to design and deploy new plug-ins.

Nova supports abstraction. *Abstraction* is the process of extracting a set of interacting elements which, together, create a well-defined computation over a given set of inputs and provide the ability to access that computation with different inputs from multiple points within the overall project. Nova's submodel and plug-in features are only two examples of its capability for abstraction. Unique to Nova are its clocked chips, which abstract an entire simulation run, and code chips, which provide new functionalities expressed in NovaScript as graphical components. In addition, submodel containers, or aggregators, manage large arrays of submodels used as agents or spatial elements in networks or cellular arrays.

Nova promotes asset reuse. Nova abstractions (submodels, plug-ins, clocked chips and code chips) may be exported and reused in other projects. It also becomes possible to create groups of reusable elements that address a particular problem area and distribute these "kits" to workers in those areas. The Nova website is planning to support an exchange to facilitate sharing of such assets.

Nova integrates with other technologies. These include R, GPS, and others in development.

Nova desktop integrates with its Web technologies: Nova models can be deployed remotely. *Nova On Line* can be used to distribute developed models through browser-resident apps. At the other end of the spectrum, *Nova On Server* can be used to implement large and complex models on servers or supercomputers.

The base model of Nova is freely distributed through NovaModeler.com. In addition to software, additional resources include a broad modeling library and a full series of training videos.

Conclusion

This chapter has presented Nova and shown how it can be used as a tool for collaborative modeling and especially as a means of promoting computational modeling to solve complex problems.

In addition to the models presented above, Nova has been used by teams of researchers in many successful projects in environmental science and epidemiology. Among these are for a model for rhino herd population viability analysis (Getz, Muellerklein et al., 2016), a model of the 2015 California measles epidemic (Getz, Carlson et al., 2016; Getz & Salter, 2015) and the 2014 African Ebola outbreak (Getz, Gonzalez et al., 2015; Getz & Salter, 2015), and a genetic algorithm-based study of foraging patterns among herding mammals (Getz, Salter & Lyons, 2015). The population viability study has resulted in an online application that can be used by investigators around the world using their own sets of parameters (Getz & Muellerklein, 2016).

Going forward, we hope that Nova will continue to facilitate the use of computational techniques in an expanding sphere of applications and, in doing so, promote collaboration on many levels.

NOTE

1. This and all models in this chapter are available as browser resident apps through www.numerusinc .com. Full Nova models are also available for download through that site. The Nova software is downloadable through novamodeller.com. These and many other models are available through that site as well. Equations and supporting NovaScript underlying the models are saved with each Nova model. Equations can be viewed using the Edit Component Equations command under Tools or exported using the Save Equations function under the File tab.

REFERENCES

Darling, N., Cohan, C. L., Burns, A., & Thompson, L. (2008). Within-family conflict behaviors as predictors of conflict in adolescent romantic relations. *Journal of Adolescence, 31*(6), 671–690. doi: 10.1016/j.adolescence.2008.10.003.

Darling, N., & Cumsille, P. (2003). Theory, measurement, and methods in the study of family influences on adolescent smoking. *Addiction, 98*(Supplement 1), 21–36.

Getz, W. M., Carlson, C., Dougherty, E., Porco, T. C., & Salter, R. (2016, April). An agent-based model of school closing in under-vaccinated communities during measles outbreaks. In *Proceedings of the Agent-Directed Simulation Symposium* (p. 10). Society for Computer Simulation International.

Getz, W. M., Gonzalez, J.-P., Salter, R., Bangura, J., Carlson, C., Coomber, M., Dougherty, E., Kargbo, D., Wolfe, N. D., & Wauquier, N. (2015). Tactics and strategies for managing Ebola outbreaks and the salience of immunization. *Computational and Mathematical Methods in Medicine.* doi. org/10.1155/2015/736507.

Getz, W. M., & Muellerklein, O. (2016). Numerus PVA: An interactive population viability analysis web app for single and multi-populations. http://www.numerusinc.com/webapps/pva.

Getz, W. M., Muellerklein, O., Lyons, A. J., Seidel, D. P., & Salter, R. (2016). A Nova web application for population viability and sustainable harvesting analyses. *World Conference on Natural Resource Modeling.* Paper 28. http://scholarexchange.furman.edu/.

Getz, W. M., & Salter, R. M. (2015). Nova transmission chain models for epidemic forecasting: Ebola and measles. Paper presented at the Impact of Environmental Changes on Infectious Diseases

Conference, Center for Discrete Mathematics and Theoretical Computer Science and Mathematics of Planet Earth, Sitges, Spain.

Getz, W. M., Salter, R., Lyons, A. J., & Sippl-Swezey, N. (2015). Panmictic and clonal evolution on a single patchy resource produces polymorphic foraging guilds. *PLOS ONE 10*(8): e0133732. doi:10.1371/journal.pone.0133732.

Getz, W. M., Salter R., & Muellerklein, O. (2015). A Nova model and web app for sustainable harvesting and population viability analyses in teaching and research. Paper presented at the DIMACS MPE 2013+ Workshop on Management of Natural Resources, Howard University, Washington, DC.

Getz, W. M., Salter, R., Seidel, D.P., & van Hooft, P. (2015). Sympatric speciation in structureless environments. *BMC Evolutionary Biology, 16*(50). doi: 10.1186/s12862-016-0617-0.

Getz, W. M., Salter, R., & Sippl-Swezey, N. (2015). The Numerus platform—An innovative simulation and modeling building environment. In L. Yilmaz, W. K V. Chan, I. Moon, T. M. K. Roeder, C. Macal, & M. D. Rossetti (Eds.) *Proceedings of the 2015 Winter Simulation Conference.* Piscataway, NJ: IEEE Press, 2015.

Getz, W. M., Salter, R. M., & Sippl-Swezey, N. (2015). Using nova to construct agent-based models for epidemiological teaching and research. In L. Yilmaz, W. K V. Chan, I. Moon, T. M. K. Roeder, C. Macal, & M. D. Rossetti (Eds.) *Proceedings of the 2015 Winter Simulation Conference.* Piscataway, NJ: IEEE Press, 2015.

Gayles, J. G., & Molenaar, P. C. M. (2013). The utility of person-specific analyses for investigating developmental processes: An analytic primer on studying the individual. *International Journal of Behavioral Development, 37*(6), 549–562. doi: 10.1177/0165025413504857.

Howe, M. L., & Lewis, M. D. (2005). The importance of dynamic systems approaches for understanding development. *Developmental Review, 25*(3–4), 247–251. doi: 10.1016/j.dr.2005.09.002.

Kunnen, S. (Ed.). (2012). *A dynamic systems approach to adolescent development.* New York: Routledge.

Laursen, B., Little, T. D., & Card, N. A. (Eds.). (2012). *Handbook of developmental research methods.* New York: Guilford Press.

NICHD CDBB [National Institute of Child Health and Human Development Child Development and Behavior Branch]. (2015). *Overview/mission statement.* http://www.nichd.nih.gov/.

Nicolson, C., Starfield, A., K, Kofinas, G., Kruse, J. (2002). Ten heuristics for interdisciplinary modeling projects. *Ecosystems, 5*, 376–384.

Raudenbush, S. W., & Bryk, A. S. (2002). *Hierarchical linear models: Applications and data analysis methods* (2nd. ed.). Newbury Park: Sage.

Salter, R. M. (2013). Nova: A modern platform for system dynamics, spatial, and agent-based modeling. *Procedia Computer Science, 18*, 1784–1793.

Starfield, A. M., & Salter, R. M. (2010). Thoughts on a general undergraduate modeling course and software to support it. *Transactions of the Royal Society of South Africa, 65*(2): 116–121.

van Geert, P. (2012). Dynamic systems. In B. Laursen, T. D. Little, & N. A. Card (Eds.), *Handbook of developmental research methods* (pp. 725–741). New York: Guilford.

Typologies and Trade-offs in FCM Studies: A Guide to Designing Participatory Research Using Fuzzy Cognitive Maps

Alexander Metzger, Steven Gray, Elpiniki Papageorgiou, and Antonie J. Jetter

During the 1960s and 1970s, the development of innovative ideas about collaborative planning and management challenged top-down approaches that had previously defined social development and environmental policy (Healey, 1997; 2003; Kapoor, 2001). Concern for stakeholders and their involvement in environmental management and decision-making became increasingly widespread among practitioners and legal mandates established during this time called for participation of stakeholders and the general public in various management situations (Voinov & Bousquet, 2010). This movement toward collaboration and participation eventually found its way into academia, countering the "ivory tower" mentality of researchers as a practice that incorporates knowledge diversity, local context, and increased legitimacy into the research process (Voinov & Bousquet, 2010).

Case studies and new methods in recent decades have linked public participation to the success of conservation and resource management projects. These cases have explored engagement of local stakeholders with diverse interests as a means of improving resource management, attributing many past failures to a lack of participation (Gleason et al., 2010; Persha, Agrawal, & Chhatre, 2011). Practitioners in this space acknowledge that managing the unique social and ecological processes of complex systems requires managers to embrace complexity and employ flexible, adaptable approaches to participation. This understanding acknowledges that there is no universally applicable type of participation or set of tools and techniques for engagement (Klein, McKinnon, Wright, Possingham, & Halpern, 2015). Additionally, there are many widely recognized fundamental challenges to participatory approaches, including mismatches in understandings between managers, researchers and stakeholders about complex systems and planning outcomes; power dynamics that lead to inequitable agency and benefit among stakeholders; and difficulty of institutionalizing and sustaining inclusive and adaptive approaches (Alpert, 1996; Barrett & Arcese, 1995; Brown, 2003; Newmark & Hough, 2000).

Participatory modeling has developed alongside the movement away from top-down management and decision-making, developing modeling approaches that enhance opportunities for broad participation in research, decision-making, and planning (Voinov & Bousquet, 2010; Voinov & Gaddis, 2008). Traditional approaches to scientific modeling that rely on scientific information alone have been rejected by decision-makers and stakeholders due to lack of local buy-in and inability to account for local priorities, values, and knowledge (Voinov & Gaddis, 2008). Additionally, complex problems within scientific disciplines often require more than traditional expert knowledge alone can offer (Funtowicz & Ravetz, 1991). Participatory modeling can expand and diversify the knowledge base involved in attempting to understand complex, interlinked social and environmental problems as well as contribute to decision-making via collective, model-based reasoning.

While a great variety of participatory modeling tools exist (Voinov & Bousquet, 2010), those that emphasize elicitation of mental models are particularly well-suited to address the need for integration of diverse stakeholder knowledge and perspectives identified by many authors (Biggs et al., 2011; Doyle & Ford, 1998; Manfredo, Teel, Gavin, & Fulton, 2014). Initiatives that emphasize diversifying the mental models used in decision-making acknowledge that model building is inherently subjective and that its legitimacy depends upon the assumptions and perspectives of the modeler (Jones et al., 2009). Here we use the term "mental models" to refer generally to an individual's internal cognitive representation of the external world, which is dynamically and iteratively constructed over time and consists largely of cause-and-effect relationships (Jones, Ross, Lynam, Perez, & Leitch, 2011). Since their original conception by Craik (1943), the concept of mental models has been further developed and applied to research on human reasoning and decision-making (Johnson-Laird, 1983) and environmental management and planning (Jones et al., 2009).

In this chapter, we introduce fuzzy cognitive mapping (FCM) as a participatory modeling tool and discuss methodological considerations for its use. FCM is commonly used to translate informal mental models of stakeholders and decision-makers into networked, cause-and-effect models that capture knowledge and understandings about the dynamics of complex systems (Gray, Zanre, & Gray, 2014; Jetter & Kok, 2014; Jones et al., 2011). Building upon earlier work that established cognitive mapping as a means of understanding and representing cognitive structure (see Axelrod, 1976; Tolman, 1948), Kosko (1986; 1988) pioneered FCM by combining neural networks consisting of nodes and signed, directional relationships with fuzzy logic, which weights those relationships from –1 to +1. While fuzzy cognitive maps are typically represented visually as a network model of components and relationships (figure 1, top), they can also be represented as an "adjacency matrix," or a grid of numerical pairwise relationships among all components (figure 1, bottom). When one or more nodes are "activated" by inputting an initial, non-zero value, this activation proceeds through the matrix following the weighted relationships. Feedback loops can cause repeated activation of a concept, introducing complex interconnectivity to the model. The activation of nodes is itcrated, using a "squashing function" to rescale node values to a 0 to 1 scale until the model reaches a stable state. The resulting node values for all concepts can then be used to interpret outcomes of a particular scenario and study the dynamics of the modeled system, which can be useful for scenario planning.

The strengths of FCM for participatory applications focusing on mental model elicitation vary by approach, but generally include:

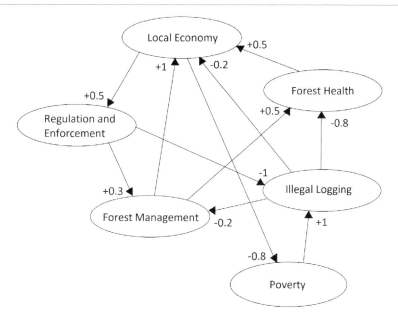

	Local Economy	Forest Health	Regulation and Enforcement	Forest Management	Illegal Logging	Poverty
Local Economy	0	0	0.5	0	0	-0.8
Forest Health	0.5	0	0	0	0	0
Regulation and Enforcement	0	0	0	0.3	-1	0
Forest Management	1	0.5	0	0	0	0
Illegal Logging	-0.2	-0.8	0	-0.2	0	0
Poverty	0	0	0	0	1	0

FIGURE 1. Example FCM and adjacency matrix for a managed forest ecosystem.

- Ability to represent, integrate and compare very diverse types of knowledge (Gray, Gray, Cox, & Henly-Shepard, 2013; Özesmi & Özesmi, 2004)
- Fast model building with low technical barriers (Özesmi & Özesmi, 2004)
- Simple enough for stakeholder involvement in model building (Gray, Gray, Cox, & Henly-Shepard, 2013; Jetter & Kok, 2014)
- Ability to support interactive scenario analysis (Gray et al., 2015; Jetter & Kok, 2014)
- Free software packages with helpful user interfaces (Gray, Gray, Cox, & Henly-Shepard, 2013)

The weaknesses of this method, which also vary by approach, include:

- Potential simplification and misrepresentation of some relationships for which advanced knowledge exists (Özesmi & Özesmi, 2004; Papageorgiou & Salmeron, 2013)
- Lack of spatial and temporal representation
- Lack of formalized and structured way to represent relationship strength

- Possible susceptibility to group power dynamics and subsequent over-reliance on a few individuals' knowledge in a group model-building setting (Jetter & Kok, 2014).

Klein and Cooper (1982), in their study of operational decision-making by army officers, were to our knowledge the first to reference a participatory mental modeling case study. The great majority of participatory FCM studies related to environmental planning have been published since Özesmi and Özesmi (2004) popularized the approach originally developed by Kosko (1986). While participatory FCM is still in its early stages, standard practices and methodological consistency are beginning to emerge in the literature. To support the continued growth of the participatory FCM method and aid in the design of future participatory FCM studies, this chapter reviews case studies of this modeling technique, creates a typology of approaches, and discusses benefits and tradeoffs of different approaches to participatory FCM.

Creating a Typology Using the "Four Ps" Framework

To organize this review of the participatory FCM literature and create a typology of approaches, we employ a framework created by Gray et al. (2017), known as the "four Ps" framework for participatory environmental modeling. This framework is intended as a way for researchers involved in participatory modeling of social-environmental systems to structure research initiatives and identify and test new hypotheses in this field by standardizing case study applications. The components of the framework can be seen in table 1. We used the four Ps framework to create a rubric that guided our development of the typology (table 2).

Constructing the Dataset

Construction of our dataset began with a general search for articles that included topics or keywords including "fuzzy cognitive map(ping)" and "participatory modeling" on the Web of Science (twenty-one results) and ScienceDirect (twenty-two results) databases. We then reduced this selection to literature that included case studies on systems with social and ecological components, models that directly represented knowledge or perspectives of people other than the researcher, and studies in which the participants were directly involved in some part of the modeling process. Citations from the resulting set of studies were used as a resource to locate more studies fitting our criteria, as were review articles by Aguilar (2005), Jetter and Kok (2014), and Papageorgiou and Salmeron (2013).

The resulting dataset includes thirty-three studies published in scientific journals, books, or dissertation databases (table 3). The case studies cover a wide variety of topics, including natural resource management, agriculture, ecology, policy and economics, and strategic decision-making. While several of the studies in the dataset were published in journals with an explicit focus on modeling techniques (e.g., *Ecological Modeling* and *Environmental Modeling and Software*), the majority of studies were published in journals covering topics related to management of coupled human and natural systems (e.g., *Ecology and Society* and *Ocean and Coastal Management*). The following section introduces the elements of our rubric, based on the four Ps framework, and process for reviewing case studies and creating a dataset.

Table 1. Description of the four Ps framework (adapted from Gray et al., 2017)

	QUESTION TO BE ADDRESSED	DIMENSION REPORTED
Purpose	Why was the PM approach selected?	1. Providing justification for why PM is used 2. Defining the issue and the purpose of the model
Partnership	Who participated and why?	1. Defining model, data, and process ownership 2. Describing the criteria for inclusion of participants 3. Describing the steps participants are involved in
Processes	How were stakeholders involved?	1. Defining the characteristics of the interaction between the participants and the model 2. Describing the level of participation 3. Defining relationship between the PM and a decision-making process
Product	What was produced by the modeling process?	1. Defining characteristics of the PM tool produced 2. Defining the social outcomes of the process 3. Defining the policy, management, or scientific insights

Table 2. Rubric elements organized by the four Ps framework

FOUR Ps FRAMEWORK ELEMENT	RUBRIC ELEMENT		
Purpose	• Research purpose		
Partnership	• Sampling of population	• Participant involvement	• Interactions with participants
Process	• Knowledge capture • Structural analyses	• Standardization and condensation • Comparative analyses	• Aggregation • Testing and simulation
Product	• Outcomes	• Recommendations for future research	• Limitations

Research Purpose

With guidance from the participatory modeling literature (see Jones et al., 2009; Voinov & Bousquet, 2010), we identified five main types of research purpose that applied to the studies in our dataset: (1) enhancing system knowledge, (2) understanding variation among participants, (3) shared learning, (4) consensus building, and (5) increasing participation. All studies in our dataset include at least one of these purpose types and many include multiple since they are not exclusive categories.

Enhancing System Knowledge

Researchers increasingly value involving local stakeholders in the research process in order to take advantage of the wealth of non-scientific knowledge they can provide, which is often referred to as "traditional" or "local" knowledge (Biggs et al., 2011; Folke, Hahn, Olsson, & Norberg, 2005; Manfredo et al., 2014). It has been suggested that, in many cases, scientific knowledge alone is not sufficient for creating a comprehensive understanding of a complex system (Funtowicz & Ravetz, 1991). Integrating local stakeholders is often thought to provide a more thorough understanding of local conditions, fine-scale dynamics, and decision-making context, which are increasingly considered valuable to research and management of these systems (Berkes & Folke, 1998; Berkes, Folke, & Gadgil, 1995). Many studies attempt to use FCM to integrate diverse sources of knowledge from scientists and non-scientists into a model that better describes the

Table 3. Source and brief description of studies included in dataset

CITATION	SOURCE	SYSTEM AND TOPIC OF FOCUS
Berbés-blázquez (2015)	Dissertation, York University, Toronto, ON	Agriculture, ecosystem services
Çelik, Özesmi, and Akdoğan (2006)	*Ecological Modeling*	Lake management, livelihoods
Douglas et al. (2016)	*Journal of Hydrology: Regional Studies*	Agriculture, irrigation management
Fairweather (2010)	*Ecological Modeling*	Dairy farming, ecosystem function
Fairweather and Hunt (2011)	*Agriculture and Human Values*	Agriculture, system management
Giordano, Passarella, Uricchio, & Vurro (2005)	*Physical and Chemistry of the Earth*	Water resources, collaborative management
Gray, Chan, Clark, & Jordan (2012)	*Ecological Modeling*	Fisheries, ecosystem function
Gray et al. (2014)	*Ocean and Coastal Management*	Coastal management, climate change
Gray et al. (2015)	*Journal of Outdoor Recreation and Tourism*	Fisheries, ecological function
Halbrendt et al. (2014)	*Global Environmental Change*	Agriculture, adoption of practices
Henly-Shepard, Gray, & Cox (2015)	*Environmental Science and Policy*	Coastal hazards, disaster planning
Hobbs, Ludsin, Knight, Ryan, & Ciborowski (2002)	*Ecological Applications*	Lake ecosystem, ecological rehabilitation
Isaac, Dawoe, & Sieciechowicz (2009)	*Environmental Management*	Agroforestry, farm management
Jetter and Schweinfort (2011)	*Futures*	Solar photovoltaic, adoption factors (2 studies)
Kafetzis, McRoberts, & Mouratiadou (2010)	*Fuzzy Cognitive Maps: Advances in Theory, Methodologies, Tools and Applications* (book)	River basin, use and policy (2 studies)
Klein & Cooper, (1982)	*Journal of the Operational Research Society*	Military wargames, decision-making
Kontogianni et al. (2012)	*Ocean and Coastal Management*	Marine system, ecosystem resilience
Kontogianni, Tourkolias, and Papageorgiou (2013)	*International Journal of Hydrogen Energy*	Hydrogen transport technology, market behavior
Mendoza & Prabhu (2006)	*Forest Policy and Economics*	Forest, sustainable management
Mouratiadou & Moran (2007)	*Ecological Economics*	River basin, water resource management
Murungweni, Wijk, Andersson, Smaling, & Giller (2011)	*Ecology and Society*	Conservation areas, livelihoods
Nyaki, Gray, Lepczyk, Skibins, & Rentsch (2014)	*Conservation Biology*	Bushmeat hunting, policy
Özesmi & Özesmi (2003)	*Environmental Management*	Lake system, ecosystem management
Papageorgiou, Markinos, & Gemptos (2009)	*Expert Systems with Applications*	Agriculture, yield prediction
Rajaram & Das (2010)	*Expert Systems with Applications*	Agro-ecosystem, sustainability factors
Ramsey & Norbury (2009)	*Austral Ecology*	Dryland ecosystem, pest management
Samarasinghe & Strickert (2013)	*Environmental Modeling and Software*	Natural hazards, public policy
Tan & Özesmi (2006)	*Hydrobiologia*	Lake ecosystem, ecosystem function
van Vliet, Kok, & Veldkamp (2010)	*Futures*	Water resources, system function
Vanwindekens, Stilmant, & Baret (2013)	*Ecological Modeling*	Grassland agriculture, management
Vasslides & Jensen (2016)	*Journal of Environmental Management*	Bay and estuary ecosystem, ecosystem function

functioning of a complex system (see Gray, Chan, Clark, & Jordan, 2012; Tan and Özesmi, 2006; Rajaram and Das, 2008).

Understanding Variation Among Participants

The mental models of stakeholder groups that are expressed in environmental planning environments can potentially be very different, causing misunderstandings and difficulty pursuing coordinated or collective action (Biggs et al., 2011). An understanding of the variation of mental models among stakeholders can be used to facilitate more productive discussion and negotiation about complex systems and decisions that involve multiple stakeholders. Using FCM as a tool to compare the knowledge, understandings, and priorities contained in mental models can make areas of mismatch and agreement explicit (Giordano, Passarella, Uricchio, & Vurro, 2005; Areti Kontogianni, Tourkolias, & Papageorgiou, 2013; Nyaki, Gray, Lepczyk, Skibins, & Rentsch, 2014).

Shared Learning

Another commonly mentioned use of FCM is to stimulate shared learning within a community (see Gray et al., 2016; Henly-Shepard, Gray, & Cox, 2015): to make explicit and distribute the knowledge each stakeholder holds about a system using FCM and use it to stimulate a learning process in which stakeholder mental models are expanded or modified. Jones et al. (2009) identify that the participation process may involve a transfer or sharing of knowledge or knowledge may be co-created by participants and researchers. Eliciting and integrating "inside knowledge" into the individual and collective understanding of a particular community is a means of initiating social learning and group processes are often used to achieve this (Pahl-Wostl, 2007). Some researchers involved in learning-oriented processes have explicitly used the concept of "learning loops," in which learning can be stimulated at a variety of levels including individual, social network, and institutional (Henly-Shepard et al., 2015; Pahl-Wostl, 2006). S. Gray et al. (2016) explore the use of citizen science to engage participants in a science-related process to create social learning outcomes. It has also been suggested that social learning within decision-making communities is an essential adaptive process for creating collective action in attempts to solve complex, multifaceted issues such as climate change (Tschakert & Dietrich, 2010).

Consensus-Building

Consensus-building involves the negotiation of a shared vision or course of action in an attempt to deal with uncertainty, complexity, or controversy (Innes & Booher, 1999). This negotiation process does not necessarily require convergence of mental models held by different stakeholders within a consensus-building process. Instead, consensus-building among a group is a process of sharing elements of individually held mental models and reconciling differences in order to develop a collective set of assumptions or a shared basis for decision-making (Mohammed & Dumville, 2001). In participatory FCM, the process of consensus-building can take the form of group model building, in which discussions and negotiations take place during the model building, or as an aggregation of models to simulate a community consensus (see Douglas et al., 2016; Hobbs et al., 2002; Klein & Cooper, 1982).

Increasing Participation

Lastly, proponents of stakeholder participation in research and management suggest that increasing the involvement of stakeholders in research and decision-making can have many benefits, but also poses significant challenges (Dietz & Stern, 2008). Beyond increasing the depth and diversity of knowledge, participation is often championed as a means of encouraging broader stakeholder buy-in, greater social capital, and greater equity in governance processes and outcomes (Berkes, Colding, & Folke, 2000; Folke et al., 2005; Walker et al., 2002). The assumption is that participants find more value in a process that includes their perspectives and increase the process's overall legitimacy and tractability by endorsing it as members of their local community. In this way, participation can increase access to the local capacity and social capital that supports the success of a project, possibly creating longer-term initiatives (Kapoor, 2001).

Partnership

To describe the different ways in which partnership was accomplished in these participatory FCM studies, we analyzed three aspects of the research design in our rubric: the characteristics of the sample population, the type of participant involvement, and the number of interactions with participants.

Sample Population

FCM modeling studies often attempt to include as many perspectives relevant to the study context as possible through careful categorization and selection of participants and participant groups. The type of participants engaged in the studies we reviewed include local experts, domain experts, practitioners, and stakeholder groups. It should be noted that these types are not mutually exclusive, and some studies include multiple types of participants in their sample population.

These participant types can be considered in terms of two different knowledge scales: one representing the level of domain knowledge about a system from formal scientific literature and the other representing the level of local knowledge about a specific system from direct experience (figure 2). In an agricultural system, for example, local knowledge may include an understanding of place-specific environmental dynamics, such as crop selection strategies for mitigating the effects of drought, and the co-influence of water resources with local farmers' water management strategies. Domain knowledge may include discipline-specific, generalizable knowledge derived through formal experimentation in social and ecological systems, such as the potential effects of climate change on broad-scale hydrology and plant physiology.

Local experts are expected to have a great deal of knowledge regarding the local system with varying amounts of domain knowledge. Some examples of local experts found in the case studies include community groups (S. R. J. Gray et al., 2014) and lay people who live within the system

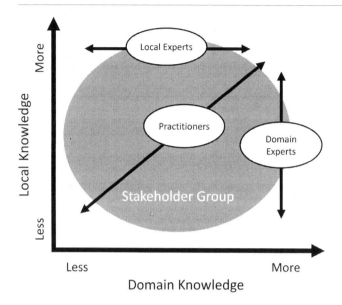

FIGURE 2. Comparison of levels of "domain" and "local" knowledge among different participant types.

contributing their experientially developed, place-based knowledge (Kontogianni, Papageorgiou, Salomatina, Skourtos, & Zanou, 2012). Domain experts are often formally trained or initiated into a particular discipline, often representing knowledge that could be applied broadly in many different contexts. Some examples of domain experts are ecologists, who were included in a study about water resource management (Mouratiadou & Moran, 2007), and fisheries scientists engaged in a study of the mid-Atlantic summer flounder fishery (Gray, Chan, Clark, & Jordan, 2012).

We define "practitioners" as participants who are directly involved in managing or interacting with specific aspects of the system being studied and are distinguished from local experts by their contribution of both local and domain-specific knowledge in the research. Practitioners may possess a variable combination of local knowledge, through experience directly with the system being studied, and domain knowledge, through education or practice in a specific discipline or occupation. Vanwindekens, Stilmant, and Baret (2013), for example, interviewed many farmers to create FCMs of the agricultural system and its management practices. Nyaki et al. (2014) engage bushmeat hunters in Tanzania to study their practices and perspectives on the bushmeat trade.

Participants that represent "stakeholder groups" in these case studies are those who affect or are affected by the system in different ways and can be distinguished from other groups based on a particular defining characteristic or type of interaction with the system. As this definition is not strictly based on different levels or types of knowledge, members of stakeholder groups can fall nearly anywhere on the graph of local and domain knowledge. Thus, members of the other groups previously mentioned (lay people, local and domain experts, and practitioners) can be considered members of a stakeholder group. Because we consider a study to include stakeholder groups if it simply delineates among multiple groups of people, studies that include stakeholder group often include at least one of the other types of participants. For example, Samarasinghe and Strickert (2013) attempt to integrate the knowledge of managers, workers, local experts, and recreational users on the effects of natural disasters in an alpine ski field. In this case, since multiple groups are defined by their types of interactions with the system and compared, we consider this study to focus on diverse stakeholder groups in addition to local experts and practitioners, since these are explicitly included. In another example, Henly-Shepard, Gray, and Cox (2015) study social learning outcomes of a modeling process that engaged a committee of residents, businesses, local organizations, law enforcement personnel, and government representatives to work closely together on elucidating and integrating their diverse knowledge regarding the outcomes of tsunami scenarios. We also consider these stakeholder groups because the members of the committee were differentiated and selected to participate based on their diverse interests and perspectives regarding tsunamis.

As noted, these types are not meant to be mutually exclusive, but to describe how researchers classify the sources of knowledge for modeling. Reality is not as clearly defined, considering that an individual participant may play multiple roles within a system, for example a local flood manager who is a hydrologist and lives and works within the system being studied. Researchers must take this into account when defining their participant population and designing their knowledge-gathering and analysis methods to ensure that they characterize knowledge in a manner that is appropriate for the research goals and acceptable to the participants. Since it is difficult or impossible to separate the multitude of influences on an individual's overall perspectives, a researcher attempting to draw distinctions between groups should be aware of these complexities and discuss the limitations and opportunities they provide. In our analysis, researchers make their classifications of participant roles clear by their description of participant groups and how they structure their analyses, but do not often discuss the issue of potential misclassification of participant knowledge.

A second challenge is determining the appropriate sample size of participants. This is typically done by monitoring whether additional data collection continues to add new insights until interviews or models yield little new information. When no new insights are being contributed by new participants, the point of saturation is reached and the data collection can be considered complete. According to Jetter & Kok (2014), many participatory FCM studies involving diverse participant populations reach saturation with approximately thirty models. When respondents are permitted to freely define concepts, saturation can be formally measured by tracking the number of new concepts introduced in subsequent interviews and estimating an accumulation curve of concept. No new respondents are added to the sample when the estimated number of new concepts introduced per interview falls below a minimum threshold (see Özesmi & Özesmi, 2004). In many FCM studies, however, researchers are constrained by practical limitations, such as time, budget, respondent availability, and the obligation to include certain participants in their study. Sample size selection based on quantitative assessments of saturation is therefore rarely reported in the literature.

Participant Involvement

The research objectives of a study primarily determine the ways in which participants are involved in participatory FCM processes. To properly frame a study, researchers may begin with initial interviews meant to determine the appropriate sample population (such as in Nyaki et al., 2014) or define some of the major concepts used in the FCMs (Murungweni, Wijk, Andersson, Smaling, & Giller, 2011). The information from these initial interviews can play an essential role in properly structuring the next stages of the research.

Model building is a phase that can take different forms for the participants involved in the research. Depending on the research objectives and other constraints of the project, researchers may choose to involve the participants in building individual or group FCMs. According to Gray, Zanre, and Gray (2014), individual models may provide a more equitable and diverse representation of knowledge within a community than group models due to the power dynamics within a group model-building process. Thus, if the goal of the study is to study knowledge diversity, an individual modeling approach would be preferable. If time and resources are limited, group model-building exercises in which multiple, distinct groups co-create FCMs may provide a less time-intensive and lower-cost method. However, this group modeling approach may come at the cost of understanding individual perspectives that contribute to a group model.

If the objectives of the study include shared learning and consensus, a group model-building process may be a very useful tool for stimulating discussion regarding differences in knowledge and perspectives and allow negotiation of a shared perspective (Gray, Zanre, & Gray, 2014). It should be noted that although some authors have deemed the process of combining individually constructed FCMs the "formation of a consensus social map" (Özesmi & Özesmi, 2004), this is only a simulated consensus rather than a true, socially constructed consensus. A socially constructed consensus can only be reached through discussion and negotiation among participants, as described in Innes and Booher (1999).

Scenario analysis is a common practice in FCM. One of the strengths of FCM is its ability to accommodate scenario analysis using a system model that has integrated diverse knowledge, providing insight into system dynamics, sensitivity of components, and system states (Aguilar, 2005; Papageorgiou & Salmeron, 2013). In a participatory context, running scenarios on models of participant knowledge can simulate the dynamics of mental models, since a model of an individual's knowledge represents their unique perspectives, priorities, and functional understandings of the system. Van Vliet, Kok, and Veldkamp (2010) engage participants in developing and analyzing a variety of scenarios using FCM in order to discuss future outcomes and stimulate social learning about participants' diverse mental models.

Interactions with Participants

Since participatory modeling often involves creating connection and collaboration between scientists and non-scientists, an important aspect of the process is contact and communication between the researcher and participants (Röckmann et al., 2012; Voinov & Bousquet, 2010). Creating a generalizable metric for connection and collaboration in participatory FCM case studies is difficult due to the diversity in methods for participant engagement. The number of interactions among researchers and participants is one metric discernable from a literature review that may indicate the amount of communication and collaboration that has taken place. The quality of these interactions, however, is also essential in strengthening relationships and trust, but would require additional data collection such as interviews with participants. While we limit our metric for interactions with participants to the number of interactions for practical reasons, we suggest that the quality of interactions is a valuable topic for future studies.

Process

Participatory FCM research requires a variety of important design decisions that characterize researchers' approach to meeting goals and objectives. Özesmi and Özesmi (2004) describe a comprehensive, nine-step process that is very model-focused in its description of how FCMs are built, validated, modified, analyzed, and applied to research. Jetter and Kok (2014) expand upon the considerations of project design and participant involvement in their six-step approach, broadening the contextual basis of FCM in the research process. Because the previous sections on purpose and partnership cover some of the processual steps described in this literature (e.g., determining objectives, sample population, and sample size) we focus more on the technical aspects and design process that determine how FCMs are built. The rubric elements in this category include:

1. Knowledge Capture
2. Standardization and Condensation
3. Aggregation
4. Structural Analyses
5. Comparative Analyses
6. Testing and Simulation

During knowledge capture, participants and researchers define system components and weighted relationships among those components, which are often used to build a fuzzy cognitive map in real time. Mental model integration requires aggregation of fuzzy cognitive maps from multiple participants, standardization of concepts, and other adjustments to represent the intended scope of the model. Moreover, the network structure of fuzzy cognitive maps and their dynamic behavior are analyzed to ensure that they reflect system knowledge in a way that is realistic and matches researchers and/or participants' understanding of the system. Once the models are created and calibrated, they may be used in a variety of ways to fulfill the research objectives, for example to simulate the impacts of different input scenarios (e.g., decision alternatives, policies) on the state of the represented system and thus support decision-making.

Knowledge Capture

Using appropriate methods for determining concepts and relationships in a participatory FCM study is critical, as it will determine the information a model contains and conveys, and how a modeled system functions in scenario analysis and system state calculations. In some modeling processes, concepts are determined entirely by participants, which is known as "open concept" design (see Çelik, Özesmi, & Akdoğan, 2006; Douglas et al., 2016). While the researcher determines the context of the model by specifying the system being modeled and sometimes the boundaries of this system, participants control what concepts and how many are included. This approach provides very little restriction in the capture of participant knowledge and can be especially beneficial if little is known about the system being modeled. However, the time-intensive nature of this approach can be a concern, especially if large numbers of participants are involved (Gray, Zanre, & Gray, 2014).

In another approach, all or some of the concepts are predetermined. In this approach, the researcher has a greater degree of control over how the system is defined and bounded. This approach can facilitate easier aggregation of multiple models into a meta-FCM that represents all individual perspectives. The degree of concept predetermination in study design varies greatly. In some studies, only one component is predefined and participants may build off this component in an unrestricted manner, while in other studies participants define relationships among a predetermined list of concepts. There is more nuance involved when the source of these predetermined concepts is considered. While the predefined components may be determined by the researcher, they can also be determined by participants in an earlier stage of research before the intent of building an FCM is introduced, providing participants an additional degree of agency. Rajaram and Das (2010) incorporate expert and practitioner perspectives on sustainability, restricting the concepts in model-building to those predetermined by the same community in a previous study that did not involve FCM. Predefining concepts can be more efficient than an open concept design with regard to time input for model building and post-modeling modification (described in the following sections), and can be useful in research meant to address specific system elements or in which sufficient knowledge of the system already exists. However, predetermination of concepts restricts the diversity of knowledge captured and can increase researchers' influence on how this knowledge is represented and contextualized (Gray, Zanre, & Gray, 2014).

Standardization and Condensation

There are many instances in which fuzzy cognitive maps require direct modification by the researcher. Standardizing components among models or condensing the model into a less-complex form by removing or combining concepts are common modifications. If multiple models are combined to form a larger, comprehensive model or compared to assess the differences among models, it may be necessary to normalize the terms used to describe components. Linguistic representation of concepts is a complex element of mental models (Miller & Johnson-Laird, 1976) and a source of uncertainty in FCM, as participants may use different language to describe concepts (Özesmi & Özesmi, 2004). Standardizing language requires interpretation by the researcher, which has been cited as a possible source of inaccuracy in how participant mental models are represented (see Giordano et al., 2005). Alternatively, to ensure that concepts are correctly interpreted according to the perspectives they represent, participants can be engaged in the standardization of concept language.

It may also be necessary to standardize relationships among components in order to combine models or present a more concise and meaningful model. In combining models, it may be desirable that the direction of causal relationships between two components is identical in all models (Özesmi & Özesmi, 2004). This can be accomplished by inverting both the relationship directions and sign of relationship. In causal concept mapping using signed, directional relationships, a positive relationship in one direction can be considered identical to a negative relationship in the opposite direction and mathematically preserves the dynamic behavior of a model (Kosko, 1986). While this modification is shown to preserve model functionality, it requires some consideration of how to preserve the logical structure of the model, for example the meaning conveyed in the direction and sign of a relationship (Özesmi & Özesmi, 2004; Zhang & Chen, 1988) or the rational sequence of events.

FCM may also require standardization in terms of non-structural, contextual aspects of the components. One example of this is the timescale at which the components operate. Although FCM is a non-temporal modeling technique, there should be an understanding of the variation in timescales of casual relationships and concepts within models. Incompatibility of timescales may introduce temporal inconsistency within the model that renders simulation meaningless. If simulation using the FCM is meant to portray system behavior in a reasonably accurate manner, the model may require normalization of concepts.

Condensing models can fulfill different purposes, for example grouping or reducing concepts down to variables directly relevant to the research context. Nakamura, Iwai, and Sawarag (1982) demonstrate the benefits of condensing a very complex model of domain knowledge into a stream-lined model directly relevant for decision-making. Some researchers in our dataset condense their models to create comprehensible visual representations of systems to serve as effective discussion and learning tools (see Tan & Özesmi, 2006; Hobbs et al., 2002). While it is widely recognized that this requires a degree of interpretation by the researcher may introduce bias to the FCM process, it is also often a means of achieving research goals (Özesmi & Özesmi, 2004).

Both of these methods may apply to attempts to address issues of functionality and concept relevance within the simulation process. It is possible that simulation of system outcomes using FCM, depending on the matrix structure of the model, leads to chaotic behavior in which the model does not reach a consistently steady state. This negates the usefulness of the FCM for studying system behavior or system state outcomes in participatory applications (Jetter & Kok, 2014; Özesmi & Özesmi, 2004). In these cases, changes to the FCM must be made through analysis and modification of the model.

Aggregation

Depending on the objectives of the study, researchers may combine multiple FCMs into aggregate models. One common purpose for combining fuzzy cognitive maps is to create a more complete system representation of a system that integrates the specialized knowledge of a diverse group of participants (see Rajaram & Das, 2010; Vanwindekens, Stilmant, & Baret 2013). They may also be combined into multiple group or community models for the purpose of generalizing and comparing the mental models of these groups (see Jetter & Schweinfort, 2011; Halbrendt et al., 2014).

Jetter and Kok (2014) describe the two different approaches to aggregating models as quantitative or qualitative. Quantitative aggregation of models involves summing the strength of relationships among each pair of components and rescaling these relationships back to a −1 to +1 scale. This provides a simple method of averaging the relationship between each pair of components defined by each member of the sample population. However, an issue with this technique lies in combining opposing perspectives: for example, when one respondent defines a positive relationship +1 between two components while another defines a negative relationship of –1. The resulting numerical values after aggregation reflect no causal relationship or, if unbalanced, cancel out one perspective and lessen the stronger-signed relationship. While this can create logical inconsistencies in a model with a small number of participants, it would not be an issue in an aggregate model that includes a large sample population that demonstrates a "wisdom-of-crowds" outcome, in which the prevailing perspective is more often true (Jetter & Kok, 2014; Surowiecki, 2004).

Qualitative aggregation, as described by Özesmi and Özesmi (2004) and Jetter and Kok (2014), can be accomplished by grouping similar concepts together into encompassing variables and creating a new aggregated map that summarizes the relationships among these variables. Both quantitative and qualitative methods often make use of standardization and condensation techniques discussed in the previous section. In our rubric, we characterize options with regard to FCM aggregation as aggregation into multiple group models, aggregation into single, "whole-system" or meta models, or not aggregated. We also assess whether aggregations are made either quantitatively or qualitatively.

Structural Analysis

A common way for researchers to assess and compare fuzzy cognitive maps at the structural level is to use a set of graph theory indices commonly used in many types of network analysis (Gray, Zanre, & Gray, 2014). A summary of these metrics from Gray, Zanre, and Gray (2014) can be seen in table 4 and more information about these metrics is available in Gray, Gray, Zanre, and Gray (2014) and Özesmi and Özesmi (2004).

Comparative Analysis

Comparing fuzzy cognitive maps created by groups or individuals can illuminate key differences in knowledge and perspectives that represent the degree of similarity of mental models. Structural comparisons can be more qualitative in nature, based on general observations related to types of concepts included and relationships present (see Douglas et al., 2016), or they may focus on the structural metrics previously discussed and use statistical analysis to more quantitatively describe differences among models (see Mouratiadou & Moran, 2007).

Testing and Simulation

One of the main benefits that sets FCM apart from other modeling techniques is its ability to integrate simple, qualitative representations of diverse mental models into quantitative models that can be used to simulate the system's dynamic behavior. This allows researchers and participants to learn about the overall system and dynamics (e.g., the different stable states it can reach

Table 4. Description of graph theory indices used as structural metrics from Gray, Zanre, & Gray (2014)

MENTAL MODEL STRUCTURAL MEASUREMENT	DESCRIPTION OF MEASURE AND COGNITIVE INFERENCE
N (Concepts)	Number of variables included in model; higher number of concepts indicates more components in the mental model. (Özesmi & Özesmi, 2004)
N (Connections)	Number of connections included between variables; higher number of connections indicates higher degree of interaction between components in a mental model. (Özesmi & Özesmi, 2004)
N (Transmitter)	Components that have only "forcing" functions; indicates number of components that effect other system components but are not affected by others. (Eden, Ackermann, & Cropper, 1992)
N (Receiver)	Components that have only receiving functions; indicates the number of components that are affected by other system components but have no effect. (Eden, Ackermann, & Cropper, 1992)
N (Ordinary)	Components with both transmitting and receiving functions; indicates the number of concepts that influence and are influenced by other concepts. (Eden, Ackermann, & Cropper, 1992)
Centrality	Absolute value of either (a) overall influence in the model (all + and - relationships indicated, for entire model) or (b) influence of individual concepts as indicated by positive (+) or negative (–) values placed on connections between components; indicates (a) the total influence (positive and negative) to be in the system or (b) the conceptual weight/importance of individual concepts (Kosko, 1986). The higher the value, the greater the importance of all concepts or the individual weight of a concept is in the overall model.
C/N	Number of connections divided by the number of variables (concepts). The lower the C/N score, the higher the degree of connectedness in a system. (Özesmi & Özesmi, 2004)
Complexity	Ratio of receiver variables to transmitter variables. Indicates the degree of resolution and is a measure of the degree to which outcomes of driving forces are considered. Higher complexity indicates more complex systems thinking. (Eden, Ackermann, & Cropper, 1992; Özesmi & Özesmi, 2004)
Density	Number of connections compared to number of all possible connections. The higher the density, the more potential management policies exist. (Özesmi & Özesmi, 2004; Hage & Harary 1983)
Hierarchy Index	Index developed to indicate hierarchal to democratic view of the system. On a scale of 0–1, indicates the degree of top-down (score 1) or democratic perception (score 0) of the mental model. (MacDonald, 1983)

and the variables that drive the system behavior), to test hypotheses about the impact of concept changes on other system elements, and to improve their decision-making by selecting alternatives that result in desired system states. To achieve these objectives, the model must be verified and tested. This step ensures that it provides a good representation of the system knowledge it encodes and exhibits the same dynamic behavior as the real-world system it represents. To this end, a variety of testing strategies, including the testing of so-called dynamic hypotheses, comparison between model and real-world data, and sensitivity analyses are available to modelers (Jetter & Kok, 2014; Papageorgiou, Markinos, & Gemptos, 2009).

Sensitivity analysis of fuzzy cognitive maps can be used to provide additional information about system behavior and simulation outcomes (Htun, Gray, Lepczyk, Titmus, & Adams, 2016). By running many iterations using various beginning state vectors, similar to the process in scenario analysis, researchers are able to determine how the dynamics of the system affect particular components, and enables them to monitor the degree to which concept values change under different conditions (Jetter & Kok, 2014). This process is used to assess the validity of the assumptions of the model, and may also be used to evaluate the cascading dynamics that changes to the system have upon concepts that are of importance to the researchers or participants (see Ramsey & Norbury, 2009; Tan & Özesmi, 2006).

The tested model can then be used to answer "what-if" questions by calculating the new stable system states that result from changes to the system that are represented by the initial state vector. Groups can thus test how variables that they are particularly interested in (e.g., regarding environmental trends, different policies, or decision alternatives) impact other variables in the system. Naturally, not all system states are equally desirable, which is why participants are often asked to describe which components of the model should increase, decrease, or stay the same, based on their priorities. This information helps the group to interpret simulation results and support decision making. For example, the simulation may show that two alternative interventions (represented by two different initial state vectors) both lead to equal improvements with regard to a stated objective. However, they may have different impacts on other desirable variables and the team would be well advised to select the intervention that improves the variables it aims to improve without deteriorating other aspects of the system (Gray et al., 2015).

Simulations can be used to predict the future state of a system. For example, Papageorgiou et al. (2009) predict future cotton yields using a co-constructed fuzzy cognitive map. In many cases, however, FCM studies do not aim to predict a single future outcome but explore a range of equally plausible, alternative futures thay may occur as trends unfold (Jetter & Schweinfort, 2011; Salmeron, Vidal, & Mena, 2012; van Vliet, Kok, & Veldkamp, 2010). In this context, FCM is not used to explore the impact of the modeling team's decisions on the system, but to provide the backdrop for planning discussions by showing how uncertain external factors could impact the system under study, referred to in this study as scenario analysis. In this context, FCM provides a valuable connection between the rich narratives that are required in scenario studies and the quantitative rigor and complexity that is provided by model calculations (Jetter & Kok, 2014). FCM-based scenario techniques for future studies vary among authors (e.g., Jetter & Kok, 2014; Jetter & Schweinfort, 2011; Kok, 2009; Kok & van Delden, 2009; Papageorgiou et al., 2009; Salmeron et al., 2012). The basic steps are described in Jetter and Kok (2012).

Simulations are thus used in varied contexts. They can define the dynamic behavior of the system and comparison of outcomes that result from policy, management or environmental change scenarios in a way that supports decision-making and prioritization of management strategies (Berbés-blázquez, 2015; Çelik, Özesmi, & Akdoğan, 2006; Gray, Chan, Clark, and Jordan, 2012; Papageorgiou et al., 2009).

Products

For our review and creation of a typology, we assess the products of the participatory modeling process by using the same basic categories as the purposes:

- A more-complete model of the system
- Identification of perspectives and differences between groups
- Occurrence of shared learning
- Better group understanding and consensus
- Other

We also seek further detail on the outcomes from the text to illustrate the broader implications of these outcomes, such as how this outcome was used or leveraged by participants. For example, in Çelik, Özesmi, and Akdoğan's (2006) study of a lake system under different management scenarios, the knowledge outcomes were incorporated into a management plan for the lake.

Results and Discussion

Using the rubric developed from the four Ps framework, we observe trends in the use of participatory FCM for research. These data allow us to better understand the current state and norms of the practice, identify needs and areas of future research, and create a typology of approaches and summary of their benefits and tradeoffs.

Purpose

The most common research purpose within our dataset could be described as enhancing system knowledge, accounting for twenty of the thirty-three case studies evaluated. Understanding participant variation was the second most common outcome, with thirteen studies stating this as a main purpose. All other research purposes (shared learning, consensus and increased participation) were only present in nine or fewer of the studies. This finding suggests that direct outcomes for participants were less common in participatory FCM than those related to a better understanding of the system and its physical and social components, which appears to be more useful in an academic sense and not surprising given the dataset reviewed. An explicit purpose of demonstrating or advancing specific methodologies was mentioned in eleven of the studies (table 5).

Voinov and Bousquet (2010) summarize the main drivers of participatory modeling research as a combination of the need to represent and share knowledge and understandings and a need to clarify and support decision-making for a particular issue. Over half of the studies whose purpose is to increase system knowledge also identify one of the other purposes (shared learning, participant variation, consensus-building, or increased participation) as an important driver of the research. Nearly all studies express an intention to develop this enhanced knowledge for the purposes of management, policy, or decision-making process, regardless of whether the research was meant to directly play a role. These findings imply that the broader motivation of participatory FCM, in terms of Voinov and Bousquet's (2010) two objectives of participatory modeling, is to use an enhanced system knowledge to support applied processes that aid in management, policy, and decision-making.

Similarly, Jones et al. (2009) suggest that the three main functions for involving stakeholders

Table 5. Rubric element frequency by number of studies in descending order

1. RESEARCH PURPOSE

COMPLETE SYSTEM MODEL	UNDERSTANDING PARTICIPANT KNOWLEDGE	METHODOLOGY	CONSENSUS	SHARED LEARNING	INCREASED PARTICIPATION
20	13	11	9	5	2

2. SAMPLE POPULATION

STAKEHOLDER GROUPS	DOMAIN EXPERTS	PRACTITIONERS	LOCAL EXPERTS
18	12	12	7

3. PARTICIPANT INVOLVEMENT

INDIVIDUAL MODEL BUILDING	INITIAL INTERVIEWS	GROUP MODEL BUILDING	RUNNING SCENARIOS
26	11	11	3

4. NUMBER INTERACTIONS WITH PARTICIPANTS

ONE	TWO	THREE	UNSPECIFIED
25	5	2	1

5. KNOWLEDGE CAPTURE

OPEN	PARTIALLY PREDETERMINED	PREDETERMINED BY PARTICIPANTS	PREDETERMINED BY RESEARCHER
21	11	1	0

6. STANDARDIZATION AND CONDENSATION

STANDARDIZED OR CONDENSED	NOT STANDARDIZED OR CONDENSED
17	15

7. AGGREGATION

GROUP MAPS	NOT AGGREGATED	QUANTITATIVE	QUALITATIVE	WHOLE SYSTEM MAP
14	11	10	10	9

8. STRUCTURAL ANALYSES

# CONCEPTS	# CONNECTIONS	DENSITY	CENTRALITY	TRANSMITTER	RECEIVER	ORDINARY	COMPLEXITY	NONE
21	21	17	16	15	13	12	12	7

9. COMPARATIVE ANALYSES

COMPONENT AND RELATIONSHIP	NONE	RELATIONSHIP ONLY
19	13	1

10. TESTING AND SIMULATION

SCENARIO ANALYSIS	OTHERS	SYSTEM STATE OR DESIRED STATE	SENSITIVITY OF COMPONENTS	NONE
22	7	5	3	6

11. OUTCOMES

UNDERSTANDING PARTICIPANT KNOWLEDGE	COMPLETE SYSTEM MODEL	METHODOLOGICAL	CONSENSUS	SHARED LEARNING	OTHER
22	13	7	7	5	1

in participatory processes can be summed up as normative, substantive, and instrumental. Normative functions focus on the legitimacy of modeling process. By including a range of stakeholders, researchers hope to create social learning and greater acceptance of outcomes. Substantive functions refer to the idea that integrating diverse stakeholder knowledge improves overall understanding of the system and its social and ecological components, resulting in better problem-solving. Instrumental functions attempt to increase collaboration and reduce conflict among modelers, stakeholders, the public, and other involved parties. Regarding FCM specifically, Codara (1998) describes the main purposes as "explanatory" when dealing with model of behavior and underlying motivations, "predictive" when applied to understanding future outcomes and actions, "reflexive" when used to examine the assumptions behind representations of a system, and "strategic" when used to better represent a complex system (as cited in Papageorgiou & Salmeron, 2013).

Based on these defined functions of participatory modeling, it is clear that the practice of participatory FCM has greatly favored substantive functions meant to clarify system function and mental models present in the social components in a way that incorporates elements of each of Codara's (1998) purposes. Enhancing system knowledge and understanding stakeholder variation are both related to better understanding the system and its components. Social learning (a normative function), consensus-building, and increasing participation (both instrumental functions) are repeatedly highlighted in the literature as processes that are essential to addressing complex issues faced globally (Adger, 2010; Biggs et al., 2011; Jones et al., 2009). These ideas are commonly cited by researchers involved in using FCM to study social-ecological systems and provide much of the rationale for their use of participatory methods. It then follows that a main concern of this field of science should be to better inform stakeholders and decision-makers through the use of these normative and instrumental processes.

Partnership

Initial interviews were only conducted in eleven of the thirty-three studies. These interviews fulfilled a variety of purposes, including determining problem context or initial model concepts and identifying or validating the target population. Regarding sample populations, diverse stakeholder groups were the most common, as found in over half of the studies. Local experts were included the least, found in only seven of the studies, and domain experts and practitioners were the most-engaged participant type, found in twelve studies (table 5).

Individual model building is the most common participant activity, used in twenty-six of the studies, while group model building is only used in eleven. Several studies incorporate both individual and group model building in different points of the research (see Papageorgiou, Markinos, & Gemptos, 2009; Rajaram & Das, 2010). Involving participants directly in the scenario analysis process is uncommon, occurring in only three studies in our dataset (see Gray et al., 2015; Murungweni et al., 2011; van Vliet, Kok, & Veldkamp, 2010) (table 5). In twenty-five of the studies, there was only one specified interaction with the participants and no study specifies more than three interactions in the course of research.

Our findings indicate that participants are most often involved in only one aspect of the modeling process: the knowledge-gathering phase. This was most often the only interaction with participants in the vast majority of studies. While some use initial interviews with participants to define the sample population, domain, or parameters of the model, these aspects of research scoping are most often decided only by the researchers. Expanding the role of participants to allow them input in identifying the appropriate sample population could help appropriately target the sources of knowledge captured in modeling and increase the degree of participation.

The finding that participant involvement in scenario analysis is uncommon within the dataset further illustrates the potential for expanding the role of participants in the research. An additional interaction in which participants are involved in scenario analysis could potentially enable troubleshooting to ensure that the model outcomes are realistic based on local knowledge of the system, encourage greater learning about system dynamics and system state outcomes, and stimulate discussion of system function that creates social learning and development of a shared knowledge base (Jetter & Kok, 2014; Gray, Chan, Clark, & Jordan, 2012; Papageorgiou & Salmeron, 2013). These attempts to further integrate participants into the modeling processes could, in other words, provide a more robust approach to research for any of the study purposes identified.

The case studies in our dataset commonly engaged diverse stakeholder groups as a knowledge-gathering strategy. The knowledge and perspectives among diverse stakeholder groups are expected to vary and potentially disagree, since each distinct group is functioning based on mental models that reflect their unique experiential and social influences (Johnson-Laird, 1983; Jones et al., 2011). Therefore, this design decision fits well with the intent of eliciting diverse knowledge about a system in which many unique interests exist. The exceptions to this strategy, or those in which fewer studies focus on diverse stakeholder groups, were:

- Group modeling with *domain experts* to increase system knowledge
- Modeling with *practitioners* for consensus-building

In group model-building for system knowledge, which engages domain experts, studies focused on management and policy dimensions of food production (Nyaki et al., 2014; Papageorgiou et al., 2009; Rajaram & Das, 2010) and ecological food webs (Ramsey & Norbury, 2009). In these applications, accurate modeling of the complex processes of agricultural management and food web dynamics requires specific knowledge domains. With the concerns expressed by some authors and participants regarding the accuracy of models constructed with stakeholder knowledge, domain experts could be considered a source of knowledge that can most accurately and cohesively depict complex system functions.

Studies that include modeling with practitioners for consensus-building, similar to the previously discussed group of studies, focus mostly on some aspect of agricultural management (Douglas et al., 2016; Fairweather, 2010; Fairweather & Hunt, 2011). For consensus-building in a system-management context, including individuals with decision-making and management capacity in the system is a logical choice. In a specialized agricultural system, many stakeholders may not be more than tangentially aware of detailed system functions or have agency to influence its management. Therefore, practitioners are important participants in an effort to build consensus on management and policy approaches.

It is also important to note that, in many FCM studies, researchers are constrained by practical limitations, such as time, budget, respondent availability, and the need to include particular individuals in their study. Therefore, determining sample size using estimates of saturation is rarely reported in the literature.

Process

In twenty-one of the studies, the concepts are unrestricted and determined entirely by participants, which is known as "open concept design" (see Çelik, Özesmi, & Akdoğan, 2006; Douglas et al., 2016) (table 5). Rajaram and Das (2010) conducted the only study in our dataset in which the concepts are predetermined prior to model-building. In this study, concepts were determined by participants from the same community in a previous study and then the relationships were mapped later. In this way, the map had a predetermined concept design but was entirely constructed by participants.

Eleven studies used a partially predetermined concept design. In many of these cases, the researchers allowed participants to add concepts; however, the researchers prompted the participants or started the mapping process with a set of concepts (see Fairweather, 2010; Mouratiadou & Moran, 2007). In some cases, this was meant to stimulate ideas in a group FCM process (see Nyaki et al. 2014) and in some to ensure that FCMs were constructed around a central theme (see Isaac, Dawoe, & Sieciechowicz, 2009).

Aggregating fuzzy cognitive maps into groups for comparison was common, with twelve studies taking this approach exclusively. Seven studies aggregated models into a whole-system map, and two of these studies (Gray, Chan, Clark, & Jordan, 2012; Özesmi & Özesmi, 2003) use both methods for different sections. Quantitative and qualitative aggregation methods are used equally. Only six of the studies in our dataset do not use structural metrics to describe or compare models created by participants. The most commonly used structural metrics were the number of concepts and connections and density of the fuzzy cognitive maps, which were used in over half of the studies. Centrality of components was also a common metric, used in just under half of the studies. Hierarchy index was the least-used metric, found in only six of the studies.

Comparing fuzzy cognitive maps among participant groups or individuals was a very common practice in our dataset, with twenty of the studies conducting some form of descriptive or quantitative analysis. Only one study compared only the relationships, as the concepts were predetermined from a previous study with the same stakeholders (van Vliet et al., 2010). Scenario analysis was by far the most common type of model simulation, appearing in twenty-two of the studies. Three studies in this dataset analyze the sensitivity of components within a model. A total of five studies in our dataset included system state or desired state calculations into their analysis (see Kontogianni et al., 2012; Özesmi & Özesmi, 2003).

Since open concept design was the standard practice for most studies within the field of participatory FCM, it is clear that there was a common effort to remove or lessen researcher influence over the knowledge capture process. Those studies that used a partially predetermined design, as mentioned, did so to ensure that the domain of knowledge being captured was clearly bounded, and usually only introduced starting concepts for participants to build upon. The partially predetermined concept design appeared most often in studies that used group modeling to increase system knowledge. Facilitation of group model-building approaches can be a challenge and predetermination of some concepts can streamline the process and ensure that model-building stays on topic in a situation where diverse perspectives and opinions could create tangential discussion (Gray et al., 2015; Murungweni et al., 2011; Nyaki et al., 2014).

Graph theory indices as structural metrics were the most common method for comparing individual or group models, likely due to their established importance in many network-based disciplines such as artificial neural networks, concept mapping, and social network analysis (Özesmi & Özesmi, 2004; Gray, Zanre, & Gray, 2014). Graph theory metrics were very useful in showing the change in mental models due to social learning (Henly-Shepard et al., 2015), indicating differences in perspectives and robustness of system knowledge among groups (Özesmi & Özesmi, 2003), and identifying key concepts and relationships (Kontogianni et al., 2012).

Different uses of scenario analysis showed a distinction between studies used for applied, instrumental purposes and those focused on representing and comparing knowledge. Scenario analysis was an important component of the participatory FCM process in all study types except in consensus building. A greater knowledge about system function was also not typically a purpose (or outcome) that co-occurred with consensus building. Consensus has been described as social negotiation of stakeholder knowledge that leads to common understanding (Innes & Booher, 1999), a process that doesn't necessarily require the building of new knowledge. These findings could suggest that consensus-focused studies in our dataset (see Douglas et al., 2016; Hobbs et al., 2002; Fairweather & Hunt, 2011) did not always strive to integrate greater system knowledge into their consensus. If consensus is intended to underlie decision-making in a complex system, the researchers and participants alike could also benefit from the integration of diverse knowledge elicited during a participatory FCM process, as seen in studies attempting to fulfill both objectives.

Products

The most common outcomes for studies in our dataset were identification and comparison of participant knowledge and understanding, found in twenty-two studies, and the creation of more complete models of the systems studied, found in thirteen studies. All other objectives (shared learning, consensus, methodological, and others) were found in seven or fewer studies. Five of the seven studies with consensus-related outcomes also highlighted shared learning outcomes.

There were discrepancies between the frequency of most purposes and outcomes in the dataset, suggesting that intentions did not always match the actual outcomes (figure 3). Characterization of participant knowledge, for example, is identified as a purpose for only thirteen studies but as an outcome of twenty-two studies. Building complete system knowledge, conversely, was an intended purpose for twenty studies, but only thirteen showed the outcome of a complete or improved system model.

Our analysis indicates that participatory FCM is a particularly effective way to elicit and learn about mental models. Our data show that learning about participant knowledge occurs even when researchers did not specifically state it as an objective. While our dataset provides some evidence that mental models could enhance system knowledge and functional understanding, it appears that this outcome has been more difficult to achieve. Studies that failed to produce what they consider a complete system model suggest various ways in which the process could be improved in future studies. Nyaki et al. (2014), for example, suggest that participant knowledge should be empirically validated in order to ensure that it is based on a correct understanding

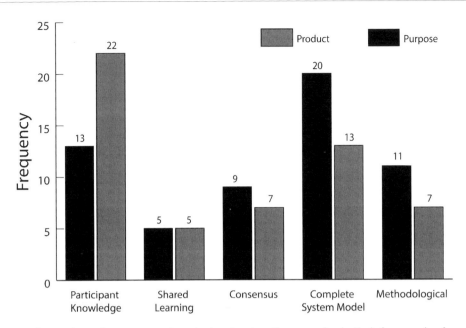

FIGURE 3. Comparison of purposes and products, showing discrepancies in their frequencies for some types.

of the system. Van Vliet, Kok, and Veldkamp (2010) suggest that, in cases where an aggregated, whole-system model did not fit with stakeholder perceptions once presented, an additional workshop should be conducted to improve the model. Gray, Chan, Clark, & Jordan (2012) suggest that new techniques for standardizing stakeholder knowledge would be beneficial, allowing for more legitimate integration and comparison.

Typologies and Tradeoffs

With the goal of creating a typology that helps to establish standards and practices for those interested in using participatory FCM techniques, we focused on the study purpose and grouped together rubric elements that commonly occurred with each study's purpose within our dataset. Table 6 details, for each study purpose, the frequency with which different partnership, process, and product rubric elements occurred. Each study purpose was commonly associated with a set of study design practices related to partnership and process and study outcomes. Of the thirteen studies on understanding participant variation, for example, ten use individual model building, eleven focus on diverse stakeholders, eleven compare model structure, and thirteen result in greater understanding of the variation among participant knowledge. We find that studies attempting to increase system knowledge consist of two sub-types: those engaging participants in individual model-building and those that utilize group model-building.

Identifying the limitations of each approach is an equally important exercise. Our typology aided in summarizing challenges encountered in each approach, which is important when selecting the optimal research design (table 7). We found the previous literature on limitations

Table 6. Summary of participatory FCM typologies

PURPOSE	PARTNERSHIP	PROCESS	PRODUCTS
Understanding Participant Variation ($n = 13$)	Individual interviews ($n = 7$) and model building ($n = 10$) with diverse groups of stakeholders ($n = 11$)	Open concept determination ($n = 8$), often aggregated into group models Robust comparisons among models ($n = 11$) and scenario analysis ($n = 8$) to study functional differences	Very effective in studying variation in participants' knowledge and understandings ($n = 13$)
More Complete System Model—Individual Approach ($n = 15$)	Individual modeling with Domain Experts ($n = 7$), Local Experts ($n = 6$), and/or Diverse Stakeholders ($n = 7$)	Open concept determination ($n = 10$) Robust comparisons among models ($n = 9$) and scenario analysis ($n = 14$) for prediction or system behavior	More complete system model ($n = 10$) and describing participant variation ($n = 10$)
More Complete System Model—Group Approach ($n = 8$)	Group modeling with Domain Experts ($n = 5$)	Partially predetermined concepts ($n = 4$) or Open concept determination ($n = 3$) Scenario analysis for prediction or system behavior ($n = 6$)	More complete system model ($n = 5$)
Consensus Building ($n = 9$)	Individual model building ($n = 7$) with no clear trend in participant types	Open concept determination ($n = 5$) or Partially predetermined ($n = 4$), models sometimes aggregated into consensus map ($n = 4$) Scenario analysis ($n = 4$) or other calculations ($n = 5$) (ex.: PCA, Resilience Metrics) conducted	Consensus outcomes often achieved ($n = 5$), but limited follow-up with groups to define next steps Participant variation outcomes ($n = 5$)
Shared Learning ($n = 5$)	Group Modeling ($n = 4$) with Small Groups (4–13)	Open concept determination ($n = 5$) and Scenario analysis ($n = 4$)	Shared learning ($n = 3$), Consensus ($n = 3$), and Participant variation outcomes ($n = 4$)

in various approaches to participatory FCM (see Gray, Chan, Clark, & Jordan, 2012; Jetter & Kok, 2014; Özesmi & Özesmi, 2004; Papageorgiou & Kontogianni, 2012) to be accurate when compared to the common findings in our dataset. For example, studies involving individual model-building often mention the additional time and expense compared to group approaches. Group model-building approaches, on the other hand, can be challenging due to the need for effective facilitation to avoid influence of power dynamics among the participants.

Our typology and table of limitations are most immediately useful for guiding researchers through the benefits and drawbacks of different approaches to participatory FCM and identifying the appropriate research design for their purpose. In a general example, a project intended to establish a set of guidelines for decision-makers addressing an urgent socio-environmental issue may be accomplished by engaging a diverse group of domain experts and stakeholders in a group workshop to quickly co-produce a fuzzy cognitive map of the issue and discuss failures and successes. Although individual modeling with open concept design may robustly represent the knowledge and perspectives of the diverse group, it may be too time intensive, as it requires building each model, standardizing for comparability, and additional group work to merge models. It may be more appropriate to use an approach similar to the "Complete System Model—Group Approach," in which initial concepts can be defined through pre-interviews,

Table 7. Limitations identified by researchers in each study type

PURPOSE	TRADE-OFFS AND LIMITATIONS	EXAMPLES
Understanding Participant Variation	Can be expensive and time-consuming to conduct Translation and ambiguity from linguistic terms introduces potential researcher bias	Berbés-blázquez, 2015; Giordano, Passarella, Uricchio, & Vurro, 2005; Kafetzis, McRoberts, & Mouratiadou, 2010; Klein & Cooper, 1982; Kontogianni, Tourkolias, & Papageorgiou, 2013; Mouratiadou & Moran, 2007; Özesmi & Özesmi, 2003
More Complete System Model—Individual Approach	Time-consuming and requires large numbers of participants Disparities in participant perspectives may introduce uncertainty in model	Douglas et al., 2016; Gray, Hilsberg, McFall, & Arlinghaus, 2015; Murungweni, Wijk, Andersson, Smaling, & Giller, 2011; Nyaki, Gray, Lepczyk, Skibins, & Rentsch, 2014; Rajaram & Das, 2010; Ramsey & Norbury, 2009; van Vliet, Kok, & Veldkamp, 2010
More Complete System Model—Group Approach	Power dynamics in group situations may bias model Group knowledge alone may not produce an accurate model	Çelik, Özesmi, & Akdoğan, 2006; Gray, Zanre, & Gray, 2014; Gray, Chan, Clark, & Jordan, 2012; Halbrendt et al., 2014; Isaac, Dawoe, & Sieciechowicz, 2009; Jetter & Schweinfort, 2011; Samarasinghe & Strickert, 2013; Tan & Özesmi, 2006; Vasslides & Jensen, 2016
Consensus Building	Merged models do not necessarily represent real consensus as achieved through group discussion/negotiation Uncertainty in model accuracy for decision-making	Fairweather & Hunt, 2011; Fairweather, 2010; Hobbs, Ludsin, Knight, Ryan, & Ciborowski, 2002; Kafetzis et al., 2010; Klein & Cooper, 1982
Shared Learning	Requires skilled facilitation to avoid group power dynamics Requires engagement and communication among diverse groups	Douglas et al., 2016; Henly-Shepard, Gray, & Cox, 2015; Van Vliet, Kok, & Veldkamp, 2010; Vasslides & Jensen, 2016

followed by a facilitated group meeting for modeling, running basic scenarios, and discussing outcomes and recommendations.

Beyond establishing standards and practices for participatory FCM, this typology will also aid in identifying ways in which the science and the practice can be further explored and improved. Shared learning outcomes, for example, were emphasized in a small portion of the studies, and only one of these studies (van Vliet et al., 2010) engaged participants in scenario exercises. Consensus building relies on individual model building in most cases, when group modeling may be more appropriate since it encourages direct participant interaction. It was also shown to be successful in just over half of the cases, perhaps due to the lack of follow-up and insufficient engagement with and among participants. These cases highlight areas of research that are critical in advancing participatory FCM.

Conclusion

The field of participatory FCM has made a great deal of progress in developing effective methods for knowledge capture and integration of knowledge into functional system models. Although relatively few case studies focus particularly on consensus-building, social learning, and other more applied appropriations of FCM, the literature suggests that standards and norms in these areas are beginning to emerge as well. Our paper, through analysis of a comprehensive dataset of participatory FCM studies and identification of several common types, has contributed to identifying these standards and norms. Our intent is that this knowledge will serve as guidance for current and future users of participatory FCM and make explicit many of the benefits and tradeoffs of tested approaches.

REFERENCES

Adger, W. N. (2010). Social capital, collective action, and adaptation to climate change. *Economic Geography, 79,* 4.

Aguilar, J. (2005). A survey about fuzzy cognitive maps papers. *International Journal of Computational Cognition, 3*(2), 27–33.

Alpert, P. (1996). Integrated conservation and development projects. *BioScience, 46*(11), 845–855.

Axelrod, R. (1976). The cognitive mapping approach to decision making. In R. Axelrod (Ed.), *Structure of Decision* (pp. 221–250). Princeton, NJ: Princeton University Press.

Barrett, C. B., & Arcese, P. (1995). Are integrated conservation-development projects (ICDPs) sustainable? On the conservation of large mammals in sub-Saharan Africa. *World Development, 23*(7), 1073–1084. http://doi.org/10.1016/0305-750X(95)00031-7.

Berbés-blázquez, M. (2015). *From ecosystem services to ecosystem benefits: Unpacking the links between ecosystems and human well-being in agricultural communities in Costa Rica* (Unpublished doctoral dissertation). York University, Toronto, ON.

Berkes, F., Colding, J., & Folke, C. (2000). Rediscovery of traditional ecological knowledge as adaptive management, *Ecological Applications 10*(5), 1251–1262.

Berkes, F., & Folke, C. (1998). Linking social and ecological systems for resilience and sustainability. *Linking Social and Ecological Systems: Management Practices and Social Mechanisms for Building Resilience, 1,* 13–20.

Berkes, F., Folke, C., & Gadgil, M. (1995). Traditional ecological knowledge, biodiversity, resilience and sustainability. *Biodiversity Conservation,* 281–299. doi: 10.1007/978-94-011-0277-3_15.

Biggs, D., Abel, N., Knight, A. T., Leitch, A., Langston, A., & Ban, N. C. (2011). The implementation crisis in conservation planning: Could "mental models" help? *Conservation Letters, 4*(3), 169–183. doi: 10.1111/j.1755-263X.2011.00170.x.

Brown, K. (2003). Three challenges for a real people-centered conservation. *Global Ecology and Biogeography, 12*(2), 89–92. doi: 10.1046/j.1466-822X.2003.00327.x.

Çelik, F. D. er, Özesmi, U., & Akdoğan, A. (2006). Participatory ecosystem management planning at Tuzla Lake (Turkey) using fuzzy cognitive mapping. *Ecological Modelling, 195*(1–2), 83–93. doi: 10.1016/j.ecolmodel.2005.11.012.

Codara, L. (1998). *Le mappe cognitive.* Roma: Carrocci Editore.

Craik, K. (1943). *The nature of explanation.* Cambridge: Cambridge University Press.

Dietz, T., & Stern, P. C. (Eds.). (2008). *Public participation in environmental assessment and decision making.* Washington, DC: National Academies Press.

Douglas, E. M., Wheeler, S. A., Smith, D. J., Overton, I. C., Gray, S. A., Doody, T. M., & Crossman, N. D. (2016). Using mental-modelling to explore how irrigators in the Murray–Darling Basin make water-use decisions. *Journal of Hydrology: Regional Studies, 6,* 1–12. doi: 10.1016/j.ejrh.2016.01.035.

Doyle, J. K., & Ford, D. N. (1998). Mental models concepts for system dynamics research. *System Dynamics Review, 14*(1), 3–29.

Eden, C., Ackermann, F., & Cropper, S. (1992). The analysis of cause maps. *Journal of management Studies, 29*(3), 309–324.

Fairweather, J. (2010). Farmer models of socio-ecologic systems: Application of causal mapping across multiple locations. *Ecological Modelling, 221*(3), 555–562. doi: 10.1016/j.ecolmodel.2009.10.026.

Fairweather, J. R., & Hunt, L. M. (2011). Can farmers map their farm system? Causal mapping and the sustainability of sheep/beef farms in New Zealand. *Agriculture and Human Values, 28*(1), 55–66. doi: 10.1007/s10460-009-9252-3.

Folke, C., Hahn, T., Olsson, P., & Norberg, J. (2005). Adaptive governance of social-ecological systems. *Annual Review of Environment and Resources, 30*(1), 441–473. doi: 10.1146/annurev. energy.30.050504.144511.

Funtowicz, S. O., & Ravetz, J. R. (1991). A new scientific methodology for global environmental issues. In R. Constanza (Ed.), *Ecological economics: The science and management of sustainability* (pp. 137–152).

Giordano, R., Passarella, G., Uricchio, V. F., & Vurro, M. (2005). Fuzzy cognitive maps for issue identification in a water resources conflict resolution system. *Physics and Chemistry of the Earth, 30*(6–7 SPEC. ISS.), 463–469. doi: 10.1016/j.pce.2005.06.012.

Gleason, M., McCreary, S., Miller-Henson, M., Ugoretz, J., Fox, E., Merrifield, M., . . . Hoffman, K. (2010). Science-based and stakeholder-driven marine protected area network planning: A successful case study from north central California. *Ocean and Coastal Management, 53*(2), 52–68. doi: 10.1016/j. ocecoaman.2009.12.001.

Gray, S. A., Chan, A., Clark, D., & Jordan, R. (2012). Modeling the integration of stakeholder knowledge in social-ecological decision-making: Benefits and limitations to knowledge diversity. *Ecological Modelling, 229,* 88–96. doi: 10.1016/j.ecolmodel.2011.09.011.

Gray, S. A., Gray, S. R. J., Cox, L. J., & Henly-Shepard, S. (2013). Mental modeler: A fuzzy-logic cognitive mapping modeling tool for adaptive environmental management. *Proceedings of the annual Hawaii international conference on system sciences,* 965–973. doi: 10.1109/HICSS.2013.399.

Gray, S. A., Gray, S. R. J., Kok, J. L. De, Helfgott, A. E. R., Dwyer, B. O., Jordan, R., & Nyaki, A. (2015). Using fuzzy cognitive mapping as a participatory approach to analyze change, preferred states, and perceived resilience of social-ecological systems. *Ecology and Society, 20*(2), 11. doi: 10.5751/ ES-07396-200211.

Gray, S. A., Hilsberg, J., McFall, A., & Arlinghaus, R. (2015). The structure and function of angler mental models about fish population ecology: The influence of specialization and target species. *Journal of outdoor recreation and tourism, 12,* 1–13.

Gray, S. A., Jordan, R. C., Crall, A., Newman, G., Hmelo-Silver, C., Huang, J., . . . Singer, A. (2016). Combining participatory modelling and citizen science to support volunteer conservation action. *Biological Conservation, 208,* 76–86. doi: 10.1016/j.biocon.2016.07.037.

Gray, S. A., Voinov, A., Paolisso, M., Jordan, R., BenDor, T., P., G., . . . Zellner, M. (2017). Purpose, processes, partnerships, and products: Four Ps to advance participatory socio-environmental modeling. *Ecological Applications, (28)*1, 46–61. doi: 10.1002/eap.1627.

Gray, S. A., Zanre, E., & Gray, S. R. J. (2014). Fuzzy cognitive maps as representations of mental models and group beliefs. *Fuzzy Cognitive Maps for Applied Sciences and Engineering SE—2, 54,* 29–48. h doi: 10.1007/978-3-642-39739-4_2.

Gray, S. R. J., Gagnon, A. S., Gray, S. A., O'Dwyer, B., O'Mahony, C., Muir, D., . . . Gault, J. (2014). Are coastal managers detecting the problem? Assessing stakeholder perception of climate vulnerability using fuzzy cognitive mapping. *Ocean & Coastal Management, 94,* 74–89. doi: 10.1016/j. ocecoaman.2013.11.008.

Hage, P., & F. Harary. (1983). *Structural Models in Anthropology.* Cambridge University Press, Cambridge.

Halbrendt, J., Gray, S. A., Crow, S., Radovich, T., Kimura, A. H., & Tamang, B. B. (2014). Differences in farmer and expert beliefs and the perceived impacts of conservation agriculture. *Global Environmental Change, 28,* 50–62. doi: 10.1016/j.gloenvcha.2014.05.001.

Healey, P. (1997). *Collaborative planning: Shaping places in fragmented societies.* Vancouver: University of British Columbia Press.

Healey, P. (2003). Collaborative planning in perspective. *Planning Theory, 2*(2), 101–123. doi: 10.1177/14730952030022002.

Henly-Shepard, S., Gray, S. A., & Cox, L. J. (2015). The use of participatory modeling to promote social learning and facilitate community disaster planning. *Environmental Science and Policy, 45,* 109–122. doi: doi: 10.1016/j.envsci.2014.10.004.

Hobbs, B. F., Ludsin, S. a, Knight, R. L., Ryan, P. a, & Ciborowski, J. J. H. (2002). Fuzzy cognitive mapping as a tool to define management objectives for complex ecosystems. *Ecological Applications, 12*(5), 1548–1565.

Htun, H., Gray, S. A., Lepczyk, C. A., Titmus, A., & Adams, K. (2016). Combining watershed models and knowledge-based models to predict local-scale impacts of climate change on endangered wildlife. *Environmental Modelling and Software, 84,* 440–457.

Innes, J. E., & Booher, D. E. (1999). Consensus building and complex adaptive systems. *Journal of the American Planning Association, 65*(4), 412–423. doi: 10.1080/01944369908976071.

Isaac, M. E., Dawoe, E., & Sieciechowicz, K. (2009). Assessing local knowledge use in agroforestry management with cognitive maps. *Environmental Management, 43*(6), 1321–1329. doi: 10.1007/ s00267-008-9201-8.

Jetter, A. J., & Kok, K. (2014). Fuzzy cognitive maps for futures studies—A methodological assessment of concepts and methods. *Futures, 61,* 45–57. doi: 10.1016/j.futures.2014.05.002.

Jetter, A., & Schweinfort, W. (2011). Building scenarios with fuzzy cognitive maps: An exploratory study of solar energy. *Futures, 43*(1), 52–66. doi: 10.1016/j.futures.2010.05.002.

Johnson-Laird, P. N. (1983). *Mental models: Towards a cognitive science of language, inference, and consciousness.* Cambridge, MA: Harvard University Press.

Jones, N. A., Perez, P., Measham, T. G., Kelly, G. J., D'Aquino, P., Daniell, K. A., . . . Ferrand, N. (2009). Evaluating participatory modeling: Developing a framework for cross-case analysis. *Environmental Management, 44*(6), 1180–1195. doi: 10.1007/s00267-009-9391-8.

Jones, N. A., Ross, H., Lynam, T., Perez, P., & Leitch, A. (2011). Mental model an interdisciplinary synthesis of theory and methods. *Ecology and Society, 16*(1), 46–46.

Kafetzis, A., McRoberts, N., & Mouratiadou, I. (2010). Using fuzzy cognitive maps to support the analysis of stakeholders' views of water resource use and water quality policy. In M. Glykas (Ed.), *Fuzzy cognitive maps* (pp. 383–402). Berlin: Springer.

Kapoor, I. (2001). Towards participatory environmental management? *Journal of Environmental Management, 63*(3), 269–279. doi: 10.1006/jema.2001.0478.

Klein, C., McKinnon, M. C., Wright, B. T., Possingham, H. P., & Halpern, B. S. (2015). Social equity and the probability of success of biodiversity conservation. *Global Environmental Change, 35,* 299–306. doi: 10.1016/j.gloenvcha.2015.09.007.

Klein, J., & Cooper, D. (1982). Cognitive maps of decision-makers in a complex game. *Journal of the Operational Research Society, 33*(1), 63–71. doi: 10.2307/2581872.

Kok, K. (2009). The potential of Fuzzy Cognitive Maps for semi-quantitative scenario development, with an example from Brazil. *Global Environmental Change, 19*(1), 122–133. doi: 10.1016/j.gloenvcha.2008.08.003.

Kok, K., & van Delden, H. (2009). Combining two approaches of integrated scenario development to combat desertification in the Guadalentín watershed, Spain. *Environment and Planning B: Planning and Design, 36*(1), 49–66. doi: 10.1068/b32137.

Kontogianni, A., Papageorgiou, E., Salomatina, L., Skourtos, M., & Zanou, B. (2012). Risks for the Black Sea marine environment as perceived by Ukrainian stakeholders: A fuzzy cognitive mapping application. *Ocean & Coastal Management, 62,* 34–42. doi: 10.1016/j.ocecoaman.2012.03.006.

Kontogianni, A., Tourkolias, C., & Papageorgiou, E. I. (2013). Revealing market adaptation to a low carbon transport economy: Tales of hydrogen futures as perceived by fuzzy cognitive mapping. *International Journal of Hydrogen Energy, 38*(2), 709–722. doi: 10.1016/j.ijhydene.2012.10.101.

Kosko, B. (1986). Fuzzy cognitive maps. *International Journal of Man-Machine Studies, 24*(1), 65–75. doi: 10.1016/S0020-7373(86)80040-2.

Kosko, B. (1988). Hidden patterns in combined and adaptive knowledge networks. *International Journal of Approximate Reasoning, 2*(4), 377–393. doi: 10.1016/0888-613X(88)90111-9.

MacDonald, N. (1983) Trees and Networks in Biological Models. John Wiley and Sons, New York.

Manfredo, M. J., Teel, T. L., Gavin, M. C., & Fulton, D. (2014). Considerations in representing human individuals in social-ecological models. In M. J. Manfredo, J. J Vaske, A. Rechkemmer, & E. A. Duke (Eds.), *Understanding society and natural resources* (pp. 93–109). doi: 10.1007/978-94-017-8959-2.

Miller, G. A., & Johnson-Laird, P. N. (1976). *Language and perception.* Cambridge, MA: Belknap Press.

Mohammed, S., & Dumville, B. C. (2001). Team mental models in a team knowledge framework: Expanding theory and measurement across disciplinary boundaries. *Journal of Organizational Behavior, 22*(2), 89–106. doi: 10.1002/job.86.

Mouratiadou, I., & Moran, D. (2007). Mapping public participation in the Water Framework Directive: A case study of the Pinios River Basin, Greece. *Ecological Economics, 62*(1), 66–76. doi: 10.1016/j.ecolecon.2007.01.009.

Murungweni, C., Wijk, M. T. Van, Andersson, J., Smaling, E. M., & Giller, K. E. (2011). Application of fuzzy cognitive mapping in livelihood vulnerability. *Ecology and Society, 16*(4), 8.

Nakamura, K., Iwai, S., & Sawarag, T. (1982). Decision support using causation knowledge base. *IEEE Transactions on Systems, Man, and Cybernetics, 12*(6), 765–777.

Newmark, W. D., & Hough, J. L. (2000). Conserving wildlife in Africa: Integrated conservation and development projects and beyond. *BioScience, 50*(7), 585. doi: 10.1641/0006-3568(2000)050[0585:CWIAIC]2.0.CO;2.

Nyaki, A., Gray, S. a., Lepczyk, C. a., Skibins, J. C., & Rentsch, D. (2014). Local-scale dynamics and local drivers of bushmeat trade. *Conservation Biology, 28*(5), 1–12. doi: 10.1111/cobi.12316.

Özesmi, U., & Özesmi, S. L. (2003). A participatory approach to ecosystem conservation: Fuzzy cognitive maps and stakeholder group analysis in Uluabat Lake, Turkey. *Environmental Management, 31*(4), 518–531. doi: 10.1007/s00267-002-2841-1.

Özesmi, U., & Özesmi, S. L. (2004). Ecological models based on people's knowledge: A multi-step fuzzy cognitive mapping approach. *Ecological Modelling, 176*(1–2), 43–64. doi: 10.1016/j. ecolmodel.2003.10.027.

Pahl-Wostl, C. (2006). The importance of social learning in restoring the multifunctionality of rivers and floodplains. *Ecology and Society, 11*(1), 10.

Pahl-Wostl, C. (2007). The implications of complexity for integrated resources management. *Environmental Modelling & Software, 22*(5), 561–569. doi: 10.1016/j.envsoft.2005.12.024.

Papageorgiou, E. I., Markinos, A., & Gemptos, T. (2009). Application of fuzzy cognitive maps for cotton yield management in precision farming. *Expert Systems with Applications, 36*(10), 12399–12413. doi: 10.1016/j.eswa.2009.04.046.

Papageorgiou, E. I., & Salmeron, J. L. (2013). A review of fuzzy cognitive maps research during the last decade. *IEEE Transactions on Fuzzy Systems, 21*(1), 66–79. doi: 10.1109/TFUZZ.2012.2201727.

Persha, L., Agrawal, A., & Chhatre, A. (2011). Social and ecological synergy: Local rulemaking, forest livelihoods, and biodiversity conservation. *Science, 331*(6024), 1606–1608. doi: 10.1126/science.1199343.

Rajaram, T., & Das, A. (2008). A methodology for integrated assessment of rural linkages in a developing nation. *Impact Assessment and Project Appraisal, 26*(2), 99–113. doi: 10.3152/146155108X323605.

Rajaram, T., & Das, A. (2010). Modeling of interactions among sustainability components of an agro-ecosystem using local knowledge through cognitive mapping and fuzzy inference system. *Expert Systems with Applications, 37*(2), 1734–1744. doi: 10.1016/j.eswa.2009.07.035.

Ramsey, D. S. L., & Norbury, G. L. (2009). Predicting the unexpected: Using a qualitative model of a New Zealand dryland ecosystem to anticipate pest management outcomes. *Austral Ecology, 34*(4), 409–421. doi: 10.1111/j.1442-9993.2009.01942.x.

Röckmann, C., Ulrich, C., Dreyer, M., Bell, E., Borodzicz, E., Haapasaari, P., . . . Pastoors, M. (2012). The added value of participatory modelling in fisheries management—what has been learnt? *Marine Policy, 36*(5), 1072–1085. doi: 10.1016/j.marpol.2012.02.027.

Salmeron, J. L., Vidal, R., & Mena, A. (2012). Expert systems with applications ranking fuzzy cognitive map based scenarios with TOPSIS. *Expert Systems With Applications, 39*(3), 2443–2450. doi: 10.1016/j. eswa.2011.08.094.

Samarasinghe, S., & Strickert, G. (2013). Mixed-method integration and advances in fuzzy cognitive maps for computational policy simulations for natural hazard mitigation. *Environmental Modelling and Software, 39,* 188–200. doi: 10.1016/j.envsoft.2012.06.008.

Surowiecki, J. (2004). *The wisdom of crowds: Why the many are smarter than the few and how collective wisdom shapes business, economies, societies and nations.* New York: Random House.

Tan, C., & Özesmi, U. (2006). A generic shallow lake ecosystem model based on collective expert knowledge. *Hydrobiologia, 563*(1), 125–142. doi: 10.1007/s10750-005-1397-5.

Tolman, E. C. (1948). Cognitive maps in rats and man. *Psychological Review, 55,* 189–208.

Tschakert, P., & Dietrich, K. A. (2010). Anticipatory learning for climate change adaptation and resilience. *Ecology and Society, 15*(2), 11.

van Vliet, M., Kok, K., & Veldkamp, T. (2010). Linking stakeholders and modellers in scenario studies: The use of fuzzy cognitive maps as a communication and learning tool. *Futures, 42*(1), 1–14. doi: 10.1016/j.futures.2009.08.005.

Vanwindekens, F. M., Stilmant, D., & Baret, P. V. (2013). Development of a broadened cognitive mapping approach for analysing systems of practices in social—ecological systems. *Ecological Modelling, 250*(2013), 352–362. doi: 10.1016/j.ecolmodel.2012.11.023.

Vasslides, J. M., & Jensen, O. P. (2016). Fuzzy cognitive mapping in support of integrated ecosystem assessments: Developing a shared conceptual model among stakeholders. *Journal of Environmental Management, 166,* 348–356. doi: 10.1016/j.jenvman.2015.10.038.

Voinov, A., & Bousquet, F. (2010). Modelling with stakeholders. *Environmental Modelling and Software, 25*(11), 1268–1281. doi: 10.1016/j.envsoft.2010.03.007.

Voinov, A., & Gaddis, E. J. B. (2008). Lessons for successful participatory watershed modeling: A perspective from modeling practitioners. *Ecological Modelling, 216*(2), 197–207. doi: 10.1016/j.ecolmodel.2008.03.010.

Walker, B., Carpenter, S., Anderies, J., Abel, N., Cumming, G. S., Janssen, M., & Lebel, L. (2002). Resilience management in social-ecological systems: A working hypothesis for a participatory approach. *Conservation Ecology, 6*(1), 1–14.

Zhang, W.-R., & Chen, S.-S. (1988). A logical architecture for cognitive maps. In *Proceedings of IEEE International Conference on Neural Networks* (pp. 231–238). San Diego, CA: IEEE.

Designing and Deploying Collaborative Models for Multifunctional Landscape Design: Geodesign in Practice

Bryan C. Runck, Carissa Schively Slotterback, David Pitt, Len Kne, David Mulla, Nicholas Jordan, Marcus Grubbs, Madeline Goldkamp, Alexander Heid, Peter Wiringa, and Yiqun Xie

Multifunctional landscapes possess a variety of aspirational characteristics, including supplying multiple ecosystem services, accounting for externalities at multiple landscape scales, and producing symbiotic relationships between humans and the environment (Lovell & Johnston, 2009; Mastrangelo et al., 2013; Naveh, 2001). A significant amount of the literature on multifunctionality comes from the agricultural context, wherein multifunctionality can be understood as land use and management practices that produce goods such as food, fuel, and fiber, along with enhanced water quality, carbon sequestration, habitat, and other ecosystem services (e.g., Boody et al., 2005; Jordan et al., 2011; Lovell et al., 2010).

Getting to multifunctional landscapes requires efforts that are both transdisciplinary and engaged. First, the literature is clear that research and management relative to multifunctionality must be transdisciplinary. Fry (2001, 161) notes the importance of "combining humanistic and natural science approaches" to better understand landscape function and how people interact with and shape landscapes. As we work toward multifunctionality, understanding the mutual relationship between people and the landscape is critical, acknowledging that natural and cultural processes shape landscape dynamics and that landscapes can be understood both objectively and subjectively at the same time (Tress & Tress, 2001; Tress, Tress, Décamps, & D'Hauteserre, 2001). When we work in a transdisciplinary manner, we have the potential to produce landscapes that are healthy, productive, attractive, and livable (Naveh 2001).

Second, achieving multifunctional landscapes requires engagement of both scientific knowledge and knowledge that is held by other stakeholders. The knowledge that stakeholders bring is characterized variously in the literature as "local," "lay," and "indigenous" knowledge (Armitage et al., 2009; Berkes, Colding, & Folke, 2000; Olsson, Folke, & Berkes, 2004). Balram et al. (2004, 1196) distinguishes local knowledge—"knowledge derived from local embedded experiences"—as complementary to technical knowledge derived from "systematic observations and experiments." Van Herzele (2004) emphasizes that stakeholders bring professional as well as sociocultural frames to participatory planning efforts, resulting in variations in how each stakeholder makes sense of issues and how they may take action. Engaging those affected by decisions is essential because of the knowledge they bring and enhances project legitimacy, justice, equity, and empowerment (Berkes, 2009).

Deliberate efforts to engage multidisciplinary experts from academia, agencies, NGOs, local government, landowners, and others have been clearly shown to generate diverse types of knowledge that can offer a base of knowledge for group decision making (Baird, Plummer, Haug, & Huitema, 2014; Deyle & Slotterback, 2009; Mandarano, 2008; Zellner et al., 2012). This chapter examines one such effort in south-central Minnesota, which convened academic, government, NGO, and community stakeholders to develop a broad-based vision for generating multifunctional landscapes. The group was facilitated by the authors via a geodesign approach that used an interactive, model-based planning tool to support a collaborative stakeholder process (Slotterback et al., 2016). Critical analysis of this case study offers important insights into the role that multiple types of knowledge play in multifunctional landscape planning and design and explores the significance of co-design approaches that deliberately engage stakeholders at two stages—model development and model application for collaborative landscape design.

Linking Geodesign and Collaborative Modeling

Geodesign systems have been positioned as a means of networking multiple types of knowledge into a common framework for design and analysis at the intersection of social and ecological systems—humans and environment—relative to planning, design, and management of rural and urban landscapes (Nyerges et al., 2016; Slotterback et al., 2016; Wissen Hayek, von Wirth, Neuenschwander, & Grêt-Regamey, 2016). Recent research indicates that geodesign may be a key tool to address the wide gap between knowledge about social and ecological systems and the local, lived effects of changing land use (Steinitz, 2012). The emerging field of geodesign can be understood as a further extension of collaborative modeling and spatial decision support systems. Geodesign shares the common objective to promote better social and ecological outcomes by balancing and incorporating multiple stakeholders' perspectives throughout decision-making processes (Langsdale et al., 2013). Where geodesign systems differ from previous decision support systems and collaborative modeling is in how they engage diverse groups of stakeholders not only in model analysis, but also in the creative exploration of how land uses can be spatially configured and aesthetically designed (Steinitz, 2012).

In the context of multifunctional landscapes, knowledge across the social, biophysical, and information sciences must be connected (Folke, Hahn, Olsson, & Norberg, 2005; Nyerges, Roderick, Prager, Bennett, & Lam, 2014). Geodesign systems can be distinguished from conventional spatial and planning decision support systems and public participation geographic information systems (Aggett & McColl, 2006; Rinner & Bird, 2009; Sheppard, 2005) by how tightly geodesign tools couple geovisualization and diverse data types with the ability to rapidly propose stakeholder-created landscape designs and receive quantitative feedback on design performance (Batty, 2013; Goodchild, 2010; Steinitz, 2012). Also, a focus on impacts and solutions is central to geodesign (Perkl, 2016).

Geodesign systems couple digital sketch capabilities with rapid simulation of biophysical and economic outcomes (Goodchild, 2010), which in theory enables stakeholders to increase the multifunctionality of subsequent sketches based on quantitative ecosystem performance feedback on previously generated sketches. The design process allows stakeholders to engage in iterative thinking and learning that is theorized to improve the designed performance among multiple landscape systems (Slotterback et al., 2016; Steinitz, 2012). Thus, through this iterative process, a geodesign system that "fits" stakeholder needs will result in a tool that enables stakeholders to progress through multiple sketches and simulations that ultimately results in increasingly multifunctional designs.

Model Fit to Facilitate Co-Design and Collaboration

Even with this potential indicated in emerging theory and practice around geodesign, there remains a risk that the geodesign systems created by scientific stakeholders will not meet stakeholder users' needs, goals, or vision (i.e., lack "fit"), a challenge experienced in numerous attempts to build models and planning support systems for stakeholder use (e.g., Uran & Janssen, 2003). Vonk et al. (2005) document a number of bottlenecks that have limited adoption and use of planning support systems, including but not limited to stakeholders' assumptions about the difficulty of operating them, accessibility and quality of input data, and mismatch with actual tasks that stakeholders are involved in. If planning support systems are going to be useful in policy-making processes, it is especially critical that they "represent the complex interactions taking place in the human—environment system" (van Delden et al., 2011, 266–267).

Understanding Users of Geodesign Systems

One established approach to protect against this lack of system "fit" in geodesign systems is human-centered design (HCD; Goodspeed et al., 2016; Haklay & Tobón, 2003; Jankowski, Robischon, Tuthill, Nyerges, & Ramsey, 2006). The specific instantiation of human-centered design emphasized here stresses that technology, such as planning support systems, needs to be co-developed with users in an iterative process whereby expert knowledge becomes directly integrated with a local vision (Sanders & Stappers, 2008). In order for expert knowledge to be useful for local stakeholders, expert and local knowledge must be integrated in a way that allows that vision to emerge (Funtowicz & Ravetz, 1993; Opdam et al., 2013; Stokols, 2006). Interaction and relationship building to facilitate social learning, trust, and respect are also critical to designing and developing usable tools (van Delden et al., 2011). Human-centered design methods provide a framework to co-develop geodesign systems and a process whereby expert and local knowledge can be repeatedly synthesized and concretized in a geodesign system.

Developing geodesign systems for stakeholder fit has not been well defined in the literature to date, though some work has been done to describe the potential components of ideal geodesign systems. Ervin (2011; 2016) describes a wide range of possible components that could be included in an ideal geodesign system. For Ervin, the technology of geodesign could consist of three sets of modular tools and helpers, each with five components, which cross the broad technological and conceptual boundaries of geodesign. Most of the characteristics of geodesign systems are currently embodied across diverse tools including web-based geographic information systems (e.g., base maps, object attributes, etc.), computer-assisted design platforms (e.g., design constraints), human-environment models (e.g., system simulation, time, etc.), or online collaboration platforms (e.g., video conferencing). Ervin catalogs these components and clearly defines the potential characteristics that could make up an ideal geodesign system.

HCD approaches further characterize how to select from and implement the components identified by Ervin (2016) in order to better fit geodesign systems with stakeholders' needs (Uran & Janssen, 2003). Widely accepted as best practice, HCD has been successfully used for generating public participatory geographic information systems. Co-development in the context of HCD specifically takes an approach that emphasizes the tool users, their goals, and their skills as the driving determinant of what components make up a geodesign system (Gottwald, Laatikainen, & Kyttä, 2016; Haklay & Tobón, 2003).

Understanding Context and Knowledge

Beyond the instrumental focus of HCD in matching tools to users' abilities and tasks, broader issues of users' context and associated knowledge are also relevant. Sanders and Stappers's (2008) conception of "co-design" is informative here, as they emphasize the importance of fitting not only tools but also outcomes to stakeholders' context. They position co-design as a subset of HCD that puts further emphasis on the particular characteristics of stakeholders' political, economic, social, and biophysical contexts, as well as their unique creative goals, raising the caution that failing to consider these factors can undermine model fit (Sanders & Stappers, 2008).

According to Sanders and Stappers (2008), stakeholders' creative goals often fit into a four-level typology. At the first level, stakeholders are interested in doing, where their primary focus is on outcomes. At this level, the objective of system development should be to create a system that leads the group to near-term measurable objectives that capitalize on existing land-use practices. At the second level, stakeholders are interested in adapting existing innovations to fit their own context. At this level, a designer (in a facilitating role) guides stakeholders to take existing work and fit it to their own needs. The third level of creativity involves making, where stakeholders use their skills in combination with existing technology in novel applications. At this level, designers provide scaffolds to support stakeholders' goals. At the fourth level, stakeholders want an opportunity to start fresh and rethink the entire system so dramatic changes can be made at the foundational level.

In the context of geodesign, co-design is akin to what Steinitz (2012) calls the "participatory design mode," which specifies a distinct process of interaction between the system designer and scientific and local stakeholders. Co-design emphasizes the position of stakeholders as partners and shifts the system designer from the role of all-knowing expert to facilitator. As we seek to design geodesign systems that better fit diverse stakeholder needs, this change in the role of the system designer is critical. The goal of the geodesign system designer becomes co-creating a geodesign system with stakeholders in a way that engages them in model development and model application, actively supporting stakeholders in designing with the support of experts

Table 1. Description of stakeholders' sectors and organizational focus that participated in geodesign activities

TOPIC FOCUS OF ORGANIZATION	NUMBER OF PARTICIPANTS
Conservation	24
Agricultural production	8
Economic development	3
Other	4
Total	*39*

ORGANIZATIONAL SECTOR	NUMBER OF ORGANIZATIONS
Public	20
Private	5
Nonprofit	13
Total	*38*

Diverse stakeholders from multiple organizations were involved in the co-design of
the geodesign system and subsequently used the system to geodesign landscapes
in a co-design mode.

and each other. By treating stakeholders as partners in the design process, co-design intends
to value and draw on the expertise that is distributed among scientific and local stakeholders.
Further, co-design enables a geodesign system that is a fit for its users and can support them in
working toward a vision that is relevant to them and their context.

Co-design, described by Sanders and Stappers (2008) and broadened here in the context of
geodesign, is directly related to the use-inspired knowledge realignment process described in
the collaborative modeling literature. This literature questions the effectiveness of stakeholder
engagement that is intended to educate or persuade wholly on the basis of scientific environmental
assessments (Landström et al., 2011). The process of providing information fit championed in
collaborative modeling intends to improve the overall quality of environmental decision making
and reduce conflict among diverse stakeholder viewpoints (see Voinov & Bousquet [2010] for
an elaborate description of the different typologies of modeling with stakeholders and their
relative merits and drawbacks). Four generic principles for collaborative modeling informed by
a cross-case comparison by Voinov and Bousquet (2010) include: (1) facilitators should focus on
supporting a flexible and iterative process that accepts uncertainty with an emphasis on social
and scientific learning; (2) the decision-making and management that emerges from this process
should be adaptive, open, and evolving; (3) facilitators should pay attention to and respond to
social dynamics including power, hierarchy, and special interests, and (4) collaborators should
accept non-traditional metrics of success, such as group perceptions. These principles are
complementary to the creative levels described above for co-design.

From Theory to Practice: Engaging Knowledge for Design in the Seven Mile Creek Watershed

The authors' engagement with a practical application of designing landscapes for multifunctionality offers a unique opportunity to explore the connection of theory to practice. It is possible
to consider how knowledge is integrated and applied as models are developed and applied in

collaborative design processes, considering the nature of co-design and its outcomes. This section considers a set of multi-year projects that used geodesign systems and co-design strategies with stakeholders during a collaborative planning process. The participants include a multi-disciplinary team of researchers at the University of Minnesota and sixty-one stakeholders from thirty-eight public, private, and non-profit interests (see table 1), approximately two-thirds of whom were engaged as collaborators across multiple meetings.

Local Opportunities for Multifunctional Landscapes

As described earlier, designing landscapes to be multifunctional is an emerging trend in the agricultural sciences, planning, and design disciplines motivated by increased societal demands for ecosystem services ranging from water quality and quantity to habitat for biodiversity as well as increased agricultural productivity (de Groot, Alkemade, Braat, Hein, & Willemen, 2010; Jordan & Davis, 2015; Slotterback et al., 2016). Multiple biophysical, cultural, market, regulatory, and technological drivers exist in the Midwestern United States, prompting the need for local consideration of how drivers intersect and either promote or detract from the creation of multifunctional landscapes (Jordan & Davis, 2015).

A multi-disciplinary team from the University of Minnesota (UMN) began thinking about the unique synergies and tradeoffs associated with multifunctionality and resulting in bio-economic development opportunities in 2007 through initial funding from the Institute on the Environment at the UMN. The team saw an opportunity to engage with ongoing participatory work to consider the impacts of biomass production in the roughly 9,700-hectare Seven Mile Creek watershed located in south-central Minnesota in Nicollet County. Previous partnering of the UMN team with local farmers and conservationists created a network of engagement in landscape planning for biomass production in the watershed, which ultimately informed a focus in the stakeholder process on multifunctional landscapes.

With the support of a geodesign system, stakeholders considered the prospects for multifunctional landscapes. The system was co-designed to enable stakeholders to knit together diverse trends that could potentially increase landscape multifunctionality. The system supported the consideration of multiple factors influencing land-use change, including how landscape patterns influence ecosystem processes (Nassauer & Opdam, 2008; Slotterback et al., 2016). The system was co-designed with the primary goal of supporting stakeholders in integrating expert and local knowledge as they considered how different land uses relate to various ecosystem service outcomes and ultimately multifunctionality. Because geodesign systems enable heterogeneous spatial data to be manipulated and visualized in an intuitive manner, diverse groups of people can engage with a common set of information that represents multiple interests in order to build overall group trust (Harvey, 2003).

Scientific and Local Stakeholders

While sharing similarities with participatory planning, the engagement process relied on network approaches from the adaptive management and boundary organizations literature to increase overall community capacity by connecting actors in social learning and deliberative processes (Jordan et al., 2016; Jordan et al., 2011; Opdam et al., 2013). The collaborative planning literature was informative as well, especially relative to the structure and facilitation of the stakeholder process, which emphasized interaction and information sharing (Innes & Booher, 1999; Margerum, 2011; Wondolleck & Yaffee, 2000). While UMN participants are considered scientific stakeholders in the process, they also played a role in facilitating goal formation and the exploration of the stakeholder driven goals. While a wide swath of interests and affiliations were present at each meeting (table 1), typical per-meeting attendance ranged from fifteen to twenty-five people across the two phases of the project. Stakeholders were updated between meetings so that those unable to attend could remain connected to the ongoing process. Among the diverse participants were some that could not participate regularly, but provided knowledge input for the geodesign system through individual or small group meetings because of their unique local or disciplinary expertise.

Geographic Area

The primary areal extent of the work described in this chapter focuses on the Seven Mile Creek watershed. The Seven Mile Creek watershed is representative of the broader Minnesota River Basin in that the dominant land use is corn and soybean production, which generates low water quality, habitat provisioning, and carbon storage (Belmont et al., 2011; Dalzell et al., 2012; Ness 2016). Incorporating perennials, cover crops, and other conservation practices in landscape management practices can increase water quality as well as upland bird habitat quality, carbon sequestration, and market return in scenarios of cellulosic feedstock production (Jordan & Warner, 2010; Jordan & Davis, 2015).

Project Phases: Goals, Skills, and Social Process

The goal of the stakeholders in the first phase was to consider the various ecological, economic, social, and aesthetic impacts of bio-economic development on the Seven Mile Creek watershed (Slotterback et al., 2016). Members of the UMN team facilitated a series of eight workshops. The first four meetings centered on social learning, where stakeholders shared their unique expertise with the whole group or in small groups to create a common understanding of the potential problems and opportunities, and the multiple ways of understanding related bio-economic development. Activities included a tour and exploration of the agricultural practices occurring in the watershed, individual presentations, and small group sharing. At the end of the first four workshops, stakeholders had developed a set of economic, social, aesthetic, and ecological "4W" (win-win-win-win) design criteria. These criteria essentially served as goals, reflecting consensus among diverse stakeholders, which could be used in identifying and evaluating potential visions for the watershed. The last four workshops focused on using two different versions of the geodesign system to explore the tradeoffs and synergies of various land use changes that could be achieved from bio-economic development. The design criteria were used to inform potential landscape designs, with small groups facilitated to work together on meeting goals such as production of biomass, profitability, and improved water quality. For a detailed overview of workshop activities, see Slotterback et al. (2016).

The goal of the second phase of the project was to build further community capacity to consider biomass production by exploring a broader array of bio-economic opportunities. The process emphasized gathering information from bio-economic innovators within a wide diversity of industries representing biofuel and bio-product production. Additionally, stakeholders explored prospects for introducing new plant species and animal agriculture in the watershed. The goal of gathering this information was to further define the ecosystem service, social, and economic impacts of potential land use changes associated with biomass production (table 2). This second phase, which ended in mid-2016, used a scenario planning process and the geodesign system in combination with regional economic development models to determine how different bio-economic development scenarios would influence landscape scale outcomes. Scenarios include considering the social, environmental, and economic impacts of:

- construction and operation of a large-scale cellulosic biomass ethanol facility drawing feedstocks from the watershed,
- a medium-sized cellulosic biomass treatment and pelleting facility for producing feed or bio-based chemicals that draws feedstock from the watershed,
- on-farm treatment of cellulosic biomass for feed,
- increased animal agriculture in the region causing increased forage demand, and
- early seeded winter annuals and cover crops.

By the end of the process, the stakeholder group produced multiple designs for the watershed that accounted for opportunities addressed in the scenarios. They also outlined implementation areas that have engaged the Seven Mile Creek stakeholders and others in ongoing working groups.

The stakeholders using the geodesign systems have been diverse in their skills, ranging from concerned citizens to farmers and conservationists to agricultural scientists and economic development professionals (table 1). As a result, the geodesign systems have been designed for users who are not trained in geographic information systems but want to explore how different agricultural land use configurations result in different ecosystem services outcomes. Additionally, the stakeholders have had diverse interests across social and physical scales, resulting in a system that intends to support design across regional, watershed, and field scales. Each version of the geodesign system has relied on simple, easy-to-use interfaces that enable in-depth consideration of scenarios and are specifically tailored to the stakeholders.

Co-Designing the Geodesign System

The geodesign system was updated between stakeholder meetings as design goals changed while considering feedback on overall usability and design. Elicitation of feedback occurred at two different points in the meetings. First, while users were actively designing alternative biomass production scenarios, UMN personnel were nearby to answer questions, make system usage observations, and record feedback. Second, at the end of the geodesign sessions, users shared

Table 2. Alignment between user-interface design principles and the Seven-mile Creek Bioeconomy project information.

| | | TRANSLATION OF USERS' GOALS AND SKILLS | | | SOFTWARE | | | | | HARDWARE | |
| | | | | | FRONT END | | | BACK END | | | |
YEAR	VERSION	LAND-USE OPTIONS	ECOSYSTEM SERVICES	SOCIAL PROCESS	DEVELOPMENT FRAMEWORKS	SKETCH CAPABILITIES	PRIMARY DATA TYPE	SERVER	SIMULATION MODELS	USER INTERFACE	SERVER
2013	1.0.1	Conservation tillage; low phosphorus application;	Carbon sequestration; upland bird habitat; water quality (sediment and phosphorus load; water yield); market return to corn production	4 meetings of social learning and design criteria development;	JavaScript; Python; SQL	Polygon drawing	Vector	Esri ArcGIS Server 10.2; PostgreSQL/PostGIS database	SWAT; InVEST Carbon & Habitat; UMN Extension Farmgate Economic Model	55" touch screens; Windows 8 processor in mobile case	Intel i7-2600 CPU; 8GB RAM; Windows 8
	1.0.2										
2014	2.0				Java; Python; SQL						
	3.0	prairie grass with biomass harvest; switchgrass with biomass harvest; corn with stover removal		4 meetings of systematic consideration of whether or not "W4" solutions were possible	JavaScript; Python; SQL						
2015	4.0	3.0 practices plus: corn/soybean with cover crop	3.0 ecosystem services plus:	meetings focused on social learning and scenario development and evaluation of scenario evaluation	JavaScript; Python; SQL	Polygons and line + buffer width	Raster				
2016	4.1										
	4.2	stover removal with cover crop	Market return to corn/soybean rotation and biomass production								
	4.3	4.2 practices plus: corn-alfalfa x3-soy rotation				Polygons and line + buffer width and parcel selection				55" touch screens, mobile and desktop computers	Windows Server 2008 Virtual Machine; 16GB RAM

Note: The version numbers describe the multiple software versions of the geodesign system and the respective translation of users' goals and skills into software and hardware deliverables. General focus of design was to identify "win-win-win," or "4W," outcomes.

feedback to reflect on scenario development, the overall experience of collaborating with other stakeholders, and the support of the geodesign system. In many respects, the ongoing process of system implementation, user feedback, geodesign system change, and re-implementation guided by user goals and objectives followed notions of co-design to enable consensus around enhancing landscape multifunctionality. UMN team members also conversed with stakeholders about the progression of their design thinking and how the collaborative process and geodesign system could enhance bio-economic development in the watershed.

Simulation Models: SWAT and InVEST

The original simulation models for the geodesign system were developed to investigate the costs of implementing various conservation practices in the Seven Mile Creek watershed. The initial models were further developed as stakeholder interests and skills evolved. The following descriptions of the technical details of the models remained consistent throughout the course of the project, unless otherwise noted.

The underlying crop yields, biomass yields, and water quality indicators were generated using the Soil and Water Assessment Tool (SWAT; Arnold & Fohrer, 2005). SWAT is a general purpose, daily time-step watershed-scale hydrologic and water quality model. Its unit of analysis is the hydrologic response unit (HRU) that captures fundamental climate, soil and topographic properties. For calibration and validation, model outputs were correlated with in-stream observations and empirical corrections for stream bank erosion were made (see Dalzell et al., 2012). SWAT has a large user base, is well maintained, and is commonly applied to study land use and land cover change in agricultural landscapes, making it an ideal option for the geodesign system.

The Integrative Valuation of Ecosystem Services and Tradeoffs (InVEST) carbon and habitat models were used to determine changes in ecosystem performance from the current to alternative land uses (Nelson et al., 2009). The carbon model examines four pools of carbon: above ground, below ground, nonliving, and atmospheric. The model assumes that a land use has been in place long enough to reach an equilibrium in each of these carbon stores. The habitat model determines habitat quality as a function of surrounding land cover opportunities present for the survival of a given species. For further technical details on the implementations of SWAT or InVEST, see Dalzell et al. (2012).

Backend Simulation Co-Design

InVEST and SWAT model output were preprocessed for a common spatial extent and then placed in the geodesign system's geographic information database that used Esri ArcGIS Server 10.2 with a series of geoprocessing, map, and feature services. To preprocess the data, the models were run for homogenous land covers. All of the data for each homogenous land cover were stored to decrease processing time from design creation to quantitative feedback. The advantage of using the SWAT and InVEST carbon models is that, while they use spatial data as inputs, the models do not account for neighborhood effects, as the properties for each HRU or cell are calculated independently. To overcome the challenge of preprocessing and neighborhood effects for the habitat quality model, results from Invest were supplemented with a similar model developed by the Minnesota Department of Natural Resources (Pitt, personal communication, June 14, 2015).

For the vector-based geodesign system, the data were calibrated to hrus. Upon conversion of the data to raster representation, all data corresponded to a thirty-square-meter grid cell size, which corresponded to the underlying land cover and soils data used in swat. Front-end landscape design drawings created by stakeholders queried the database using the selected land use changes inherent in the designs and examined summations of ecosystem service delivery for the entire watershed. Performance outputs could be reported to geodesign users in a real-time perspective, allowing users to generate future design proposals based on conversation with other stakeholders and informed by the implications of each design iteration.

As stakeholders shifted their goals, new land cover options were added to the geodesign system. In the first version of the geodesign system, the land uses available for design included corn production with conservation tillage, low phosphorus application corn production, mixed prairie, corn production with 60 percent stover removal, and switchgrass. As the umn and community stakeholder groups continued to consider alternative bioeconomic development scenarios, they became increasingly interested in the opportunities represented by cover cropping to mitigate the impacts of stover removal. An additional design scenario integrating cover cropping with stover removal was generated in swat and Invest and added to the geodesign system. Further discussions with a local dairy farm around procurement of alfalfa from local sources made the group wonder about the potential for alfalfa to create environmental and economic benefits. This led the team to examine and validate additional cropping system scenarios for a corn, alfalfa (three years), and soy rotation, representing the common practices of the dairy and their growers. These new opportunities for bio-economic developments were then considered as a part of the on-going scenario planning process.

Originally, prices in the geodesign system were fixed in the preprocessed data. Stakeholders showed considerable interest in being able to alter the economic assumptions underlying the model, to reflect potential future conditions driven by market or policy changes. Incorporating this capacity into the geodesign model led the umn team to separate the evaluation of economic values of a given design scenario from the biophysical values. This change enables stakeholders to change slider bars for crop and biomass prices, and evaluate how commodity value changes influence the overall profitability of a land use change (figure 1c).

Front-End User Interface Technical Description and Co-Development

The front end of the geodesign system was built in JavaScript as a web application capable of running in most modern web browsers. It consists of three main screens: Draw, Results, and Compare. The first window a user sees when entering the web application is a request for a group name (figure 1a). After entering the group information, users are brought to the Draw screen with the design system (figure 1b). The design system allows users to select from the land cover options and sketch it on the aerial map of the landscape. Areas that are not drawn remain in the existing land use. After users finish creation of their design, they can assign a design name and submit it for processing. After processing, users are shown the Results screen (figure 1c).

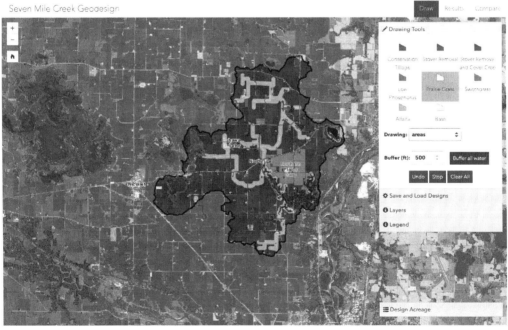

FIGURE 1A. Geodesign system group name screen.

FIGURE 1B. The draw screen allows users to redesign land use. Areas not designed remain in current land uses.

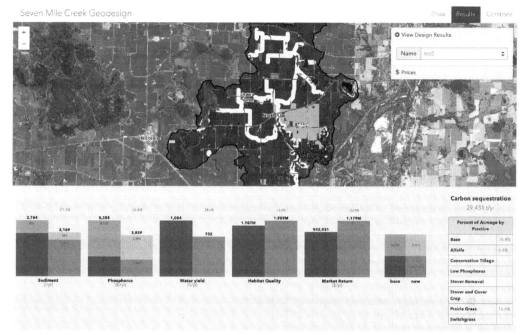

FIGURE 1C. The results screen, with market manipulations in the upper-right corner.

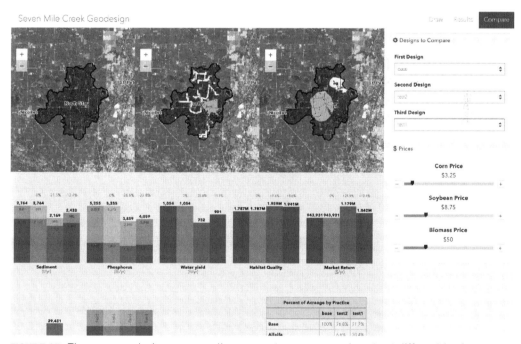

FIGURE 1D. The compare designs screen allows users to compare and contrast different landscape designs side by side.

From the Results screen, users can go back to the Draw screen or advance to the Compare screen, which allows users to visualize three designs at one time and compare the performance of the three designs to the current land cover (figure 1d). Users returning to the Draw screen are able to continue working from their last-processed state.

The Esri JavaScript application programming interface generates the maps and sketch tools. Originally, the geodesign system only provided the ability to draw polygons for the different land uses. In discussion with stakeholders, they desired the ability to draw lines that would perform a buffer operation around the lines at a predetermined distance, so this feature was added. Midway through the second set of meetings, the Minnesota legislature passed a vegetative buffer law requiring perennial grass buffers around waterways depending on their classification (http://www.bwsr.state.mn.us/buffers/). As a result, a water feature buffering tool was added to the interface. The details of the buffer requirement and what constitutes an equivalent practice are under ongoing consideration and will thus likely drive further user interface and practice changes in the geodesign system.

In the first three versions of the system, visualizations were generated using the programming libraries Dojo and AMcharts, which underlie Esri's technology. In later versions, D3 is used for visualizing graphs but the web maps still use Esri's technology. Graph visualization tools are used primarily in the Results and Compare screens of the system. The group decided to switch to D3 for graph visualization because it is open source, is widely used in information visualization, and provides more flexibility. Graph visualizations include the percent of each land use in the watershed, market return, phosphorus loading, sediment loading, water yield, habitat quality, and carbon sequestration. Originally, a pie chart was used to visualize the percentage of the landscape in each practice. With continued use, stakeholders preferred a table view of these practices. In order to facilitate scenario design, a table view was added to the design page to provide real-time estimates of biomass produced from the landscape and the total acreage in each land use.

Since version 1 of the system, ecosystem services have been visualized as bar charts. However, as the process continued, stakeholders became concerned about some of the results of the model. Ecosystem service performance did not correspond to their mental models of how the biophysical system was functioning. The primary concern was over the impact of conservation tillage on water quality. The crux of this concern related to where sediment and phosphorus were originating in the watershed. The Seven Mile Creek is a relatively flat and productive watershed and farmers' daily experiences do not include physically seeing a lot of soil erosion in their fields. Instead, a significant portion of the pollution comes from stream bank erosion (Dalzell et al., 2012). The challenge is that the stream bank erosion is caused by the amount of in-stream water flow, which is largely determined by land management practices in the upland.

In order to respond to this concern and help stakeholders consider the complex interactions among land use, spatial configuration, and hydrologic responses, the UMN team separated field and stream sources of pollution by creating a stacked bar chart display. Doing so enabled stakeholders to have richer and more informed conversations and provides an example of how co-design can integrate knowledge to not only inform the underlying modeling, but also improve the fit of the model information for actual use.

FIGURE 2. Image of stakeholders working on a geodesign system in a workshop showing the ability for multiple stakeholders to communicate easily around the 55-inch touch displays.

In total, since 2013, the geodesign system has gone through four major version changes and eight minor changes, with the rate of versioning increasing rapidly since major version 4. U-Spatial, a center at UMN, has played a key development role in this process, providing highly skilled and affordable developers for the project who are students in the Master of Geographic Information Science Program (U-Spatial, 2016). Such long-term co-design efforts would have been impossible without institutional support and specific development expertise.

Hardware and Technical Support

The geodesign software is a web-based application originally optimized for an InFocus fifty-five-inch multi-touch display running Windows 8 housed in a mobile case (figure 2). While the user interface is now responsive and highly usable across device sizes, the fifty-five-inch multi-touch displays are consistently used during design meetings with stakeholders. From a human-computer interaction standpoint, the displays encourage communication around a common map document because their size enables multiple people to work jointly on the same product (figure 2). The fifty-five-inch multi-touch displays were chosen over a table design because they are easier to transport in contained cases, allowing facilitators to travel to communities, as opposed to placing the burden on stakeholders to travel to the university. For meetings, three to five of the displays were loaded onto a truck and moved to the meeting location. During the meetings, technical support staff from U-Spatial were present to monitor server and display performance and provide technical support if needed. During the first phase of the geodesign system, considerable amounts of technical support were required, though as the application has advanced, it has become significantly more stable, thus requiring less technical support during meetings.

Geodesign System Outcomes

The overall objective of the geodesign system is to enable diverse groups of people to efficiently and effectively engage in a collaborative design process where social learning takes place and multifunctional landscape designs are produced. The primary outputs from the geodesign sessions are the landscape designs that stakeholders produced during the collaborative and iterative design process. By considering the design trajectories, it is possible to assess how well the geodesign system enabled stakeholders to explore opportunities for landscape multifunctionality.

To determine how well the geodesign system served this purpose, we collected and compiled design data from one design session from the first phase of landscape design where the fewest technical challenges happened (figure 3). Figure 3 provides an example of what a spider web chart would look like for a multi-functional design with improvements across all ecosystem service indicators. Figure 3 also shows one group's design progression from design one to design six over a forty-five-minute design session. The design evolution shows that the system allowed the group to respond to the simulation feedback and update their designs to obtain better design performance. In terms of the spatial configuration of each design, two distinct design strategies were used to achieve greater landscape multifunctionality. Designs one to three illustrate designs that appear to be based on the geodesign system overlays and rely on one to three practices. At design four, the group transitioned to a different design strategy relying on vegetative buffers around waterways, which they combined with other practices to further improve market return (designs four through six). Design data from other groups' design sessions show similar design trends and trajectories. The design data illustrates the potential of the geodesign system to enable groups to iteratively design landscapes and increase the overall landscape multifunctionality as measured by finding win-wins that achieve economic benefits as well as enhanced ecosystem services. The observations from qualitative analysis of the geodesign design outcomes fits with the broader conclusions of Slotterback et al. (2016) that geodesign systems are likely able to engage diverse groups of people, assist in knowledge sharing, and make collaborative decisions that lead to multifunctional landscape designs.

Conclusions

Multifunctional landscapes offer a path toward bio-economic development as well as enhanced ecosystem services. Achieving multifunctionality requires the engagement of knowledge from multiple disciplines, as well as the critical professional and contextual knowledge that stakeholders can bring to the table. Engaging this knowledge, whether from academics and regulators or from environmental advocates and farmers, calls for much more explicit attention to the practices of co-design. It is well-recognized that stakeholders can benefit from planning support systems and other tools and technologies to engage their knowledge and make better decisions. Applying co-design practices impacts how we support stakeholders in working

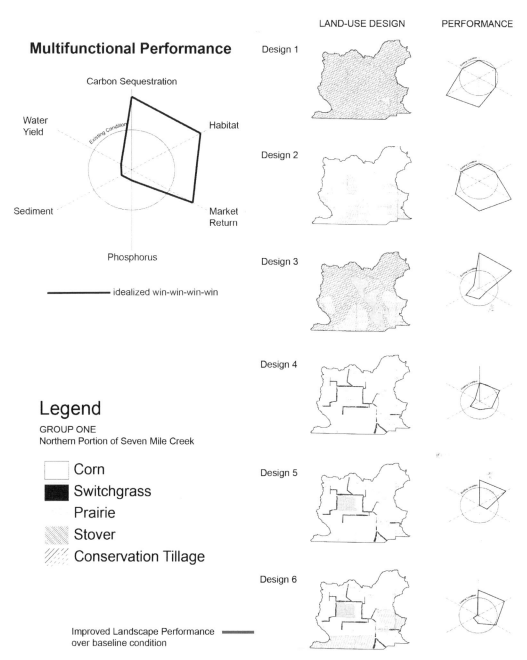

FIGURE 3. The spider web chart shape of a multifunctional landscape where every ecosystem service indicator is greater than the baseline land use, shown by the bold, black circle in the center. The first three design iterations used a common strategy to explore different land uses. Stakeholders switch to an alternative design strategy. Importantly, in comparing designs 1 and 6, stakeholders began to achieve multifunctionality by finding spatial "win-wins," which was their design goal. A seventh design is not shown because it was nearly identical to design six.

together and how we design support systems that enhance collaboration and improve decision outcomes.

This chapter describes co-design in the context of a geodesign system and the subsequent co-emergence of a vision for a multifunctional agricultural landscape in south-central Minnesota by a diverse stakeholder group. Co-design approaches in geodesign systems offer one potential social process to build technical systems that fit stakeholder goals and in turn enable stakeholders to co-design multifunctional landscapes. This preliminary evidence suggests that when geodesign engages knowledge from multiple disciplines and values academic and local knowledge through co-design, it may be a fundamental approach to support groups of people to explore the infinite solution space of the future and generate consensus-driven, multifunctional landscape designs.

Despite the great promise of geodesign and the preliminary evidence of use and outcomes presented here, the specific social mechanisms of why such systems produce these outcomes have been minimally characterized. Thus, knowledge of how to transfer collaborative geodesign processes to other contexts is still more art than science. Additionally, a multifunctional landscape design does not mean that a group will be able to generate plans and policies that will produce multifunctional landscapes. The process of collaborative geodesign must be embedded within a larger socio-cultural and institutional context in order for the designs that are created to result in changes in the material world (Jordan et al., 2013). Engaging stakeholders in a distributed manner online, similar to decision support tools such as those in Cravens (2016) work on marine management, may be a way to create common language and understanding across a larger portion of stakeholders. This kind of broader, distributed approach to engagement will require additional considerations of the broad knowledge systems that need to become integrated and more accessible to decision makers by using a geodesign system (Klerkx, Schut, Leeuwis, & Kilelu, 2012; Nyerges et al., 2014). Further, broader application of geodesign in other geographies, with other groups, and in other issues will offer further insights about relevant socioecological data, varied cultural and community contexts, and the viability of replication of the outcomes observed here. The data presented here provide an indication of what additional, comprehensive empirical studies could reveal. Such future work will offer further insights on the impacts of geodesign systems on stakeholder collaboration, learning, and ability to generate multifunctional landscape designs.

BIBLIOGRAPHY

Aggett, G., & McColl, C. (2006). Evaluating decision support systems for PPGIS applications. *Cartography and Geographic Information Science, 33*(1), 77–92. doi: 10.1559/152304006777323163.

Armitage, D. R., Plummer, R., Berkes, F., Arthur, R. I., Charles, A. T., Davidson-Hunt, I. J., . . . Wollenberg, E. K. (2009). Adaptive co-management for social-ecological complexity. *Frontiers in Ecology and the Environment, 7*(2), 95–102. doi: 10.1890/070089.

Arnold, J. G., & Fohrer, N. (2005). SWAT2000: Current capabilities and research opportunities in applied watershed modelling. *Hydrological Processes, 19*(3), 563–572. doi: 10.1002/hyp.5611.

Baird, J., Plummer, R., Haug, C., & Huitema, D. (2014). Learning effects of interactive decision-making processes for climate change adaptation. *Global Environmental Change, 27*(1), 51–63. doi: 10.1016/j. gloenvcha.2014.04.019.

Balram, S., Dragićević, S., & Meredith, T. (2004). A collaborative GIS method for integrating local and technical knowledge in establishing biodiversity conservation priorities. *Biodiversity and Conservation, 13*(6), 1195–1208. doi: 10.1023/B:BIOC.0000018152.11643.9c.

Batty, M. (2013). Defining geodesign (= GIS + design ?). *Environment and Planning B: Planning and Design, 40*(1), 1–2. doi: 10.1068/b4001ed.

Belmont, P., Gran, K. B., Schottler, S. P., Wilcock, P. R., Day, S. S., Jennings, C., . . . Parker, G. (2011). Large shift in source of fine sediment in the Upper Mississippi River. *Environmental Science & Technology, 45*(20), 8804–8810. doi: 10.1021/es2019109.

Berkes, F. (2009). Evolution of co-management: Role of knowledge generation, bridging organizations and social learning. *Journal of Environmental Management, 90*(5), 1692–1702. doi: 10.1016/j. jenvman.2008.12.001.

Berkes, F., Colding, J., & Folke, C. (2000). Rediscovery of traditional ecological knowledge as adaptive management. *Ecological Applications, 10*(5), 1251–1262. doi: 10.1890/1051-0761(2000)010[1251:ROTE KA]2.0.CO;2.

Boody, G., Vondracek, B., Andow, D. A., Krinke, M., Westra, J., Zimmerman, J., & Welle, P. (2005). Multifunctional agriculture in the United States. *BioScience, 55*(1), 27–38. doi: 10.1641/0006-3568(2005)055[0027:maitus]2.0.co;2.

Cravens, A. E. (2016). Negotiation and decision making with collaborative software: How MarineMap "changed the game" in California's marine life protected act initiative. *Environmental Management, 57*(2), 474–497. doi: 10.1007/s00267-015-0615-9.

Dalzell, B., Pennington, D., Polasky, S., Mulla, D., Taff, S., & Nelson, E. (2012). *Lake Pepin watershed full cost accounting project.* Minnesota Pollution Control Agency. http://www.pca.state.mn.us/.

de Groot, R. S., Alkemade, R., Braat, L., Hein, L., & Willemen, L. (2010). Challenges in integrating the concept of ecosystem services and values in landscape planning, management and decision making. *Ecological Complexity, 7*(3), 260–272. doi: 10.1016/j.ecocom.2009.10.006.

Deyle, R., & Schively Slotterback, C. (2009). Group learning in participatory planning processes. *Journal of Planning Education and Research, 29*(1), 23–38. doi: 10.1177/0739456X09333116.

Ervin, S. (2011). A system for geodesign. In *Digital landscape architecture conference* (pp. 1–14). http:// www.gsd.harvard.edu/.

Ervin, S. M. (2016). Technology in geodesign. *Landscape and Urban Planning, 156,* 12–16. https://www. researchgate.net/publication/265011735_A_system_for_GeoDesign.

Folke, C., Hahn, T., Olsson, P., & Norberg, J. (2005). Adaptive governance of social-ecological systems. *Annual Review of Environment and Resources, 30*(1), 441–473. doi: 10.1146/annurev. energy.30.050504.144511.

Fry, G. L. A. (2001). Multifunctional landscapes—towards transdisciplinary research. *Landscape and Urban Planning, 57*(3–4), 159–168. doi: 10.1016/S0169-2046(01)00201-8.

Funtowicz, S. O., & Ravetz, J. R. (1993). Science for the post-normal age. *Futures, 25*(7), 739–755. doi: 10.1016/0016-3287(93)90022-L.

Goodchild, M. F. (2010). Towards geodesign: Repurposing cartography and GIS? *Cartographic Perspectives,* (66), 7–21.

Goodspeed, R., Riseng, C., Wehrly, K., Yin, W., Mason, L., & Schoenfeldt, B. (2016). Applying design thinking methods to ecosystem management tools: Creating the Great Lakes aquatic habitat explorer. *Marine Policy, 69,* 134–145. doi: 10.1016/j.marpol.2016.04.017.

Gottwald, S., Laatikainen, T. E., & Kyttä, M. (2016). Exploring the usability of PPGIS among older adults: challenges and opportunities. *International Journal of Geographical Information Science, 8816*(May), 1–18. doi: 10.1080/13658816.2016.1170837.

Haklay, M. M., & Tobón, C. (2003). Usability evaluation and PPGIS: Towards a user-centred design approach. *International Journal of Geographical Information Science, 17*(6), 577–592. doi: 10.1080/1365881031000114107.

Harvey, F. (2003). Developing geographic information infrastructures for local government: The role of trust. *The Canadian Geographer/Le Geographe Canadien, 47*(1), 28–36. doi: 10.1111/1541-0064.02e10.

Innes, J. E., & Booher, D. E. (1999). Consensus building and complex adaptive systems. *Journal of the American Planning Association, 65*(4), 412–423. doi: 10.1080/01944369908976071.

Jankowski, P., Robischon, S., Tuthill, D., Nyerges, T., & Ramsey, K. (2006). Design considerations and evaluation of a collaborative, spatio-temporal decision support system. *Transactions in GIS, 10*(3), 335–354. doi: 10.1111/j.1467-9671.2006.01001.x.

Jordan, N. R., & Davis, A. S. (2015). Middle-way strategies for sustainable intensification of agriculture. *BioScience, 65*(5), 513–519. doi: 10.1093/biosci/biv033.

Jordan, N. R., Dorn, K., Runck, B., Ewing, P., Williams, A., Anderson, K. A., . . . Johnson, G. (2016). Sustainable commercialization of new crops for the agricultural bioeconomy. *Elementa: Science of the Anthropocene, 4,* 81. doi: 10.12952/journal.elementa.000081.

Jordan, N. R., Slotterback, C. S., Cadieux, K. V., Mulla, D. J., Pitt, D. G., Olabisi, L. S., & Kim, J.-O. (2011). TMDL Implementation in agricultural landscapes: A communicative and systemic approach. *Environmental Management, 48*(1), 1–12. doi: 10.1007/s00267-011-9647-y.

Jordan, N., Schulte, L. A., Williams, C., Mulla, D., Pitt, D., Shively-Slotterback, C., . . . Bringi, B. (2013). Landlabs: An integrated approach to creating agricultural enterprises that meet the triple botom line. *Journal of Higher Education Outreach & Engagement, 17*(4), 175–200.

Jordan, N., & Warner, K. D. (2010). Enhancing the multifunctionality of US agriculture. *BioScience, 60*(1), 60–66. doi: 10.1525/bio.2010.60.1.10.

Klerkx, L., Schut, M., Leeuwis, C., & Kilelu, C. (2012). Advances in knowledge brokering in the agricultural sector: Towards innovation system facilitation. *IDS Bulletin, 43*(5), 53–60. doi: 10.1111/j.1759-5436.2012.00363.x.

Landström, C., Whatmore, S. J., Lane, S. N., Odoni, N. A., Ward, N., & Bradley, S. (2011). Coproducing flood risk knowledge: Redistributing expertise in critical "participatory modelling." *Environment and Planning A, 43*(7), 1617–1633. doi: 10.1068/a43482.

Langsdale, S., Beall, A., Bourget, E., Hagen, E., Kudlas, S., Palmer, R., . . . Werick, W. (2013). Collaborative modeling for decision support in water resources: Principles and best practices. *Journal of the American Water Resources Association, 49*(3), 629–638. doi: 10.1111/jawr.12065.

Lovell, S. T., DeSantis, S., Nathan, C. A., Olson, M. B., Ernesto Méndez, V., Kominami, H. C., . . . Morris, W. B. (2010). Integrating agroecology and landscape multifunctionality in Vermont: An evolving framework to evaluate the design of agroecosystems. *Agricultural Systems, 103*(5), 327–341. doi: 10.1016/j.agsy.2010.03.003.

Lovell, S. T., & Johnston, D. M. (2009). Creating multifunctional landscapes: How can the field of ecology inform the design of the landscape? *Frontiers in Ecology and the Environment, 7*(4), 212–220. doi: 10.1890/070178.

Mandarano, L. A. (2008). Evaluating collaborative environmental planning outputs and outcomes: Restoring and protecting habitat and the New York—New Jersey harbor estuary program. *Journal of Planning Education and Research, 27*(4), 456–468. doi: 10.1177/0739456X08315888.

Margerum, R. D. (2011). *Beyond consensus: Improving collaborative planning and management.* Cambridge, MA: MIT Press.

Mastrangelo, M. E., Weyland, F., Villarino, S. H., Barral, M. P., Nahuelhual, L., & Laterra, P. (2013). Concepts and methods for landscape multifunctionality and a unifying framework based on ecosystem services. *Landscape Ecology, 29*(2), 345–358. doi: 10.1007/s10980-013-9959-9.

Nassauer, J. I., & Opdam, P. (2008). Design in science: Extending the landscape ecology paradigm. *Landscape Ecology, 23*(6), 633–644. doi: 10.1007/s10980-008-9226-7.

Naveh, Z. (2001). Ten major premises for a holistic conception of multifunctional landscapes. *Landscape and Urban Planning, 57*(3–4), 269–284. doi: 10.1016/S0169-2046(01)00209-2.

Nelson, E., Mendoza, G., Regetz, J., Polasky, S., Tallis, H., Cameron, Dr., . . . Shaw, Mr. (2009). Modeling multiple ecosystem services, biodiversity conservation, commodity production, and tradeoffs at landscape scales. *Frontiers in Ecology and the Environment, 7*(1), 4–11. doi: 10.1890/080023.

Ness, E. (2016). Phosphorus in the Minnesota River Basin: The debate over its source and ways to mitigate impacts. *CSA News, 61*(6), 4. doi: 10.2134/csa2016-61-6-1.

Nyerges, T., Ballal, H., Steinitz, C., Canfield, T., Roderick, M., Ritzman, J., & Thanatemaneerat, W. (2016). Geodesign dynamics for sustainable urban watershed development. *Sustainable Cities and Society, 25*, 13–24. doi: 10.1016/j.scs.2016.04.016.

Nyerges, T., Roderick, M., Prager, S., Bennett, D., & Lam, N. (2014). Foundations of sustainability information representation theory: Spatial-temporal dynamics of sustainable systems. *International Journal of Geographical Information Science, 28*(5), 1165–1185. doi: 10.1080/13658816.2013.853304.

Olsson, P., Folke, C., & Berkes, F. (2004). Adaptive comanagement for building resilience in social-ecological systems. *Environmental Management, 34*(1), 1251–1262. doi: 10.1007/s00267-003-0101-7.

Opdam, P., Nassauer, J. I., Wang, Z., Albert, C., Bentrup, G., Castella, J.-C., . . . Swaffield, S. (2013). Science for action at the local landscape scale. *Landscape Ecology, 28*(8), 1439–1445. doi: 10.1007/s10980-013-9925-6.

Perkl, R. M. (2016). Geodesigning landscape linkages: Coupling GIS with wildlife corridor design in conservation planning. *Landscape and Urban Planning.* doi: 10.1016/j.landurbplan.2016.05.016.

Rinner, C., & Bird, M. (2009). Evaluating community engagement through argumentation maps—a public participation GIS case study. *Environment and Planning B: Planning and Design, 36*(4), 588–601. doi: 10.1068/b34084.

Sanders, E. B.-N., & Stappers, P. J. (2008). Co-creation and the new landscapes of design. *CoDesign, 4*(1), 5–18. doi: 10.1080/15710880701875068.

Sheppard, S. R. (2005). Participatory decision support for sustainable forest management: A framework for planning with local communities at the landscape level in Canada. *Canadian Journal of Forest Research, 35*(7), 1515–1526. doi: 10.1139/x05-084.

Slotterback, C. S., Runck, B., Pitt, D. G., Kne, L., Jordan, N. R., Mulla, D. J., . . . Reichenbach, M. (2016).

Collaborative geodesign to advance multifunctional landscapes. *Landscape and Urban Planning, 156,* 71–80. doi: 10.1016/j.landurbplan.2016.05.011.

Steinitz, C. (2012). *A framework for geodesign: Changing geography by design.* Redlands, CA: Esri Press.

Stokols, D. (2006). Toward a science of transdisciplinary action research. *American Journal of Community Psychology, 38*(1–2), 63–77. doi: 10.1007/s10464-006-9060-5.

Tress, B., & Tress, G. (2001). Capitalising on multiplicity: a transdisciplinary systems approach to landscape research. *Landscape and Urban Planning, 57*(3–4), 143–157. doi: 10.1016/S0169-2046(01)00200-6.

Tress, B., Tress, G., Décamps, H., & D'Hauteserre, A. (2001). Bridging human and natural sciences in landscape research. *Landscape and Urban Planning, 57*(3–4), 137–141. doi: 10.1016/S0169-2046(01)00199-2.

Uran, O., & Janssen, R. (2003). Why are spatial decision support systems not used? Some experiences from the Netherlands. *Computers, Environment and Urban Systems, 27*(5), 511–526. doi: 10.1016/S0198-9715(02)00064-9.

van Delden, H., Seppelt, R., White, R., & Jakeman, A. J. (2011). A methodology for the design and development of integrated models for policy support. *Environmental Modelling & Software, 26*(3), 266–279. doi: 10.1016/j.envsoft.2010.03.021.

Van Herzele, A. (2004). Local knowledge in action: Valuing nonprofessional reasoning in the planning process. *Journal of Planning Education and Research, 24*(2), 197–212. doi: 10.1177/0739456X04267723.

Voinov, A., & Bousquet, F. (2010). Modelling with stakeholders. *Environmental Modelling & Software, 25*(11), 1268–1281. doi: 10.1016/j.envsoft.2010.03.007.

Vonk, G., Geertman, S., & Schot, P. (2005). Bottlenecks blocking widespread usage of planning support systems. *Environment and Planning A, 37*(5), 909–924. doi: 10.1068/a3712.

Wissen Hayek, U., von Wirth, T., Neuenschwander, N., & Grêt-Regamey, A. (2016). Organizing and facilitating geodesign processes: Integrating tools into collaborative design processes for urban transformation. *Landscape and Urban Planning, 156,* 59–70. doi: 10.1016/j.landurbplan.2016.05.015.

Wondolleck, J. M., & Yaffee, S. L. (2000). *Making collaboration work: Lessons from innovation in natural resource management.* Washington, DC: Island Press.

Zellner, M. L., Lyons, L. B., Hoch, C. J., Weizeorick, J., Kunda, C., & Milz, D. C. (2012). Modeling, learning, and planning together: An application of participatory agent-based modeling to environmental planning. *Urisa Journal, 24*(1), 77–92.

Collaborative Modeling Institute: A Conception, Paradigm and Protocol for Transdisciplinary Integrative Team Science

Stuart J. Whipple and Bernard C. Patten

Introduction: Why do we need CMI?

Scores of new environmental problems are continuously emerging in our world and a great deal of time, effort, and resources are expended to recognize, study, and develop management solutions for them. In many cases, solutions are developed in an ad-hoc, reactionary, short-term, and case-by-case manner, which often provides for immediate, strategic, but often non-optimal, long-term solutions.

What Is Wrong with This Paradigm?

Ad-hoc, short-term response does not provide for effective long-term planning or long-term, iterative improvement of solutions. It is the environmental equivalent of emergency room treatment of human health problems versus long-term care aimed at disease prevention and lifestyle modification. Much of the time, effort, and resources expended in a model-making effort are left fallow in drawers and computer disks, with no permanent home to allow them to be revisited for reuse, improvement, and learning. Many of the relationships are not maintained or allowed to ramify without a permanent institution to nurture them. Response to emerging environmental problems is diminished because there is no existing institutional capital, such as models, data, and relationships, poised for suitable modifications, to respond to new problems. Local scientists and stakeholders depend on regional or national regulatory and management agencies to respond. This is often a slow and tedious process, with remote and weakly connected staff reducing effectiveness to address local problems.

Is There a Viable Approach Providing Solutions to These Problems?

A set of locally distributed, site-specific collaborative modeling institutes (CMI), with the paradigm of institutionalized model-making (IMM) as their operating template, could provide a

101

more effective response to emerging environmental problems. By providing a permanent home for local or regional model-making products and data, CMIs provide a mechanism by which addressing environmental problems becomes a part of an ongoing iterative feedback cycle of problem specification, model-making, empirical study, and site-specific management.

In environmental modeling, the process of model-making has potentially as much, or even more value than its products, which are conceptual or mathematical models themselves. CMIs allow for the ongoing capture, documentation, and repeated improvement of the process of environmental modeling. In ways similar to those first articulated as "adaptive management" (Holling, 1978), CMI facilitates individual and institutional learning through the use of its assets to direct experiential learning programs for scientists, students, and stakeholders. The model-based information stored in the CMIs would provide the organizational and operational template for CMI.

Environmental Science Joined with Team Science

Collaborative model-making for environmental problem solving is a complex process entailing two fields. First is modeling, the science of applying general systems theory, mathematics, and ecology to construct representations of socioecological systems. Second is the social science field of team science, investigating the formation and functioning of transdisciplinary teams. The authors' expertise lies primarily in ecological modeling; however, as Fiore (2008) states: "it has been recognized that team science is a challenge *as much if not more from the activity of teamwork, that is the interpersonal and coordinative standpoint, as it is from the scientific standpoint*" (262, emphasis added). Our response is to provide an analysis of how our IMM-CMI approach to collaborative model-making is associated with the concepts and findings of team science.

This chapter describes how collaborative modeling in CMIs would be organized and carried out and what the IMM-CMI paradigm contributes to the field of collaborative model-making.

Elements of IMM-CMI

IMM is a paradigm and a protocol for conducting multidisciplinary integrative science (Sage, Patten, & Salmon, 2003). IMM was developed over forty years by Patten and colleagues at the University of Georgia. Key periods include a five-year (1975–1980) collaborative modeling study of the Yugoslav Adriatic coastal ecosystem; a US National Science Foundation (NSF) Long-Term Ecological Research (LTER) program (1975–1985) entailing integrated studies of the Okefenokee Swamp ecosystem; and a collaboration (1990–2001) with Richard Sage of the State University of New York's Adirondack Ecological Center to produce a comprehensive ecosystem-based simulation model focused on white-tailed deer (*Odocoileus virginianus*). These experiences in collaborative model-making and those of Whipple at the University of Toronto (1996—1998), the US National Marine Fisheries Service Woods Hole lab (1999–2000), and Skidaway Institute of Oceanography (2001–2006) provide the background for the synthesis of ideas presented in this chapter. IMM is a staged procedure that involves a series of choices about model types and

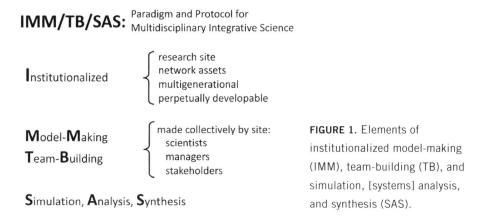

IMM/TB/SAS: Paradigm and Protocol for Multidisciplinary Integrative Science

Institutionalized
{
research site
network assets
multigenerational
perpetually developable
}

Model-**M**aking
Team-**B**uilding
{
made collectively by site:
scientists
managers
stakeholders
}

Simulation, **A**nalysis, **S**ynthesis

FIGURE 1. Elements of institutionalized model-making (IMM), team-building (TB), and simulation, [systems] analysis, and synthesis (SAS).

the details of group-oriented construction that follow. The IMM/TB/SAS paradigm and protocol is composed of three main elements as illustrated in figure 1.

Home Institution

CMI serves as the center of activity, a vehicle for staged model development, and the repository for storage and use of modeling products. A core group of CMI scientists and staff is responsible for the maintenance of model-formatted infrastructure in the form of databases, computer code, and materials generated in ongoing model-making workshops and in applications to planning, management, and outreach activities. The larger community extending from the core group includes other scientists, managers, and stakeholders who serve as collaborating members of model-making teams.

Team-building and Model Making

The second component is the protocol for team-building through model making. This ongoing process is the core of IMM, details for which are elaborated in later sections of this chapter. Figure 2 provides an overview of the principal stages involved. Stages 1 and 2 entail conceptual modeling workshops during which sets of research and management questions are defined and sets of conceptual models are developed by collaborative teams that include scientists, managers, and local stakeholders. Stages 3 and 4 involve the building of mathematical and computer models.

Application and Perpetuation

The final stage of the IMM protocol is ongoing model application and improvement. Activities include simulation, systems analysis, and synthesis, and results are used to set priorities for further scientific research and development, as well as to guide management decisions and institutional outreach. A key feature of figure 2 is iteration, wherein early and subsequent stages may be revisited many times during the life of a project.

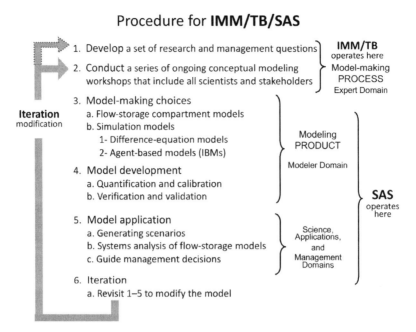

FIGURE 2. Flow diagram of basic processes involved in institutionalized model-making (IMM), team-building (TB), and simulation and [systems] analysis and synthesis (SAS).

Sketch of IMM State-Space Framework

At its core, the framework employed as the basic structuring mechanism behind conceptual and simulation modeling in IMM is state-space system theory (figure 3). This formal mathematical theory, adapted from Zadeh & Desoer (1963), lays out in elemental terms how all systems behave in response to forces to which they are exposed, both within and without. The universality of these elements makes the state-space formulation suitable for all classes of systems and open, dissipative environmental systems in particular. The component-level objects in these systems, called "abstract objects" to emphasize they are models, are "state variables" (x). The functional forms and numerical values for these are taken from a state space (X). System states expressed by the state variables are driven by inputs (z, elements of sets Z) to generate outputs (y, elements of sets Y) to the environment outside the system boundary. Inputs change exogenously over time in response to un-modeled influences outside the system. States and outputs change endogenously, governed as modeled by existing states and received inputs. Therefore, the state space framework provides an explicit emphasis on open-system modeling incorporating realistic representations of environmental linkages provided by systemic inputs (z) and outputs (y).

As depicted in figure 3, state-transition functions (ϕ), generate state dynamics, and response or output functions (ρ), which are formulated as algebraic equations, generate system outputs. The state transition function provides the theoretical basis for the development of functions that define the time behavior of the compartment storages of the model in mathematical simulation form; in many instances the equations will be difference equations, but in agent-based models, algebraic state transition rules govern model time behavior.

State-Space Determinism

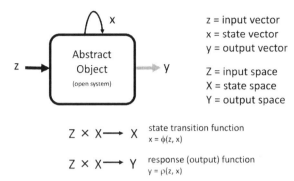

z = input vector
x = state vector
y = output vector

Z = input space
X = state space
Y = output space

$Z \times X \longrightarrow X$ state transition function
$x = \phi(z, x)$

$Z \times X \longrightarrow Y$ response (output) function
$y = \rho(z, x)$

FIGURE 3. Elements of L. A. Zadeh's state-space system theory.

4 Cs of Modeling

In IMM, the state-space scheme is operationalized in model scoping and conceptualization workshops and in all stages of the modeling process to follow. The original concepts framed by the multidisciplinary teams in workshops are thereby carried over into the subsequent more technical steps in the process. State-space structuring of workshops takes place by mapping the state-space elements into what IMM calls the "4 Cs" of model making—currency, compartments, connections, and controls, which provide the concrete framework within which workshop dynamics are staged and structured. The "box-and-arrow" diagram depicted in figure 4 shows how the compartments (rectangles), connections (arrows), and controls (valves) of the 4 Cs protocol are combined. These correspond to the iconography of the popular system-dynamics software STELLA (Richmond & Peterson, 1994).

"Currencies" are conservative quantities (e.g., energy, mass, money) to be transferred between the compartments of the model(s) to be developed. In multicurrency systems, different kinds of substances transferred in different model sectors are interrelated by the use of stoichiometric correspondence coefficients.

Compartment Model Specification
4 Cs approach

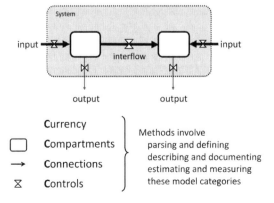

Currency
Compartments   Methods involve
Connections   parsing and defining
                  describing and documenting
Controls   estimating and measuring
                  these model categories

FIGURE 4. The 4 Cs model specification of compartment models, showing correspondences with STELLA diagramming: currency, compartments, connections, and controls.

"Compartments" are storage elements (e.g., standing stocks, natural or economic capital), n in number, that serve as the system's compartments or state variables (in vector form, state vectors, $x = (x_i)$, $i = 1, \ldots, n$ compartments).

"Connections" are links formed by transactions, which are zero-sum currency exchanges ("flows," f_{ij}) between compartments. "Flows" are the directed arrow input, output, and interflow connections shown in figure 4 and can also be represented in an adjacency matrix representation of the system, with 1 representing an existing flow and 0 representing no flow between the two compartments.

"Controls" are constant or time-varying coefficients and other parameters that directly or indirectly regulate model variables. Controls in mathematical models are algorithms that are formulated to regulate the magnitude of flows (inputs, outputs, interflows) in model systems.

The 4 Cs of IMM are used to structure and guide the work of the team workshops in which conceptual and mathematical models are created. The organization of model groups and subgroups will be described below in the team function section.

IMM-CMI Model Making: Team Formation and Function

The formation of project-oriented IMM teams is one of the primary functions of a CMI. In many instances, scientists, managers, and stakeholders available for model teams are limited, imposing constraints on the formation of optimal teams and shifting the emphasis to team function. Whenever a large pool of potential participants can be recruited, criteria for optimum team formation should be pursued; these are described in the paragraphs below.

Incubator Effect

Adding a potential member to a project team requires a personal assessment involving the individual's risk-proneness and an evaluation of past successes of other team members in which potential rewards for the team member to join are shown to outweigh risks (Pennington, et al., 2013). Team science is inherently riskier than many alternatives available to potential team members and Pennington et al. (2013) describes team science as volatile, uncertain, complex, and ambiguous. In the CMI context, we posit that these characteristics argue for a permanent institution to serve as an incubator for projects to give them a "safe space" to develop with adequate resources and time.

Assigning Credit

A strong motivating factor enabling scientists, managers, and stakeholders to agree to participate as team members is to receive professional credit for their contributions to group processes. As Kaushal and Jeschke (2013) point out, if only individual contributions are tracked, incentives for contributions to team science are reduced. CMIs provide an ideal mechanism for combatting this problem because they are fundamentally about group processes in the first place. In assigning credit, appropriate descriptive information is attached so it is clear to future users what each originator's contributions were; therefore, the CMI takes on some functions of a traditional academic library. Software tools to enable tracking and credit assignment for diverse materials, sometimes called "altmetrics" (http://altmetrics.org/tools/; Piwowar, 2013), have been developed. To ensure this process means allocating enough time for ongoing and repeated interactions to occur in stable institutional environments.

Group Member Diversity

Diversity of team members tends to emerge on its own in model-making because of need for experts from different scientific fields, management, and community stakeholders. Fostering certain types of diversity should result in more effective team function, and the two main types of diversity desired are career stage/experience diversity and disciplinary/viewpoint diversity (Cheruvelil et al., 2014; Guimera et al., 2005; Leung et al., 2008; McLeod et al., 1996). Social relationships developed over time in iterative model making in CMIs would leverage experienced team members' social networks to attract and retain returning members and recruit new members to maintain disciplinary and viewpoint diversity of model teams.

Communication

Establishing effective communication patterns, and face-to-face interactions in particular, among the members of a model-making team has been found to be the single most important factor for ensuring a high-functioning group. After group assembly, it is important to allow sufficient time for interpersonal relationships to develop (Hackett et al., 2008; LINX collaborators, 2014; Olson & Olson, 2000; Pentland, 2012; 2014). The interactive nature of IMM model-making team projects, involving repeated engagement of many of the same team members, allows time for relationships to develop among team members and between team members and permanent CMI staff.

Pentland (2012) describes two communication characteristics of successful teams: (1) members engage each other directly and side conversations are important—that is, team leaders

Hierarchical Categories

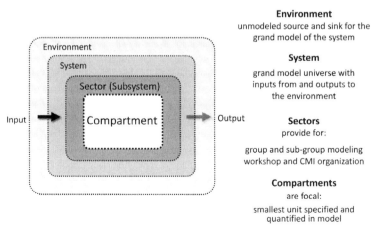

Environment
unmodeled source and sink for the grand model of the system

System
grand model universe with inputs from and outputs to the environment

Sectors
provide for:

group and sub-group modeling workshop and CMI organization

Compartments
are focal:

smallest unit specified and quantified in model

FIGURE 5. Hierarchical categories used in IMM conceptual modeling. Four levels are shown for working purposes.

do not dominate interactions; and (2) members break and explore to have conversations with people outside their team. Successful teams oscillate between exploration and discovery of new information and engagement with other team members to integrate shared knowledge into the group's mental model. In the IMM-CMI context, alternating small group teamwork on submodels (sectors; figure 5) with larger group interactions provides for an alternating engagement-and-exploration dynamic within the project team.

If CMI model-making groups were subjected to Pentland's (2014) "reality mining" behavioral monitoring using sociometric badges and other tools, maps of social interactions could be created and used to provide feedback to model teams that could adapt their social network to create more effective communication patterns. In a permanent CMI, the results of this work become assets of the institute and serve to improve future team function.

Organization of Modeling Groups: State Space Theory

CMIs are organized bottom-up scientifically, operationally, and administratively around multiple IMM projects structured by the hierarchical application of state-space formalism. The grand model is hierarchically represented in figure 5 as the system, with submodels or sectors within that, and compartments as the fundamental unit. Within the grand model, compartments or state variables are sorted into submodels (sectors; figure 5) with respect to topical or disciplinary areas. An ecological example of three sectors by topic (with two example compartments and disciplines in parentheses) might include nutrients (N, P; biogeochemistry), plants (mosses, ferns; botany), and insect herbivores (beetles, aphids; entomology) sectors. Sectors appear as block-diagonal elements $(X_1, X_2, \ldots, X_{k \leq n})$ in an adjacency matrix representation of the grand (system-level) model under construction (figure 6). Team members may often participate in the development of more than one submodel. The constructed adjacency matrix carries all the way back through the 4 Cs (figure 4) to the defining state-transition function (figure 3). Once sectors and their compartments are defined, subgroups of the full project team can be assigned to work on the block diagonal subnetwork that represents each sector. At periodic intervals, after work on each sector has progressed, each subteam interacts with other subteams whose sectors are linked by inflows or outflows. In the ecological example just described, the nutrients sector would have outflows that become inflows to plants; also, the plants sector would have outflows that become inflows to insect herbivores. In this way, the modeling work is distributed to subgroups, but the outflow-inflow coupling of the block diagonal sectors maintains whole-system coherence. This subgroup structuring and interaction enables the engagement-and-exploration communication dynamic described by Pentland (2012) to be realized in the IMM-CMI context.

Creating Trust

Building trust among team members is considered by most team science researchers to be critical to effective group function (Olson & Olson, 2000; Poteete, Janssen, & Ostrom, 2010). Established relationships among team members reflect developed trust and members work together more productively in future teamwork assignments (Rousseau, Sitkin, Burt, & Camerer, 1998; Shrum,

IMM/TB — Sector Interaction
(4 Cs procedure — matrix format)

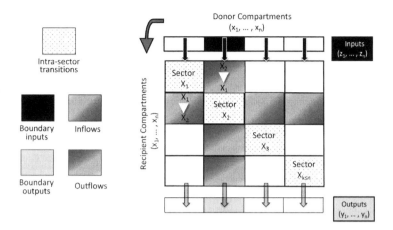

FIGURE 6. Matrix representation of within-system interactions partitioned by model sectors, $k \leq n$ in number, where n is the number of system compartments. The flows are oriented from columns to rows. Within-sector interactions are denoted by the block diagonal entries $X_1, X_2, \ldots, X_{k \leq n}$. Between-sector interactions are denoted by the off-diagonal blocks. Sector 2 is the focal sector in the figure; the inflow from Sector 1 to Sector 2 and the outflow from Sector 2 to Sector 1 are explicitly labelled. Other Sector 2 pairwise interactions are shown in the row 2 (inflows) and column 2 (outflows) in two different gradient patterns.

Chompalov, & Genuth, 2001; Adler & Birkof, 2002). In their theory of collective action, Poteete et al. (2010) posit the centrality of trust to establishing necessary conditions for effective cooperation in groups. Four of the six group variables they identify as increasing trust were shown to be generally conducive to group work: (1) known reputations of group members (familiarity or experience working together); (2) long time horizons (value of long term group interactions); (3) voluntary participation (members choose to enter or exit teams); and (4) face-to-face communication between and among all team members. These four conditions for establishing trust are integral to how the IMM process would operate in a CMI.

Creating Shared Mental Models

Communicating individual mental models and developing shared mental models across entire model-making teams are among the most important early tasks in collaborative team modeling (Senge, 2006). The World Café Conversation Method (Brown & Issacs, 2005; World Café Community Foundation, 2015) is an effective method to create shared mental models. Populating the support staff of CMIs with individuals who are knowledgeable and experienced in methodologies like IMM, the World Café process and numerous others (e. g., Holman, Devane, & Cady, 2007) would make effective use of individual and institutional time in eliciting the shared mental models necessary for collaborative model making.

Conflict Resolution

To sustain optimal team functioning, mechanisms for conflict resolution must be available. Ongoing effective communication and leadership are key factors in this, but prior planning for dealing with specific sources of conflict as they arise should pay dividends for the project. A major source of conflict in team science is lack of transparency and planning concerning team members' roles and responsibilities; related issues are credit, authorship, and control of project products (LINX collaborators, 2014). The iterative dynamic of IMM projects facilitates development of team guidelines specifying roles and expectations of team members at the start of their collaboration. Newly established groups could fine-tune existing CMI guidelines to tailor them to their particular requirements.

Leveraging CMI Assets

Shared mental models can be codified in the form of a computer-based ontology (e.g., Bowden, Song, Kosheleva, & Dubach, 2012) so that diverse domain vocabulary and concepts can be understood by team members from different disciplines. Model structures, model data, and model metadata can be included in ontologies. CMI team members engage in team learning by co-creating model-making ontologies with information technology experts and these ontologies provide a means to collaborate. In CMIs, because ontologies developed over a suite of IMM projects would have much in common, a general institutional ontology framework would tend to develop and be continually improved and updated as a permanent CMI asset.

CMI Model-Facilitating Personnel

Modeling support personnel, who may be drawn from the permanent CMI staff or from project team personnel, play important roles in and provide experienced leadership for the model-making process. Team members may perform one or more model support functions during the project. Richardson and Andersen (1995) identify five model support roles: (1) facilitator, (2) modeler/reflector, (3) process coach, (4) recorder, and (5) gatekeeper. Permanent model support personnel such as those just described are among many new types of positions needed at a CMI to carry out functions that transcend traditional academic or research areas (e.g., Kueffer et al., 2012). These integrative personnel sustain IMM projects between periods of active development in collaborative groups and conduct activities that sustain the institutional center—administration, fundraising, IT activities, stakeholder engagement, and public relations work—and provide a potential career track for collaborative team members of diverse disciplines.

Value of Long-Term CMI Assets

Many studies have shown that collaborative research benefits from long-term relationships (Barreteau, Bots, and Daniell, 2010; Cash et al., 2003; Dietz & Stern 2008; Kueffer, 2006; Kueffer et al., 2012; Pohl & Hirsch Hadorn, 2007; Roux, Rogers, Biggs, Ashton, & Sergeant, 2006). Most team modeling projects only continue for restricted time periods corresponding to funding cycles. When the money ends, the projects end and, with or without some publication, their core products find their way into (usually participants' personal) dead files as team members move to new, funded projects. What was done is lost to further development. IMM is the operational foundation for CMIs proceeds to be stored in permanent homes where activities and products— modeling information capital—are conserved in states poised for further development, even if the original project is resource- and funding-dependent. Permanence in and of itself serves to make CMIs as scoped herein attractive places for team members to work.

Institutional Learning: Organization and Operation of CMIs

To be effective and efficient in use of time and resources, socioecological research and management requires individual and group learning. Collaborative transdisciplinary team science creates a novel set of information capital, and the creation, nurturing, and dissemination of this capital is a central function of a CMI. Social capital involves two main forms of personal learning. First is learning produced by the experience of scientists, managers, and stakeholders who engage in CMI collaborative model-making activities. Second is the social relationships built among these project team members and with those encountered from outside the project group involved in model-making. Accumulation of social capital provides a positive feedback benefit because new team members interacting with experienced team members can utilize this accumulated social capital.

CMI cultural capital is the total information stored by the CMI from its project team activities. In addition to the traditional scientific literature products, a set of group- and team member-created project materials are archived at CMIs for future use. In pursuing its activities, CMIs build inter-institute capital by forming relationships with existing institutions to provide access to insights and expertise needed by project teams and CMI staff, while also providing insight and expertise to outside institutes. Reciprocal exchange of project team members and CMI staff with staff from outside institutes is an effective way to build inter-institute capital. The mission, methods, and a portion of the institutional learning is brought with the person to be shared with the other institute. CMI group learning can be further enhanced by establishing training and mentoring programs for students (K–12, undergraduate, graduate), non-student scientists, managers, and stakeholders (e.g. Bosque-Perez et al., 2016; Tamura & Uegaki, 2012; Weik, Withycombe, & Redman, 2011; Yarime et al., 2012).

Model-Guided CMI Organization and Operation

Using models and associated assets as a set of evolving mission documents for CMI operation requires a strong commitment to the IMM-CMI paradigm—it takes quite a leap of faith to put the models in charge. The CMI concept, anchored in the grassroots of collective model-making, requires a reshaping from the bottom-up, of how traditional scientific institutions are directed and operate, from the top-down. Few human organizations have ever been run quite so "democratically" as envisioned in the crowd sourcing that is IMM conducted in dedicated CMIs. A brief example illustrates.

Our example of model-based CMI operation is the US Manhattan project, whose goal was tightly focused on operationalizing nuclear physics to produce a functional atomic bomb for the US military during WWII. Project development is best illustrated as a set of feedback cycles in a learning-centered collaborative environment. The first cycle was assembly of a multidisciplinary science, engineering, and administrative team; feedback occurred to select the group that could function together as a tight-knit team, with physicist J. R. Oppenheimer as its charismatic leader. The second feedback cycle concerned operation of the team. As each physics or engineering development was produced, it was guided by theoretical physics and chemistry, but tested to determine if it brought the group closer to producing a functional bomb. If yes, the product or process was encouraged with positive feedback, otherwise it was discouraged, and other avenues explored. The reason that this tight feedback structure was so effective was that the urgency of the problem during WWII provided virtually unlimited resources and access to the best personnel in the country.

This example provides a useful analogy to the use of socioecological models for environmental management and problem solving. Although the special circumstances of the Manhattan project will not be duplicated in CMIs, the same feedback processes can operate in a different context. Collaborative model-making brings together a diverse team of people to address urgent problems in need of solutions. Models, associated materials, and the consensus they represent emerge from theories, scientific data, and stakeholder knowledge. Actions resulting from model-making work are subjected to the harsh judge of field management applications. To the extent that they bring the group closer to solutions, positive feedback will favor those aspects of the modeling process in CMI operation. This is what the phrase "put the models in charge" means.

CMI-Like Exemplars: Lessons and Comparison to CMI

In this section, we describe two other paradigms for collaborative model-making. Still others exist, certainly, with the earliest in principle in the ecological domain probably being "adaptive management" first described in Holling (1978). We also describe two academic institutes and a research project that embody the spirit and approach that we have described for our IMM-CMI paradigm. We mainly want to stress there are other approaches to this subject and the aggregate elements in them are in the main congruent with IMM-CMI, and so could be molded to form a consistent, comprehensive approach.

Mediated Modeling

"Mediated modeling" (MM) is a collaborative team modeling approach in which team leaders guide the process by functioning as facilitators, mediators, and modelers (van den Belt, 2004). MM workshops, usually conducted over the course of several days, typically involve the development of a group consensus on problems, purposes, and implementable policies. Group model-building aids consensus-building by making system components, their interrelationships, and possible dynamics explicit (van den Belt, 2004).

MM uses the "system dynamics" (sd) paradigm originated by Forrester (1961) and implemented with stella software (Richmond & Peterson, 1994). In the van den Belt (2004) approach, scenarios generated by parameter manipulations express the effects of manipulating change levers. Team learning and team-created conclusions are workshop products. Because workshops are typically short-term (days), scoping models, designed to enhance understanding of system structure and dynamics are emphasized. Many features of mm are similar to and consistent with the imm scheme of this chapter and could easily fit into the cmi framework. Scoping and conceptualization in workshops are indistinguishable from the early stages of imm; however, continuance is an important difference. If mm is focused on short-term strategic workshops, imm is designed to extend this process into all the subsequent phases of modeling and throughout the life of the institution.

Integrated Modeling

Voinov and Bousquet (2010) have called for a community approach to model building, called "integrated modeling" (im), which is a form of collaborative team model-making with two basic stages. At the decision/policy stage, the problem is defined and possible management or policy solutions and their resource constraints are explored and developed; this stage is coupled to the modeling/monitoring stage, in which conceptual and detailed modeling solutions are developed (Laniak et al., 2013). A synthesis of findings aims at providing management solutions. The whole process is intended to involve feedback and iteration properties (Laniak et al., 2013), essentially like those identified above for imm. State-space grounding and permanent institutionalization are the two basic differences between im and imm.

Modeling Organizations and Consortia

We provide a brief description of three consortia that provide umbrella organizations to facilitate collaborative modeling in diverse fields. We realize that many organizations of this type exist, but we provide a few examples to compare to the imm-cmi paradigm. In later subsections, we provide a detailed description of three organizations: two academic institutes (nceas and Mitchell Center for Sustainability), and a collaborative research association (linx project), that reflect many of the characteristics described for imm-cmi.

CSDMS

Kettner and Syvitski (2013) describe the mission of Community Surface Dynamics Modeling System (csdms) as promoting the sharing and reuse of existing modeling software by providing a model repository and software to allow for existing models to be linked into larger meta-models. CSDMS is targeted primarily to earth systems science; however, its focus on earth surface systems provides for a breadth of possible modeling topics. Many parts of the mission and activities of csdms mirror the cmi activities of archiving the products of collaborative model-making in ontology databases and providing for their use and modification for other purposes; the main difference is that csdms is a remote repository and the cmi, as proposed in this chapter, is a local site-specific institution.

CUAHS

The Consortium of Universities for the Advancement of Hydrologic Science (CUAHS) is a collaborating group of universities with a focus on hydrologic science. In addition to promoting multidisciplinary collaboration and education, CUAHS developed an initiative to support community modeling tools to facilitate study and modeling of hydrologic systems by local or regional research organizations or NGOS (https://www.cuahsi.org). Much of the CUAHS mission is consistent with our IMM-CMI approach and organizations such as this would be ideal partners for a network of local CMIS.

NCAR

The National Center for Atmospheric Research (NCAR) serves a research center for atmospheric research in the USA. Support of collaborative science in universities and other labs along with NCAR's long-term institute lifetime serve to provide ongoing research integration and opportunities for institute-level learning (https://ncar.ucar.edu). NCAR's mission and activities are very consistent with the IMM-CMI paradigm of this chapter; however, NCAR is a continental scale institute, which contrasts with the local scale envisioned for CMI. Of course, collaboration between a set of CMIS and centers like NCAR would provide a further enhancement of the missions of both organizations.

NCEAS

The National Center for Ecological Analysis and Synthesis (NCEAS; Hackett et al., 2008; https://www.nceas.ucsb.edu/) was founded to provide a place (University of California, Santa Barbara) for ecological research collaborations. Participants travel to NCEAS for intensive several-day to week-long working group sessions. In addition to working groups, visiting scientists are hosted, but there is no permanent science faculty. To facilitate collaboration, NCEAS has developed computer tools to increase team productivity and potential for successful outcomes (Hackett et al., 2008).

In their review of characteristics contributing to NCEAS group productivity and scientific impact, Hampton and Parker (2011) found that a high frequency of face-to-face interactions is most important. Second in importance are NCEAS resident scientists (post-docs, sabbatical fellows) who increase the productivity of working groups by providing social and scientific skills acquired while at NCEAS. These characteristics are consistent with IMM bottom-up design and process methodologies that translate individual expert and stakeholder knowledge into CMI social and institute capital.

At NCEAS, working group interactions are of short duration and assembled to address very specific problems (Hampton & Parker, 2011), whereas CMIS are permanent sites where modeling, management, and outreach are focused on long-term solution to site-specific problems of local stakeholder interest. In IMM, NCEAS-style working groups could include experts from other regions to augment intramural CMI strengths. The wider perspectives brought in could then be incorporated into the permanent CMI framework for continuing development and application.

LOTIC INTERSITE NITROGEN EXPERIMENTS (LINX)

The LINX project (http://lter.kbs.msu.edu/) was a distributed-team, multi-institutional project forming intersite teams consisting of personnel from the separate research sites (LINX collaborators, 2014). The project-level team and sub-teams had frequent face-to-face meetings and also communicated remotely on a regular basis. This worked because there was a long history of collaboration among the stream ecologists, particularly those at the US Long Term Ecological Research sites. Models and model-making played a central role in planning and synthesis. Senior scientists assumed leadership roles, but major decisions were reached by sharing information and data to reach consensus . In LINX I, post-doctoral scientists circulated between sites to cross-fertilize and coordinate the project. Open planning of roles and responsibilities with respect to data sharing and authorship also served to unify the project (LINX collaborators, 2014).

Several LINX features are built into IMM processes and procedures. First, institutional permanence of the CMI improves on the coordination achievable by circulating personnel, and enhances the possibilities for team and institute learning. Second, LINX establishment of roles and responsibilities through data sharing and authorship is captured automatically in CMIS because IMM models are conceptualized by the same individuals who will later provide the data to quantify them; existing protocols are revised and refined to establish model team protocols. The third characteristic, effective leadership and communication, is facilitated by the natural evolution of model-making protocols in the CMI by continuing collaborations between team members and leaders.

MITCHELL CENTER FOR SUSTAINABILITY SOLUTIONS

The three goals of the Mitchell Center for Sustainability Solutions at the University of Maine (https://umaine.edu/mitchellcenter/) are: (1) to engage experts and stakeholders in evaluations of dynamics of socioecological change; (2) to conduct research to identify parameters to be manipulated to steer socioecological change; and (3) to foster innovation in institutional structures and processes to facilitate interdisciplinary team science (Hart et al., 2015). In its first decade, the Mitchell Center supported initiatives involving hundreds of faculty members and students from universities, high schools, and over 300 stakeholder organizations (Hart et al., 2015). Several lessons learned are relevant for the operational design of CMIS.

The first lesson is spatial. Attention to local-scale systems was found to be conducive to framing questions whose answers could be used to guide managers and stakeholders (Hart et al., 2015). This contrasts with "big science" projects focused on systems at larger spatial scales. The Mitchell Center experience argues for CMIS to be local in spatial reach, but capable of collaborating with regional or national networks to extend local results to larger scales.

The second lesson is temporal. The repeated assembly of scientists, managers, and stakeholders to advance projects is expensive in human and financial resources. Hart et al. (2015) report that existing university-stakeholder relationships can be leveraged to advance progress on projects, and this is time and cost effective. Permanent CMIS anchored by resident staff enabling extra-institutional resources to be spread out over time to be used when needed makes sense scientifically and fiscally. It also enables ongoing revision of project plans based on changed objectives or changed conditions in the subject systems. CMI projects can take a long time to

Conceptual Model of CMI Teamwork and Outreach

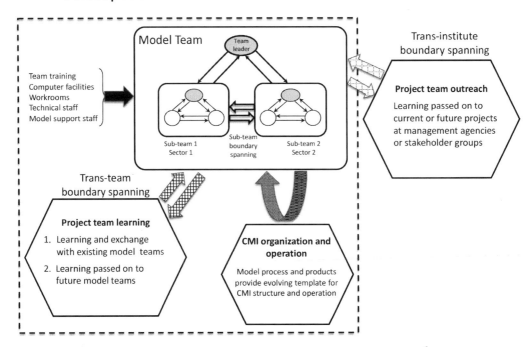

FIGURE 7. Flow diagram for a model team (upper, large, rounded rectangle) within a CMI; CMI boundary is indicated by the dashed rectangle. Gray ovals indicate team and subteam leaders. The solid arrow represents inputs of resources from the institution to the team. Dark, diamond-filled arrows indicate team learning and exchange with other model teams, and stippled, diamond-filled arrows the same but between CMI and other institutions. A dark-stippled, curved arrow returning to model team represents feedback of stored CMI model information to guide CMI operation. Unfilled black arrows denote exchange of products or information between subteams. Within the upper rounded rectangle, subteams 1 and 2 correspond to the $k = 1$ and 2 block diagonal sectors (Figure 6) of the overall model to be developed. Interactions between subteam 1 and 2 represent the off-diagonal regions (Figure 6).

play out, and in such protracted circumstances, institutional permanence rather than project discontinuance is the preferred alternative.

Summary and Conclusions

As previous sections of this chapter show, many of the individual conceptual components of IMM-CMI have been and are being carried out in many different types of organizations (e.g., the aforementioned CMI-like exemplars). However, as with models themselves, it is the emergent properties of the complete IMM-CMI paradigm, where these individual concepts are combined and operationalized over the lifetime of a set of CMIs, that provide the essence of what the approach has to offer the collaborative modeling community.

Figure 7 shows the basic structure of a CMI model team and its subteam components embedded within a CMI. This diagram shows the hierarchical interactions within CMI as well as interactions with other institutions. At the team level, subteams working on model sectors interact to produce a coherent whole system model. Existing teams within a CMI exchange information and new teams are able to harvest information of existing and past teams to prime the pump and enhance their capabilities. Within the CMI boundary, figure 7 shows a feedback that indicates the use of model team process and product learning to guide the structure and operation of the CMI, perhaps its most distinguishing feature. The mosaic of ongoing model projects provides a blueprint for how a CMI is articulated with its ecoregion and human social system context.

Why Do CMIs Need to Be Local or Site-Specific?

The reason CMIs must be local and site-specific is that local stakeholders, local issues, and local contexts matter (e.g., Hart et al., 2015). A good analogy is the success of the local (mostly county-based) US Department of Agriculture Cooperative Extension Service (USDA-CES) offices set up to provide for the dissemination of agricultural research results to farmers in their communities (https://nifa.usda.gov). The key points of this analogy follow.

First, USDA-CES extension agents, as local people living in the community, become trusted sources of information based on long-term relationships with farmers (https://nifa.usda.gov). This is analogous to CMI permanent staff and associated model group scientists building relationships with local stakeholders. Second, USDA-CES forms partnerships with local and regional institutions such as land-grant universities, federal agencies, NGOs, and private-sector businesses to carry out its mission. CMI partnerships similarly build social capital and provide for the trust and familiarity required for effective communication and model group function. Third, the spread of the USDA-CES model into many other countries over the past decades and interest shown in adopting its organizational structure and operational methods by health care organizations (Berwick, 2003; Grumbach & Mold, 2009) provides supporting evidence that a set of local, site-based networked institutes such as CMIs would be an effective paradigm for conducting collaborative model-making.

Why Is Putting the Models in Charge Better?

Collaborative model-making done for a local site molds the organization and operation of the CMI to the best practices to address local environmental problems. An agriculture analogy is instructive. A USDA-CES agent in Hawai'i requires a different set of research findings, economic data, and outreach methods to collaborate with a pineapple farmer than another agent in Georgia requires to collaborate on problem solutions with a peanut farmer. The farmers' environmental contexts are different; therefore, local, site-based, long-term interaction provides the best results.

Evolving, model-driven mission documents for local CMIs provide for an efficiency and focus of operation that cannot be obtained by traditional hierarchical management, particularly if control is by a distant, centralized bureaucracy. Guidelines for operations, such as what type of data to collect, what staff are needed, or what experiments are needed are driven by the models archived at the CMI. Models point out gaps in data and system understanding and the CMI is organized to respond with new or modified initiatives and programs as they emerge from local collaborative model development. Because local stakeholders are involved, problems identified in the local context are not ignored, but are brought into the CMI to demand a response.

What Makes IMM-CMI different?

IMM-CMI is unique in the following ways:

- CMI state-space theoretical structure affords coherence to model-making and CMI organization and operation.
- CMI configuration and function is consistent with many of the findings of team science (e.g., communication, group and subgroup structuring, trust).
- Local CMIs provide long-term iterative engagement of scientists, managers, and stakeholders, with archived model process and products enhancing the effectiveness of new model-making groups.
- CMIs provide an ideal environment for individual and group experiential learning.
- Model-based CMI organization and operation.

Conclusions

To address complex environmental systems, the fundamentals of the scientific method for reductive science—hypothesis-testing, systematic empirical observation, and controlled experimentation—may have to be supplemented with other modes of knowledge generation for environmental systems of concern. Scenario-generation and analysis of model systems, rather than the empirical systems themselves, may become at least the transitional methodology working toward an ultimate science of holism. Collective model-making, rooted in formalism, in dedicated institutions of some permanence like CMIs, could be an effective approach to deal with long-term environmental management.

REFERENCES

Adler, P. S., & Birkhoff, J. E. (2002). *Building trust: When knowledge from "here" meets knowledge from "away."* Portland: National Policy Consensus Center. www.policyconsensus.org.

Barreteau, O., Bots, P. W. G., & Daniell, K. A. (2010). A framework for clarifying "participation" in participatory research to prevent its rejection for the wrong reasons. *Ecology and Society, 15*(2), 1.

Berwick, D. M. (2003). Disseminating innovations in health care. *Journal of the American Medical Association, 289*(15), 1969–1975.

Bosque-Perez, N. A., Klos, P. Z., Force, J., Waits, L. P., Cleary, K., Rhoades, P., . . . Holbrook, J. D. (2016). A pedagogical model for team-based, problem-focused interdisciplinary doctoral education. *Bioscience, 66*(6), 477–488.

Bowden, D., Song, E., Kosheleva, J., & Dubach, M. F. (2012). NeuroNames: An ontology for the BrainInfo portal to neuroscience on the web. *Neuroinformatics, 10,* 97–114.

Brown, J., & Issacs, D. . (2005). *The World Café book: Shaping our futures through conversations that matter.* San Francisco: Berrett-Koehler Publishers.

Cash, D.W., Clark, W.C., Alcock, F., Dickson, N.M., Eckley, N., Guston, D.H., Jager, J., Mitchell, R.B. (2003). Knowledge systems for sustainable development. *Proceedings of the National. Academy of Science, 100*(14), 8086–8091.

Cheruvelil, K. S., Soranno, P. A., Weathers, K. C., Hanson, P. C., Goring, S. J., Filstrup, C. T., & Read, E. K. (2014). Creating and maintaining high-performing collaborative research teams: The importance of diversity and interpersonal skills. *Frontiers in Ecology and the Environment, 12*(1), 31–38.

Dietz, T., & Stern, P. C. (2008). *Public participation in environmental assessment and decision making.* Washington, DC: National Academies Press.

Fiore, S. M. (2008). How the science of teams can inform team science. *Small Group Research, 39*(3), 251–277.

Forrester, J. (1961). *Industrial dynamics.* Waltham, MA: Pegasus Communications.

Grumbach, K., & Mold, J. W. (2009). A health care cooperative extension service—Transforming primary care and community health. *Journal of the American Medical Association, 301*(24), 2589–2591.

Guimera, R., Uzzi, B., Spiro, J., & Amaral, L. A. N. (2005). Team assembly mechanisms determine collaborative network structure and team performance. *Science, 308,* 697–702.

Hackett, E. J., Parker, J. N., Conz, D. Rhoten, D, & Parker, A. (2008). Ecology transformed: The national center for ecological analysis and synthesis and the changing patterns of ecological research. In Olson, G. M., Zimmerman, A., & Bos, N. (Eds.), *Scientific collaboration on the internet* (pp. 277–296). Cambridge, MA: MIT Press.

Hampton, S. E., & Parker, J. N. (2011). Collaboration and productivity in scientific synthesis. *Bioscience, 61*(11), 900–910.

Hart, D. D., Bell, K. P., Lindenfeld, L. A., Jain, S., Johnson, T. R., Ranco, D., & McGill, B. (2015). Strengthening the role of universities in addressing sustainability challenges: The Mitchell Center for Sustainability Solutions as an institutional experiment. *Ecology and Society, 20*(2), 4. doi: 10.5751/ ES-07283-200204.

Holling, C. S. (Ed.) (1978). *Adaptive environmental assessment and management.* Chichester: Wiley.

Holman, P., Devane, T., & Cady, S. (Eds.). (2007). *The change handbook: The definitive resource on today's best methods for engaging whole systems.* (2nd ed.). San Francisco: Berrett-Koehler.

Kaushal, S. S., & Jeschke, J. M. (2013). Collegiality versus competition: How metrics shape scientific communities. *Bioscience, 63*(3), 155–156.

Kettner, A. J., & Syvitski, J. P. M. (2013). Editorial—Modeling for environmental change. *Computers and Geosciences, 53,* 1–2.

Kueffer, C. (2006). Integrative ecological research: case-specific validation of ecological knowledge for environmental problem solving. *Gaia, 15,* 115–120.

Kueffer, C., Underwood, E., Hirshch Hadorn, G., Holderegger, R., Lehning, M., Pohl, C., . . . Edwards, P. (2012). Enabling effective problem-oriented research for sustainable development. *Ecology and Society, 17*(4), 8.

Laniak, G. F., Olchin, G., Goodall, J., Voinov, A., Hill, M., Glynn, P., . . . Hughes, A. (2013). Integrated environmental modeling: A vision and roadmap for the future. *Environmental Modeling and*

Software, 39, 3–23.

Leung, A. K., Maddux, W. W., Galinsky, A. D., & Chiu, C. (2008). Multicultural experience enhances creativity. *American Psychologist, 63,* 169–181.

LINX collaborators (2014). The Lotic intersite nitrogen experiments: An example of successful ecological research collaboration. *Freshwater Science, 33*(3), 700–710.

McLeod, P.L., Loel, S.A., & Cox, T.H. (1996). Ethnic diversity and creativity in small groups. *Small Group Research,* 27, 248–264.

Olson, G. M. & Olson, J. S. (2000). Distance matters. *Human-Computer Interaction, 15,* 139–178.

Pennington, D. D., Simpson, G. L., McConnell, M. S., Fair, J. M., & Baker, R. J. (2013). Transdisciplinary research, transformative learning, and transformative science. *Bioscience, 63*(7), 564–573.

Pentland, A. (2012, April). The new science of building great teams. *Harvard Business Review,* 61–70.

Pentland, A. (2014). *Social physics: How good ideas spread–The lessons from a new science.* New York: Penguin Press.

Piwowar, H. (2013). Value all research products. *Nature, 493,* 159.

Pohl, C., & Hirsch Hadorn, G. (2007). *Principles for designing transdisciplinary research.* Munich, Germany: Odkon.

Poteete, A. R., Janssen, M. A., & Ostrom, E. (2010). *Working together: Collective action, the commons, and multiple methods in practice.* Princeton: Princeton University Press.

Richardson, G. P., & Andersen, D. F. (1995). Teamwork in group model building. *System Dynamics Review, 11*(2), 113–137.

Richmond, B., & Peterson, S. (1994). *STELLA documentation.* Hanover: High Performance Systems.

Rousseau, D. M., Sitkin, S. B., Burt, R. S., & Camerer, C. (1998). Not so different after all: A cross-discipline view of trust. *Academy of Management Review, 23*(3), 393–404.

Roux, D. J., Rogers, K. H., Biggs, H. C., Ashton, P. J., & Sergeant, A. (2006). Bridging the science-management divide: Moving from unidirectional knowledge transfer to knowledge interfacing and sharing. *Ecology and Society, 11*(1),4.

Sage, R. W., Patten, B. C., & Salmon, P. A. (2003). Institutionalized model-making and ecosystem-based management of exploited resource populations: A comparison with instrument flight. *Ecological Modelling, 170,* 107–128.

Senge, P. M. (2006). *The fifth discipline: The art and practice of the learning organization.* New York: Doubleday.

Shrum, W., Chompalov, I., & Genuth, J. (2001). Trust, conflict, and performance in scientific collaborations. *Social Studies of Science, 31*(5), 681–730.

Tamura, M., & Uegaki, T. (2012). Development of an educational model for sustainability science: Challenges in the mind-skills-knowledge education at Ibaraki University. *Sustainability Science, 7,* 253–265.

van den Belt, M. (2004). *Mediated modeling: A system dynamics approach to environmental consensus building.* Washington, DC: Island Press.

Voinov, A., & Bousquet, F., (2010). Modelling with stakeholders. *Environmental Modelling & Software, 25* (11), 1268–1281.

Weik, A., Withycombe, L., & Redman, C. L. (2011). Key competencies in sustainability: A reference framework for academic program development. *Sustainability Science, 6,* 203–218.

World Café Community Foundation. (2015). *Café to go: A quick reference guide for hosting World Café.* www.theworldcafe.com.

Yarime, M., Trencher, G., Mino, T., Scholz, R. W., Olsson, L., Ness, B., . . . Rotmans, J. (2012). Establishing sustainability science in higher education institutions: Towards an integration of academic development, institutionalization, and stakeholder collaborations. *Sustainability Science, 7* (Supplement 1), 101–113.

Zadeh, L. A. & Desoer, C. A. (1963). *Linear system theory: The state space approach.* New York: McGraw-Hill.

PART 2

Applications in Collaborative Modeling

Using Participatory System Dynamics Modeling of Agricultural-Environmental Systems in a Developing Country Context

Robert B. Richardson, Laura Schmitt Olabisi, Kurt B. Waldman, Naomi Sakana, and Nathan G. Brugnone

The global population is projected to increase to nine billion by 2050 and the increasing demand for food is driving both land conversion for agricultural expansion and unsustainable agricultural intensification, reducing the resilience of rural households dependent on agriculture and the landscapes that support their livelihoods. The UN World Population Prospects estimates the current population in Africa at 925 million (United Nations, 2012). Africa has the highest population growth rates in the world, and the continent's population is projected to reach more than 2 billion people by 2050 (Cleland, 2013). The population of Zambia is projected to more than double in the next generation, rising from 16.2 million in 2015 to 44 million by 2050. Population growth, along with rising incomes, will have significant implications for the amount of land and resources required to meet demands for agriculture, energy, and food.

Meeting the needs of such a growing population while minimizing the impacts on the environment and on the critical ecosystem services that support and sustain life remains one the greatest challenges facing human society today. Global food production has increased dramatically in recent decades, in large part due to agricultural intensification, often involving the increased use of agricultural inputs and high-yielding crop varieties to produce more food per unit of land. However, there are growing concerns about the long-term sustainability and environmental consequences of the intensification of agricultural systems (Matson et al., 1997; Tilman et al, 2002).

The objective of this project was to advance the understanding of the linkages between adoption of sustainable intensification (SI) practices and forest conservation. This study examined the agricultural-environmental linkages in Zambia, with a focus on the implications of farm-level decisions for landscape-level impacts. The complex nature of the linkages between agricultural and ecological systems requires the consideration of non-linear relationships, feedback loops, and uncertainty. System Dynamics Modeling is a quantitative modeling approach that uses systems thinking to analyze the impact of feedback loops in complex and dynamic systems. Participatory system dynamics modeling was used in this study to examine the linkages between field and farm-scale sustainable intensification interventions and forest conservation.

Agriculture faces tremendous pressure to supply the growing and also wealthier population with more food, fiber, and fuel (Tilman et al., 2011). Food security remains a long-standing problem throughout sub-Saharan Africa (SSA), which has lagged behind other regions of the world in terms of agricultural productivity. The population of SSA has grown at a faster rate than agricultural productivity in the region over the past century, which has exacerbated problems related to hunger, malnutrition, and food insecurity (Sanchez & Swaminathan, 2005; Hazell & Wood, 2008).

Most farmers in SSA are smallholder farmers who cultivate small plots for subsistence agriculture and face an array of challenges related to agricultural productivity, including depleted soil fertility, costly fertilizer inputs, low marginal returns (i.e., profitability), and declining agricultural productivity (Giller et al., 1997). Intensification of agriculture has been cited as a plausible pathway to increase food security for poor households in Africa and elsewhere (Angelsen & Kaimowitz, 2001), but inputs such as fertilizer are often costly and only marginally profitable for the rural poor (Tittonell & Giller, 2013).

High demand for food coupled with both low-input conventional agricultural and input-intensive agricultural intensification practices are potentially leading to agricultural land degradation, land conversion, and greenhouse gas emissions. National policies often promote input-driven intensification, which have been found to increase yields and productivity, but unsustainable agricultural practices render the soil unproductive (Giller et al., 1997) and contribute to land degradation (Sanchez et al., 1997). Once land becomes degraded and scarce, farmers put more pressure on protected areas and marginal hillsides (Headey & Jayne, 2014). Unsustainable practices can also force smallholders to acquire new fertile lands (often marginal lands in forested areas) through land conversion. The transition to intensive agriculture may also reduce total soil carbon stocks and increase emission of greenhouse gases such as carbon dioxide, methane, and nitrous oxide, thus exacerbating climate change. The net effect of unsustainable agriculture intensification is a reduction in the food security and resilience of agricultural households and the ecosystems on which their livelihoods depend.

Sustainable intensification practices, however, have the potential to mitigate the impact of agriculture on the landscape by intensifying agricultural production without increasing deforestation or land clearing (Garnett et al., 2013). It is common to think of intensification in terms of land as the key input and improving yields as the key objective. Sustainable intensification involves the processes or systems where agricultural yields are increased without adverse environmental impact and without the conversion of additional non-agricultural land (Pretty & Bharucha, 2014). SI approaches must lead to higher yields on the existing agricultural footprint, because most arable land with agricultural potential consists mainly of forests, wetlands, or grasslands whose conversion would greatly increase emissions of greenhouse gases and loss of biodiversity (Garnett et al., 2013). Increasing the land area in agriculture would also have significant environmental costs in terms of carbon sequestration, flood protection, wildlife habitat, and other ecosystem services.

Numerous SI practices and technologies have been identified in the literature, including agroforestry, cereal-legume intercropping, conservation agriculture, integrated pest management, and organic farming (Pretty et al., 2011; Agriculture for Impact, 2013). These practices are intended to harness ecosystem services to improve productivity by increasing soil organic matter, reducing competition between crops and increasing mutual benefits among crops, such as nitrogen fixation. However, there is much debate about the efficacy (and impacts) of SI in practice. While nitrogen-fixing agroforestry trees potentially increase farm productivity, especially under conditions of resource scarcity in regions such as SSA, it is unclear if these systems indeed contribute to low-emission agricultural development (Rosenstock et al., 2013). Similarly, conservation agriculture has been vigorously promoted in countries like Zambia as a form of SI, although the impacts have been hotly debated (Baudron et al., 2012). Where SI technologies like agroforestry and conservation agriculture are adopted, it is not clear whether the benefits lead to slower land degradation and compel farmers to stay on their farms, thereby easing pressure on forests from land clearing, or whether increased agricultural income from adoption of more profitable farming technologies causes farmers to expand their agricultural land holdings through deforestation or attracts new farmers to agriculture. This question was the primary motivation for the project.

The study sites for this project were Eastern Province and Lusaka Province in Zambia, chosen because they are identified as the Zone of Influence of the US Government's Feed the Future initiative and a priority area for biodiversity conservation initiatives that are supported by the US Agency for International Development. The landscape is rich in biodiversity and primarily consists of Miombo woodlands, which are dominated by tropical grasslands, savannas, and shrublands. Most smallholder farmers in the region cultivate maize for subsistence agriculture on small plots in rainfed systems.

Traditional approaches to rural development programming often use farm-level or household-level metrics to measure the outcomes of their programs (Brouder & Gomez-McPherson, 2014; Ngoma et al., 2015), without considering the impact on the larger landscape. Likewise, decisions regarding resource use at the landscape scale (e.g., forest conservation for climate change mitigation) do not usually consider the impact of such decisions on smallholder farmers or rural livelihoods. This integrated study on the impacts of sustainable intensification on landscapes and livelihoods aims to advance understanding of these linkages in order to design effective integrated projects and interventions to promote sustainable development.

The study began with a review of literature and datasets related to sustainable intensification and forest resources in Zambia, discussed later. Information from these publications and datasets provided variables and other data that were used to parameterize the system dynamics model. The structure and parameters of the model were validated through participatory stakeholder workshops and used to simulate deforestation scenarios including drought, increasing maize yields, full electrification, and adoption of fuel-efficient stoves over a fifty-year period (2010–2060).

Sustainable Intensification

Sustainable intensification has been promoted as a means to simultaneously address food insecurity and ensure environmental sustainability (Phalan et al., 2011; Pretty et al., 2011; Garnett et al., 2013). The concept of SI has attracted widespread attention from policy makers, donors, and the international agricultural development community, but there is no consensus on a theoretical foundation for the term or on the specific practices or techniques that are implied by the phrase. Pretty et al. (2011) define SI as "producing more output from the same area of land while reducing the negative environmental impacts and at the same time increasing contributions to natural capital and the flow of environmental services" (7).

Sustainable intensification practices take many forms and do not involve a prescriptive set of agricultural technologies. It is often assumed that smallholder farmers who face low yields in degraded soil environments subsequently abandon their fields and clear new land (Angelsen & Kaimowitz, 2001). Therefore, SI practices that increase yields or produce fuelwood would presumably reduce deforestation pressures. However, others have raised concerns that promoting agricultural innovation could enhance the profitability of agriculture, thereby encouraging deforestation and the expansion of agricultural land (Villoria et al., 2014).

Two commonly promoted SI practices include conservation agriculture (CA) and agroforestry. A dominant theory of change in international agricultural development suggests that by adopting CA, smallholder farmers will enjoy higher yields, which would reduce need for land conversion. Furthermore, by adopting agroforestry, farmers would produce on-farm fuelwood, further reducing demand for forest resources. This study examined this theory of change by exploring the evidence of linkages between these two on-farm SI practices and landscape-scale deforestation.

CA is widely promoted as an example of sustainable intensification and a solution to low productivity and soil degradation problems in SSA (Giller et al., 2009; Grabowski and Kerr, 2014). CA is designed to improve farm productivity by combining three principles: (1) minimum soil disturbance, (2) permanent organic soil cover, and (3) crop rotation and crop diversification (FAO, 2012; Andersson & D'Souza, 2014). CA is a set of practices that is a possible avenue for intensifying agriculture to improve food security amid heightened environmental challenges and population increase (Corbeels et al., 2014). CA has also been highlighted as one of the major avenues for climate change adaptation and mitigation in agriculture within the Intergovernmental Panel on Climate Change and has been shown to help stabilize crop yields in variable rainfall areas.

The CA technologies practiced in Zambia involve dry-season land preparation using minimum tillage or no-till methods (e.g., ox-drawn ripping, hand-hoe planting basins, and zero tillage) and permanent soil cover through the retention of crop residues, crop rotation, and agroforestry (Baudron et al., 2007). CA practices in Zambia were initially promoted on the premise that they would improve crop yields because of the potential to rejuvenate soils. Empirical evidence on the impact of CA on smallholder productivity is mixed (Giller et al., 2009; Andersson & D'Souza 2014; Brouder & Gomez-McPherson, 2014). More recently, these practices are increasingly seen as strategies for enhancing the capacity of smallholders to adapt to the effects of climate change (Pretty et al., 2011; Arslan et al., 2014; Corbeels et al., 2014).

Despite the promotion of CA over the last two decades, overall adoption rates remain low and inconsistent in Zambia (Arslan et al., 2014). Some reports, however, indicate that where promotion has been sustained, adoption levels are significantly higher (Kasanga & Daka, 2013). Many CA adoption studies focus on farmers' use of minimum tillage to prepare the land as the most essential and most observable indicator of adoption. Arslan et al. (2014) use panel data from two rounds of household surveys that were implemented in 2004 and 2008 to show that the percentage of households using minimum tillage as the main land preparation method on at least one plot increased from 8 percent in 2004 to 14 percent in 2008 nationwide.

In recent years, CA practices have been actively promoted at a national scale by the Zambian government and international donors with a target of achieving 40 percent adoption by 2016 (GRZ, 2013) but there is little empirical evidence that these efforts are resulting in increased adoption rates (e.g., Arslan et al. [2014] documented high levels of disadoption between 2004 and 2008). Because there is little evidence demonstrating that CA improves yields, the linkage between adoption of CA practices and reducing land clearing and deforestation would appear to be weak. From this review, the only evidence to demonstrate that CA improves yields is derived from the minimum-tillage practice of ripping (as opposed to conventional tillage), particularly when combined with early land preparation prior to the onset of rains (Ngoma et al., 2015).

"Agroforestry" is the deliberate integration of trees and woody shrubs into farms and productive landscapes in order to diversify and increase production, while promoting social, economic and environmental benefits for land users. Agroforestry can improve the resilience of agro-ecosystems by enhancing nutrient supply through biological nitrogen fixation and nutrient cycling, improving soil structure and water infiltration, serving as an erosion control measure, and increasing the efficiency of resource capture and use (Albrecht & Kandji, 2003; Chirwa et al., 2007; Ajayi et al., 2011). Agroforestry systems can take a range of forms and provide an array of benefits, including fertilizer trees for land regeneration, soil health, and food security; fruit trees for nutrition and income; fodder trees that improve smallholder livestock production; and timber and fuel wood trees for shelter and energy (Garrity, 2004). Given its multiple uses and benefits, agroforestry is widely considered pertinent to achieving sustained growth in agricultural production of smallholder systems (Garrity et al., 2010), particularly in maize-based cropping systems on depleted soils in southern Africa (Kwesiga & Coe, 1994).

Agroforestry systems have been promoted for over two decades in most southern African countries but few quantitative studies on the adoption of individual tree species exist. Adoption studies in Malawi and Zambia show an increasing adoption of intercropping of fertilizer trees on farms, including *Faidherbia albida* (Akinnifesi et al., 2010). Keil et al. (2005) found that 75 percent of farmers who initially tested fertilizer trees in Zambia eventually adopted the practice. An impact assessment in the region also indicated that farmers have generally increased the land under agroforestry (Akinnifesi et al., 2010). Moreover, a study of the impact of fertilizer tree fallows in Zambia reported that the average size of fertilizer tree fallow fields increased from 0.07 hectares (ha) in 1997 to 0.20 ha in 2003 (Ajayi et al. 2003).

Agroforestry systems also have the potential to provide on-farm fuelwood and other household wood requirements (Akinnifesi et al., 2008; Winterbottom et al., 2013). Kwesiga et al. (1999) confirm the provision of fuelwood from *Sesbania sesban* fallows in Eastern Zambia. Trimmings of branches of *Gliricidia sepium* provide firewood to women (Winterbottom et al., 2013). The volume of firewood from these agroforestry systems, however, varies among species. For example, tree species of *Leucaena leucocephala* supply wood at a rate of 20–60 m^3 per hectare per year (Winterbottom et al., 2013). Assuming an average density of 750 kg per m^3 (UNEP, 2015), *Leucaena* could produce at least 7,050 kg of fuelwood per year. This quantity of fuelwood should be enough to meet the fuelwood requirement of small rural households of about five members. The on-farm fuelwood provision is of particular benefit to women and children in rural Zambia by reducing their burden of walking long distances to collect firewood due to local scarcity (Neufeldt et al., 2015).

Forests in Zambia

Zambia is endowed with abundant forest resources compared to most of the other Miombo countries in southern and eastern Africa. The national Integrated Land Use Assessment (ILUA 2005–2008) inventory classifies the national vegetation into three categories: Miombo woodlands, deciduous forests, and shrub thickets (Kalinda et al., 2008). With its relatively small population, the available forested land per capita is estimated at about 3.5 hectares, compared to 1.7 in Zimbabwe, 1.6 in Mozambique, and 0.2 in Malawi (World Bank, 2008). There is, however, a high level of variation in the estimates of national forest cover in Zambia. Recent estimates of the remaining forest cover range between 39 million (CSO, 2013) and 50 million ha (Kalinda et al., 2008). Based on these estimates, forest cover represents between 52 and 65 percent of the total land area, estimated at 75.3 million ha (World Bank, 2008). Zambia has a large standing stock of wood biomass, estimated at about 2,941 million m^3, with a re-growth rate of 568 million per year (Kalinda et al., 2008; Mukosha & Siampale, 2009; Bwalya, 2011). Over 2,700 million m^3, or 94.7 percent of this national stock, are in forests, with over 70 percent in Miombo woodlands (Mukosha & Siampale, 2009).

The indigenous forests in Zambia are rich in biodiversity. They are home to approximately 5,500 species of flowering plants, 146 species of ferns, and 88 species of mosses (GRZ, 1997). The landscape is dominated by Miombo woodlands, which are primarily characterized by savannah grasslands and tree species that are well suited for charcoal production (Chidumayo, 1990; Mulenga et al., 2014). These forest resources provide sources of energy, construction materials, and wild food that support local livelihoods, especially in rural areas in Zambia (Kalinda & Bwalya, 2014; Zulu & Richardson, 2013). A wide range of non-timber forest products are collected from these resources, including raw materials for construction, thatching, crafting, wild foods (e.g., bushmeat, edible caterpillars, fruits, honey, mushrooms, and tubers), as well as medicinal products. Non-timber forest products not only provide important sources of food and materials for subsistence, they also significantly contribute to rural household income (Bwalya, 2011; Mulenga et al., 2014). Environmental benefits of forests include erosion control and sediment retention, agricultural support services, and carbon storage and sequestration (GRZ, 2011).

While Zambia does have a relatively high amount of forested land per capita, annual deforestation rates are ten times higher than in most other Miombo-dominated countries (Dewees et al., 2011), and estimates range widely (Stringer et al., 2012). Recent estimates of deforestation rates range from 167,000 ha or 0.3 percent per year (FAO, 2010) to 540,000 ha per year (Pohjonen, 2004). But the most recent and widely reported estimates were on the order of 250,000 ha per year to 445,800 ha per year (FAO, 2005). The ILUA reported estimates of 250,000 to 300,000 ha per year, or a relative annual decline of the total forest cover of 0.62 percent (Kalinda et al., 2008; Mukosha & Siampale, 2009).

The most recent estimates by UN-REDD and the ILUA provided a more conservative rate of deforestation of 300,000 ha per year, or an annual relative decline of 0.33 percent (ZFD, 2008). We calculated an average deforestation rate of about 303,000 ha per year using the most recent estimates between 2005 and 2010. This estimate is similar to that reported in the World Bank indicators for Zambia (World Bank, 2008).

Forest loss is mainly driven by wood extraction, agricultural expansion, infrastructure development, and illegal timber extraction (Kalinda et al., 2008; Vinya et al., 2011). Wood extraction frequently leads to deforestation because thinning for firewood or charcoal production facilitates subsequent clearing of land for agriculture (UN-REDD, 2010). Land clearing for agricultural expansion and charcoal production are among the largest drivers of wood extraction and the primary cause of forest degradation in Zambia (Clarke & Shackleton, 2007, Vinya et al., 2011). Timber and wood products are also extracted from forests in Zambia for housing and road construction (UNEP, 2015). Mining and forest fires also contribute to forest loss and degradation in Zambia (Mwitwa & Makano, 2012).

Charcoal is the primary source of energy for cooking among urban households in Zambia, as well as throughout much of SSA (Zulu & Richardson, 2013). About 5.8 million tons of wood biomass was used to produce charcoal in 2008 (Kalinda et al., 2008). Charcoal production accounted for one-quarter of the annual deforestation rate nationwide (Kalinda et al., 2008) and estimates from Chongwe District in the 1990s and Nyimba District in the 2000s suggest rates of about 30 percent of total deforestation (Chidumayo, 2001). Based on a conservative estimate of the rate of deforestation of 300,000 ha per year (World Bank, 2008), the rate of deforestation attributed to charcoal production is estimated at approximately 75,000 ha per year. The rate of deforestation attributed to charcoal varies between provinces and districts (Vinya et al., 2011), but it tends to be localized and closer to urban areas for easier access to markets. Charcoal production may not always lead to deforestation, however, because of the ability of many Miombo tree species to regenerate quickly after harvesting (Chidumayo & Murunda, 2010).

Firewood is the main source of energy in rural areas, with over 90 percent of rural households depending on wood to meet their energy requirements (Bwalya, 2011). Firewood is often collected from dead wood and rarely cut down from live trees. The estimated total dead wood biomass is around 434 million tons in Zambia (Kalinda et al., 2008). If the existing dead wood meets the rural energy demand, the impact of firewood harvesting on forest loss is presumably negligible. However, evidence shows that commercial harvesting of firewood in some parts of the country leads to high rates of extraction and hence to forest degradation (World Bank, 2008).

Estimates of forest cover loss from agricultural expansion are as high as 90 percent in Zambia (Vinya et al., 2011), though such estimates are inconsistent with other estimates of deforestation, such as that for charcoal production (Chidumayo, 2001). Forest loss from agricultural expansion is often associated with smallholder agriculture and unsustainable farming practices such as shifting cultivation (UN-REDD, 2010, Bwalya, 2011). There is also evidence of widespread encroachment into forest reserves and conversion of forest into agriculture. An estimated 78 percent of the total forested land has been openly accessed as a result of poor forest management (Chidumayo et al., 2001; Bwalya, 2011).

The two main drivers of forest loss—charcoal production and agricultural expansion—have been found to work in tandem in Zambia (UNEP, 2015). Wood extraction for charcoal is often followed by land clearing for agriculture because of the low marginal labor requirements to convert the land after the trees have been removed. Alternatively, the wood biomass from land cleared for agriculture may be used to produce charcoal, generating income for the smallholder farmer. There is, however, variation in the levels and causes of deforestation across the country and a poor understanding of causality (Dewees et al., 2011).

Charcoal Production and Use

Small-scale charcoal production typically involves cutting big trees into smaller logs and burning them in an earthen kiln. It is primarily the work of men and older boys in rural villages (Zulu & Richardson, 2013). Commercial production of charcoal involves greater mechanization and employs wage laborers, which is an important source of household income in rural areas.

Clarke and Shackleton (2007) found that charcoal producers practiced selective harvesting of preferred tree species in areas with abundant wood biomass and low demand for charcoal and clear-cutting harvesting in areas of high demand for charcoal. The former contributes to forest degradation, whereas the latter directly leads to deforestation. For example, Chidumayo (1993) attributed the removal of more than 50 percent of woody biomass in Miombo woodlands for charcoal production in Zambia. A variety of tree species are selectively cut for charcoal production, with preferred species in Miombo ecosystems being of the genera *Brachystegia*, *Julbernadia*, and *Isoberlinia* (Chidumayo, 1993; Dewees et al., 2011). The selection is determined by the density of the wood and tends to be associated with slower-growing trees.

Charcoal is a major source of income, a significant contributor to national energy balances, and a potential renewable energy source capable of powering significant economic growth (Arnold et al., 2006; Zulu & Richardson, 2013). Charcoal production and marketing are lucrative activities for both rural and urban households, and they are also coping strategies for the rural poor with limited livelihood options. A lack of alternative livelihoods makes the charcoal production business more attractive to young and unemployed people. Demand for transportation and marketing of charcoal creates jobs in both rural and urban areas (Mwitwa & Makano, 2012; Zulu & Richardson, 2013).

In Zambia, between 50 and 70 percent of urban low and middle-income households reportedly depend on charcoal for their cooking energy (Kalinda et al., 2008; Bwalya, 2011; Atteridge et al., 2013). There is a wide range of estimates of average monthly consumption of charcoal per household in Lusaka. Estimates range from an average of 58 kg (Chidumayo et al., 2001) to 114 kg per household per month (Atteridge et al., 2013). The widespread use of charcoal is driven by limited access to and high cost of electricity (Kalinda et al., 2008). Few rural households, however, use charcoal as a cooking source because of the loss in efficiency and additional labor required to produce charcoal from wood, as well as the availability of dead wood.

Alternative sources of energy are not widely available in Zambia. Adoption of available alternative energy sources is constrained by the high fixed costs of adoption. Electricity is a substitute for charcoal for some urban households, but regular supply disruption and high costs keep adoption relatively low. The supply is limited to only one-fifth of the population across the country (Foster & Dominguez, 2010) since many households are unable to afford the high connection fee (Haanyika, 2008). Few of the alternative sources of cooking fuel such as kerosene or liquid petroleum gas are used in Zambia. This may be due to a combination of strong preferences for charcoal and relatively low prices. Small 10-watt off-grid solar systems are available in Lusaka for about $240 (Atteridge et al., 2013), although there is limited information on adoption.

Methods

We used participatory system dynamics modeling to simulate the drivers of deforestation over a fifty-year period, 2010 to 2060. System Dynamics Modeling (SDM) is a quantitative modeling approach that uses systems thinking to analyze the impact of feedback loops in complex and dynamic systems. SDM has been applied in a variety of complex system contexts, ranging from business dynamics (Sterman, 2000) to environmental systems (Ford, 1999). SDM has been applied to the adoption and diffusion of new agricultural technologies (Kopainsky et al., 2012), agricultural development (Saysel et al., 2002), global climate change (Sterman, 2011), forest fire management (Collins et al., 2013), and water resource management (Simonovic, 2002; Stave, 2003), among other topics.

SDM captures the essential temporal self-regulating feature of many systems. This means that feedbacks among the system components incrementally adjust the state of the system. A change in one part of the system affects another that then affects others with some delay. Some of these changes will eventually feedback to amplify or dampen the effect of the original change. SD modeling recognizes that changes do not occur in isolation and many systems do not respond instantaneously to these changes.

Interactions between the system components are represented with causal feedback loops, which describe closed chains of cause-and-effect relationships. Two types of feedback loops exist: (1) positive or reinforcing feedback that gives rise to exponential growth or exponential decline (e.g., population growth is exponential because more people make more people) and (2) negative or balancing feedback that balances out change (e.g., an increase in deforestation leads to less available wood, thus potentially decreasing the absolute rate of change in deforestation). The result is often one of two outcomes. When a balancing feedback loop dominates, there is an oscillating or stable equilibrium. When a positive feedback occurs, there is exponential change. An important component of feedback loops are levels of stocks that change through their respective rates of flows. To measure the dynamics of changing levels of stocks and rates of flows, SD models solve a system of simultaneous differential equations.

Participatory modeling has grown in popularity in recent years as a tool to investigate environmental systems and generate consensus among stakeholders around environmental problems. System dynamics has been consistently used to incorporate stakeholder input into the model-building process and is easily adaptable to a participatory format (van den Belt, 2004). We used participatory system dynamics modeling as a framework to integrate stakeholders' knowledge with scientific analysis and develop a discussion among them about model dynamics.

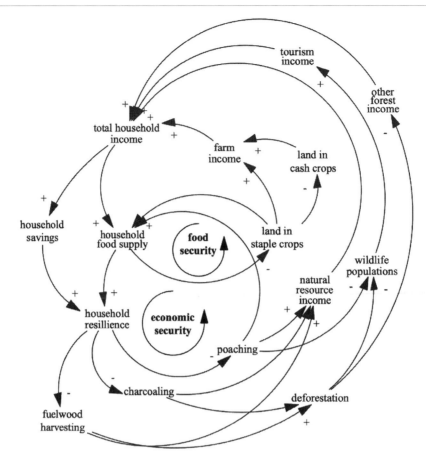

FIGURE 1. Causal loop diagram depicting the structure of the system dynamics model.

This approach is particularly useful for analyzing coupled human-environment systems with dynamic connections between social and ecological systems.

Participatory modeling is a broad field with a diverse set of methods, but generally the goal of constructing a model in collaboration with stakeholders is to elicit their views of a system and how it operates, and to use that information to inform the model. Interviews, textual analysis, focus group discussions, and participatory mapping and diagramming exercises are all techniques that are commonly used (Andersen & Richardson, 1998). We used group diagramming and scenario-building exercises in combination with key stakeholder interviews to build the participatory system dynamics model for this project. We did this to garner a diverse set of views and knowledge on the system, while drawing on the specialized knowledge of stakeholders who were unable to attend the group meetings. The model-building process was iterative, meaning that it involved the modeling team returning to the stakeholders repeatedly for further model development and feedback on what had been done so far.

We first identified and recruited stakeholders from partner organizations through purposive sampling. Approximately thirty-five representatives were identified from regional non-governmental organizations, international agricultural research centers, Zambian research institutes,

Table 1. Baseline values for model parameterization of national- and provincial-level models in Zambia

BASELINE VARIABLE	NATIONAL	EASTERN PROVINCE	LUSAKA PROVINCE	SOURCE
Miombo woodlands (ha)	34,145,000	2,892,450	556,251	ZFD (2008)
Deciduous and evergreen forests (ha)	15,823,000	1,548,800	297,850	ZFD (2008)
Grass and shrub lands (ha)	12,140,000	687,214	132,159	ZFD (2008)
Agricultural land (ha)	7,787,000	1,368,140	659,867	ZFD (2008)
Total area in maize (ha)	1,311,295	276,444	30,110	Tembo & Sitko (2012)
Total cotton area (ha)	131,691	1,463	2,107	Tembo & Sitko (2012)
Total groundnuts area (ha)	223,298	55,891	2,408	Tembo & Sitko (2012)
Average maize yield for small- and medium-scale farmers (kg/ha)	2,082	1,696	1,725	Tembo & Sitko (2012)
Average land cleared by new farmers (ha/year)	2.25	2.05	2.20	Jayne (2008)
Population (persons)	13,217,000	1,707,730	2,138.910	CSO (2011)
Rural population (persons)	7,996,285	1,392,338	336,318	CSO (2011)
Urban population (persons)	5,220,715	98,103	1,854,907	CSO (2011)
Average household size (persons)	5.3	5.0	4.8	CSO (2011)
Average electrification rate	23%	3%	48%	Singh et al. (2013)
Per capita fuelwood consumption per month, rural (kg/person)	85.42			Kalumiana (1997)
Per capita charcoal consumption per month, urban (kg/person)	7.45			Mulenga et al. (2014)

and local implementation organizations. We then organized two workshops that were held in May 2014 in Mfuwe (Eastern Province) and Lusaka (Lusaka Province) with these representatives. Workshop participants were asked to identify the drivers of the problems that their organizations work on related to agriculture and the environment. They generated different causal loop diagrams representing processes driving food security, economic security, energy security, land management, and population pressures. These causal loop diagrams were later integrated into one diagram that became the conceptual map used to build the system dynamics model (figure 1).

We used the synthesized causal loop diagram to construct a system dynamics model of land use change in Zambia using Vensim, a simulation software for modeling complex systems. The reference mode of behavior is the continuous cultivation of maize by smallholder farmers, and SI practices were modeled as alternative agricultural technologies. Model parameters were drawn from the literature and existing datasets, including rural household survey data and land use data (Kalumiana, 1997; Jayne, 2008; ZFD, 2008; CSO, 2011; Tembo and Sitko, 2012; Mulenga et al., 2014). Many of these parameters are discussed earlier in the reviews of literature on SI and forests in Zambia. Datasets included information on land area by category, agricultural land area by crop, population at various scales, and per capita consumption of firewood and charcoal for rural and urban households, respectively. Baseline values for model parameterization of national- and provincial-level models are presented in table 1.

The national-level model consists of three subsystems: (1) landscape, (2) population, and (3) agriculture and drought. Each of these modules represents stocks and flows. At the core of the landscape module is a chain of different types of forest stocks disaggregated into three categories:

(1) Miombo woodlands, (2) deciduous and evergreen forests, and (3) grass and shrub land. The disaggregation follows the classification of forest types used in the ILUA (ZFD, 2008). The flows represent rates of change in forest cover types at the following five stages: (1) natural regrowth, (2) conversion into agricultural land, (3) deforestation for charcoal and firewood, (4) land and forest degradation, and (5) land abandonment. The model assumes that each of the three land cover types can be converted into agricultural land and can lead to degraded land over time with unsustainable farming practices. Degraded land is restored through fallowing and regeneration processes to any of the three forest types. The restoration was simulated using separate rates of regrowth. For example, the rate of regrowth for Miombo woodlands was set at 1.93 m^3 per ha per year, per Chidumayo (1988). Miombo woodland and deciduous forests are degraded through selective cutting for charcoal production or industrial round wood. Deadwood and trimmings of branches are harvested for fuelwood, with a small proportion of households that cut down live tree in degraded natural forests.

Other exogenous variables in the model affect the rates of flow, including urban charcoal demand, rural demand for firewood, efficiency of charcoal kilns, deadwood biomass, relative price of electricity, and electrification rate among others. The structure described above forms the core of the landscape module for all three models.

A third stakeholder workshop was held in August 2014 in Chisamba, Zambia and focused on validating the assumptions and parameters used in the national landscape-level model. Small group discussions centered on the initial model behavior and dynamics and interventions, which would disrupt the model behavior. Discussion also focused on the assumptions and data underlying the model and scenarios or policies that might change the operation of the model. We attempted to validate stakeholder feedback with other data and literature before we incorporated it into the model. For example, during the workshop, participants expressed skepticism that rural fuelwood gathering was contributing significantly to deforestation (as the model then depicted), since most believed that rural Zambians collect deadwood to burn rather than cutting live trees. Consequently, using findings from literature, we changed the model algorithm to reduce the amount of deforestation associated with fuelwood collection by rural households.

The feedback from these workshops was used to develop two provincial-level models for Eastern Province and Lusaka Province. These models were validated in a fourth interaction with stakeholders via a conference on improving integration among agriculture, forestry, and land tenure, held in Lusaka in June 2015. This conference was attended by many of the same stakeholders who participated in the earlier workshops and included presentations on the contributions of the stakeholder organizations to integrated programming to address agricultural-environmental linkages.

Throughout the participatory modeling process, the interventions discussed by participants focused on three broad categories: more-efficient energy sources, energy governance (such as legalization and enforcement of charcoal production and marketing), and social programs targeting fuelwood consumption such as community-based natural resources management. Scenarios identified that needed further exploration ranged from human-environment conflict to exogenous market scenarios and development-led scenarios.

Model Sensitivity Analysis and Validation

We conducted a sensitivity analysis on the model by varying each input variable between +50 percent and –50 percent of its baseline input value and observing the effect on deforestation trends. Fifty values of the input variable were selected for the sensitivity analysis across a random uniform distribution of between +50 percent and –50 percent of baseline input value.

The model was validated in three ways, following best practices for system dynamics model validation (Barlas, 1996): (1) through expert opinion, by interviewing stakeholders with key insights into real-world trends and variables depicted in the model; (2) by comparison with other estimates of deforestation rates in Zambia drawn from the Zambian government, the World Bank, and published literature; and (3) through testing model behavior in "extreme" scenarios to observe internal model consistency.

Findings and Simulation Scenarios

We first present the baseline scenario for the national-level model, which represents how the system is likely to perform with no interventions. In the baseline scenario, we simulated deforestation by each of the main national drivers, including charcoal production and forest clearing for fuelwood harvesting from cutting down live trees, extraction of wood for construction and timber production, as well as agricultural expansion. We built two provincial-level models for Eastern and Lusaka Provinces using the same basic structure of the national-level model. Then we ran four additional scenarios that are related to the relative contribution of both agriculture and wood fuels to deforestation. We simulated the effects of drought, maize yield increase, full electrification, and fuel-efficient stoves on forest cover in Zambia in each province. The drought scenario included an assumption that a moderate drought occurs every eight years and affects 40 percent of the total agricultural land and a severe drought occurs every forty years and affects 70 percent of the area under cultivation. The maize yield-increase scenario included an assumption that maize yields would increase three-fold primarily from the practice of sustainable intensification. The electrification scenario included an assumption of full provision of electrification nationwide. Finally, the fuel-efficiency scenario included an assumption of 100 percent adoption of efficient stoves, which are estimated to use 55 percent less charcoal (Luganda, 2013).

Results and Discussion of National-Level Model

The results of the baseline scenario on forest loss by forest type over a fifty-year period (from 2010 to 2060) are presented in figure 2 for the national model, including simulated national deforestation rates for deciduous and evergreen forest (2a) and Miombo woodlands (2b). The national model simulated an area loss of 156,364 ha of all forest types in 2010. The simulated deforestation rate is lower than those reported by FAO (2010) at 167,000 ha in 2010 or even the range of 250,000 to 300,000 ha reported in the ILUA study by Kalinda et al. (2008) and Mukosha and Siampale (2009). The slightly lower rate may be attributed to the exclusion of mining and

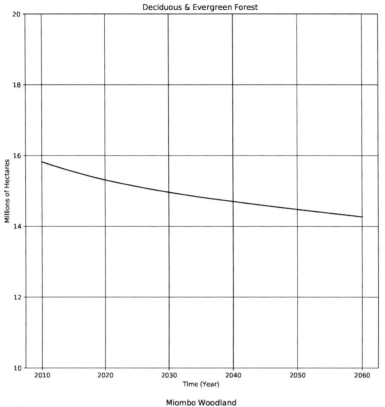

FIGURE 2A. Simulated national deforestation rates for deciduous and evergreen forest in the baseline scenario.

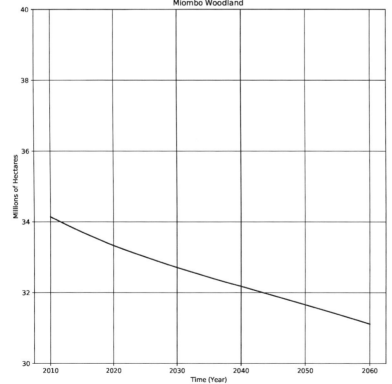

FIGURE 2B. Simulated national deforestation rates for Miombo woodlands in the baseline scenario.

infrastructure development, as well as the additional demand for wood by agriculture and industry in Zambia (Vinya et al., 2011). CSO (2013) estimated an additional 1.2 million tons of firewood and 48,000 tons of charcoal used in agriculture, industry, and mining in 2010. In terms of relative decline in the total forest cover, the model reported a simulated value of 0.33 percent in 2010, which is consistent with that reported by World Bank (2008).

The deciduous and evergreen forest type would decline by 2.84 million ha or 18 percent in 2060, suggesting a deforestation rate of approximately 56,880 ha per year. The Miombo woodland areas would reduce by 14 percent, or 4.77 million ha over a fifty-year period, which translates to a loss of 95,000 ha of Miombo area per year. Applying the estimated rate of 79.37 tons of wood produced per ha in intact forests (Kalinda et al., 2008), a total of over 12 million tons of wood per year would be produced from the simulated total area of 153,350 ha in both forest cover types. Assuming an average density of 750 kg per m^3 (UNEP, 2015), this suggests a minimum extraction of over 16 million m^3 of wood per year across the country. Considering the additional wood demand in the agricultural and mining sectors, the annual wood extraction would rise over 17.6 million m^3, representing the lower bound of wood extraction.

Figures 3a and 3b depict the deforestation by each driver at the national level. Agricultural expansion accounted for the largest proportion of deforestation in 2010. The model simulated approximately 28,000 ha cleared for agriculture compared to about 7,000 ha of forest lost to charcoal production. The model simulated an increase of about 40 percent in agricultural expansion in 2060. The contribution of charcoal production to deforestation would nearly quadruple from approximately 8,500 ha per year to more than 34,000 by 2060 (figure 3a). Our results support the prevalence of both charcoal production and agricultural expansion as national drivers of deforestation reported in various studies in Zambia (Kalinda et al., 2008; Vinya et al., 2011; Mulenga et al., 2014). At the national level, the simulations showed similar patterns for most drivers in the Miombo woodlands, with the exception of commercial timber harvesting (figure 3b). The simulations revealed that the contribution of agricultural expansion to deforestation would increase slowly, while the share from charcoal production would more than quadruple to nearly 70,000 ha/year.

Results and Discussion of Eastern Province Model

The results of the baseline model for Eastern Province are summarized in figure 4. The Eastern Province model simulated a loss of over 11,000 ha of deciduous and evergreen forest in 2010 or a rate of 0.74 percent per year (4a). Similarly, the simulation suggested a lower relative decline in Miombo woodlands at 0.54 percent, but a higher deforested area of over 15,000 ha in 2010 (4b). Having applied the estimated rate of 79.37 tons of wood per ha produced in intact forests (Kalinda et al., 2008), the simulation results suggest the extraction of at least 2.1 million tons of wood in all forest types in 2010. Assuming an average density of 750 kg per m^3 (UNEP, 2015), this would translate into approximately 2.75 million m^3 of wood biomass harvested in 2010.

The model further simulated a total forest loss of 350,000 to 490,000 ha in Eastern Province over the next fifty years. Such loss represents an estimated annual deforestation rate between 7,000 and 9,800 ha per year in deciduous and Miombo woodlands, respectively. Figure 5a

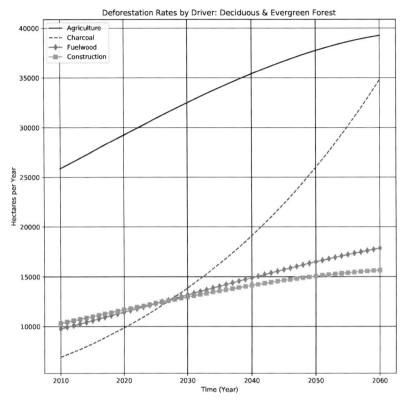

FIGURE 3A. National deforestation rates by driver for deciduous and evergreen forest in the baseline scenario in Zambia.

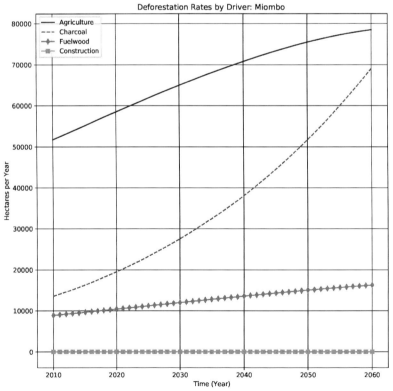

FIGURE 3B. National deforestation rates by driver for Miombo woodlands in the baseline scenario in Zambia.

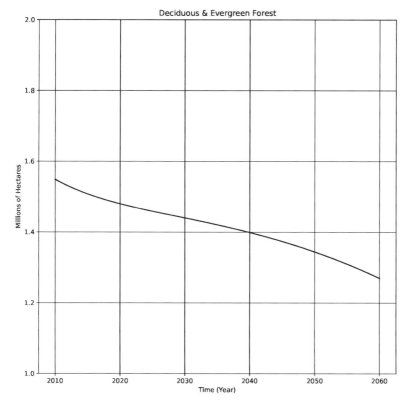

FIGURE 4A. Simulated deforestation rates for deciduous and evergreen forest in the baseline scenario in Eastern Province.

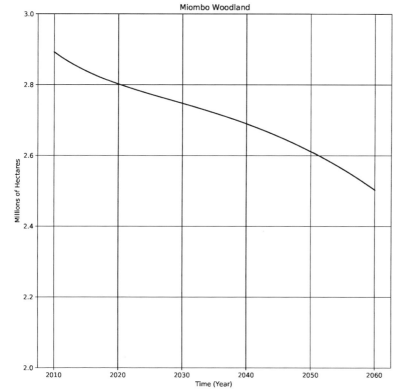

FIGURE 4B. Simulated deforestation rates for Miombo woodlands in the baseline scenario in Eastern Province.

illustrates that forest loss in Eastern Province is mainly driven by agricultural expansion and charcoal production. The model simulated a quadrupling of deforestation from charcoal production, rising up to 15,000 ha per year in 2060. Agricultural expansion would increase by 120 percent over the fifty years to approximately 11,000 ha in 2060. The simulation results suggested charcoal production would induce more deforestation than agricultural expansion by about 2045.

The simulation further showed similar patterns for the drivers of deforestation of the Miombo woodland, but with even greater contributions from land clearing for agriculture and charcoal production (figure 5b). The simulation suggests that charcoal production would require the clearing of over 26,000 ha of Miombo woodland in Eastern Province in 2060. Similarly, land clearing for agriculture in all forest types increased by 48 percent in Miombo woodland alone in 2010, doubling by 2060. The large clearing of Miombo woodland for charcoal production supports the preference of tree species of the genera *Brachystegia*, *Julbernadia*, and *Isoberlinia* for charcoal production reported by many studies like (Chidumayo, 1993; Dewees et al., 2011).

Scenario Analysis for Eastern Province

The first scenario simulated for the Eastern Province model is the effect of drought on forest cover change. The model reported negligible effects of both moderate and severe droughts on forest cover loss, even if all maize farmers practice CA. Grabowski and Kerr (2014) reported an average maize yield of 1,260 kg per ha for poor farmers in rural areas. The model assumes production loss of 40 percent or 70 percent of the maize area depending on the drought severity, which is translated into a total loss of production for the portion of farmers who use drought-prone land. The main impact of drought on forest loss in the model occurred among farmers who experience crop losses and turned to charcoal production as a coping strategy.

We also simulated a three-fold increase in maize yield on forest cover change and the scenario revealed no change in the current rate of land clearing in both deciduous and evergreen forests as well as in Miombo woodlands. Assuming an average maize yield of 1,696 kg per ha for rural smallholder, the yield-increase simulation suggests a smallholder maize yield of over 5,000 kg per ha. Attaining such levels of productivity would require a tailoring of agricultural technologies that suit specific locations across the country. These may include no-till methods, crop protection, integrated soil fertility management, drought-tolerant and high-yielding crop varieties, water harvesting, and/or a combination of improved technologies. Thus, the model reported only negligible effects of both moderate and severe droughts and increased maize yields on forest cover loss in Eastern Province. In fact, these effects do not appear on graphs depicting the simulations.

The next scenario we simulated was the impact of full electrification coverage on forest cover change. Full electrification would have marginal effects on deforestation in Eastern Province (figure 6). The model reported a reduction in lost forest cover of deciduous and evergreen forest of about 250,000 ha over the fifty-year period compared with the baseline scenario. This loss reduction averaged 350,000 ha in the Miombo woodland over the same time period. Full electrification would conserve about 6,000 ha of forest cover per year in Eastern Province. This

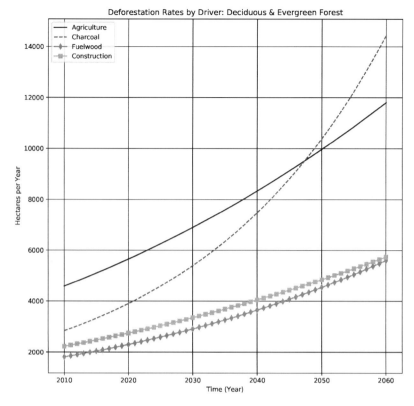

FIGURE 5A.
Simulated
deforestation
rates by driver for
deciduous and
evergreen forest
in the baseline
scenario in Eastern
Province.

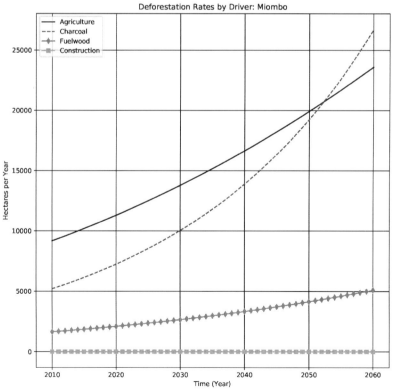

FIGURE 5B.
Simulated
deforestation
rates by driver for
Miombo woodlands
in the baseline
scenario in Eastern
Province.

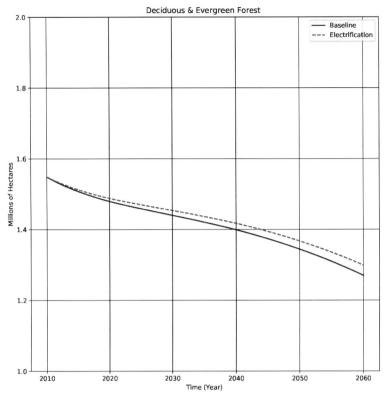

FIGURE 6A1.
Simulated results of the effects of full electrification on land cover change for deciduous and evergreen forest in Eastern Province.

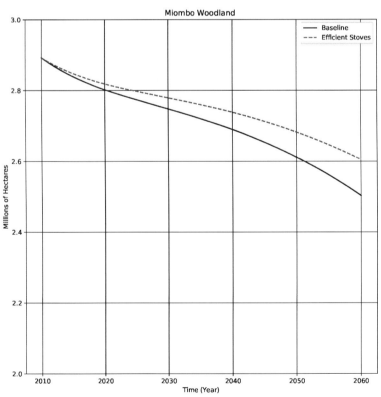

FIGURE 6A2.
Simulated results of the effects of full electrification on land cover change for Miombo woodlands in Eastern Province.

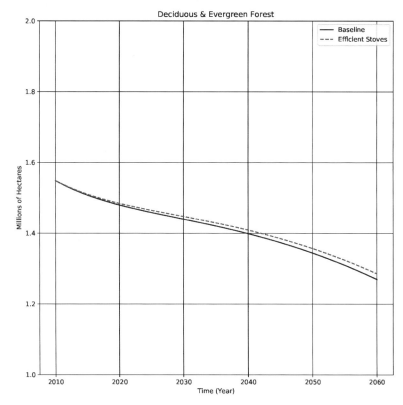

FIGURE 6B1. Simulated results of the effects of efficient cook stoves on land cover change for deciduous and evergreen forest in Eastern Province.

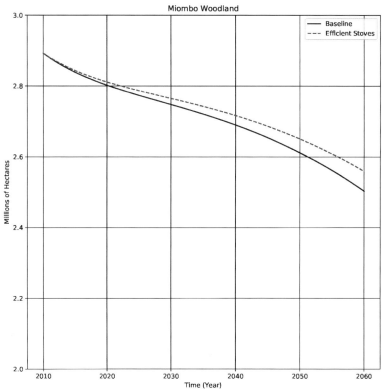

FIGURE 6B2. Simulated results of the effects of efficient cook stoves on land cover change for Miombo woodlands in Eastern Province.

low reduction is explained by the greater proportion of rural population in Eastern Province for whom electrification would not replace woodfuels as a primary source of energy.

The final scenario we simulated for the Eastern Province model was widespread use of more fuel-efficient stoves on forest cover change. The use of efficient stoves would induce marginal reductions in forest loss in Eastern Province. The model reported reduced loss in forest cover over time for both forest cover types compared with the baseline scenario (figure 6b). The reduction in forest loss was about 62,500 ha in deciduous and evergreen forest type over the simulation time period. This suggests an average loss reduction of approximately 1,250 ha per year in the same forest type. Loss reductions in Miombo woodland are four times that in the deciduous forest, simulated at 250,000 ha. The use of efficient stoves would conserve about 5,000 ha of Miombo woodland area per year.

Results and Discussion of Lusaka Province Model

The baseline model for Lusaka Province illustrates a total forest loss of about 3,600 ha, or 1.23 percent of deciduous and evergreen forest in 2010. Higher losses were simulated in the Miombo woodlands, reaching 5,170 ha, or 0.93 percent of forest cover in the same year (figure 7). If we apply the estimated rate of 79.37 tons of wood produced per ha in intact forests by Kalinda et al. (2008), the simulation results suggest a partial extraction of over 700,000 tons of wood in both the deciduous forests and Miombo woodlands in 2010. Assuming an average density of 750 kg per m^3 (UNEP, 2015), this would represent approximately 930,000 m^3 of wood biomass harvested in 2010. The simulation results suggest forests and woodlands in Lusaka province are overexploited (e.g., Chidumayo, 2001), despite their seemingly low loss rates. Lusaka, therefore, likely relies heavily on imports from forest-rich provinces to supply both charcoal and timber needs.

The model further showed a sharp decline in both forest and woodland cover types over time. Each of these forest cover types is projected to decline by at least 87 percent by 2060. This suggests an average loss of about 260,000 ha in deciduous and evergreen forests over fifty years, or about 5,170 ha per year. Loss in Miombo woodland would almost double that in deciduous forest, simulated at 487,000 ha over fifty years, or over 9,700 ha per year. The results indicated a sharp increase in the rate of deforestation by 44 to 88 percent in simulated forest and woodland cover types over time. The model further suggested a complete collapse of the forest and woodland in the next sixty to seventy years. The total land clearing of 14,870 ha by 2060 would represent over 1.5 million m^3 of wood biomass, which suggests that meeting the charcoal and timber demand in Lusaka province would require a clearing of over 10,000 ha of land in other provinces.

The simulation showed that charcoal production is the most important driver of deforestation in deciduous and evergreen forests, increasing exponentially over time. Land clearing for charcoal production would increase by over eleven-fold, or 1025 percent, from 2,000 ha in 2010 to 22,500 ha by 2060 (figure 8a). Charcoal production alone would require over 2.38 million m^3 of biomass wood in 2060. The second important driver was land conversion for agriculture, which would increase by 3.5-fold, from about 2,000 to over 7,000 ha of land clearing by 2060. Fuelwood and wood harvesting for construction showed similar patterns of marginal increases over the simulation time.

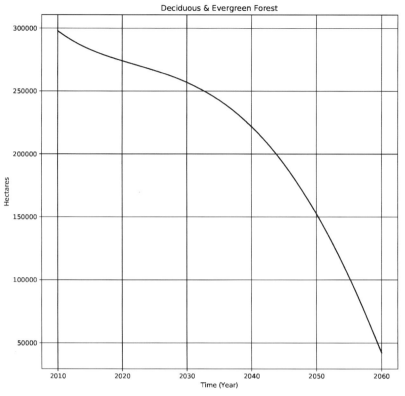

FIGURE 7A.
Simulated deforestation rates for deciduous and evergreen forest in the baseline scenario in Lusaka Province.

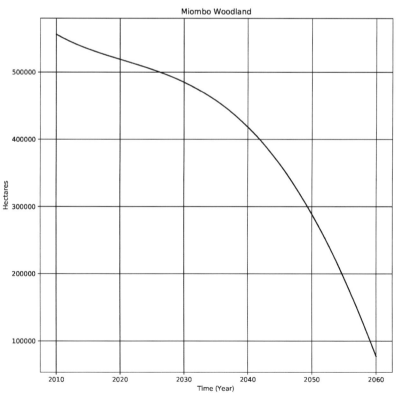

FIGURE 7B.
Simulated deforestation rates for Miombo woodlands in the baseline scenario in Lusaka Province.

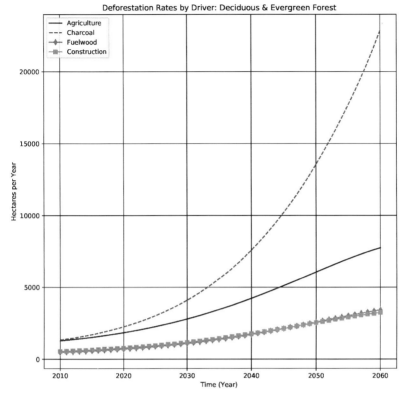

FIGURE 8A. Simulated deforestation rates by driver for deciduous and evergreen forest in the baseline scenario in Lusaka Province.

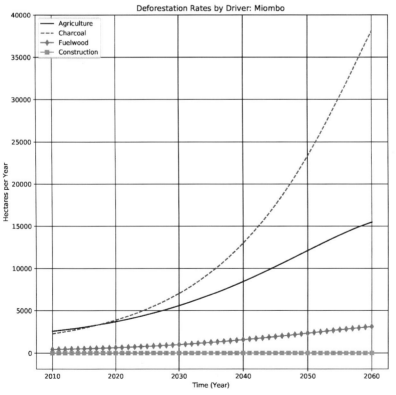

FIGURE 8B. Simulated deforestation rates by driver for Miombo woodlands in the baseline scenario in Lusaka Province.

The model showed the same pattern in the Miombo woodlands, with higher levels of land clearing than in other forest types (figure 8b). Charcoal production would increase land clearing by around nineteen-fold, rising up to 38,000 ha by 2060 in the Miombo woodlands. Similarly, land conversion for agriculture would increase up to 10,000 ha, increasing by five-fold over the fifty-year time period. The simulation results support the findings that charcoal production is the most important driver of deforestation in Lusaka province (Vinya et al., 2011). It further emphasizes the preference of Miombo woodlands for charcoal production as well as its vulnerability to overexploitation of wood extraction (e.g., Dewees et al., 2011). Moreover, the exponential increase in land clearing for charcoal production over time reflects the exponential growth in energy needs of the urban population. Our findings are consistent with studies in many other countries in ssa, where charcoal demand is expected to increase for several decades with the fast growing urbanization (Arnold et al., 2006; Zulu and Richardson, 2013).

Scenario Analysis for Lusaka Province Model

The first scenario simulated was the effects of drought on forest cover change. Similar to Eastern Province, the model reported negligible effects of both moderate and severe droughts and increased maize yields on forest cover loss if all maize farmers practice ca in Lusaka Province. The same result was revealed for the scenario that simulated the effect of a three-fold increase in maize yields. The effects of both moderate and severe droughts and increased maize yields on forest cover loss in Lusaka Province were so minor that they do not appear on graphs depicting the simulations.

The next scenario we simulated was the impact of full electrification coverage in Zambia on forest cover change. Full electrification showed significant effects on land cover loss in Eastern Province (figure 9a). The model reported a total reduction in the loss of both deciduous forests and Miombo woodlands of about 487,500 ha over five decades compared with the baseline scenario. This suggests that full electrification would conserve about 9,750 ha of the total forest cover per year in Lusaka Province. In addition, over 75 percent of this total loss reduction would occur in Miombo woodlands over the same time period. The simulation suggests that full electrification is likely to reduce more than half the current rate of deforestation in simulated forest types over the next fifty years in Lusaka Province. The loss reduction is higher in the Miombo woodlands, estimated at 68 percent of the area being currently cleared in the Province. These loss reductions are attributable to the large population of urban dwellers in Lusaka province, and the high use of charcoal among them. Curbing charcoal use would therefore have a disproportionate impact on conserving forest in Lusaka province.

The final scenario we simulated was the impact of widespread use of fuel-efficient stoves on forest cover change. The use of efficient stoves would induce significant reductions in forest loss in Lusaka Province. The model reported increased loss reductions in forest cover over time compared with the baseline scenario, totaling 237,500 ha by 2060 (figure 9b). Over two-thirds of the projected loss reduction would occur in Miombo woodlands alone, with a simulated area of 150,000 ha over the five decades, or 3,000 ha per year. About 87,500 ha would be conserved in the deciduous forest, representing an average annual loss reduction of 1,750 ha over the same

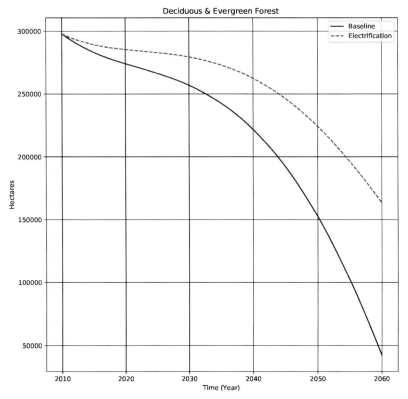

FIGURE 9A1. Simulated results of the effects of full electrification on land cover change for deciduous and evergreen forest in Lusaka Province.

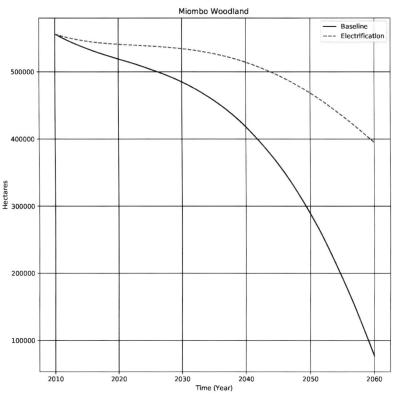

FIGURE 9A2. Simulated results of the effects of full electrification on land cover change for Miombo woodlands in Lusaka Province.

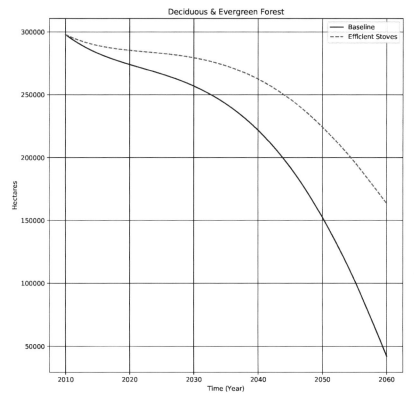

FIGURE 9B1.
Simulated results
of the effects of
efficient cook
stoves on land
cover change for
deciduous and
evergreen forest in
Lusaka Province.

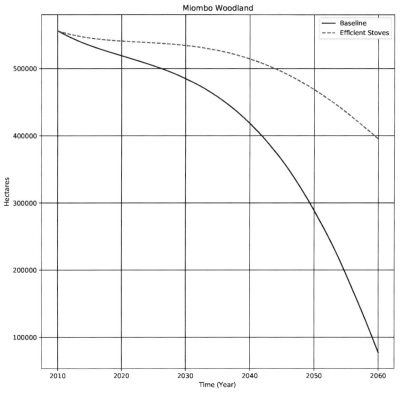

FIGURE 9B2.
Simulated results
of the effects of
efficient cook
stoves on land cover
change for Miombo
woodlands in
Lusaka Province.

time period compared with the baseline. The simulation suggested that efficient stoves would reduce the current rate of deforestation by 69 percent in all forest types, rising up to 71 percent in Miombo woodlands alone. Our results support ongoing initiatives of fuel-efficient cook stoves by various NGOs in urban areas. It is, however, important to note that such initiatives should be spatially targeted in order to yield desirable outcomes.

Results of Sensitivity Analysis and Validation

Model results at the national level and for both provinces were highly sensitive to changes in population growth rates, which is logical as all forms of deforestation are driven by population growth in the model. This implies that, if Zambia were to experience dramatic changes in projected population growth rates over the coming decades, the model results may no longer be valid. However, the United Nations Population Division estimates of Zambia's population growth do not range widely over the next fifty to one hundred years, as they do for other countries in ssA (United Nations, 2012). All estimates of population growth, including those assuming the presence of interventions targeted at reducing birth rates, depict high population growth and urbanization rates for Zambia.

The Lusaka model and the national model results are highly sensitive to efficiencies of charcoal production, and all models are somewhat sensitive to electrification rates and stove efficiency, as described in some detail above. These variables were targeted for intervention through our scenario analysis.

The process of stakeholder consultation that facilitated the building the model served as a form of validation, with Zambian experts confirming the model's underlying logic. As described above, estimates of deforestation in our model were largely consistent with other estimates of deforestation rates in the country. Historical, longitudinal data sets are sparse in Zambia, so we were unable to "backcast" with our model. We did conduct the following "extreme-scenario" tests for the national level model: halting all deforestation in Zambia; population doubling due to in-migration; and massive and frequent drought on a nationwide scale. For each of these extreme scenarios, model behavior was consistent with internal logic (respectively, widespread clearing of grassland for agriculture and an end to charcoal production; much higher rates of deforestation; and more frequent "spikes" in charcoal production activity caused by household income-earning activities during drought years).

Conclusions

This study examined the agricultural-environmental linkages in Eastern and Lusaka Provinces in Zambia with a focus on the implications of farm-level decisions for landscape-level impacts. A comprehensive literature review reveals that these agricultural-environmental linkages in the context of Zambia are complex and dynamic, especially in light of rapid population growth and urbanization. The results of the participatory system dynamics model demonstrate that agricultural expansion is currently the largest contributor to forest loss, but in the future, charcoal production will soon outstrip expansion. At the provincial level, there are different patterns.

Charcoal production dominates in Lusaka Province throughout the fifty-year simulation time, primarily because of urban demand. By contrast, agricultural expansion dominates in Eastern Province until about 2045, at which point charcoal production becomes the dominant driver.

Charcoal production is driven by urban population growth and energy demand. Agricultural expansion is driven by rural population growth, as opposed to low yields and/or land abandonment. Currently, wood is extracted in an unsustainable way from forests and woodlands, posing a threat to the remaining forest and woodland resources across the country. Moreover, Miombo woodlands are the most vulnerable to deforestation of all forest cover types in Zambia despite their ability to regenerate. The results support other projections of the expected increase in charcoal demand as a result of rapid urbanization (e.g., Zulu and Richardson, 2013). Reducing charcoal consumption would likely involve coordinated policies that address rural household dependence on charcoal as an income source in addition to policies that seek to reduce urban charcoal demand.

The main objective of the project was to examine evidence of linkages between SI practices and climate change mitigation and forest conservation. For the reasons described in the summary of agricultural-environmental linkages, the overall conclusion is that there is no evidence of linkages between adoption of sustainable intensification practices (such as CA and agroforestry) and environmental objectives in terms of climate change mitigation, forest protection, and wildlife conservation. There is theoretical and empirical evidence that agriculture can have negative implications on wildlife when promoted in areas where human-wildlife conflict is likely (Richardson et al., 2013). However, the cause is related to encouraging agricultural activities in sensitive areas more generally, not the promotion of SI or CA specifically. Agroforestry appears to have a net positive effect on biodiversity (for some species), and on-farm fuelwood provision from agroforestry is of particular benefit to women and children in rural Zambia by reducing their burden of walking long distances to collect firewood due to local scarcity. However, given the minimal contribution of firewood collection in rural areas to overall deforestation, the results suggest that agroforestry will contribute little to reduce the largest driver of deforestation, which is the rapidly rising demand for charcoal consumption in urban areas. Therefore, we conclude that in the context of agricultural development in Zambia, there is little evidence of linkages between adoption of SI practices and either forest protection objectives associated with climate change mitigation or forest conservation.

The findings of this study highlight the fact that linkages between farm-scale practices and landscape-level impacts on ecosystems are not well understood. In many cases, closely held (but poorly examined) assumptions often influence or guide agricultural development investments intended to achieve sustainable intensification. Participatory system dynamics modeling can be used to test those assumptions and determine priorities for development investments. In this case, the dominant theory of change guiding the promotion of CA and agroforestry was based on the assumption that adoption of these practices would reduce need for land conversion, but the findings of the study revealed that rural population growth and urban demand for energy were the dominant drivers of deforestation.

Given the high uncertainty in the data surrounding deforestation rates in Zambia and the often-conflicting narratives surrounding sustainable intensification, it was critical that we involved a wide variety of stakeholders with intimate knowledge of Zambian forestry and agricultural systems in the construction of the model. Bringing together this diverse group to discuss the long-term dynamics of Zambian landscapes revealed key areas of disagreement (for example, regarding the benefits of CA), as well as the inaccuracy of some of the assumptions the modelers made (regarding rates of fuelwood harvesting, as described above). There were numerous examples of the benefits of using the participatory modeling approach, including interactions in which participants expressed skepticism about particular model assumptions; when their skepticism was validated in the literature, we changed the model algorithm to reflect the shared agreement about the assumption. This study highlights one often-overlooked but important reason to do participatory modeling—when data is uncertain and unavailable, local scientists and stakeholders who work within the systems being modeled can provide important context and information that enhances the model's accuracy. If we had performed a purely expert-driven modeling exercise, we would also have missed the opportunity to define model variables in ways that were important and relevant to Zambian scientists.

In spite of the advantages of constructing the model in a participatory manner, some members of the project team were initially skeptical of the approach. Participatory modeling is time-consuming, and for those unfamiliar with the process, it can be difficult to see the end result based on initial diagramming exercises, which seemed frivolous and not sufficiently rigorous to some team members. However, by the end of the model-building process, when the interactive model and the results were presented, previously skeptical team members saw the utility of both the tools and the process. Learning from this experience, we suggest that participatory modeling teams take special care to explain the process and the steps involved to all relevant team members at the beginning of the project.

ACKNOWLEDGMENTS

This research was made possible by funding from the United States Agency for International Development (USAID), which supports research and programming in sustainable intensification, climate change mitigation, and biodiversity conservation.

REFERENCES

Agriculture for Impact. (2013). *Sustainable intensification: A new paradigm for African agriculture: A 2013 Montpellier Panel Report.* https://ag4impact.org/.

Ajayi, O. C., Franzel, S., Kuntashula, E., & Kwesiga, F. (2003). Adoption of improved fallow soil fertility management practices in Zambia: Synthesis and emerging issues. *Agroforestry Systems, 59*(3), 317–326.

Ajayi O. C., Place, F., Akinnifesi, F. K., & Sileshi, G. W. (2011). Agricultural success from Africa: the case of fertilizer tree systems in Southern Africa (Malawi, Tanzania, Mozambique, Zambia and Zimbabwe). *International Journal of Agricultural Sustainability, 9,* 129–136.

Akinnifesi, F. K., Ajayi, O. C., Sileshi, G., Chirwa, P. W., & Chianu, J. (2010). Fertilizer trees for sustainable food security in the maize-based production systems of East and Southern Africa: A review. *Agronomy* for Sustainable Development, 30, 615–629.

Akinnifesi, F. K., Chirwa, P., Ajayi, O. C., Sileshi, G. W., Matakala, P., Kwesiga, F., Harawa, R., & Makumba, W. (2008). Contributions of agroforestry research to livelihood of smallholder farmers in southern Africa: Part 1. Taking stock of the adaptation, adoption and impacts of fertilizer tree options. *Journal of Agricultural Research, 3,* 58–75.

Albrecht, A., & Kandji, S. T. (2003). Carbon sequestration in tropical agroforestry systems. *Agriculture, Ecosystems & Environment 99,* 15–27.

Andersen, D. F., & Richardson, G. P. (1998). Scripts for group model building. *System Dynamics Review, 13*(2), 107–129.

Andersson, J. A., & D'Souza, S. (2014). From adoption claims to understanding farmers and contexts: A literature review of Conservation Agriculture (CA) adoption among smallholder farmers in southern Africa. *Agriculture, Ecosystems & Environment, 187,* 116–132.

Angelsen, A., & Kaimowitz, D. (2001). *Agricultural technologies and tropical deforestation.* New York: CABI Publishing.

Arnold, J. E. M., Köhlin, G., & Persson, R. (2006). Woodfuels, livelihoods, and policy interventions: changing perspectives. *World Development, 34* (3), 596–611.

Arslan, A., McCarthy, N., Lipper, L., Asfaw, S., & Cattaneo, A. (2014). Adoption and intensity of adoption of conservation farming practices in Zambia. *Agriculture, Ecosystems & Environment, 187,* 72–86.

Atteridge, A., Marcus, H., & Senyagwa, J. (2013). Transforming household energy practices among charcoal users in Lusaka, Zambia: A user-centered approach. Working Paper 2013–04, Stockholm Environment Institute.

Barlas, Y. (1996). Formal aspects of model validity and validation in system dynamics. *System Dynamics Review, 12*(3): 183–210.

Baudron, F., Mwanza, H.M., Triomphe, B., & Bwalya, M. (2007). *Conservation agriculture in Zambia: A case study of Southern Province.* Nairobi: African Conservation Tillage Network.

Baudron, F., Tittonell, P., Corbeels, M., Letourmy, P., & Giller, K. E. (2012). Comparative performance of conservation agriculture and current smallholder farming practices in semi-arid Zimbabwe. *Field Crops Research, 132,* 117–128.

Brouder, S.M., & Gomez-McPherson, H. (2014). The impact of conservation agriculture on smallholder agricultural yields: a scoping review of the evidence. *Agriculture, Ecosystems & Environment 187,* 11–32.

Bwalya, S. M. (2011). Household dependence on forest income in rural Zambia. *Zambia Social Science Journal, 2*(1).

Chidumayo, E. N. (1988). Estimating fuelwood production and yield in regrowth of dry Miombo woodland in Zambia. *Forest Ecology and Management, 24*(1), 59–66.

Chidumayo, E. N. (1990). Above-ground woody biomass structure and productivity in a Zambezian woodland. *Forest Ecology and Management, 36,* 33–46.

Chidumayo, E. N. (1993). Zambian charcoal production: Miombo woodland recovery. *Energy Policy, 12,* 586–597.

Chidumayo, E. N. (2001). Land cover transformation in central Zambia: role of agriculture, biomass energy and rural livelihoods. Paper presented at the Kyoto International Community House Symposium "Area Studies: Past experiences and Future Visions." Kyoto University, Kyoto, Japan.

Chidumayo, E. N., Masaileti, I., Ntalasha, H., & Kalumiana, O. S. (2001). *Charcoal potential in southern Africa (CHAPOSA)—report for Zambia.* Stockholm: Stockholm Environment Institute.

Chidumayo, E. N., & Murunda, C. (2010). Dry forests and woodlands in sub-Saharan Africa: Context and challenges. In Chidumayo, E. & Gumbo, D. (Eds.), *The dry forests and woodlands of Africa: Managing for products and services* (pp. 1–10). London: Earthscan.

Chirwa, P. W., Ong, C. K., Maghembe, J., Black, C. R. (2007). Soil water dynamics in intercropping systems containing *Gliricidia sepium,* pigeon pea and maize in Southern Malawi. *Agroforestry Systems, 69,* 29–43.

Clarke, C., & Shackleton, J. (2007). *Research and management of Miombo woodlands for products in support of local livelihoods.* Johannesburg: Genesis Analytics.

Cleland, J. (2013). World population growth: Past, present, and future. *Environmental and Resource Economics, 55*(4), 543–554.

Collins, R. D., de Neufville, R., Claro, J., Oliveira, T., & Pacheco, A. P. (2013). Forest fire management to avoid unintended consequences: A case study of Portugal using system dynamics. *Journal of Environmental Management, 130,* 1–9.

Corbeels, M., de Graaff, J., Ndah, T. H., Penot, E., Baudron, F., Naudin, K., Andrieu, N., Chirat, G., Schuler, J., Nyagumbo, I., Rusinamhodzi, L., Traore, K., Mzoba, H. D., & Adolwa, I. S. (2014). Understanding the impact and adoption of conservation agriculture in Africa: A multi-scale analysis. *Agriculture, Ecosystems & Environment, 187,* 155–170.

CSO [Central Statistical Office]. (2011). *Zambia 2010 census of population and housing: Preliminary population figures.* Lusaka: Central Statistical Office.

CSO [Central Statistical Office]. (2013). *Energy statistics 2000–2011.* Lusaka: Central Statistical Office.

Dewees, P., Campbell, B. M., Katerere, K., Sitoe, A., Cunningham, A. B., Angelsen, A., & Wunder, S. (2011). *Managing the Miombo woodlands of southern Africa: Policies, incentives and options for the rural poor.* Washington, DC: World Bank.

FAO [Food and Agriculture Organization]. (2005). *Global forest resource assessment 2005: Country report, Zambia.* FRA 2005/062. Rome: Food and Agriculture Organization of the United Nations.

FAO [Food and Agriculture Organization]. (2010). *Global forest resources assessment 2010: Country report, Zambia.* FRA 2010/233. Rome: Food and Agriculture Organization of the United Nations.

FAO [Food and Agriculture Organization]. (2012). *What is CA? Principles of CA. Benefits of CA.* http://www.fao.org/.

Ford, F. A. (1999). *Modeling the environment: An introduction to system dynamics models of environmental systems.* Washington, DC: Island Press.

Foster V., & Dominguez, C. (2010). *Zambia's infrastructure: A continental perspective.* Washington, DC: International Bank for Reconstruction and Development.

Garnett, T., Appleby, M. C., Balmford, A., Bateman, I. J., Benton, T. G., Bloomer, P., B. Burlingame, Dawkins, M., Dolan, L., Fraser, D., Herrero, M., Hoffmann, I., Smith, P., Thornton, P. K., Toulmin, C., Vermeulen, S. J., & Godfray, H. C. J. (2013). Sustainable intensification in agriculture: premises and policies. *Science, 341*(6141), 33–34.

Garrity, D. P. (2004). Agroforestry and the achievement of the millennium development goals. *Agroforestry Systems, 61,* 5–17.

Garrity, D. P., Akinnifesi, F. K., Ajahi, O. C., Weldesemayat, S. G., Mowo, J. G., Kalinganire, A., Larwanou,

M., & Bayala, J. (2010). Evergreen agriculture: A robust approach to sustainable food security in Africa. *Food Security, 2*(3), 197–214.

Giller, K. E., Cadisch, G., Ehaliotis, C., Sakala, W. D., & Mafongoya, P. L. (1997). Building soil nitrogen in Africa. In Buresh, R. J., Sanchez, P. A., & Calhoun, F. (Eds.), *Replenishing soil fertility in Africa* (pp. 151–191). Madison: Soil Science Society of America.

Giller, K. E., Witter, E., Corbeels, M., & Tittonell, P. (2009). Conservation agriculture and smallholder farming in Africa: The heretic's view. *Field Crops Research, 114*, 23–34.

Grabowski, P. P., & Kerr, J. M. (2014). Resource constraints and partial adoption of conservation agriculture by hand-hoe farmers in Mozambique. *International Journal of Agricultural Sustainability, 12*(1), 37–53.

GRZ [Government of the Republic of Zambia]. (1997). *Preliminary first draft national report on the implementation of the Convention on Biological Diversity.* Ministry of Tourism, Environment and Natural Resources. Lusaka, Government Printers.

GRZ [Government of the Republic of Zambia]. (2011). *Sixth national development plan 2011–2015.* Lusaka: Government Printers.

GRZ [Government of the Republic of Zambia]. (2013). *Fees and prices for indigenous forest produce. Statutory Instrument No. 52 of 2013. The Forests Act (Laws, Volume 12, Cap. 199); the Forest Amendment Regulations, 2013. Appendix (Regulation 2).* Lusaka: Government Printers.

Haanyika, C. M. (2008). Rural Electrification in Zambia: A policy and institutional analysis. *Energy Policy, 36*(3), 1044–1058.

Hazell, P., & Wood, S. (2008). Drivers of change in global agriculture. *Philosophical Transactions of the Royal Society, Land, B: Biological Sciences, 363*, 495–515.

Headey, D. D., & Jayne, T. S. (2014). Adaptation to land constraints: Is Africa different? *Food Policy, 48*, 18–33.

Jayne, T. S., Chamberlin, J., & Headey, D. (2014). Land Pressures, the evolution of farming systems, and development strategies in Africa: a synthesis. *Food Policy, 48*, 1–17.

Kalinda, T., & Bwalya, S. M. (2014). Utilization of forest products and services for livelihoods among households in Zambia. *Research Journal for Environmental and Earth Sciences, 6*(2), 102–111.

Kalinda, T., Bwalya, S. M., Mulolwa, A., & Haantuba, H. (2008). *Use of Integrated Land Use Assessment (ILUA) data for environmental and agricultural policy review and analysis in Zambia.* Lusaka: Forest Management and Planning Unit of the Forestry Department; FAO and the Zambian Forestry Department; Ministry of Tourism, Environment and Natural Resources.

Kalumiana O. S. (1997). *Study of the demand and supply of firewood and charcoal—Lusaka Province.* Provincial Forestry Action Program Publication No. 22. Ndola, Zambia: Provincial Forestry Action Programme.

Kopainsky, B., Tröger, K., Derwisch, S., & Ulli-Beer, S. (2012). Designing sustainable food security policies in sub-Saharan African countries: How social dynamics over-ride utility evaluations for good and bad. *Systems Research and Behavioral Science, 29*(6), 575–589.

Kasanga, J., & Daka, O. (2013). *Broad-based survey to establish baseline conditions and collection of data for monitoring the impact of the second phase of the Conservation Agriculture Programme (CAP II) survey results 2013.* Lusaka: Conservation Farming Unit. http://conservationagriculture.org/.

Keil, A., Zeller, M., & Franzel, S. (2005). Improved tree fallows in smallholder maize production in

Zambia: Do initial testers adopt the technology? *Agroforestry Systems, 64,* 225–236.

Kwesiga, F., & Coe, R. (1994). The effect of short-rotation *Sesbania sesban* planted fallows on maize yield. *Forest Ecology and Management, 64* (2–3), 199–208.

Kwesiga, F., Franzel, S., Place, F., Phiri, D., & Simwanza, C. P. (1999). Sesbania sesban improved fallows in Eastern Zambia: Their inception, development and farmer enthusiasm. *Agroforestry Systems, 47*(1–3), 49–66.

Luganda, P. (2013). Efficient Uganda charcoal stoves see surge in popularity. *Thomson Reuters Foundation News.* http://news.trust.org/.

Matson, P. A., Parton, W. J., Power, A. G. & Swift, M. J. (1997). Agricultural intensification and ecosystem properties. *Science, 277*(5325), 504–509.

Mukosha, J., & Siampale, A. (2009). *Integrated land use assessment, Zambia 2005–2007.* Lusaka: Ministry of Tourism, Environment and Natural Resources and Forestry Department; Government of the Republic of Zambia; Food and Agriculture Organization of the United Nations.

Mulenga, B., Richardson, R. B., Tembo, G., & Mapemba, L. (2014). Rural household participation in markets for non-timber forest products in Zambia. *Environment and Development Economics, 19*(4), 487–504.

Mwitwa, J., & Makano, A. (2012). *Charcoal demand, production and supply in the Eastern and Lusaka Provinces.* Ndola, Zambia: Mission Press.

Neufeldt, H., Dobie, P., Liyama, M., Njenga, M., Mohan, S., & Neely, C. (2015). *Developing sustainable tree-based bioenergy systems in sub-Saharan Africa.* ICRAF Policy Brief No. 28. Nairobi, Kenya: World Agroforestry Centre (ICRAF).

Ngoma, H., Mason, N. M., & Sitko, N. J. (2015). Does minimum tillage with ripping or planting basins increase maize yield? Meso panel data evidence from Zambia. *Agriculture, Ecosystems & Environment, 212,* 21–29.

Phalan, B., Onial, M., Balmford, A., & Green, R. E. (2011). Reconciling food production and biodiversity conservation: Land sharing and land sparing compared. *Science, 333*(6047), 1289–1291.

Pohjonen, V. M. (2004). *Zambia forest resources assessment 2004.* Vantaa, Finland: EU Forest Support Programme in Zambia.

Pretty, J., & Bharucha, Z. P. (2014). Sustainable intensification in agricultural systems. *Annals of Botany, 114*(8), 1571–1596.

Pretty, J., Toulmin, C., & Williams, S. (2011). Sustainable intensification in African agriculture. *International Journal of Agricultural Sustainability, 9*(1), 5–24.

Richardson, R. B., Fernandez, A., Tschirley, D., & Tembo, G. (2012). Wildlife conservation in Zambia: impacts on rural household welfare. *World Development, 40*(5), 1068–1081.

Rosenstock, T. S., Rufino, M. C., Butterbach-Bahl, K., & Wollenberg, E. (2013). Toward a protocol for quantifying the greenhouse gas balance and identifying mitigation options in smallholder farming systems. *Environmental Research Letters, 8*(2), 021003.

Sanchez, P. A., Buresh, R. J., & Leakey, R. R. B. (1997). Replenishing soil fertility in Africa. *Philosophical Transactions of the Royal Society, B352,* 949.

Sanchez, P. A., & Swaminathan, M. S. (2005). Hunger in Africa: The link between unhealthy people and unhealthy soils. *Lancet, 365,* 442–444.

Saysel, A. K., Barlas, Y., & Yenigum, O. (2002). Environmental sustainability in an agricultural development project: A system dynamics approach. *Journal of Environmental Management, 64*(3), 247–260.

Simonovic, S. P. (2002). World water dynamics: global modeling of water resources. *Journal of Environmental Management, 66*(3), 693–792.

Singh, G., Nouhou, S. A., & Sokona, M. Y. (2013). *Zambia renewables readiness assessment.* Abu Dhabi: International Renewable Energy Agency.

Stave, K. A. (2003). A system dynamics model to facilitate public understanding of water management options in Las Vegas, Nevada. *Journal of Environmental Management, 67*(4), 303–313.

Sterman, J. D. (2000). *Business dynamics: Systems thinking and modeling for a complex world.* Boston: Irwin/McGraw-Hill.

Sterman, J. D. (2011). Communicating climate change risks in a skeptical world. *Climate Change, 108*(4), 811–826.

Stringer, L., Mungoli, M., Dougill, A., Mkwambisi, D., Dyer, J., & Kalaba, F. (2012). Challenges and opportunities for carbon management in Malawi and Zambia. *Carbon Management, 3*(2), 159–173.

Tembo, S., & Sitko, N. (2012). *Technical compendium: Descriptive agricultural statistics and analysis for Zambia.* IAPRI Working Paper 76. Lusaka: Indaba Agricultural Policy Research Institute.

Tittonell, P., & Giller, K. E. (2013). When yield gaps are poverty traps: The paradigm of ecological intensification in African smallholder agriculture. *Field Crop Research, 143,* 76–90.

Tilman, D., Balzer, C. Hill, J., & Befort, B. L. (2011). Global food demand and the sustainable intensification of agriculture. *Proceedings of the National Academy of Sciences, 108*(50), 20260–20264.

Tilman, D., Cassman, K. G., Matson, P. A., Naylor, R., & Polasky, S. (2002). Agricultural sustainability and intensive production practices. *Nature, 418,* 671–677.

UNEP [United Nations Environment Programme]. (2015). *Benefits of forest ecosystems in Zambia and the role of REDD+ in a green economy transformation.* Nairobi, Kenya: United Nations Environment Programme.

United Nations. (2012). *World population prospects: 2012 revision.* New York: Department of Economic and Social Affairs, Population Division. http://www.un.org.

UN-REDD. (2010). *National programme document—Zambia.* Geneva, Switzerland: UN-REDD Programme. http://wedocs.unep.org/.

van den Belt, M. (2004). *Mediated modeling: A system dynamics approach to environmental consensus building.* Washington, DC: Island Press.

Villoria, N. B., Byerlee, D., & Stevenson, J. (2014). The effects of agricultural technological progress on deforestation: What do we really know? *Applied Economic Perspectives and Policy, 36*(2), 211–237.

Vinya, R., Syampungani, S., Kasumu, E. C., Monde, C., & Kasubika, R. (2011). *Preliminary study on the drivers of deforestation and potential for REDD+ in Zambia.* Lusaka: Forestry Department and FAO; UN-REDD+ Programme Ministry of Lands and Natural Resources.

Winterbottom, R., Reif, C., Garrity, D., Glover, J., Hellums, D., McGahuey, M., & Scherr, S. (2013). *Improving land and water management.* Washington, DC: World Resources Institute. http://www.worldresourcesreport.org.

World Bank (2008). *Managing the Miombo woodlands of southern Africa: Policies, incentives and options for the rural poor.* Washington, DC: Sustainable Development Department. Environment and Natural

Resources Management Unit, African Region.

ZFD [Zambia Forestry Department]. (2008). *Integrated Land Use Assessment (ILUA) 2005–2008: Republic of Zambia*. Lusaka: Ministry of Tourism, Environment and Natural Resources.

Zulu, L. C., & Richardson, R. B. (2013). Charcoal, livelihoods, and poverty reduction: evidence from sub-Saharan Africa. *Energy for Sustainable Development, 17*(2), 127–137.

Co-Designing a Role-Playing Game to Characterize and Parametrize an Agent-Based Model on Coexistence of Farming Activities and Wildlife Conservation in the Periphery of the Sikumi Forest, Zimbabwe

Arthur Perrotton, Christophe Le Page, and Michel de Garine-Wichatitsky

Mainstream ecological modeling produces predictive models based on expert knowledge so that decision makers can better understand the "natural functioning" of a given system and choose the best, optimal management decision. In recent years, environmental sciences have acknowledged more and more the necessity to consider social and ecological dynamics as entwined components of complex systems, hence the emergence of new analytical frameworks, such as social-ecological systems (SES; Epstein et al., 2013) or coupled human and natural system (CHANS; Alberti et al., 2011). Environmental modeling has also evolved to focus more on the relationships between human actors (referred to as "local actors" or "stakeholders" hereafter) and their environment, taking account of intertwined social and ecological dynamics that shape SESs. This chapter describes how participatory modeling can be used to model and address a particular type of socioecological issue: coexistence of different land uses.

Within an SES, one finds a potentially high diversity of local actors, each with his or her own world vision, production system, objectives, practices, and governance system. This diversity sometimes leads to misunderstandings, tensions, and conflicts. Issues surrounding natural resources use and the coexistence of the local actors sharing them are many. Taking the simple example of a river, Webber (1998) explains how the fisherman's, engineer's, geographer's and ecologist's river are different, although they rely on the same environmental feature. Keeping this example, we can easily imagine conflicts among actors concerning the management of this river. In other words, the plurality of stakeholders interacting around common resources brings with it the question of coexistence. More than the sum of interactions and outcomes, coexistence is a key driver of SESs (Guerbois et al., 2013). In cases where the coexistence of different actors results in reciprocal benefits, we can expect local actors to collaborate to maintain these benefits. But when one or more actors dominate and achieve their own objectives at the expense of others, we can expect the emergence of conflicts, along with an increase in individualism and rule avoiding mechanisms that can *in fine* threaten the system as a whole (Tompkins & Adger, 2004). Studying socioecological problems and providing recommendations and tools to solve them is therefore necessary.

Coexistence can be classified as a "wicked problem." Originally coined by Churchman (1967) and later redefined by Rittel and Webber (1973), this term denotes problems for which uncertainties and conflicting cultural values prevent the definition of an optimal solution. As expressed by Balint (2011), environmental wicked problems defy simple solutions and are characterized by uncertainty, incomplete scientific knowledge, competing cultural values, and interconnections with other problems (Balint, 2011). In terms of research and environmental management, wicked problems are highly challenging. Due to the intense socioecological feedbacks happening within SESS, every action engaged is consequential and outcomes are often irreversible. With environmental sustainability and human well-being at stake, a classical trial-error approach is impossible.

The use of models is an alternative, but their design is questioned by the "wickedness" of the problems to solve. First, we need an appropriate type of modeling. Among the modeling techniques available, agent-based models (ABMs) are particularly promising (Janssen & Ostrom, 2006). Indeed, ABMs enable the researcher to represent heterogeneous agents that are virtual representations of actors or groups of actors, each having individual internal reasoning and cognitive capacities. Agents interact among themselves and with a virtual environment in which they evolve. In other words, ABMs simulate virtual societies. This form of modeling is implemented more and more to understand and propose solutions to socioecological issues (Bousquet & Le Page, 2004). In the companion modeling approach, role-playing game settings are used to let the decisions of the agents be made by the local actors themselves in an interactive way (Etienne, 2014). But how can we design a model despite the inherent ambiguities and the lack of knowledge characterizing a wicked problem? And how can the model be relevant enough to local actors when part of the problem stems from the inaccessibility of local cultural values to an external researcher? The answer is to be found in the creation of an "extended peer community" (Funtowicz & Ravetz, 1993), that is, a team of researchers and local actors who share their knowledge and co-design the model.

The case study described here presents a participatory modeling experiment. With the objective of studying a typical case of a coexistence issue within a protected area and its rural periphery, we adopt the companion modeling approach, mixing anthropological fieldwork, a participatory process, and computer modeling to ultimately co-design a computer-based role playing game (RPG) that enables us to understand the local farming and cattle herding strategies that shape interactions between the different actors of the socioecological system. A particularity of our work is that, whereas most participatory models and RPGs are built and used by the same individuals, we decided to co-design, with a group of selected individuals, a game that could be used with any members of the same rural community. More broadly, we address the following question: How and to what extent can participation foster the inclusion of endogenous perceptions and knowledge and meet local actors' expectations while maintaining scientific relevance? Drawing lessons from our work, we provide guidelines to promote the inclusion of local actors and produce efficient participatory modeling.

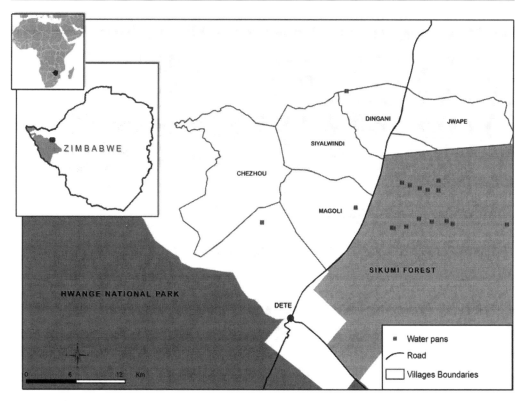

FIGURE 1. Study area, villages adjacent to Hwange National Park and Sikumi Forest, Zimbabwe.

Study Area

The study area is located in the Kalahari sand dune system of southern Africa (Stokes et al., 1997). More precisely, this work was conducted at the interface of Hwange National Park and the Sikumi Forest, two protected areas managed respectively by the Zimbabwean Parks and the Zimbabwean Forestry Commission, and the surrounding villages of Magoli, Siyalwindi, Chezhou, Dingani, and Jwape within ward 15 of the Hwange District, western Zimbabwe (see figure 1). The area receives between 450 and 650 millimeters of rain per year and is characterized by the presence of "dry spells" and droughts, which added to poor soils make this area poorly suited for agriculture (Matarira & Jury, 1992). Nevertheless, rural households rely on agriculture, with maize, millet, and sorghum being the main food crops, and livestock keeping (Perrotton et al. 2016; de Garine-Wichatitsky et al., 2013). Our study area shows classic coexistence issues: human-wildlife conflicts (Metcalfe and Kepe 2008), poaching (Muboko et al. 2014), cattle incursions in restricted protected areas, illegal wood harvesting, livestock predation by wild carnivores and crops raiding (e.g. Guerbois et al. 2012) along with disease transmission between domestic livestock and wildlife (de Garine-Wichatitsky et al. 2013).

If local communities have no right of access to any natural resources use of or extraction from Hwange national park, the severe droughts of the early 1990s (Maphosa, 1994) led the forestry commission and local traditional leaders to negotiate a right of access for communities neighboring the Sikumi forest. Herders obtained the right to graze their cattle within the forest (Guerbois et al., 2013), although the official authorized distance remains unclear and, depending on the informant, ranges from 2 kilometers according to a Forestry manager, to 3 kilometers according to Guerbois et al. (2013), and up to 7 kilometers according to local herders. The right of access to the forestry's land is essential for livestock owners and simultaneously constitutes a form of land claiming on a territory that used to be used by the villagers until 1972. On the other hand, forestry managers are concerned about the possible consequences of such an agreement: overgrazing to the detriment of wildlife and opportunistic activities, such as illegal wood harvesting or poaching. The right of access is a bone of contention between traditional leaders and the forestry commission. This particular context justifies our focus on cattle herding as the main activity shaping coexistence between these two land uses.

Tensions around cattle driving at the interface between the Sikumi Forest and neighboring rural community show characteristics of wicked problems: uncertainty (climate, resources availability), incomplete scientific knowledge (e.g., how do herders drive cattle? What is the vegetation structure in the forest? How do cattle impact vegetation in the forest?), ambiguity maintained by local actors (what is the legal right of access?), competing cultural values (rural livelihood versus wildlife conservation and timber production), and interconnections with other problems (unemployment, droughts). Such a context justified the implementation of a companion modeling approach that allows the acquisition of data through the enhancement of communication between local actors and researchers.

Companion Modeling

Participation can be a way to address wicked problems (Roberts, 2000; Davies et al., 2015) by bringing together local actors and experts in a joint dynamic, turning the first from passive objects to partners of research, natural resources management or development (Eversole, 2003). The potential benefits of participation are summarized by Stringer et al (2006). Participation uses perspectives from a range of sources and can produce more robust factual bases, therefore reducing uncertainty. Grassroots actors provide local, social, ethical, and political insights that cannot be achieved through scientific approaches. Finally, involving local stakeholders can promote democratic ideals in natural resources management, empower the "marginalized," and facilitate long-term collaboration among local stakeholders. The objects used for and produced through participation (e.g., models, sketches, tables, or maps) are boundary objects linking different actors who belong to different social worlds but are involved in a common dynamic (Daré, 2005; Vinck, 2009; Daré et al., 2010).

The Companion Modeling (ComMod) approach developed in the 1990s by researchers from the French Center for Agricultural Research for Development (CIRAD; Bousquet et al., 2002; Etienne, 2014) aims to identify the various points of views and knowledge that local actors implicitly refer to and use in their relationship with their environment, working out—together with local stakeholders—a common vision of a given SES in order to understand its functioning or facilitate stakeholders' decision-making processes using a common resource. These objectives are achieved by co-constructing and using ABMs and RPGs with the local actors of a SES to reflect the expectations and constraints of the actors involved and enhance discussion and co-operation among the local actors as well as and between the local actors and researchers. Up to six types of human protagonists can take part in a ComMod approach (Etienne, 2014). The first four are endogenous actors: (1) "grassroots actors," who draw their knowledge from their empirical experience of the world, (2) "researchers," who draw their knowledge from their academic background, (3) "technicians," who are generally exterior to the system but are occasionally consulted on precise matters, and (4) "institutionals," who are, for example, policy makers and have their own vision and knowledge of their system. Two types of exogenous human protagonists are found in ComMod processes: (1) "ComModians," researchers who have mastered the approach and its ethical implications and rules, and (2) "students," who are learner ComModians and who will, through the implementation of a ComMod approach, test their scientific knowledge and build their own vision of the ComMod approach, and master it in turn.

Kulayinjana, an Overview of the Participatory Modeling Process

Although issues around cattle involve diverse local actors, this study focuses on rural communities for several reasons. Rural communities are the owners of cattle and the ones making decisions about herding strategies, whereas the Sikumi Forest managers are institutional actors. Furthermore, decision-making processes concerning forestry management are centralized and take place either in Bulawayo (regional office) or Harare (national office), rarely in the local office. We are conscious that forestry actors will have to be involved in future work, but with the idea of initiating a long-term collaboration with local stakeholders, creating an arena for rural communities to express themselves freely was the necessary first step to a fair potentially long-term ComMod approach.

The co-design of *Kulayinjana* was a long process, which involved several sets of fieldwork methods, from social, ecological and computer sciences. In the following paragraphs, we describe and explain these steps.

Anthropological Fieldwork

The first step of the project consisted of in-depth anthropological fieldwork. For over a year, we shared local villagers' lives by living among them, hosted by a local family. Direct and participant observation along with individual questionnaires, interviews, and informal discussions, was crucial for the initiation of the participatory modeling process. This first step had two major objectives. Although we assumed that part of the local reality was ungraspable due to our exogenous nature, it was still necessary to acquire the basic knowledge about cattle-herding strategies in order to play our role in the co-design process. This would also help us achieve the second objective: acquiring legitimacy in the eyes of the future co-design team. This legitimacy is necessary to justify our position of leaders of a participatory process and secure the commitment of the future co-design team. For that, we had to prove that we had a minimal understanding of cattle herding and what was at stake in the community-forestry interactions in order to build the trust necessary to create the extended peer community.

At the end of this first step, in consultation with the local traditional authorities, we proposed ten local villagers to join the co-design team. These people had been identified for their knowledge of the area and the relationship we had built with them, but also for their social position (e.g., some were village heads). The co-design team was therefore composed of two "researchers" and one PhD "student" (the ComModians) and ten "grassroots actors" (villagers from our study area). Ages ranged from thirty-nine to fifty-seven years old. All but one were household heads, three were village heads, one was the secretary of a village head, two were involved in dip-tank committees, and one was the local chairman of a community project developing goat husbandry. They originated from the different villages of the study area. Our local translator was also part of the team.

In order to initiate the ComMod process, we used the knowledge we had gathered to design a "launch version" (Vo) of the RPG. This first version of the game was not a collective production, as only the researchers were involved in its design. The Vo was brought by the researchers as an entry point to initiate the co-design process. Starting the co-design process with an object that already took the form of an RPG was more engaging and accessible to participating local farmers than starting with a conceptual model. The main challenge was to come up with a game that was realistic enough to legitimize us as facilitators of the ComMod process, catch the interest of the future co-design team members by showing the potential outcomes of their participation, and encourage them to improve it. The Vo was computer-based and developed using CORMAS, a simulation platform developed by the CIRAD (Le Page et al., 2012). The Vo was a simplified representation of the studied system because a complex object would have been harder to appropriate, deconstruct, or improve by the future team.

Following Barnaud's (2012) advice, the virtual environment did not realistically represent the study area to allow stakeholders to create distance from reality and issues that come with it, such as the conflicting authorized distance allowed for cattle in the Sikumi Forest. In other words, a conceptualized environment was chosen so stakeholders could project themselves in a conflict-free world within which they could devise their own rationales about cattle herding. The virtual environment proposed consisted of a grid and exposed characteristics similar to reality, such as a communal area where farms were located and a forest. The principle of the Vo game was simple: on a game board divided into thirteen paddocks, forming the "village" and nine forming the "forest," each player was in charge of a farm, each with five fields and an initial herd of five heads of cattle. The game was played on monthly time steps, starting in October and finishing in September the year after (centered on the agricultural season). Each round (each "month"), players had to signal whether they wanted to plough or harvest any of their fields, which paddock they wanted their herd to graze in, and whether they wanted the herd to be herded or not. Each player was also given an initial number of tokens at the beginning of the game. These were used to pay for the various actions, such as planting fields, herding cattle (whose price varied depending on the distance covered by the herd), and guarding the cattle. Players could also gain tokens either through their harvests or by selling cows. Players' wealth and the environment (fodder quality) evolved according to players' decisions. Although the Vo set the basics of the future game, it was voluntarily incomplete and its functioning, meaning the ecological and social dynamics we had designed, contained discordances with reality that

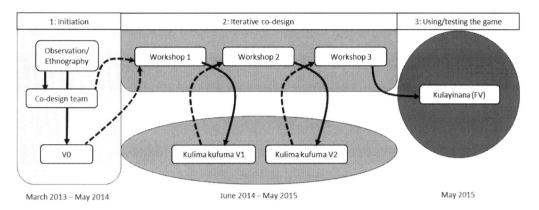

FIGURE 2. The RPG co-design process. Plain arrows represent creation or (re)design phases; dash arrows represent testing phases.

would help engaging the debates with participants. Starting with an incomplete and partly discordant representation of reality also helped highlight the need for local actors' help to fill in the knowledge gaps, therefore breaking the "foreigner white-male positionality of researchers" (Stringer et al., 2006).

Iterations and Co-Design of Kulayinjana

The full iterative process is described in figure 2. All co-design workshops were held at the Magoli community hall. We assume that the success of participatory processes partly relies on the researchers' capacity to create an atmosphere of mutual trust as much as a fair and balanced arena between researchers and non-researchers. Although it necessitated the transport and use of a generator and involved technical complications, the venue was chosen so that the local members of the team could easily come to that place and feel confident there.

The first workshop was crucial, as it was the moment when we initiated the ComMod process and start creating the "team spirit." Once the different members of the team were introduced, we presented the research project and the specific objectives of the co-design process. After exposing the principles of the Vo by asking a local member to play a test month, the rest of the first day was used to play with all the members. A first debriefing was done at the end of the day, during which the team shared impressions about the game and decided a list of topics to be discussed the day after.

The second day of workshop was dedicated to a collective redesign of the game. Local members of the team proposed a series of improvements and modifications. Rules concerning livestock predation by lions were entirely redesigned. A major constraint to agriculture was absent in Vo and added by local members: elephants. A simplified elephant behavior was designed by the team, along with field protection modalities. The cost of actions was thought to constrain players and force them to prioritize their actions in the game. Although the principle was maintained by the team, the rules of costs-benefits were also improved and the cattle selling and purchase rules were formalized. The crop submodel wasn't satisfying for most of the members of the team

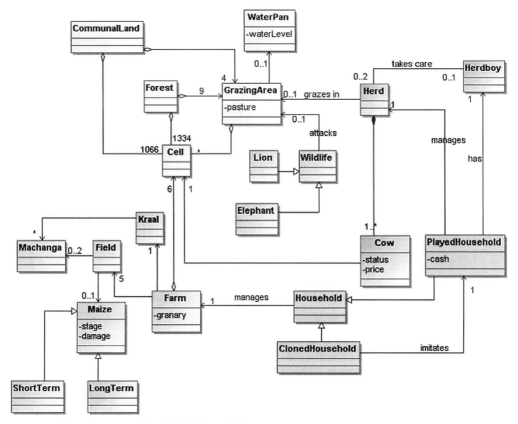

FIGURE 3. Class diagram of the Kulayinjana ABM.

and was therefore intensively discussed and redesigned. The idea of having only one type of crop was kept, but development stages were added, along with the possibility of crop failures due to droughts or floods (figure 3). Absent in Vo, a new action was added: when harvesting, players would be able to either collect crop residues and feed their cattle later with it or leave them in the fields where any cattle could eat them. The Vo included a rainfall calendar. Based on local rain records (2012–2013), the weekly rainfalls were only displayed retrospectively at the end of each month. The local members of the team asked for the availability of a weather forecast at the beginning of the month. They justified by explaining that, in real life, they had access to short-term weather forecasts through newspapers, radio, or traditional weather forecasting methods. The game should therefore display the weather forecast of the first week of each month.

Finally, the biggest contribution of this first workshop to the game concerned livestock grazing management. The subdivision of the environment in paddocks was kept, as was the rule that each player could use one paddock per month to graze his cattle. A completely new submodel of grazing resources dynamics was designed and worked around the notion of carrying capacity. It was decided that the effects of grazing on a paddock would depend on the land use (communal land or forest), with slightly better pastures in the forest and on the season. The name "Kulima Kufuma" ("farming to get rich" in ChiNambiya, one of the local languages) was chosen by local members of the team at the end of the first workshop.

Following the first workshop, V0 was modified to include the team decisions about the game. The first co-designed version (V1) was born. The participatory design continued through an iterative process alternating tests and improvements and redesign of the game. Two other workshops were held, one in November 2014 and one in April 2015. Each workshop resulted in a new version of the game. During these workshops, the core of the game (e.g., rules, submodels) were collectively redesigned and rethought in order to create a game that was realistic and could easily be played by novice villagers. Some of the final submodels were collectively built during workshops and some were tabulated functions designed by researchers and validated by the team. A second climatic year also relying on meteorological data collected in Hwange (1921–1922) was added, proposing a much-contrasted climatic year with low rainfalls and dry spells. A full game session thus covered two years, played one after the other: the "good year" first (2012–2013), followed by the "bad year" (1921–1922). The co-designers also thought about the best physical support for the game. Computer-free (V1) and computer-based (V0, V2, FV) versions of the game were tested. From a projection on the wall (V0), the game became a horizontally projected playing board with pawns to move (V2, FV), enhancing interactions between the game and the players and among the players. In all members' opinions, the use of pawns, together with the automation of processes over which the players do not have control, made the game easier to understand by potential novice players and also more fun and faster to play. Additionally, the computer support allowed the recording of every playing decision.

At the end of the third workshop, about two years after the beginning of the project, the team agreed that the game was ready to be played by other villagers. Almost a year after initiating the co-design, the game had been radically transformed and a new name was proposed by local members of the team: *Kulayinjana*, meaning "teaching each other" in ChiNambiya.

Implementation: Playing Sessions with Novice Villagers

The use of a co-designed RPG with novice players was one of the challenges of our approach. Pushing participation further, five local members of the team volunteered to facilitate the playing sessions with villagers. Two days were dedicated to the preparation of playing sessions. An introduction speech for the game was collectively written in ChiNambiya and in isiNdebele (another main local language) and a blank game was played as a training game with workers of a neighboring hotel as players.

Four playing sessions were organized and a total of twenty-eight villagers played *Kulayinjana*. Playing sessions were held in local languages. The villagers (hereafter referred to as "players") were appointed by the facilitators and the researchers, covering the different villages of our study area. Players were neighbors or friends and, except for two players, direct family links with the facilitators were avoided.

Evaluating the Co-Design Process and the Final Game

Four dimensions of the ComMod process were assessed: (1) the effective inclusion of local actors' views of the system, (2) the extent to which the co-designed game met local members' expectations,

(3) the scientific effectiveness and relevance of the co-designed game, and (4) its usability with novice players and effectiveness in gathering relevant data to model and simulate cattle herding.

Two questionnaires were designed. These contained open-ended questions that did not restrain opinions to predefined answers, along with ranking questions. Individual questionnaires were carried with local members of the co-design team (N = 10 villagers + 3 researchers) once the VF was produced. The co-designer questionnaire assessed the team members' opinion about the initiation of the process, the workshops, the final game and their perspective about this participatory process. Villagers who played the game (N = 28) in May 2015 also answered a specific questionnaire to evaluate the final version of the game. Their questionnaire contained open and ranking questions. The players' questionnaire covered their experiences of the game, their opinions about the game, and their opinions about the facilitation of the gaming session.

Results

Kulayinjana: The Model behind the Game

The following section presents the final version of the game, *Kulayinjana,* the one played with villagers to gather their herding strategies. A full description of the model, such as an ODD format (Grimm et al., 2010) would be too long; therefore, only the key elements are presented here in order for the reader to have a general understanding of the game.

Kulayinjana is a computer-based RPG supported by CORMAS, an agent-based simulation platform developed by the CIRAD (Le Page et al., 2012). As such, the game consists of agents, some of whom are controlled by the players, evolving in a virtual environment (the playing board) taking the form of a spatial grid. The structure of the game is presented in figure 4. The virtual environment is shared between a communal area and a forest and divided into thirteen grazing areas, numbered C1 to C4 in the communal land and F1 to F9 in the forest. There are six water pans on the board, one in communal land (C4), and five in the forest (F2, F3, F5, F6, F8, and F9). The communal area is where the farms are, eight of which are controlled by players and fifteen of which are controlled by the computer. Each played farm has its kraal colored according to the player in charge (two played farms by communal grazing area), with the five fields appear in orange (five orange cells around the kraal). Each player starts the game with a herd of five heads of cattle. The computerized farms do not have cattle.

At the initiation of the game, players choose, from predefined locations, which farm they want to manage. Then the simulation is scheduled by month. The model presented here supports an RPG and, as a result, is not run "continuously" but is stopped and resumed for players to make their decisions (figure 5).

The game covers twelve months, and each round consists of decisions to take for one month. A round goes as follows: At the beginning of the round, a weather forecast is given for the first week of the coming month. Four types of weekly rainfalls are possible: dry week (< 5mm), small rains (5–20mm), medium rains (20–40mm), or heavy rains (> 40mm). The first set of decisions concerns field management. Players signal with pawns whether they want to plant one or several fields (up to five). During the co-design, the team decided that, although local farmers

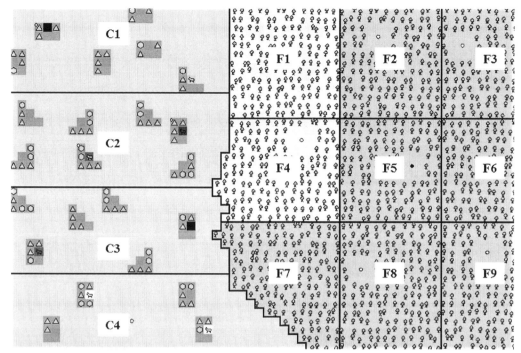

FIGURE 4. The virtual environment. The grazing areas names are showed for illustrative purpose; they do not appear during the game. Farms with a colored paddock are to be managed by players. The figure shows three of the four different forage levels: "poor" (F1 and F4), "medium" (C1 to C4), and "good" (F2, F3, F5, F6, F7, F8 and F9). These levels change during the game according to players' actions.

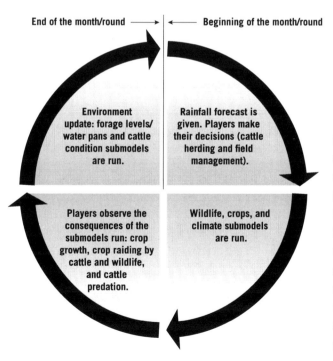

FIGURE 5. Sequential mobilization of the submodels during the playing session. A round of playing, that is a month in the model, is done in four steps. During steps 1 and 3, the model is paused for players to observe the consequences of their actions and make their decisions, while during steps 2 and 4, the model is run and translates players' decisions into socioecological effects.

plant maize, sorghum, and millet, only one "crop" would be included in the game. Nevertheless, there are two types of pawns corresponding to the two types of crops chosen by the team, short season and long season. These differ by the time needed to grow and their resistance to drought and floods (figure 3).

If some of the fields are ready to be harvested, the players can choose to harvest. In that case, they have to choose whether to leave the crop residue (*machanga*) in the field (to be used by any cattle) or store the crop residue within the kraal. Once stored, players can use the residue to feed their cattle when they want. The second set of decisions concerns cattle management and herding. Each player has to decide in which grazing area he wants his cattle to graze for the next four weeks and whether his herd is to be guarded by a herd boy. Each grazing area has its own level of forage that can be depleted, poor, medium, or good. The transition between these levels relies on a tabulated function considering the grazing pressure in the previous months and the amount of rainfall received in the month. Each round, players have access to a cattle market where they can buy and sell cattle. These actions have a cost. Players are initially given forty-eight tokens. These represent both seeds to plant their fields and money to pay for their different actions. For instance, planting one field costs six tokens, taking cattle costs up to five tokens per month (depending on the grazing area used), protecting the field from elephants costs one token per month, and buying a cow costs between six and eighteen tokens depending on the body condition of the cow. Players can also gain tokens either from the harvests or from selling cattle.

After all these decisions are made, they are entered into the computer interface and the different submodels are run. The climate model displays the weekly rainfalls on the board, which impact the growth and failures of crops. The wildlife submodel is run and players eventually have their cattle attacked by lions and crops raided by elephants. Crops grow and can be raided by cattle grazing in the communal area without being herded. Players are directly informed of the outcomes of their actions.

During the fourth and final step of the round, cattle body conditions are updated according to the grazing areas they used. Finally, the forage level of each grazing area is updated, as are the water pans.

Analysis of the Co-Design Process

When asked about their motivation for joining the process, six local members answered that it was curiosity and the will to learn, three answered that they wanted to share ideas, and one wanted to help researchers whom he knew. All acknowledged a high degree of freedom in giving individual ideas during the co-design of the game and everyone could recall at least one personal idea that had been kept in the final game. As one local member remarked, "It was said to be our game and we made it like that." The atmosphere during the workshops was given an average ranking of 8.5/10 (±1.5).

When asked about the final version of the game, the whole team declared being satisfied, with a few of them suggesting possible improvements, such as the inclusion of seasonal rivers proposed by three local members or the use of alternative sources of climatic information like

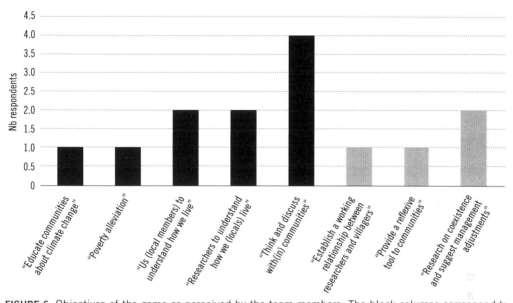

FIGURE 6. Objectives of the game as perceived by the team members. The black columns correspond to the local members' opinions ($N = 10$); the grey columns correspond to the researchers' answers ($N = 3$).

birds songs that farmers "use here to know when it is about to bring rain; they are our reporters." This last suggestion was supported by one of the researchers and echoes previous research (Perrotton et al. 2016). The three researchers of the team agreed on the necessity to pursue the calibration of the foraging submodel.

The analysis of questionnaires highlights the appropriation of the process by local team members during the participatory process. One year of collaboration led local members to find their own objectives of the game (figure 6), and at the end of the co-design, only 20 percent of the local members ($N = 10$) still saw the game as a tool for researchers to understand local farming strategies, which was the initial objective.

The co-design process and its product was transformed by local actors into the creation of an endogenous reflexive tool that could help local team members understand their own strategies, and the communities to "think and discuss," "educate (themselves) about climate change" and "alleviate poverty." One of the members explained how creating the game had "opened [their] minds widely and [led them to] think more." Local members also saw an opportunity for them to better understand their own life. Unsurprisingly the main objectives mentioned by researchers were coherent with the initial research objectives: establishing a working relationship with local communities and study coexistence within the study area.

First Results of the Playing Sessions and Modeling Perspectives

Four playing sessions were organized at the Magoli community hall in May 2015, and a total of twenty-eight players were invited to play *Kulayinjana* (figure 7). As explained earlier, the organization of playing sessions was done jointly by a researcher and local members of the

FIGURE 7. The facilitator describing the playing board before starting the game in *Magoli*. Photo by A. Perrotton, January 5, 2015.

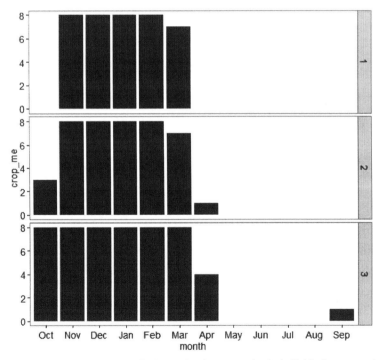

FIGURE 8. Crops management. Number of players having crops in their fields for every playing session (1, 2 and 3).

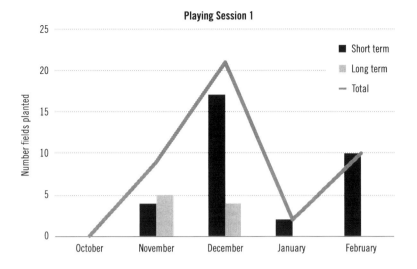

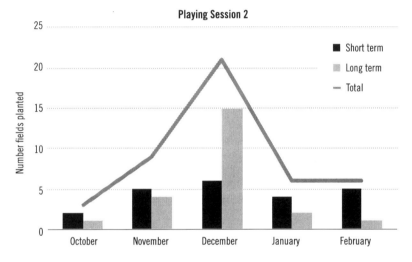

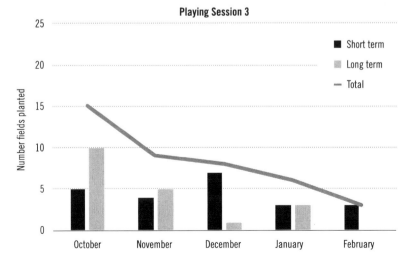

FIGURE 9. Number of fields and type of crops planted per round in the three playing sessions.

co-design team. As we write this chapter, the analyzes of the herding strategies are still ongoing. We therefore only present preliminary results. Using data from the first climatic year (good rains) of the first three playing sessions (twenty-four players), our aim here is to show the type of data that can be gathered with the game.

The first set of data concerns fields management. Each playing session showed slightly different planting patterns. As showed by figure 8, the agricultural season lasted between five months (session 1) and seven months (sessions 2 and 3). The dry planting rate was also different between the second and the third playing session, with only three players planting in October during the second session, against eight in the third session. Completed with detailed data about the choice of crop planted (figure 9), we will be able to conduct in depth analysis of planting strategies.

We also gathered date about cattle herding strategies. The analysis of cattle herding strategies focuses on the opposition between communal and forest grazing areas, and considers three seasons, the agricultural season that is during the months during which at least one player has at least crops in one field, the cold and dry season covering approximately from May to July, and the hot and dry season covering August and September. The objective is to gain a better understanding of the way cattle used these two types of grazing areas throughout the game. For instance, in average, during the twelve months covered by the first climatic scenario, each one of the twenty-four players: used in average 4.17 different grazing areas (min = 3; max = 7), and spent 1.4 month per grazing area (min = 1, max = 7). During the agricultural season, 88 percent of players sent their cattle to graze in the forest, all but one keeping cattle in the first or second line of grazing areas (avoiding F3, F6 and F9). Although the forest was used all year long by some of the players, a significant shift happened after the end of harvests.

Indeed, as shown in figure 10, during the cold and dry season, about 70 percent of cattle herds grazed in the communal land, this figure being reduced to about 60 percent during the hot and dry season, when the forage level of communal areas became too low (see previous section), and crops residues decreased. This pattern is consistent with results obtained by Valls-Fox et al (2018). During their study, conducted in the same area with some of the villagers, they deployed eleven GPS collars, and monitored cattle for over a year. By comparing the two graphs, we can observe a similar yearly evolution of the use of the environment by cows. Indeed, Valls-Fox et al show that cows spend 84.72 percent of the grazing time in the forest during the rainy season (that corresponds approximately to the agricultural season), 21.63 percent during the hot and dry season during which cows feed on crop residues and 27.63 percent during the hot and dry season. Such consistency with GPS collars participates to the validation of the use of the RPG to elicit cattle herding strategies.

One question needs to be asked: to what extent did players reproduce their actual strategies? A first dimension to explore is then the relevance of the virtual environment for local villagers. Indeed, the major assumption of our work was that co-design would allow us to better capture reality and therefore bring players to re-enact their everyday practices. As expressed by a player, "it's not a game, it's [their] real life." Although they mentioned some differences with reality, none of the players answered negatively to the question about the global realism of the game. Opinions about possible differences between the game's submodels and reality varied between the submodels. Unsurprisingly, the climate submodel (based on empirical data) was realistic or very

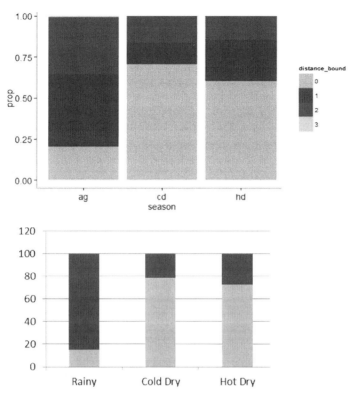

FIGURE 10. Played strategies and data from GPS collars. Top: The figure represents aggregated data from the three playing sessions and is shared between the three seasons. The use of the environment is characterized by the distance to the boundary of the forest. Communal grazing areas are coded as 0; grazing areas F1, F4, and F7 are coded 1; grazing areas F2, F5 and F8 are coded 2; and grazing areas F3, F6, and F9 are coded 3. Bottom: The figure represents the percentage of time spent in the communal area (light grey) and in the forest (dark grey) by 11 cattle followed by Valls-Fox et al (2018) in the same villages with GPS collars.

realistic for 93 percent of the player, and 82 percent of the players validated the crops dynamics submodel, although two thought the game was missing crop raiding birds such as the queleas (*Quelea quelea*). Wildlife in the game presented no difference at all or slight differences with reality for 85 percent of the players. Some players thought that the game's lions were attacking too often (11 percent), others not enough (21 percent). The confinement of lions to the forest was criticized by 18 percent of the players who acknowledge occasional attacks in the communal area. Three players (11 percent) answered that elephants would enter the communal land more often in reality, but cause less loss than in the game. Although validated by 68 percent of the players, the livestock submodel was the one obtaining the most shared opinions from the players, with 32 percent of the players mentioning real differences between their gaming experience and reality. These differences were not always explicit and for some players it was just a feeling. Players who could point precise differences explained that the difference of pasture availability between the communal land and the forest was underestimated in the game (16 percent), that livestock body condition was decreasing too fast in the game (26.3 percent), or that on the contrary livestock was staying "fat" longer in the game compared to their experience of real life (26.3 percent). Finally, a comment was shared by 17 percent of the players who suggested that unlike in the game, not all farmers have cattle and that this was the origin of social interactions (lending, fostering and bartering) missing during the playing sessions.

Out of the twenty-eight players, 61 percent acknowledge having reproduced exactly " their farming and cattle herding strategies while playing and 36 percent declared that their playing strategies were "almost" similar to their real life strategies. The differences were said to be due to the discovering of the game for 66 percent of the players. Only 4 percent of the players answered that their playing strategies were "not really" similar to their actual practices. The computer-based nature of the game allowed researchers to automatically record all individual strategies of all playing sessions. The general pattern of cattle herding identified during our anthropological fieldwork was reproduced by players, therefore confirming our field observations. Playing sessions are currently being analyzed and will result in cattle herding strategies simulations (Perrotton et al., 2016).

Discussion

In the following paragraphs, we draw several lessons from our experience. We show how co-designing an RPG allowed us to better involve local actors and later improve appropriation. We also try to demonstrate why such approaches are relevant when dealing with socioecological issues and provide advice on how to better co-design research tools such as *Kulayinjana*.

Achieving Participation and Appropriation

Participatory processes are long (Mansbridge, 1973) and ours took more than eighteen months. As expressed by d'Aquino and Bah (2013), the success of such processes depends on the facilitators' awareness of the social background. The long ethnographical fieldwork that took place before the co-design contributed to the success of the endeavor by providing crucial information about the context, practices, and coexistence issues in our study area. Like Becu et al. (2005), we assume that the ethnographic approach enables a more trusting relationship between researchers and local actors. Through these months of sharing life of rural populations, we became part of the local social network, which obviously played a role in the motivation of local members of the team to join the process. The consensus within the co-design team around *Kulayinjana* and the members' appreciations of the co-design process are indications that we achieved the creation of a fair relationship between researchers and local actors. The reason lies at the very core of our method. The efficiency of participation relies on appropriation by local actors involved (Chlous-Ducharme & Gourmelon, 2011). The method described in this chapter is flexible by nature and gives a high degree of freedom to local members. Once the process was started, the co-design process and the team were maintained as collectively and non-hierarchically as possible, therefore empowering the local members involved (Desouza, 2012). The definition of endogenous objectives both results from and enhances appropriation, as was the will of local members to facilitate playing sessions. Through this participatory process, we therefore created more than a research-oriented RPG.

We would like to insist here on the opportunities that result from such a process of appropriation. Using a popular metaphor (although a bit dark), the RPG is like Dr. Frankenstein's creature: we lacked key parts to create our "monster" (epistemic uncertainty) and we resorted to parts from other people (local knowledge and frames). Along the design process, we somehow lost control, with the emergence of local actors' objectives. This is not a bad thing. On the contrary, to us, appropriation of the object by local actors is proof of a fair collaboration in which lay actors and researchers are equals. The changing of the name of the game marked this appropriation process, as "teaching each other" translates local objectives and put the local member at the heart of an active co-learning process. Volunteering to facilitate playing sessions is further evidence of the appropriation process by local members. Three said that they were proud of the game and wanted to show it to other villagers and solicit their opinions. As one of them said, it was a way to "help [his] community to improve the way people drive their cattle."

The Added Value of an RPG

One could wonder what the game's added value is compared to "classical" approaches to understanding and modeling cattle-herding strategies, such as ethnographical fieldwork alone or the use of GPS collars on livestock.

Cattle-related decision-making processes are complex. Cattle husbandry and herding strategies are normed and structured in our study area. Owners and herders have to respect a set of endogenous norms (defined by the communities) concerning cattle herding inside the communal area, such as *xotshela*, the date before which cattle should not be left to stray in the village, and exogenous norms (defined mostly by the Forestry commission) concerning the use of the protected area, such as the maximum distance within the forest that cattle have access to (although this fluctuates somewhat). The ethnographic part of our work was crucial and provided key knowledge about the system. Could it have been sufficient to reach our objectives? Our answer is "no." Actually, not only would ethnographical fieldwork not have been enough, but the use of the RPG enabled us to corroborate some of our observations, such as the use of the forest as a way to avoid loss of crops due to incursions in fields. By talking with people, we could understand these rules and we began observing discrepancies between the rules and the actions.

Differences between normative rules and observed and real practices are very common. The theory of situatedness (Clancey, 1997) stands that knowledge can only be represented once a person has actually put his or her knowledge into use. Adapting Simon's (1947) perspective, what matters for modeling human activities is how people are observed to behave, not how they are supposed to. In a very normed coexistence situation with written rules and enforcing entities—forestry rangers, police, traditional authorities)—studying these discrepancies is challenging because they are hard to observe (informants will do what they are supposed to do, say what they are supposed to say). If individuals are key elements of a system, behaviors are influenced by collective dynamics. A knowledge elicitation exercise must therefore include these two dimensions. We do not argue that it is necessarily the best solution, but a co-designed RPG is a relevant tool. Unlike individual interviews, the game brings players to play in a representative virtual alter ego of their reality (situated actions) and triggers collective as individual actions having potential actions on the others. When used with a modeling exercise, the added value of a participatory design of an RPG is that while co-designing the game, the team actually co-formalizes a virtual environment and defines a first step of parameters to include in the model and that will belong to or interact with the agents.

The question of the relationship between what happens during the game and reality must be asked (Daré, 2005): that is, do players reproduce their reality or do they use the game as a training arena? As explained in our results, the playing strategies were recorded and discussions and individual questionnaires were conducted after playing sessions. Asking villagers to play their own roles in an artificial environment coherent with their reality allowed players to take a step back from their reality, offering them an arena where they could act freely. Of course, one could wonder if, in that case, the strategies played are representative of "real" strategies. The RPG was complemented by discussions and individual interviews and the results allowed us to answer this question in the affirmative.

Supporting Experiential Learning in Virtual Worlds

Derived from J. Heller's novel (1961), a "catch-22" is a paradoxical situation from which an individual cannot escape because of contradictory rules. Among the ten characteristics of wicked problems is the fact that every action is consequential (Rittel & Webber, 1973). For managers or policy makers, this means that implementing a solution to a wicked problem will leave "traces" that cannot be undone. In other words, you cannot try plan A and have plan B in case plan A fails, because plan A will change the system in a way that is likely to make plan B irrelevant. This is the catch-22 of wicked problems: you cannot learn about the problem without trying solutions, but every solution attempt is consequential.

The same applies to researchers who want to study and therefore propose solutions to a wicked problem involving human beings and their real lives, such as coexistence issues between a protected area and its periphery. Wicked problems limit the feasibility of experimentations. Every modification of the system—including experimentations—has lasting consequences that may endanger human well-being and spawn new wicked problems. Transposed to our work in exploring alternative coexistence scenarios, shutting down the villagers' access to the Sikumi Forest or extending it, for instance, could both provide a solution to the concerns expressed by local actors but present risks of critically impacting local actors' livelihoods. If policy makers or managers are responsible for their actions, their position and their mandates give them some sort of legitimacy to change the system. How can we get out of the deadlock we are facing when dealing with reality? We propose that a solution is to conduct research in an experimental reality, a virtual reality. In other words, we need simulations. Different definitions of "simulation" can be found in the literature (Treuil et al., 2008). The one that best represents our approach is probably Shannon's (1998, 7), which states that "*simulation* is the process of designing a model of a real system and conducting experiments with this model to understand and/or evaluate various strategies for the operation of the system. . . . It is critical that the model be designed in such a way that the model behavior mimics the response behavior of the real system to events that take place over time." In a virtual environment, we can try plan A, reset, and try plan B. The consequences of each experiment can be recorded and lessons drawn without impacting the real subject system.

As one challenge is met, another appears: how can we design this virtual ersatz of reality? How can we capture the essence of the reality as seen by actors? In the case of wicked problems, how can we consider uncertainties? If "all models are wrong" (Box, 1976), we need a way to build a model that is "fruitfully wrong" (Epstein, 2008). A participatory approach like ours enables researchers to deal with this major constraint to our understanding of wicked problems.

Three categories of uncertainty can be distinguished: (1) epistemic uncertainties related to the lack of knowledge about a given system (we do not know everything), (2) ontological uncertainty related to the intrinsically unpredictable nature of social-ecological systems (our scientific understanding does not allow us to predict all of the dynamics and properties; Walker et al., 2003), and (3) ambiguities coming from the fact that different actors have different views and opinions of a given reality, therefore voicing different but still valid interpretations (Dewulf et al., 2005; Brugnach et al., 2008). This type differs from previous types of uncertainty, as it is not based on an incomplete knowledge but on the fact that there are many possible interpretations of a given situation. In our case, the rural communities, protected-area managers, and researchers each have their own frame, that is, their own sense-making process, that mediates the interpretation of reality by adding meaning to a situation (Weick, 1995), and each actor has his own reality. These uncertainties are an inherent and necessary part of life, definitional to the problem at hand (Brugnach et al., 2008). In the work presented here, we chose the negotiation approach (Leeuwis, 2000) to deal with uncertainties. Uncertainty is inevitable and should be included in the research process, so we decided to strategically transform it with local actors.

Our research tool is an RPG, that is, a virtual erzatz of reality, and we needed to include some sort of uncertainty in it. Co-designing the game was therefore a way to collectively negotiate a consensual uncertainty. Our vision of the system, that is, our frame, necessarily differed from those of local actors. The ethnographical fieldwork contributed to a partial understanding of endogenous frames, but a deeper understanding of local frames was necessary. An exogenous research tool used to collect data and simulate a social-ecological system is a manifestation of the researcher's frame and using it with people who have different frames would generate ambiguities. Co-designing an RPG to collect data for modeling rather than directly running the simulation model was a way for us to optimize the inclusion of divergent frames in the model. From a relatively high level of ambiguity-related uncertainty due to the different frames used by researchers and local actors to analyze reality, we collaboratively created a consensual frame. The three types of uncertainty were negotiated. For instance, researchers did not know how cattle grazing impacted forage availability in the study area, nor the specific composition of the grazing lands used (epistemic uncertainties) or how regeneration worked (ontological uncertainties). To cope with our lack of knowledge, we collectively negotiated a forage submodel for the game based on the crossed experiential knowledge of researchers and local members of the team who are custodians of the system. As the exact dietary regime of cattle is complex, multifactorial (age, diseases, physiological and reproductive status), and adaptive in space and time, we proceeded in a similar way to negotiate the submodel describing the dynamics of cattle body condition. The whole game, that is, all the submodels supporting it, was designed the same way. By doing so, we were able to design a virtual reality that was relevant for all the members of the co-design team despite the initial uncertainties.

Towards a Formalization of Research Tools Co-Design

In the field of environmental sciences, participation has become so inescapable that some authors spoke out about the "tyranny of participation" (Cooke & Kothari, 2001). Participatory empirical modeling still needs to be framed and formalized (Janssen & Ostrom, 2006). Our work allows us to draw several lessons participating in the formalization of empirical participatory modeling.

A GOOD AWARENESS OF THE CONTEXT

A time of observation and immersion is necessary, or at least greatly advisable. Beyond contextual information, it represents the first steps to create links between the project facilitators and local stakeholders. This step has consequences on the engagement of local actors and the effective collaboration within the working team (Mathevet et al., 2011).

BUILDING LEGITIMACY

The question of the legitimacy of external agents to conduct participatory processes is highlighted by Barnaud and Van Paassen (2013). Social-ecological systems are complex and involving actors is not neutral. Power asymmetries must be considered when engaging local stakeholders, resulting in the dilemma of participation for the authors. When designers of a participatory process claim a neutral posture, ignoring these power asymmetries, they are accused of being manipulated by the most powerful stakeholders, therefore reinforcing asymmetries. On the other hand, what is their legitimacy when a non-neutral posture empowers particular stakeholders? Such a dilemma isn't solved with a method, but by being reflective about our posture (Daré et al., 2010; Barnaud & Van Paassen, 2013). Transposed to our study, local communities and protected areas managers are all equally concerned with coexistence issues and the choice could have been to involve them equally. Other research activities are conducted by our team with the Hwange National Park and Sikumi Forest authorities, and while it legitimizes us in their eyes it also leads rural communities to see researchers as conservation agents. With the objective of initiating collaboration between researches and local actors in the study area, we chose to start by involving rural communities only and assume this posture. Our legitimacy was built according to ComMod view, which is that legitimacy is the product of an iterative and adaptive co-construction between local actors and researchers (Barnaud, 2013). Our choice of living in one of the villages is in accordance with this position. We do not claim that our approach was the "right" one, but the positive perception of the co-design process by local team members, the appropriation that occurred, and their expressed will to pursue collaboration are good signs of an acquired legitimacy.

SIMPLY PREPARE COMPLEXITY

Co-designing a model with people who are not used to manipulating such objects is challenging. The initiation of participation defines the relationship between participants for the whole co-design process. The popular "keep it simple, stupid" adage encourages one to start with the simplest possible model and only move to a complex one if forced to. As argued by Edmond and Moss (2005), it is sometimes critical to start with a model that relates to the target phenomena in the most straightforward way possible, which is rarely simple. In the case of a co-design with grassroots actors, we advocate for the use of a simple launch version, like the V0 we used. Simplicity serves three purposes: (1) easing the understanding of the project expectations by local members, (2) legitimizing the researchers, and (3) facilitating the improvement process. The choice of elements put in and left out of it is critical. The choices have to show your knowledge of the system without overinfluencing the design. The V0 brought for the first workshop displayed enough elements to show local members our understanding of the system, although observed elements of the SES studied were purposely left out. This eased the initiation of a critique-redesign dynamic from local members. Starting simple doesn't mean keeping it simple forever and this launch version has to be designed for complexity. In other words, the launch version is a complex structure of simple elements articulated around obvious gaps. The participation process then consists of filling the gaps and adding new elements.

Social Responsibility of Researchers and Benefits of Participation

The RPG presented is a boundary object built by heterogeneous actors coming from different social worlds but joining together to produce a shared representation of reality. The empowerment during the process and the appropriation of the game led local actors to define their own objectives and researchers to define new ones. Engaging local stakeholders triggers social dynamics (Gurung et al., 2006) and gives responsibilities to project researchers. When given an arena to think, conceptualize, share, and implement their ideas, local actors develop their own objectives. Emergent objectives have to be considered, discussed, and prioritized within the team and a balanced dynamic has to be found to satisfy all stakeholders. As shown in this chapter, the life of a boundary object can transcend the achievement of initial objectives. In our case, although we obtained the data needed to proceed to the next steps of our research, it is our responsibility to answer local partners' expectations. The game is ours, not "ours" as in the researchers'" but as in "the thirteen people who worked together." Strong human relationships were built and we believe that, as researchers, it is our moral duty to make sure that even after the end of this project and the end of our funding we do our best to help local members of the team achieve their objectives. The main challenge will be to produce a computer-free version of *Kulayinjana* that can be played by local communities without our technical support (generator, computer, and video projector).

Conclusion

At the origin of our work was the question of the coexistence of a protected area and the rural communities living in its periphery. Spending time living in the study area, partly within the villages where these communities live, led us to realize the complexity of addressing this issue. Uncertainties were high and different angles could be chosen. The central role of cattle in interactions between the two areas quickly appeared and we decided to focus our attention on cattle herding practices. The interdisciplinarity and participation at the heart of our work were a way for us to cope with the inherent complexity of social-ecological dynamics and our gaps in of knowledge. In order to study cattle practices, and with the capabilities necessary to model them, we co-designed a research tool that took the form of an RPG. This game is the central result of our work and its implementation has allowed us to better understand how people living next to the Sikumi Forest drive their cattle using the forest. We showed how participatory modeling could be used to overcome the wickedness of this socioenvironmental problem. We engaged ourselves in a collaboration that goes beyond this research project and this should not be "wasted." In 2016, we played *Kulayinjana* with the local managers of Hwange National Park and the Sikumi Forest. Having played the role of farmers, all acknowledged the potential interest of the game to mitigate local conflicts through playing and sharing ideas and opinions. It was then collectively decided to develop a version of the game that explicitly includes the role of protected area managers. As cattle-related issues on the edge of protected areas are found elsewhere in the country, we hope that this new version of *Kulayinjana* will be a key component of future outscaling studies.

REFERENCES

Alberti, M., Asbjornsen, H., Baker, L. A., Brozovic, N., Drinkwater, L. E., Drzyzga, S. A., Jantz, C. A., Fragoso, J., Holland, D. S., Kohler, T. A., Liu, J., McConnell, W. J., Maschner, H. D. G., Millington, J. D. A., Monticino, M., Podestá, G., Pontius, R. G., Redman, C. L., Reo, N. J., Sailor, D., & Urquhart, G. (2011). Research on Coupled Human and Natural Systems (CHANS): Approach, challenges, and strategies. *Bulletin of the Ecological Society of America, 92*(2), 218–228.

d'Aquino, P., & Bah, A. (2013). A participatory modeling process to capture indigenous ways of adaptability to uncertainty: Outputs from an experiment in West African drylands. *Ecology and Society, 18*(4).

Balint, P. J. (Ed.). (2011). *Wicked environmental problems: Managing uncertainty and conflict.* Washington, DC: Island Press.

Barnaud, C. (2013). La participation, une légitimité en question. *Natures Sciences Sociétés, 21*(1), 24–34.

Barnaud, C., Le Page, C., Dumrongrojwatthana, P., & Trébuil, G. (2012). Spatial representations are not neutral: Lessons from a participatory agent-based modelling process in a land-use conflict. *Environmental Modelling & Software, 45,* 150–159.

Barnaud, C., & Van Paassen, A. (2013). Equity, power games and legitimacy: Dilemmas of participatory natural resource management. *Ecology and Society, 18*(2), 21.

Becu, N., Barreteau, O., Perez, P., Saising, J., & Sungted, S. (2005). A methodology for identifying and formalizing farmers' representations of watershed management: A case study from northern Thailand. In Bousquet, F., Trebuil, G., & Hardy, B. (Eds.), *Companion modeling and multi-agent systems for integrated natural resource management in Asia* (pp. 41–62). Los Baños, Philippines: International Rice Research Institute.

Bousquet, F., & Le Page, C. (2004). Multi-agent simulations and ecosystem management: a review. *Ecological Modelling, 176*(3–4), 313–332.

Bousquet, F., Le Page, C., & Müller, J.-P. (2002). Modélisation et simulation multi-agent. Paper presented at *deuxiemes assises du GDRI3*, Nancy, France, December 2002.

Box, G. E. P. (1976). Science and statistics. *Journal of the American Statistical Association, 71*(356), 791–799.

Brugnach, M., Dewulf, A., Pahl-Wostl, C., & Taillieu, T. (2008). Toward a relational concept of uncertainty: About knowing too little, knowing too differently, and accepting not to know. *Ecology and Society, 13*(2), 30.

Chlous-Ducharme, F., & Gourmelon, F. (2011). A companion modelling: Appropriation of the approach by various partners and consequences. *VertigO-la revue électronique en sciences de l'environnement, 11*(3).

Churchman, C. W. (1967). Wicked problems. *Management Science, 4*(14), 141–142.

Clancey, W. (1997). *Situated cognition: On human knowledge and computer representations.* New York: Cambridge University Press.

Cooke, B., & Kothari, U. (2001). *Participation: The new tyranny?* London: Zed Books.

Daré, W. (2005). *Comportements des acteurs dans le jeu et dans la réalité: Indépendance ou correspondance? Analyse sociologique de l'utilisation de jeux de rôles en aide à la concertation.* (Unpublished doctoral dissertation.) Agro ParisTech, Paris.

Daré, W., Barnaud, C., D'Aquino, P., Etienne, M., Fourage, C., & Souchère, V. (2010). La posture du commodiens: un savoir être, des savoir-faire. *La modélisation d'accompagnement: Une démarche en appui au développement durable.* Paris: Quae éditions.

Davies, K. K., Fisher, K. T., Dickson, M. E., Thrush, S. F., & Le Heron, R. (2015). Improving ecosystem service frameworks to address wicked problems. *Ecology and Society, 20*(2).

Desouza, S. 2012. The strength of collective processes: An "outcome analysis" of women's collectives in India. *Indian Journal of Gender Studies, 19*(3), 373–392.

Dewulf, A., Craps, M., Bouwen, R., Taillieu, T., & Pahl-Wostl, C. (2005). Integrated management of natural resources: Dealing with ambiguous issues, multiple actors and diverging frames. *Water science and technology, 52*(6), 115–124.

Edmonds, B., & Moss, S. (2005). From KISS to KIDS–an "anti-simplistic" modelling approach. *Lecture Notes in Artificial Intelligence 3415,* 130–144.

Epstein, G., Vogt, J. M., Mincey, S. K., Cox, M., & Fischer, B. (2013). Missing ecology: Integrating ecological perspectives with the social-ecological system framework. *International Journal of the Commons, 7*(2), 432–453.

Epstein, J. M. (2008). Why model? *Journal of Artificial Societies and Social Simulation, 11*(4), 12.

Etienne, M. (Ed.). (2014). *Companion modelling: A participatory approach to support sustainable development.* Dodrecht, Netherlands: Springer.

Eversole, R. (2003). Managing the pitfalls of participatory development: Some insight from Australia. *World Development, 31*(5), 781–795.

Funtowicz, S., & J. R. Ravetz, J. R. 1993. Science for the post-normal age. *Futures* 25(7):739–755.

de Garine-Wichatitsky, M., Miguel, E., Mukamuri, B., Garine-Wichatitsky, E., Wencelius, J., Pfukenyi, D. M., & Caron, A. (2013). Coexisting with wildlife in transfrontier conservation areas in Zimbabwe: Cattle owners' awareness of disease risks and perceptions of the role played by wildlife. *Comparative Immunology, Microbiology and Infectious Diseases, 36*(3), 321–332.

Grimm, V., Berger, U., DeAngelis, D. L., Polhill, J. G., Giske, J., & Railsback, S. F. (2010). The ODD protocol: A review and first update. *Ecological Modelling, 221*(23), 2760–2768.

Guerbois, C., Chapanda, E., & Fritz, H. (2012). Combining multi-scale socio-ecological approaches to understand the susceptibility of subsistence farmers to elephant crop raiding on the edge of a protected area. *Journal of Applied Ecology, 49*(5), 1149–1158.

Guerbois, C., Dufour, A.-B., Mtare, G., & Fritz, H. (2013). Insights for integrated conservation from attitudes of people towards protected areas near Hwange National Park, Zimbabwe. *Conservation Biology, 27*(4), 844–855.

Gurung, T. R., Bousquet, F., & Trébuil, G. (2006). Companion modeling, conflict resolution, and institution building: Sharing irrigation water in the Lingmuteychu Watershed, Bhutan. *Ecology and Society, 11*(2), 36.

Janssen, M. A., & Ostrom, E. (2006). Empirically based, agent-based models. *Ecology and Society, 11*(2), 37.

Le Page, C., Becu, N., Bommel, P., & Bousquet, F. (2012). Participatory agent-based simulation for renewable resource management: The role of the cormas simulation platform to nurture a community of practice. *Journal of Artificial Societies and Social Simulation, 15*(1), 10.

Leeuwis, C. (2000). Reconceptualizing participation for sustainable rural development: Towards a negotiation approach. *Development and Change, 31*(5), 931–959.

Mansbridge, J. J. (1973). Time, emotion, and inequality: Three problems of participatory groups. *The Journal of Applied Behavioral Sciences, 9*(2–3), 351–368.

Maphosa, B. (1994). Lessons from the 1992 drought in Zimbabwe: The quest for alternative food policies. *Nordic Journal of African Studies, 3*(1), 53–58.

Matarira, C., & Jury, M. (1992). Contrasting meteorological structure of intra-seasonal wet and dry spells in Zimbabwe. *International Journal of Climatology, 12*(2), 165–176.

Mathevet, R., Antona, M., Barnaud, C., Fourrage, C., Trébuil, G., & Aubert, S. (2011). Contexts and dependencies in the ComMod process. In M. Etienne (Ed.), *Companion modelling: A participatory approach to support sustainable development* (pp. 103–126). New York: Springer.

Metcalfe, S., & Kepe, T. (2008). "Your elephant on our land": The struggle to manage wildlife mobility on Zambian communal land in the Kavango-Zambezi Transfrontier Conservation Area. *Journal of Environment & Development, 17*(2), 99–117.

Muboko, N., Muposhi, V., Tarakini, T., Gandiwa, E., Vengesayi, S., & Makuwe, E. (2014). Cyanide poisoning and African elephant mortality in Hwange National Park, Zimbabwe: A preliminary assessment. *Pachyderm,* (55), 92–94.

Perrotton, A., Garine-Wichatitsky, E. McKey, D. Mukamuri, B., & De Garine-Wichatitsky, M. (2016). Reading the environment: Dynamics of the ethno-meteorological knowledge system of a multicultural community farming in a semi-arid area of Zimbabwe. Unpublished manuscript.

Rittel, H. W., & Webber, M. (1973). Dilemmas in a general theory of planning. *Policy Sciences, 4,* 155–169.

Roberts, N. (2000). Wicked problems and network approaches to resolution. *International Public*

Management Review, 1(1), 1–19.

Shannon, R. E. (1998). Introduction to the art and science of simulation. In *Proceedings of the 30th conference on winter simulation* (pp. 7–14). Los Alamitos, CA: IEEE Computer Society Press.

Simon, H. A. (1947). *Administrative behavior: A study of decision-making processes in administrative organizations.* New York: The Free Press.

Stokes, S., Thomas, D. S. G., & Washington, R. (1997). Multiple episodes of aridity in southern Africa since the last interglacial period. *Nature 388*(6638), 154–158.

Stringer, L. C., Dougill, A. J., Fraser, E., Hubacek, K., Prell, C., & Reed, M. S. (2006). Unpacking "participation" in the adaptive management of social–ecological systems: A critical review. *Ecology and Society, 11*(2), 39.

Tompkins, E. L., & Adger, N. W. (2004). Does adaptive management of natural resources enhance resilience to climate change? *Ecology and Society, 9*(2), 10.

Treuil, J.-P., Drogoul, A., & Zucker, J.-D. (2008). *Modélisation et simulation à base d'agents: Exemples commentés, outils informatiques et questions théoriques.* Malakoff, France: Dunod.

Valls-Fox, H., Chamaillé-Jammes, S., de Garine-Wichatitsky, M., Perrotton, A., Courbin, N., Miguel, E., Guerbois, C. Caron, A., Loveridge, A., Stapelkamp, B., Muzamba, M., & Fritz, H. . (2018). Water and cattle shape habitat selection by wild herbivores at the edge of a protected area. *Animal Conservation, (21)5*, 365–375.

Vinck, D. (2009). De l'objet intermédiaire à l'objet-frontière: Vers la prise en compte du travail d'équipement. *Revue d'anthropologie des connaissances, 3*(1), 51.

Walker, W. E., Harremoës, P., Rotmans, J., van der Sluijs, J. P., van Asselt, M. B. A., Janssen, P., & von Krauss, M. P. K. (2003). Defining uncertainty: A conceptual basis for uncertainty management in model-based decision support. *Integrated Assessment, 4*(1), 5–17.

Webber, J. (1998). Environnement, développement et propriété, Une Approche Epistemologique. In F. Aubert & J-P. Sylvestre (Eds.), *Ecologie et société* (pp. 61–74). Dijon, France: Educagri.

Weick, K. E. (1995). *Sensemaking in organizations.* Thousand Oaks: Sage Publications.

Participatory Complex Systems Modeling for Environmental Planning: Opportunities and Barriers to Learning and Policy Innovation

Moira Zellner, Leilah Lyons, Daniel Milz, Joey T. R. Shelley, Charles Hoch, Dean Massey, and Joshua Radinsky

I n 2009, our research team embarked on a project to study how complex systems modeling could help stakeholders plan for persistent environmental problems. We knew that providing decision-makers with information alone would not be enough to effect lasting and meaningful change. Stakeholders often hold out for "more information," hoping that previously hidden data will simplify their decisions, when even in the presence of perfect information, most planning decisions require the deep consideration of tradeoffs. Beyond characterizing the problem and anticipating future outcomes, we hypothesized that it was important for stakeholders to learn how local resource use (e.g., land, water) decisions interact with environmental processes (e.g., water flow) to cause system-wide impacts in order to acknowledge and understand the tradeoffs stemming from those effects and to collectively design more effective approaches to such problems (Zellner, 2008; Zellner et al., 2012).

We thus designed and tested a participatory modeling approach to environmental planning inspired by the collaborative planning, planning support systems, participatory modeling, human-computer interaction, and social learning literatures. Several challenges need to be overcome for such a setup to succeed.

The first challenge involves communicating across a range of expertise, such that stakeholders can use expert knowledge to inform their own decisions and not just be beholden to expert recommendations. Expert modelers are trained to distill complex systems into appropriate (and, ideally, elegant) abstractions, which requires a facility with spatial reasoning and systems thinking skills (Railsback & Grimm, 2011). Experts are not typically trained to communicate with the general public and citizens are often excluded from modeling and policy design. Moreover, citizens make decisions and provide public input based on simplifications that, although necessary, may not map appropriately onto the complexities of the real world. The typical development process of models—wherein modelers dive deep into the problem space and select and implement their simplifying abstractions in isolation—means that the stakeholder voice is often inadvertently lost in the midst of the modeling process (Zellner, 2008; Basco-Carrera et al., 2017).

Spatial thinking and computer modeling are difficult for most novice users, even as such technology is becoming increasingly ubiquitous (Milz, 2015; Hoch et al., 2015; Golledge, Marsh, & Battersby, 2008). When the public is only able to consume modeling outputs rather than participate in the modeling activity, however, there is a greater likelihood of confirmatory bias; that is, models that provide desired or expected results are more likely to be favored and trusted while those that challenge them are not, making it hard to use such tools to support meaningful deliberations and the formulation of concrete policy (Pahl-Wostl, 2007). Without such support, conflicts arising from diverse or vague interpretations of the problem and the effect of potential solutions are typically resolved through consensus-building around a concept of sustainability that is so generalized that anyone can co-opt it to support their individual interests, whether those interests include improving well-being or not.

Given the above, we designed our approach to "unbox" the models. We situated complex systems simulations within ordinary planning activities. Supportive interfaces and facilitation structures were designed to translate specialized expertise into useful knowledge for practical judgment and to improve complex systems understanding. The intent was to reorient participants from consumers to co-constructors of knowledge. Fostering curiosity about causes rather than seeking "proof" for favored, predetermined policies should promote joint inquiry and creative problem solving, leading to policy innovation through collaborative learning rather than through political shortcuts. To support participants, we must be very sensitive to what they need to know (i.e., what information is present in the models), the process by which they discover that knowledge (i.e., how interaction design can make knowledge available to them for discovery), and how they need to share and negotiate their insights with their co-planners (i.e., how we can structure the social processes of the planning activity).

In the following sections, we provide an overview of the literature supporting our work, followed by the progressive design of our participatory modeling protocol applied to groundwater supply and urban flooding, and three main lessons that came out of this progression: (1) keep models and interfaces simple, (2) make both biophysical processes and values visible and tangible, and (3) explicitly structure the social aspects of the simulation's use. We derive implications for participatory modeling applied to environmental planning, emphasizing the need to support group goal deliberation, empathy, and negotiation, beyond enhanced cognition.

Background on Tools for Collaborative Modeling and Planning

The research on Planning Support Systems (PSS) and participatory modeling has focused more on the computational aspects than on the more mundane and practical aspects of making plans (Jones et al., 2009; Pelzer et al., 2015). While computational tools are novel and efficient, their use in planning is more strongly tied to the fact that making plans has always been supported by nonhuman actors (Klosterman, 2007; Beauregard, 2012). Planners adopt digital planning tools more because they are useful cognitive aids than because they provide exacting predictions of future conditions (Klosterman, 2012; Hoch et al., 2015; Milz, 2015; Zellner et al., 2012). The literature on PSS emerged in the 1960s as planning analysts sought to use new computational tools to develop predictive models of urban systems (Harris, 1960; 1965). After a period of disrepute (Lee,

1973), such tools have now again taken center stage with the advent of cheaper computational capacity, widespread access to mobile technology, online and open source applications, and Big Data (Goodspeed, 2015a). Similarly to the 1970s critics of comprehensive urban modeling, a new wave of scholars cautions against the rising tide of technophilia (Goodspeed 2015a; 2016; 2015b; Milz, 2015; Pelzer & Geertman, 2014; Pelzer, Geertman, & van der Heijden, 2015; Zellner, 2008; Zellner et al., 2012; te Brömmelstroet, 2010; te Brömmelstroet & Schrijnen, 2010). This counter narrative has focused on how computational tools support planning instead of replacing planners (Geertman, 2006).

Collaboration, Consensus, and Compromise

Planning is no longer a solo enterprise, if it ever was. Participatory planning emerged in the mid-twentieth century in reaction to the corruption and power imbalances associated with the technocratic planning models of that era (Arnsteinm, 1969; Davidoff, 1965). Democratic reforms, buttressed by communicative planning theories (Innes, 1995; Machler, Leonard, & Milz, 2015), embraced the authentic representation of a diversity of interests through dialogue and debate (Innes & Booher, 2010; Forester, 2009). Collaborative planning allowed communities to identify and commit to future actions, often in instances when individuals might otherwise have chosen different alternatives for themselves (Hoch, 2009).

However, this democratic imperative has not lived up to expectations (Cain, 2014). On the one hand, robust participation is difficult to achieve in practice and, on the other hand, too many voices can paralyze deliberative processes since no plan, policy, or action can satisfy all participants (Quick & Feldman, 2011). How can planning processes account for these challenges and encourage inclusive participation?

Participatory planning meetings adopt a variety of formats and use a range of activities to engage stakeholders (Chambers, 2002). Some strive to create more social interactions than others. Some adhere to strict parliamentary conventions and others do not (Susskind & Cruikshank, 2006). Some planning meetings are designed to accommodate large numbers of participants and others are suited to more intimate settings. Vacik et al. (2014) collated and reviewed forty-three activities planners often used in participatory planning meetings. They evaluated activities and found that some are useful for three things: (1) helping stakeholders identify problems through conversation, for example, World Café (Brown, 2010); (2) representing the problem in maps and models, for example, Planning for Real (Kingston et al., 2000); and (3) helping stakeholders develop solutions, for example, Open Space Technology (Owen, 2008). Which activities to use and which technologies to draw on to support them are critical questions to answer while designing participatory processes and planning meetings (Bryson et al., 2012). We drew on lessons from Learning Sciences and Human-Computer Interaction to design our participatory modeling activities and answer these critical questions.

LEARNING AND REASONING

Carried along with the rest of planning field, scholars of PSS have adopted the theories and techniques of social learning scholars to show what stakeholders and planners learn as a result of using PSS (Pelzer & Geertman, 2014; Pelzer, Geertman, & van der Heijden, 2015; Goodspeed, 2015b). Many have adopted Argryis and Schon's model of social learning (Argyris & Schön, 1996), which includes two interrelated loops of learning. A third loop, or "order" as described by Innes (1998) and Pahl-wostl and colleagues (2007), includes the foundational and cognitive aspects of social learning and hints at the practical behavior changes that accompany a collaboratively rational process. Pelzer and colleagues (2014), for instance, show how digital interfaces supported double-loop learning (i.e., questioning assumptions and goals, beyond assessing outcomes relative to pre-established goals) in cases in the Netherlands across three levels. They illustrated how stakeholders individually understood the problem and the perspectives of the other stakeholders, and how groups of stakeholders improved their ability to collaborate, communicate, build consensus, and craft plans efficiently. Finally, they observed how PSS informed the quality of plans and subsequent decisions.

Other scholars have adopted Wenger's (1998) communities of practice to describe learning the ongoing evolution of stake holding groups. Butler and Goldstein (2010), for instance, describe the US Forest Service's Fire Learning Network as a community of practice. They describe the ways that interactions between members of that community at the national level translated to practical changes on the ground and vice versa.

Much of this research has implicitly (and explicitly, in some cases) adopted the tenets of communicative action concomitant with the communicative turn in planning theory (Innes, 1995). As a consequence, this research often characterizes PSS as communication devices. The tools facilitate communication and thus stand between an expert analyst and nonexpert stakeholder, planner, or policy maker. In other words, this perspective has not overcome the division of labor described above, stunting the tools' capacity to augment individual and joint information processing.

SUPPORTING SHARED WORK: LESSONS FROM HUMAN-COMPUTER INTERACTION

The challenge of supporting collaboration is common in the field of Human Computer Interaction—to the extent that there are two subfields devoted to it, Computer Supported Cooperative Work (CSCW) and Computer Supported Collaborative Learning (CSCL). Both hold lessons for those who attempt to support collaborative planning activities with digital technologies. Here, we review two of the major theories these fields employ to define and design for "collaboration," demonstrate how those perspectives can have very different implications for the design of supportive software, and argue that, while some of these software design ideas can be profitably adopted to support collaborative planning activities, there are aspects of planning which necessitate new collaborative software designs.

The theory of "distributed cognition" has been proposed as particularly helpful for guiding the design of CSCW software systems (Rogers & Ellis, 1994). Distributed cognition takes as a given that collaborators are working towards a shared goal and that the "work" of collaboration involves distributing the subtasks among the participants and coordinating the execution of those tasks so as to reach that goal. The canonical example is that of a navy crew working together to navigate a ship (Seifert & Hutchins, 1992). CSCW research that adopts this perspective, then, is often focused on designing software supports that can improve coordination

(Schmidt & Simonee, 1996), like dashboards that help team members monitor one another (Biehl et al., 2007).

As technologies have evolved away from desktop systems, researchers have explored how to use platforms like mobile devices, tangible interfaces, and interactive tabletops to support distributed work. For example, by combining individual workspaces supported via handheld mobile devices with a shared workspace, which can be either a large screen (Myers, 2001) or a tabletop (Sugimoto, Hosoi, & Hashizume, 2004), individual collaborators can take on subtasks and do their own work while maintaining awareness of the group's activities. Collaborators can retreat to their individual interfaces to explore an idea or complete a subtask before migrating back out with the group via the shared workspace.

Most environmental planning problems are not simple (Rittel & Webber, 1973). The complex interactions that produce human settlements and the drama of organizing collective interests means that crafting plans is no simple task with a clear goal or end point (Zellner & Campbell, 2015). Consequently, while cscw designs like dashboards and distributed interfaces can be helpful for planning, the interface designs cannot be adopted wholesale. Participants cannot be assumed to be working together towards the same fixed outcome; rather, the outcome they are working towards is one they are actively negotiating. So shared workspaces need to be repositioned from being repositories of completed actions to sites of proposed actions, and dashboards need to give feedback not on task completion, but on participants' valuation of the various aspects of a plan. Moreover, because the ultimate outcome is unknown, it becomes less critical to support coordination and more important to support joint exploration of a problem space, with all of the messiness that this process entails.

CSCL has placed a bit more emphasis on producing interfaces that support joint exploration. The theory of Convergent Conceptual Change (ccc) positions the main purpose of collaboration not as attaining a goal, as cscw does, but as attaining a shared understanding of a concept (Roschelle, 1992), which can involve highly elliptical explorations. As a consequence, many cscl interfaces are designed to support the creation and iterative refinement of a shared artifact (e.g., a document, a map, a diagram), which represents the best current model of what the collaborators understand about the problem space. Urban planning interfaces designed in accordance with this idea of shared exploration have used tabletop activities enhanced with tangible objects that participants can move and manipulate as a way of representing the current arrangement of plan elements (Maquil, 2016). With our work, we use a similar template, which allows participants to propose plan elements in a socially visible way via a tangible interface. However, because a proposed plan may *not* represent a best current model of the plan (at least, according to some participants), it is also important to maintain records of the plans that have been proposed, and different participants' valuation of them, as well as to provide support for comparing the current plan against previous plans.

Planning Support Systems and Practical Judgment

Our approach seeks to blend learning and computer supported collaborative work (Radin-sky et al., 2016). We view collaborative practices as a form of distributed cognition (albeit a sometimes-conflictive cognition, given the competing goals of individual participants) situated in participatory planning meetings. Models of complex socio-environmental systems enable practical inquiry and imaginative play that prompt a more robust consideration of the tradeoffs necessary to make better plans in the face of wicked problems (Zellner & Campbell, 2015).

At the outset of this project and based on the review of the literature, we expected that an increasing progression of tool sophistication would lead to deeper engagement and policy innovation; shared digital interfaces alone would prompt collaboration and learning, and our tools would support more open and collaborative dialogue leading to better plans.

We use three examples to show the ways in which our experiences did and did not align with these initial expectations. First, we note that highly sophisticated tools did support learning about the challenges of planning for water resources. However, increasing the sophistication of the tools led participants away from deeper engagement and learning, especially as model outputs challenged the conventional wisdom of the groups included in this study. Second, we note that the introduction of shared workspaces (paper maps) and individual workspaces (tablets) enhanced stakeholder judgments and led to greater collaboration and compromise. Finally, we observe that the structure of the planning activities was vital for improving learning and planning. Activities that were either heavily structured and instructional, or too unstructured and participant-led, frustrated participants, while facilitated experiences promoted deeper learning through subtle provocation and not outright confrontation. We refined our model interfaces, components and facilitation guidelines to support learning and compromise-seeking behavior as a result of each lesson learned.

Small Is Beautiful: Groundwater Sustainability

We approached some communities in Northeastern Illinois as the region was planning for its long-term water supply. A US Supreme Court decree and the Great Lakes Compact limits the amount of water communities in Northeastern Illinois can withdraw from Lake Michigan, to address the increased stress from regional growth (Annin, 2006). Many communities thus rely on groundwater aquifers for their water supplies and were concerned about their ability to sustain these supplies, in light of economic and climate uncertainty (Meyer et al., 2012).

We partnered with some of these communities to develop and try a progression of models to support collaborative learning and uptake of agent-based modeling as a way to understand the system-wide effects of social and natural interactions and to develop a way to systematically examine how groups of participants learn with these tools and how such learning might translate into policy innovation (Zellner et al., 2012; Hoch et al., 2015). The progression ranged from simple land-use change models to help participants understand how residential and commercial location preferences could lead to different urbanization patterns in an exurban area, to more detailed models that linked land-use with the groundwater flow processes and water consumption behavior, to geographically relevant representations of the communities' processes based on stakeholders' feedback (figure 1). Stakeholders explored the models in pairs or in threes around a laptop, and on occasion, we prompted them to "look under the hood" of the models so that they could inspect, inform, and derive meaning from them.

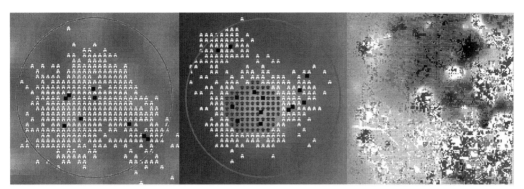

FIGURE 1. An illustration of the progression of simulated environments—from stylized land use, to stylized land use coupled with groundwater flow, to geographically detailed coupled systems— developed with stakeholders to explore water supply issues in Northeastern Illinois. (Note: different landscape shades represent levels of natural beauty (left) or groundwater (center and right); black squares = service center agents, houses = resident agents, those in water deficit are shown in darker color). Source: Zellner et al. (2012).

What Stakeholders Learned

In these trials, we observed that hands-on exploration and model development enabled participants to have open discussions about their assumptions about how their world works. For example, participants in a no-growth community realized that there was, in fact, residential development occurring within its boundaries, prompting the group to share knowledge of which others were unaware and increasing the relevance of the model being developed. Some participants also insisted that there was no groundwater scarcity and resisted the modeling process to explore such problems until another participant questioned this position in light of the conservation efforts already underway in their community. Working with the models allowed users to develop an understanding of how water flows in the region and how it is intercepted by residential and commercial areas, partially from the models themselves and partially from the information-sharing conversations the models inspired. Once a shared understanding of water flow was established, participants thus were able to anticipate, without even modeling it on the computer, how connecting communities to Lake Michigan water would affect neighboring communities, based on their upstream or downstream location.

Participants also moved their conversation towards increasingly concrete solutions as they explored them with the models, rather than more general recommendations of conservation, cluster development, etc. In particular, they were interested in seeing how enhanced recharge could help them prevent groundwater depletion in their region and the modeling forced them to specify the location, size, and capacity of such recharge areas for them to have an impact. Participants quickly realized that such localized solutions could not provide a safeguard for a regional problem and that they would have to work with neighboring communities to coordinate the management of the shared resource. In another case, the modeling prompted users to suggest injecting water back into the aquifer, a measure that was not in practice and that was

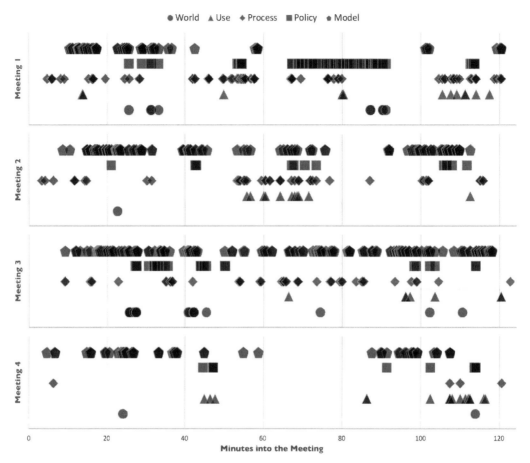

FIGURE 2. Frequency of coded discourse in each one of the four participatory modeling meetings. (Note: Each panel represents a two-hour meeting; each symbol corresponds to a dialogue target: model/software, policy, model use, participatory modeling process, real world).

proposed with some hesitation when nothing other than drastically reducing per capita water consumption would work (Zellner et al., 2012).

Despite these encouraging signs of learning, policy design, and innovation, by the end of our first series of four meetings with each case there was a general sense of disconnection, bewilderment, and uncertainty. We had hoped that these communities would want to take on this effort and eventually be able to completely own the process, but this did not happen. There was a general sense of hopelessness when participants realized that their favored solutions (e.g., purely local plans like conservation or clustering urban development) would not work the way they had expected (Zellner et al., 2012; Hoch et al., 2015). Even when facing the evidence from the models—which had been built with their information and assumptions—they rejected the implications, displaying a mixture of skepticism about the specific model (perhaps "more data" would "fix" the model to align it with their expectations) or about models in general (that they cannot be trusted).

What (and How) Researchers Learned

We studied the discourse in our meetings, developing a methodology drawn from the Learning Sciences (Radinsky et al., 2016). This approach required video recording each meeting, transcribing all dialogue, and coding it for the dimensions of interest to our study: how the modeling tools mediated the conversations towards an understanding of the complex problem, how participants derived meaning from the modeling, how participants shifted from localized to system-wide perspectives, and how the tools supported policy innovation and implementation. These five dimensions guided the coding of dialogue content, called "targets," shown in figure 2: (1) aspects of the model and software, (2) the real world, (3) policy, (4) the use of the model, and (5) the process of participatory modeling.

We also attempted to capture the nature of the discussion based on the conversational function of each statement (called moves), including: observation, objection, agreement, clarification and request for clarification, and explanation and request for explanation. Figure 3 shows a representation of the sequence of targets that were referred to around model objections.

Both views of coded dialogue help us look at the events in the sequence of meetings in an unfamiliar way and identify patterns that we might have not have perceived by direct observation. Figures 2 and 3 correspond to one of our cases, where we were able to tape all meetings. In both figures, we observe an initial predominance of the conversation around the software and the model, as there were many questions about how the models worked and what they represented. As more relevant and detailed models were introduced in subsequent meetings, the models still remained a central aspect of the conversation, but other targets became more present in the dialogue, most notably, the world and policy. The peak of this conversation was the third meeting, and in the fourth meeting all dialogue was greatly reduced, returning to the predominance of modeling and software.

We can explain this "collapse" in several ways. The model progression was good for learning, initially. By the fourth meeting, the number of moving parts in the models (both in their internal structure and on their interface) seemed to impose too big of a cognitive burden on participants. It was hard for them to make sense of the outcomes, given the many mechanisms that contributed to them, which added to the sense of uncertainty and distrust in the collaborative modeling effort and led to participants' demand for validation with data. Other sources of resistance added to this rejection of the process and the tools. Prior expectations of what plans should work trumped any dissonant insights from the simulations they experienced, especially because it was hard to explain the dissonance. Planning practice also operates within a culture of optimization and predictability, stemming from relying on external experts and consultants to conduct sophisticated analyses, rather than on collaborative exploration, anticipation, and innovation (Zellner, 2008; Zellner & Campbell, 2015). A predictable future allows us to be certain in our optimal solution. However, complex systems are often uncertain and the best we can do is find robust solutions that can work reasonably well in a range of future scenarios (Bankes, Lempert, & Popper, 2002). The discomfort and disappointment with such uncertainty led participants to demand for increased model relevance with more data, not realizing that this would further increase the same model complication and system intractability from which they

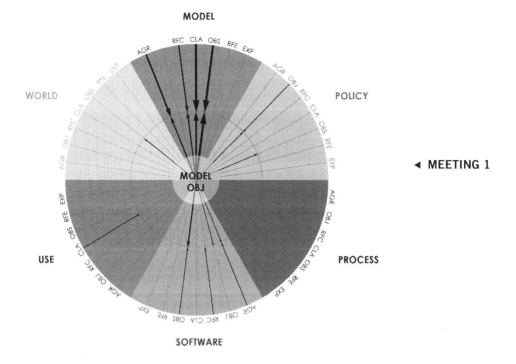

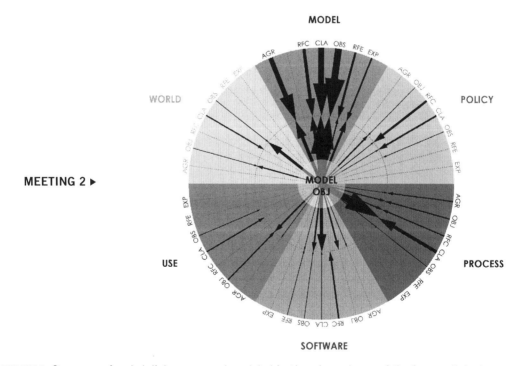

FIGURE 3. Sequence of coded dialogue around model objections in each one of the four participatory modeling meetings. (Note: each circle corresponds to a two-hour meeting; each shade corresponds to a dialogue target, and each radius corresponds to the type of move: AGR = agreement, OBJ = objection, RFC = request for clarification, CLA = clarification, OBS = observation, RFE = request for

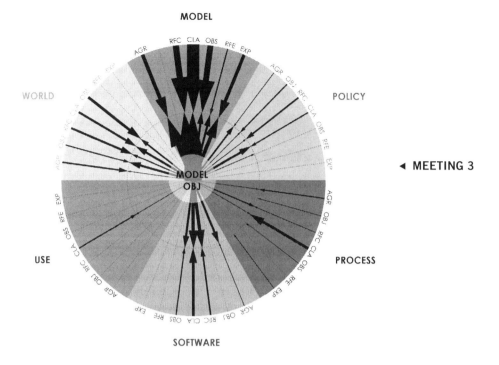

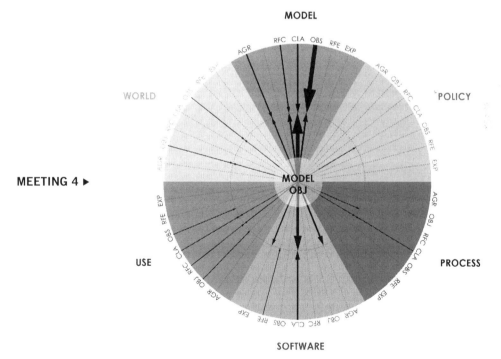

explanation, EXP = explanation; arrows show the direction of the sequence of dialogue, while arrow thickness shows the frequency of such sequence, e.g., model objections followed model agreement a total of three times in Meeting 1).

wanted to move away. When the models failed to clarify, the resistance was directed toward the researchers. The instructional social setting did not help in this respect: instead of creating a more collaborative and exploratory environment, it pitted the participants against the researchers.

Lessons for Improvement

In sum, the model progression approach was useful for learning, but only up to a certain point. Once the models became too complicated, they ceased to be useful. While working in small groups around a laptop and then interacting in large group discussions was helpful, it was hard for all participants to engage at equally via a single mouse. Finally, we realized we needed to make our social setup more interactive, rather than instructional, to allow participants to freely confront their own expectations and explore options, instead of being confronted with an externally imposed tool and outcomes. Instruction got in the way of planning.

The main lessons learned from this experience were fundamental in shaping our subsequent development. After these experiences, we met with our community partners and collectively revised our strategy. We thus shifted to a more visible problem that required fewer assumptions and interactions and thus could be supported with simpler modeling and visualization tools, and less need for instruction. We focused on urban flooding and the role of green infrastructure in addressing it. We addressed the tensions we had observed in our groundwater cases by redesigning the social setting for participatory mapping and modeling, moving towards a more familiar facilitated process of exploration, rather than a tutorial approach. This would be an entry point for the communities to engage and become familiar with collaborative modeling before delving into more complicated problems and their representation.

Making the Invisible Visible: Moving to Urban Flooding

In this phase of our work, we became increasingly aware of the two aspects of collaborative modeling that needed to be visible. The first, as in our prior work, was the underlying biophysical and socioeconomic processes, in this case, of urban flooding. We adapted the Landscape Green Infrastructure Design model (L-GrID), a neighborhood-level, spatially explicit, process-based model we had developed to answer questions about how much green infrastructure is needed to mitigate urban flooding and in what spatial configurations given different storm and landscape conditions (Zellner et al., 2016). While other models are primarily either site-specific (e.g., stormwater calculators for particular land parcels), or watershed-scale and data-intensive, L-GrID was meant to simulate hypothetical conditions, where surface flow could be easily visualized during a simulated storm, without needing as much data (and therefore, resources) to run, and stylized enough to simulate controlled experiments to generalize recommendations towards policy.

The details of the model are reported elsewhere (Zellner et al. 2016), but a summary is provided here for self-containment. The original version of L-GrID modeled a single, stylized form of green infrastructure that incorporates features common to various types, mainly stormwater storage and infiltration. The model allows users to modify storm duration and intensity, landscape size, placement of green infrastructure, sewer configuration, and proportions for different land cover types (with corresponding soil types) in the landscape. After the configuration is set, the user can run simulations and compare the outcomes in terms of flooded area and runoff volumes directed to sewers, green infrastructure, and downstream areas. The processes in L-GrID include precipitation (following a hyetograph), dynamic infiltration (decreasing with increasing soil saturation), sewer intake (limited by intake and treatment capacity), evaporation and evapotranspiration, surface flow, and outflow drainage downstream of the neighborhood simulated. The model runs for up to one additional day, or until all accumulated water leaves the surface, whichever comes first.

L-GrID simulations allowed us to derive generalized guidelines for the amount and spatial layout of green infrastructure to increase its effectiveness in reducing flooding, taking into consideration the spatial interactions between elevation, land cover, storm type, regional drainage, road layout, etc. Simulations alone, however, cannot provide answers to complex environmental problems. Tradeoffs across variables are inevitable and difficult to resolve, most notably monetary and environmental costs, differential impacts across populations, physical constraints, and people's values and preferences that might limit some options or make others possible. A computer can process a tremendous amount of data and scenarios, but the solution space is usually large, and by the time computing is completed, conditions or participants' values are likely to have changed. Additionally, we knew from our initial trials that when model outputs do not match stakeholder expectations, the model's validity is strongly challenged and can only be tested by opening the model for examination, a difficult task for novice users. Looking for the best (optimal) solution is a very costly and time-consuming endeavor and can create resistance when outsourced to a computer or set of experts. Instead, finding a good-enough solution that stakeholders can all live with, with an understanding of what is given up and what can be done about it, might be more meaningful and practical, supporting the necessary transformations towards sustainability.

The design of visualization tools and the way they are used in planning need to attend to this friction in decision-making processes. We needed to develop a way to support both collaborative solution building *and* compromise among diverse stakeholders, making visible not just the biophysical and socioeconomic processes that give rise to a complex problem, but also the diverse values around the problem and possible solutions. For compromise to happen, participants first need to acknowledge where they stand, how their values affect the way they see the problem and the solutions, and then share that with others. Participants then need to collectively evaluate different candidate solutions with variables of their interest. The visualization of both processes and outcomes through interactions with both tools and people is a scaffold, an entry point into the problem and a problem-solving space, as well as to other people's perspectives.

We thus shifted our focus to designing interfaces to support simultaneous collaborative use of hydrological simulations with mobile devices and paper-based tangible user interfaces. We simplified our simulations and model interfaces to allow novice users to explore on their own, with fewer interventions from the researchers, keeping the representation of biophysical dynamics reasonable (if not fully accurate) and relevant to the diverse interests of stakeholders. We developed a tangible interface representing the geography of interest to allow participants to propose solutions to the environmental problem, by laying out arrangements of green infrastructure to test using simulations. The performance of the proposed plans was made available via a mobile tablet application that lists all tested plans and their associated simulation outcomes, allowing users to sort and resort the plans based on specific outcomes (e.g., damage costs, spatial extent of impact). The mobile tablet included several other features to enable it to function akin to a CSCW "dashboard," albeit a dashboard for progress made with mutual plan satisfaction rather than progress made with task execution. The interface allows users to prioritize the results by what outcomes users might consider more important, as a platform to prompt discussion with others the benefits and costs of each scenario from different stakeholder perspectives, and to collectively design solutions that can address the participants' diverse goals.

Stakeholders and experts were involved in the iterative design and conceptual validation of models, interfaces, and facilitation guidelines. Progressively refined versions were made available to different stakeholder groups in self-contained workshops, so that participants could come together and jointly design and test several environmental planning scenarios in a typical two-hour meeting, while providing feedback on the features of the protocol that worked well and the ones that needed refinement.

Paper-Based Interfaces

By allowing participants to place and move tokens on a shared tabletop map to reconfigure a plan, we ensured it would be clear when participants were proposing changes to the plan—purely digital interfaces can make it easier for participants to make changes unnoticed. More visible proposed changes become topics of conversation and debate more easily. Indeed, an early experiment we conducted showed that working around a paper map representing the urban neighborhood on which participants placed green infrastructure tokens was more effective and led to more exploration and better collaboration than manipulating a mouse on a computer (Shelley et al., 2010; 2011). Participants generally preferred this to mouse-based manipulations, even more so when they did not know each other well. Learners also used hand gestures around the tangible interface to bring into discussion dynamic, emergent outcomes, like the way runoff patterns changed, and generate solutions incorporating knowledge of these dynamics (Kwah, Lyons, & Ching, 2013). Moreover, in experimental trials with these tools, users were able to design solutions that were as, or more, effective than those proposed by experts.

These findings informed our design of the paper-based interface, a representation of the same neighborhood in the simulation (figure 4). Participants would then place wooden tokens on the map, representing different green infrastructure: rain barrels, bioswales, permeable pavement, and roof gardens. These could be placed in allowed areas on the map. So, for example, bioswales could only be placed wherever there was soil, lawns or driveways; rain barrels and roof gardens could be located on cells covered by buildings, and permeable pavement could be placed on driveways, alleys, and parking lots. Once participants collectively decide on a design, a software application we developed can take a snapshot and convert it into an L-GrID input (figure 4). L-GrID can then import the scenario and run a simulation, generating outputs that were then downloaded onto mobile interfaces, described in more detail below.

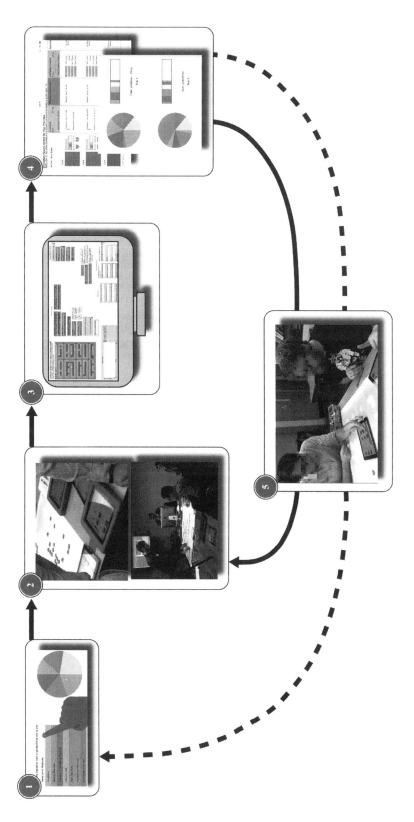

FIGURE 4. Stakeholders sort their preferences for variables of interest on a personalized iPad (1), then collectively design green infrastructure (GI) scenarios on a paper map of their neighborhood (2). An iPad application takes a picture of a GI scenario participants want to test and feeds it into the L-GrID simulation (3). Simulation results are delivered to each participant's iPad and sorted according to their preferences (4), allowing participants to compare their favored scenario to the valuation of others (5). Participants use this information to discuss tradeoffs and seek compromise, feeding back into the process by testing new arrangements (2), and/or readjusting their priorities (1).

Consistent with CSCL software intended to promote CCC, this tangible interface allowed them to explore the problem space by iteratively refining a shared artifact—the current plan proposal. Unlike CSCL software, which is commonly devoted to evolving a shared artifact, we also made sure to keep records of each plan that was proposed. In this way, participants could compare a current proposal against a past proposal, decide to revert to an earlier plan, or decide to incorporate elements of an older plan into the new plan. Perhaps most importantly for a planning problem space, this record-keeping helps prevent the suppression of "crazy" ideas: each proposal is only a trial, freeing participants to try out ideas with nothing lost.

Mobile Interfaces

Each user has a mobile interface, showing different information tied to the urban flooding simulation. The first challenge we faced was how we could create a dashboard that gave participants feedback on plan satisfaction; the system would need to know something about what outcomes the different participants valued. Thus, on the first screen (figure 4, point 1; figure 5), users are asked to rank their values relative to the outputs of the simulation (e.g., minimizing basement damage, maximizing efficiency of green infrastructure, etc.), in this way defining a Concern Profile for themselves.

The tablet software then uses the Concern Profile forced ranking to adjust how the outputs are seen by each user on the second screen, so that outputs that are more important to that user are seen first and weigh more in a composite score applied to each plan (figure 4, point 4; figure 6). This second page presents the simulation results from proposed plans as filtered through these output orderings and accompanied by weighted composite scores, so that users can quickly evaluate how a plan performed relative to their concerns. Some of the visualizations of simulation outputs also allow users to revisit how the output changes over the course of a storm (e.g., the accumulation of stormwater), and define different flooding thresholds, depending on what magnitude of flooding participants are willing to tolerate. Users can sort the presented plans by their composite scores, the order in which they were designed, or any of the individual outcome metrics by tapping the corresponding column. By making this interface interactive, we support exploration of the plan results, allowing users to alternate between deep dives exploring a specific outcome and a more gestalt presentation.

A third screen, not shown here, contains a guidebook that shows the neighborhood map with legends and references, as well as other aspects of the landscape not shown on the paper-based interface, such as slope. At the request of users, we also included information on the unit cost of each type of green infrastructure.

Lessons for Improvement

The easier access to the simulations allowed participants to question the simulation assumptions. In contrast with our initial trials where researchers set up an instructional modeling progression, in this trial the researchers only addressed questions when they were raised. Typically, users were reassured by our clarifications, although we recorded a few instances of skepticism.

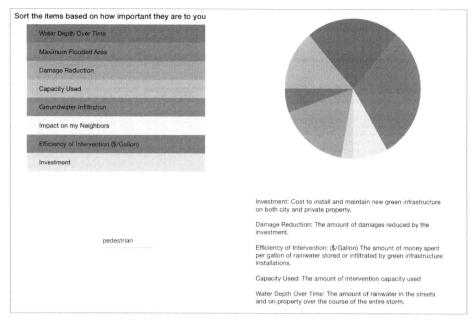

FIGURE 5. Forced ranking and definitions in the first page of the mobile application allows users to create a Concern Profile to filter the simulation results according to their priorities and preferences.

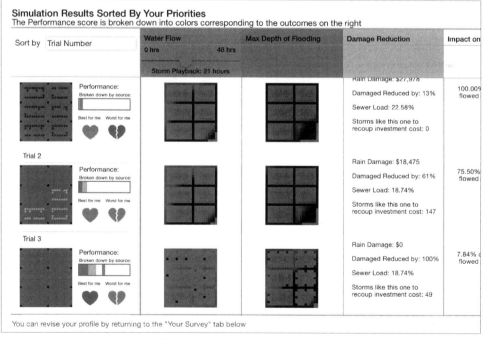

FIGURE 6. Simulation results for different green infrastructure scenarios (as shown on the left), composite score, and variables of interest for a specific user. Users can name the different scenarios and choose their favorite one by clicking on the heart icon. The screen can be scrolled to the right to view other variables that are less important to them.

When offering to open up the model for inspection by showing its code, however, we encountered resistance and did not pursue it further. As they manipulated the interfaces, users became increasingly aware of landscape constraints to the implementation of green infrastructure in specific locations (e.g., the presence of utility infrastructure). This awareness, however, led them to discuss how to address some of these constraints.

As in preliminary trials, we observed participants using gestures to follow the flow of water through the landscape and in this way inform the placement of green infrastructure to intercept it. For example, one participant directly referred to the flow path outputs on the iPad to understand how the slope in the landscape was influencing water flow and how they could locate green infrastructure to intercept that flow before it accumulated in the lower areas of the landscape. Participants were also able to engage in mental modeling and imagine different performance of stormwater infrastructure if some of the specifications changed. For example, some speculated on whether they should be increasing the capacity of rain barrels or even building underground storage tanks to store enough of the stormwater to have a greater impact on flooding.

Perhaps more revealing is the fact that participants quickly learned that green infrastructure could not, by itself, solve the problem locally unless they spent a lot of money. This realization required them to think out of the box: "Perhaps we need to think of moving the houses out of [the floodplain]."

Despite the evidence of increased understanding and ability to expand solution-building beyond familiar ideas, participants had a hard time finding solutions that would improve the flooding situation in the simulated community. As researchers and observers, we did not want to impose a predefined solution and instead focused on giving stakeholders visualization tools to develop their own according to their values, so we only explained how the interfaces and simulation worked, but then let them explore their own scenarios. The many moving parts often led groups to focus on only one variable to optimize (e.g., reducing damages or reducing downstream runoff), an easier task than negotiating tradeoffs. Participants still found the exercise overwhelming and it was hard for them to converge on a preferred solution or even a strategy.

Like in our initial trials, some users asked for more detail, which ran counter to their need for simplicity to make sense of the simulations. In another case, they asked if the computer could come up with the optimal solution for each Concern Profile. Even if that were possible, participants did not realize that letting the computer produce an optimal solution for each perspective would eliminate the in-between exploration and deliberation that would support a productive compromise. They would also not be able to explore the solution space for themselves and trust the outcome.

Moving forward, we realized that we had to keep the number of participants small, to around five people per map. Large groups made it hard for people to coordinate strategies and have a sense of what the others were thinking. We also needed new metrics of interest, such as the distance of streets that were flooded (as an indicator of public damage), and separate metrics for damage and investment (rather than separating public from private costs). We discovered that we had inadvertently introduced bias by projecting on the shared screen the return on green infrastructure investment (an additional variable of interest that was excluded from the composite score to prevent double-counting), which tended to draw more attention than the entire suite of output variables shown on the mobile interfaces of each participant. These limitations resulted in participants not fully exploring the variable space and the possibilities within it. Finally, in our attempt to create a planning session that contrasted with our earlier, more instructional approach, we may have gone too far to make the experience participant-led and open-ended. The participants needed a bit more orientation to the problem space, so we decided that we needed to start with drastically different profiles for them to understand how different stakeholders could interpret results differently. A set of predefined strategies and scenarios in the form of pre-existing plans for users to examine with their mobile interface would also be helpful, giving them tips on how to explore the solution space and prompting specific kinds of exploration, particularly around metrics they might have overlooked.

Where Is the Good News?

While both paper-based and mobile interfaces greatly improved access to the simulations and supported learning, our interactional style proved too unstructured for participants to feel they were making progress towards a concrete solution. They often felt overwhelmed by the many moving parts involved: different green infrastructure types that could go in many different locations, which would influence their effectiveness under different storm and upstream conditions. A facilitation structure was needed to help users navigate the process more effectively within the time-span of a two-hour workshop. For such facilitation to work, however, the group sizes around a shared simulation needed to stay small, at around five people. We attempted to run parallel sessions, which required a dedicated facilitator for each small group.

Each session started by introducing the problem of flooding and the purpose for the participatory simulation and then immediately explaining the tools and interfaces. We preconfigured "canonical" Concern Profiles based on archetypical stakeholders such as pedestrians (who are primarily concerned with how deep the water is and how it effects their walking paths), homeowners (who are primarily concerned with the amount of damage reduced by the intervention), environmental activists (who are concerned with the amount of water returning to the ground water supply) and public officials (who are concerned with balancing the cost and benefits of an intervention). These profiles were designed to assist the participants in exploring the variable space more completely as well as to provide them with an opportunity to use the interface in a low-stakes way. Once they tried these out in a role-playing game with two contrasting green infrastructure scenarios, they were given the chance to see how these scenarios could be valued differently depending on what kind of stakeholder they represented and to explain the differences. Participants could become comfortable with both interpreting results based on their Concern Profiles and incorporating others' Concern Profiles into discussion.

Every participant was then given the option to modify their Concern Profile to reflect their actual values and to design new green infrastructure scenarios. Participants were given printed worksheets to keep track of which variables were improving across scenarios, which ones were declining, and which ones they wanted to improve and how. In this way, we hoped they could pay close attention to tradeoffs across a broader range of variables.

We also gave them sample strategies for exploration, including finding compromises across different concern profiles, exploring effects of one green infrastructure type at a time (e.g., all rain barrels versus all bioswales), exploring effects of the spatial arrangement of green infrastructure (e.g., scattered versus clustered), and combining strategies.

Periodically, we asked them to choose their preferred scenario so far and give reasons for their preference to give them an opportunity to synthesize the findings of their exploration, which they did on a board next to their table.

Finally, we also added an exercise that allowed them to connect their neighborhood to the larger landscape by adding inflows from upstream areas into the landscape in the L-GrID simulation. This gave participants the chance to think about regional coordination and collaboration beyond local actions.

Learning and Compromise

Our protocol helped participants reflect and have more explicit discussions on tradeoffs between, for example, investment in green infrastructure and damages, and how that was different for different people, as exemplified by the following dialogue:

> **Jo:** "Oh wow, that's much better . . . for you."
> **Nina:** "I guess it matters what your priorities are!"
> **Kevin:** "Damage was reduced by 87% . . . but we were over budget by 1.2 million."

To justify their final decision of which trial was best for their group, they reported considering both investment and damage reduction and trying to select a scenario that balanced between the two. This compromise might not have occurred if the worksheet had not prompted strategic reflection and the mobile interface had not supported that reflection by highlighting how different participants were being affected differently by these variables.

Our guidelines helped participants engage in a more systematic exploration of the design and trial of scenarios:

> "Let's start by going crazy, putting a lot of stuff on here, and then pare back from there."
> "We can run multiple simulations, so let's run this one and then try that."

With a more structured facilitation, stakeholder groups did arrive at a preferred solution, although with some hesitation. Participants still wondered if there was an optimal solution out there that they were missing. The participatory simulation process and the learning that goes with it take time, much as a planning process takes time and several meetings. The fact that such collective learning, innovation, and convergence happened within standalone two-hour meetings gives us hope that, over a series of meetings typical of a planning process, this protocol can support collective decision-making for complex environmental problems. Moreover, one participant shared their excitement to continue working with the tools outside of the meeting time, while others wanted to hold more workshops with communities: "I want to take this back to work and play with this."

This is a significant improvement over prior trials, where the realization that their favorite solutions would not work as anticipated inevitably led to stakeholders' hopelessness, uncertainty, denial, and disengagement (Zellner et al., 2012; Hoch et al., 2015). In contrast, these recent trials have prompted planning agencies in the Chicago region to partner with us to further refine and adopt our protocol in their planning practice.

Implications for Planning and Future Work

When we started out with our scaffolded approach to participatory modeling and planning, we quickly learned that exposing a group of stakeholders to complex systems simulations fostered innovation through trial and error in a collaborative effort shared with others. While this setup was enough to support some complex systems learning and derive implications for policy, it was not enough to support the uptake or adoption of the lessons learned and transform them into practical measures on the ground (Zellner et al., 2012; Hoch et al., 2015). We encountered several barriers that explained the reticence. The first was the difficulty of manipulating and making sense of complicated models, requiring participants to deal with heavy cognitive loads to interpret the effects of multiple moving parts and interacting with the computer simulation and all its parameters and outputs. Also, the most common experience ended with a sense of doom and gloom for the participants: the future looked bleak unless drastic changes took place that conflicted with their beliefs.

As researchers, we were excited about the learning and innovation observed that shook up outdated and false assumptions. But what is the point of learning if it leads to paralysis or denial of new insights? The dissonance between what participants experienced through modeling and what they expected was too great and too uncomfortable for them to accept and own. We realized this was a deeply human experience, where computers and models are prostheses for human exploration, supporting the re-evaluation of expectations, judgment, and responsibility. Our tools need to be designed to support, not replace, this very human activity.

The process of iterative design to build our protocol allowed us to design tools and practice guidelines with the potential user in mind. This road was not always smooth, but it was helpful for creating meaningful interactive experiences that translated into successful practice. Participants more explicitly worked towards designs they were able to concretize in moments of synthesis, addressing specific tradeoffs for each scenario. We learned that, as much as the visualization tools were critical for users to interact and learn with the simulation, structured facilitation was equally critical to help participants explore the various moving parts of the complex problem they were facing, and guide them in the discovery of appropriate solutions. To that end, we are planning an additional screen in the mobile application to support the work of facilitators, tracking participants' use of their individual applications and synthesizing their explorations as actionable information to support productive deliberations.

Many planning workshops are designed to bring people to consensus, to find an average of the point of the view of the participants. Instead, our protocol allows communities to honor the multiplicity of the participants' viewpoints, even if—or perhaps especially if—they are not in concordance with one another. We have come to recognize that, unlike much of cscw and cscl software, the main purpose of our approach is not to support users as they collaboratively construct a product. While our users certainly do construct planning proposals, the main activity we are supporting with our collaborative modeling design is comparison, not construction. In order for participants to have a truly useful dashboard of their progress towards a compromise plan, they need to be able to compare plans against their own priorities, compare plans against other plans, and compare plans' performance against other participants' priorities. To support comparison, we have developed a fourth screen in the mobile application that allows users to see their preferred scenario and how that scenario is valued by other participants according to *their* preferences. Initial experimental testing has shown that this additional visualization is conducive to further compromise-seeking behavior, as users understand how differing values lead to discrepancies in which plans are preferred, giving them an opportunity to resolve those differences.

We envision this set of tools and guidelines as an initial prototype for use in conjunction with other, more sophisticated models for the application to urban flooding. The initial exposure to simplified simulations and analysis provides a scaffold to allow stakeholders to explore and learn about a system and its common patterns of interaction and to build a simple mental model of the problem space, which sets the stage for them to make sense of the outputs of more complicated models and propose meaningful interventions with such understanding. Such collaborative, multi-modeling framework could be transferred to other complex environmental problems for which appropriate model simplifications, visualization tools, and facilitation structures would need to be developed. The experience here provides a guide for both building these tools and putting them into practice in planning settings.

People have habits of practice and thought that distract them from discovering new possibilities. Visualizing both complex biophysical processes at play and tradeoffs around diverse values can empower participants to see gaps and differences and discuss whether and how to address them. Far too often, when communities work on developing compromise plans, they move further and further away from specifics until what emerges is a generalized "best practice" that may be able to gain consensus, but is so vague that it no longer holds any meaningful guidance (e.g., going from "we should put a specific type of green infrastructure here" to "whenever possible, we should favor green infrastructure"). It pushes back conflict but does not resolve it (Innes, 2004).

Models, interfaces, and facilitation can be designed to aid exploration and the evolution of understanding and valuation. Innovation happens through relationships with other people and can be enhanced by the use of tools as cognitive "prosthetic devices" (Hoch et al., 2015). Models offer a technical enhancement for groups of people to explore new possibilities, examine their expectations, and make practical judgments to plan for the future. There is no technical fix without social learning. Reliance on predictive models strips away opportunity and responsibility. Humans are good with nuance and judgment. Computers can inform such judgments, but their computations should not be given final authority in decision-making scenarios, especially scenarios with outcomes that are valued very differently by different people. Guided facilitation is key to helping participants (including facilitators) make sense of, be creative around, and seek compromises for complex problems.

We believe the consequences to be significant. The insights that came out of our trials, like "we need to take houses out of there" or "we need to stop growth" or "we need to work with neighbors," are a major and promising departure from standard policy. Perhaps more importantly, our approach supports a democratic process of working with difference, rather than trying to eliminate it. This is where innovation happens, and planning tools and the social protocols around their use can be designed to support it.

ACKNOWLEDGMENTS

UIC colleagues and research assistants: Emily Minor, Ben O'Connor, Kelsey Pudlock, Brian Slattery, Lisa Cotner, Priscilla Jimenez, Jen Weizeorick, Carl Kunda, Ethan Brown, Lissa Domoracki, April Schneider.

UIC funding sources: Urban Planning and Policy, Great Cities Institute, Institute for Public and Civic Engagement, UIC Chancellor Discovery Fund.

External partners: Chicago region stakeholders, Howard Reeves (USGS), Tim Loftus (CMAP).

National Science Foundation OCI program #1135572, and DRL REESE program #1020065.

REFERENCES

Annin, P. (2006). *The Great Lakes water wars.* Washington, DC: Island Press.

Argyris, C., & Schön, D. A. (1996). *Organizational learning II: Theory, method, and practice.* (2 vols.) Reading, MA: Addison-Wesley.

Arnstein, S. R. (1969). A ladder of citizen participation. *Journal of the American Institute of Planners, 35*(4), 216–224. doi: 10.1080/01944366908977225.

Bankes, S., Lempert, R., & Popper, S. (2002). Making computational social science effective. *Social Science Computer Review, 20*(4), 377.

Basco-Carrera, L., Warren, A., van Beek, E., Jonoski, A., & Giardino, A. (2017). Collaborative modelling or participatory modelling? A framework for water resources management. *Environmental Modelling & Software, 91* (May), 95–110. doi: 10.1016/j.envsoft.2017.01.014.

Beauregard, R. A. (2012). Planning with things. *Journal of Planning Education and Research, 32*(2), 182–190. doi: 10.1177/0739456x11435415.

Biehl, J. T., Czerwinski, M., Smith, G., & Robertson, G. G. (2007). FASTDash: A visual dashboard for fostering awareness in software teams. In *Proceedings of the SIGCHI conference on human factors in computing systems* (pp. 1313–1322). New York: Associations for Computing Machinery.

Brömmelstroet, M. te. (2010). Equip the warrior instead of manning the equipment: Land use and transport planning support in the Netherlands. *Journal of Transport and Land Use, 3*(1).

Brömmelstroet, M. te, & Schrijnen, P. M. (2010). From planning support systems to mediated planning support: A structured dialogue to overcome the implementation gap. *Environment and Planning B: Planning and Design, 37*(1), 3–20.

Brown, J., & Isaacs, D. (2010). *The World Café: Shaping our futures through conversations that matter.* San Francisco: Berrett-Koehler Publishers.

Bryson, J. M., Quick, K. S., Slotterback, C. S., & Crosby, B. C. (2012). Designing public participation processes. *Public Administration Review. 73(1),* 23–34. doi:10.1111/j.1540-6210.2012.02678.x.

Butler, W. H., & Goldstein, B. E. (2010). The US fire learning network: Springing a rigidity trap through multi-scalar collaborative networks. *Ecology and Society, 15*(3), 21.

Cain, B. E. (2014). *Democracy more or less*. Cambridge: Cambridge University Press.

Chambers, R. (2002). *Participatory workshops: A sourcebook of 21 sets of ideas and activities*. London: Routledge.

Davidoff, P. (1965). Advocacy and pluralism in planning. *Journal of the American Institute of Planners, 31*(4), 331–338.

Forester, J. (2009). *Dealing with differences: Dramas of mediating public disputes*. New York: Oxford University Press.

Geertman, S. 2006. Potentials for planning support: A planning-conceptual approach. *Environment and Planning B: Planning and Design, 33*(6): 863–880.

Golledge, R., Marsh, M., & Battersby, S. (2008). A conceptual framework for facilitating geospatial thinking. *Annals of the Association of American Geographers, 98*(2), 285–308. doi:10.1080/00045600701851093.

Goodspeed, R. (2015a). Smart cities: Moving beyond urban cybernetics to tackle wicked problems. *Cambridge Journal of Regions, Economy and Society, 8*(1), 79–92. doi:10.1093/cjres/rsu013.

Goodspeed, R. (2015b). Sketching and learning: A planning support system field study. *Environment and planning B: Planning and design, 43*(3), 444–463. doi:10.1177/0265813515614665.

Goodspeed, R. (2016). Digital knowledge technologies in planning practice: From black boxes to media for collaborative inquiry. *Planning Theory & Practice, 17*(4), 577–600. doi:10.1080/14649357.2016.12 12996.

Harris, B. (1960). Plan or projection: An examination of the use of models in planning. *Journal of the American Institute of Planners, 26*(4), 265–272.

Harris, B. (1965). New tools for planning. *Journal of the American Institute of Planners, 31*(2), 90–95.

Hoch, C. (2009). Planning craft: How planners compose plans. *Planning Theory, 8*(3), 219–241. doi:10.1177/1473095209105528.

Hoch, C., Zellner, M., Milz, D., Radinsky, J., & Lyons, L. (2015). Seeing is not believing: Cognitive bias and modelling in collaborative planning. *Planning Theory & Practice, 16*(3), 319–335. doi:10.1080/146493 57.2015.1045015.

Innes, J. E. (1995). Planning theory's emerging paradigm: Communicative action and interactive practice. *Journal of Planning Education and Research, 14*(3), 183–189. doi:10.1177/0739456x9501400307.

Innes, J. E. (1998). Information in communicative planning. *Journal of the American Planning Association, 64*(1), 52–63. doi:10.1080/01944369808975956.

Innes, J. E. (2004). Consensus building: Clarifications for the critics. *Planning Theory, 3*(1), 5–20. doi:10.1177/1473095204042315.

Innes, J. E., & Booher. D. E. (2010). *Planning with complexity: An introduction to collaborative rationality for public policy*. New York: Routledge.

Jones, N. A., Perez, P., Measham, T. G., Kelly, G. J., d'Aquino, P., Daniell, K. A., Dray, A., & Ferrand, N. (2009). Evaluating participatory modeling: Developing a framework for cross-case analysis. *Environmental Management, 44*(6), 1180–1195. doi:10.1007/s00267-009-9391-8.

Kingston, R., Carver, S., Evans, A., & Turton, I. (2000). Web-based public participation geographical information systems: An aid to local environmental decision-making. *Computers, Environment and Urban Systems, 24*(2), 109–125. doi:10.1016/S0198-9715(99)00049-6.

Klosterman, R. E. (2007). Deliberating about the future. In L. D. Hopkins & M. Zapata (Eds.), *Engaging the future: Forecasts, scenarios, plans, and projects* (pp. 199–220). Cambridge, MA: Lincoln Institute of Land Policy.

Klosterman, R. E. (2012). Simple and complex models. *Environment and Planning B: Planning and Design, 39*(1), 1–6.

Kwah, H., Lyons, L., & Ching, D. (2013). Interface Tangibility and Gesture in Mediating Individual Agency Within Group Spatial Problem Solving with an Ecosystem Simulation. In Nikol Rummel, M. Nathan, & S. Puntambekar (Eds.), *Proceedings of the 10th International Conference on Computer-Supported Collaborative Learning (CSCL 2013)* (Vol. 1, pp. 264–271). Madison, WI.

Lee, D. B. (1973). Requiem for large-scale models. *Journal of the American Institute of Planners, 39*(3), 163–178.

Machler, L., & Milz, D. (2015). *The evolution of communicative planning theory.* Groningen, Netherlands: InPlanning. http://www.inplanning.eu.

Maquil, V. (2016). Towards understanding the design space of tangible user interfaces for collaborative urban planning. *Interacting with Computers, 28*(3), 332–351. doi:10.1093/iwc/iwv005.

Meyer, S. C., Wehrmann, H. A., Knapp, V. H., Lin, Y-F., Glatfelter, F. E., Angel, J. R., Thomason, J. F., & Injerd, D. A. (2012). *Northeastern Illinois water supply planning investigations: Opportunities and challenges of meeting water demand in Northeastern Illinois.* Champaign, IL: Prairie Research Institute.

Milz, D. (2015). *Mismatched scales, mismatched intentions: Regional wastewater planning on Cape Cod, Massachusetts, USA.* (PhD Thesis) University of Illinois at Chicago.

Myers, B. A. (2001). Using handhelds and PCs together. *Communications of ACM, 44*(11), 34–41. doi:10.1145/384150.384159.

Owen, H. (2008). *Open space technology: A user's guide.* San Francisco: Berrett-Koehler Publishers.

Pahl-Wostl, C. (2007). The implications of complexity for integrated resources management. *Environmental Modelling & Software, 22*(5), 561–569. doi:10.1016/j.envsoft.2005.12.024.

Pahl-Wostl, C., Craps, M., Dewulf, A., Mostert, E., Tabara, D., & Taillieu, T. (2007). Social learning and water resources management. *Ecology and Society, 12*(2), 5. doi: 10.5751/ES-02037-120205.

Pelzer, P., Arciniegas, G., Geertman, S., & Lenferink, S. (2015). Planning support systems and task-technology fit: A comparative case study. *Applied Spatial Analysis and Policy, 8*(2), 1–21. doi:10.1007/s12061-015-9135-5.

Pelzer, P., & Geertman, S. (2014). Planning support systems and interdisciplinary learning. *Planning Theory & Practice, 15*(4), 527–542. doi:10.1080/14649357.2014.963653.

Pelzer, P., Geertman, S., & van der Heijden, R. (2015). Knowledge in communicative planning practice: A different perspective for planning support systems. *Environment and Planning B: Planning and Design, 42(4)*, 638–651. doi: 10.1068/b130040p.

Pelzer, P., Geertman, S., van der Heijden, R., & Rouwette, E. (2014). The added value of planning support systems: A practitioner's perspective. *Computers, Environment and Urban Systems, 48*, 16–27. doi:10.1016/j.compenvurbsys.2014.05.002.

Quick, K. S., & Feldman, M. S. (2011). Distinguishing participation and inclusion. *Journal of Planning Education and Research, 31*(3), 272–290. doi:10.1177/0739456X11410979.

Radinsky, J., Milz, D., Zellner, M., Pudlock, K., Witek, C., Hoch, C., & Lyons, L. (2017). How planners and stakeholders learn with visualization tools: Using learning sciences methods to examine planning processes. *Journal of Environmental Planning and Management, 60*(7), 1296–1323. doi:10.1080/0964 0568.2016.1221795.

Railsback, S. F., & Grimm, V. (2011). *Agent-based and individual-based modeling: A practical introduction.* Princeton: Princeton University Press.

Rittel, H. W. J., & Webber, M. M. (1973). Dilemmas in a general theory of planning. *Policy Sciences, 4*(2), 155–169. doi:10.1007/BF01405730.

Rogers, Y., & Ellis, J. (1994). Distributed cognition: An alternative framework for analysing and explaining collaborative working. *Journal of Information Technology, 9*(2), 119–128.

Roschelle, J. (1992). Learning by collaborating: Convergent conceptual change. *Journal of the Learning Sciences, 2*(3), 235–276. doi:10.1207/s15327809jls0203_1.

Schmidt, K., & Simonee, C. (1996). Coordination mechanisms: Towards a conceptual foundation of CSCW systems design. *Computer Supported Cooperative work (CSCW), 5*(2–3), 155–200. doi:10.1007/BF00133655.

Seifert, C. M., & Hutchins, E. L. (1992). Error as opportunity: Learning in a cooperative task. *Human-Computer Interaction, 7*(4), 409–435.

Shelley, T., Lyons, L., Shi, J., Minor, E., & Zellner, M. (2010). Paper to parameters: Designing tangible simulation input. In *Proceedings of the 12th ACM international conference adjunct papers on ubiquitous computing—adjunct* (pp. 431–432). New York: Association for Computing Machinery.

Shelley, T., Lyons, L., Zellner, M., & Minor, E. (2011). Evaluating the embodiment benefits of a paper-based TUI for educational simulations. In *CHI '11 extended abstracts on human factors in computing systems* (pp. 1375–1380). New York: Association for Computing Machinery.

Sugimoto, M., Hosoi, K., & Hashizume, H. (2004). Caretta: A system for supporting face-to-face collaboration by integrating personal and shared spaces. In *Proceedings of the SIGCHI conference on human factors in computing systems* (pp. 41–48). New York: Association for Computing Machinery.

Susskind, L., & Cruikshank, J. L. (2006). *Breaking Robert's rules: The new way to run your meeting, build consensus, and get results.* Oxford: Oxford University Press.

Vacik, H., Kurttila, M., Hujala, T., Khadka, C., Haara, A., Pykäläinen, J., Honkakoski, P., Wolfslehner, B., & Tikkanen, J. (2014). Evaluating collaborative planning methods supporting programme-based planning in natural resource management. *Journal of Environmental Management, 144*, 304–315. doi:10.1016/j.jenvman.2014.05.029.

Wenger, E. (1998). *Communities of practice: Learning, meaning, and identity.* New York: Cambridge University Press.

Zellner, M. (2008). Embracing complexity and uncertainty: The potential of agent-based modeling for environmental planning and policy. *Planning Theory & Practice, 9*(4): 437–457.

Zellner, M., & Campbell, S. (2015). Planning for deep-rooted problems: What can we learn from aligning complex systems and wicked problems? *Planning Theory & Practice, 16*(4), 457–478. doi:10.1080/14649357.2015.1084360.

Zellner, M., Lyons, L. Hoch, C., Weizeorick, J., Kunda, C., & Milz, D. (2012). Modeling, learning, and planning together: An application of participatory agent-based modeling to environmental planning. *URISA Journal, 24*(1), 77–92.

Zellner, M., Massey, D., Minor, E., & Gonzalez-Meler, M. (2016). Exploring the effects of green infrastructure placement on neighborhood-level flooding via spatially explicit simulations. *Computers, Environment and Urban Systems, 59*, 116–128. doi:10.1016/j.compenvurbsys.2016.04.008.

Developing a Collaborative System Dynamics Model of College Drinking Events: Finding a Common Language

John D. Clapp, Kevin M. Passino, Luis Felipe Giraldo, Danielle R. Madden, and Hugo J. Gonzalez Villasanti

This chapter details a three-year collaboration between a team of social scientists and a team of engineers to develop a system dynamics framework to study and model drinking events. Beyond the goal of advancing knowledge, the collaboration is geared toward informing the development of real-time solutions to address alcohol-related problems as they happen. Much of our work has focused on young adults and college students—one of the heaviest drinking demographics in society. Prior to discussing our modeling approach, we provide some background on drinking among college students, research related to drinking events and why that focus is important, and where the field is heading given recent technological advances.

College Drinking

From the earliest days of higher education, college students have consumed alcohol in excess and experienced negative consequences. As early as the 1300s, college students were involved in alcohol-fueled riots (Koenig, 2011). Currently, college students are the heaviest non-clinical drinking cohort in society (McCaig & Burt, 2005). The majority of students (82 percent) report having tried alcohol at least once in their lives, with 71 percent of those trying alcohol drinking to intoxication (Johnston, O'Malley, Bachman, & Schulenberg, 2011). In national surveys, over 70 percent of college students report consuming alcohol within the past thirty days (Johnston et al., 2011), and approximately 40 percent have engaged in binge drinking during the past two weeks (Johnston, O'Malley, Bachman, Schulenberg, & Patrick, 2013). The National Institute of Alcohol Abuse and Alcoholism (NIAAA [2004]) defines "binge drinking" as the consumption of five or more drinks for men or four or more drinks for women within a two-hour period. It is a pattern of drinking that results in a blood alcohol concentration (BAC) of 0.08 percent or more.

The consequences of binge drinking are readily apparent on campuses across the United States. In general, heavy alcohol consumption has been linked to consequences that can range from less severe (e.g., hangover) to very severe (e.g., death). Alcohol use fuels behavior that places students most at risk for disciplinary infractions and is among the most common reasons students seek medical assistance. Approximately 600,000 students are injured each year as a result of drinking and 1,825 of those students die from their alcohol-related, unintentional injuries (NIAAA, 2015). It is estimated that over 3 million students between the ages of eighteen and twenty-four drive while under the influence of alcohol each year (Hingson, Zha, & Weitzman, 2009; Teeters, Pickover, Dennhardt, Murphy, & Martens, 2014). Intoxicated students are also known to damage property, disrupt neighborhoods, and require police intervention (Wechsler et al., 2002).

Students' alcohol use can impact their fellow peers as well. Each year, 690,000 students are victims of assaults perpetuated by other intoxicated students. Alarmingly, 97,000 students are victims of sexual assaults in which alcohol is involved (NIAAA, 2015). Binge drinking has also been linked to poorer academic outcomes (Wolaver, 2002). On average, 25 percent of students report academic issues that result from binge drinking (NIAAA, 2015). These students are more likely to miss class, avoid work, and fall behind (Wechsler et al., 2002). Furthermore, students who regularly consume large amounts of alcohol are at a decreased likelihood of graduating on time (Renna, 2007).

As a result, binge drinking can strain already-meager institutional budgets for campus health and security. Large universities may incur emergency department costs of over $500,000 for alcohol-related injuries per year (Mundt & Zakletskaia, 2012). Other costs have not yet been systematically quantified, but the financial implications for property damage and security can be substantial (Perkins, 2002).

Why Are Drinking Events Important?

Drinking events are direct antecedents to numerous acute alcohol-related problems, including but not limited to injuries, sexual and other violence, burns, falls, crashes, and crime (NIH, 2000). In aggregate, drinking events represent patterns of consumption that drive disease and premature death (Holder, 2006). Acute problems have a huge global impact (Rehm et al., 2009); for instance, approximately 25 percent of all unintentional and 10 percent of intentional injuries in the world can be attributed to drinking events. When alcohol-related disease and death are considered, 3–4 percent of all deaths in the world are alcohol related (Rehm et al., 2009).

Approaches to Studying Drinking Events

The scientific study of alcohol use and its related problems is broad and inherently interdisciplinary—ranging from genetic studies and neuroscience on the micro level (Gacek, Conner, Tennen, Kranzler, & Covault, 2008; Kaufman et al., 2007; Covault et al., 2007) to large-scale economics and policy studies on the macro level (Rosen, Miller, & Simon, 2008; Anderson & Baumberg, 2006; Lenk, Erickson, Nelson, Winters, & Toomey, 2012; Anderson, 2004). Over the past half-century, a subfield of alcohol research has emerged with the goal of better understanding the ecology of drinking behavior as it naturally occurs. Reflecting the inherent multidisciplinary nature of alcohol research, such studies vary in conceptual foci, methods, and operational definitions. Independently, studies on "drinking contexts," "drinking situations," and "drinking environments" offer related but unique insights into drinking behavior in situ. Recent work has focused on drinking at the event level as a way of examining drinking as it occurs (Wells et al., 2015; Verster, Benjaminsen, van Lanen, van Stavel, & Olivier, 2015; Thrul & Kuntsche, 2015; Clapp, Reed & Ruderman, 2014). It is important to note that most of this work focuses on drinking as a social function and does not address the etiology of chronic heavy drinking. That is, the work tends to be focused on acute behavior and its attendant problems like drunk driving. As a collective body of work, such studies suggest the need and offer the empirical basis for a conceptual modeling approach reflecting the complex and dynamic nature of drinking events.

Our understanding of the etiology of alcohol related problems at the event level has—to date—emerged only from rudimentary ecological approaches. Although conceptual models and theory have long guided social science in general (Lewin, 1951; Kuhn, 1974) and alcohol studies specifically (Gusfield, 1996; Denzin, 1987), models for drinking events rarely build on previous work or transcend levels of abstraction in ways that integrate theoretical streams or acknowledge dynamics and complexity (e.g., non-linearity, feedback loops). Although there is a small body of system dynamics alcohol studies at the community level (Holder, 2006; Gorman, Speer, Gruenewald, & Labouvie, 2001; Scribner et al., 2009; Gruenewald, 2006), and some recent notable exceptions employing agent-based modeling at the population and event levels (Gorman, Mezic, Mezic, & Gruenewald, 2006; Fitzpatrick & Martinez, 2012), dynamical modeling in alcohol research is still largely underdeveloped. At the event level, this may well be an artifact of the difficulty of measuring drinking events (Kuntsche, Dietze, & Jenkinson, 2014; Clapp et al., 2007).

The conceptualization, definition, and measurement of drinking events began over thirty years ago when NIAAA published a monograph titled *Social Drinking Contexts* (Harford & Gaines, 1982b). In the introduction to that collection of conference papers, Harford and Gaines note, "While context, or frame of reference, may hold the key to understanding drinking behavior, no single idiom describes context" (1). The authors go on to say that the multidisciplinary nature of alcohol studies related to context reflect a spectrum of terms and units of analysis. The nomenclature and taxonomies used today to frame drinking events still reflect such diversity.

In that same monograph, drawing from the basic social psychology theory of Lewin (1951), Jessor (1982) offers a simple linear multilevel representation (person x environment leads to drinking behavior). Jessor's simple path model explicitly defines "context" as "environment" and he conceptualizes environment as having five types of elements: (1) physiogeographic (e.g., geospatial); (2) group-level (e.g., demographics, size, gender ratio); (3) social or situational (e.g., a party); (4) theoretical (e.g., alcohol availability, social control, norms); and (5) perceptual (i.e., how the environment is perceived by the individuals embedded in it). In his discussion, he notes two important considerations. First, the environment "persists in being a concept of disturbing *complexity*" (230; emphasis added). Second, "the dynamics of situations give rise to changes in situations and behavior over time.... An obvious source of such change is ... alcohol ingestion ... and its disinhibition effects" (231). Understanding drinking event dynamics and complexity associated with individuals, groups, social context, the built environment and shifting blood alcohol content remains a vexing problem.

Since the publication of *Social Drinking Contexts* (Harford & Gaines, 1982b), there has been great variation in the conceptualization, measurement, and analysis of drinking events. The implicit notion of a drinking event is often embedded in another conceptual focus. For instance, a number of studies have examined behaviors conceptually couched in drinking events such as "pre-gaming" (Reed et al., 2011) or "drinking games" (Borsari et al., 2007). Others have correlated typical drinking settings with drinking behaviors or problem outcomes (Saltz, Paschall, McGaffigan, & Nygaard, 2010). Alcohol epidemiology—quantity, frequency, variability measures (e.g., heavy episodic drinking)—is also a simple form of enumerating drinking events (Wechsler, Davenport, Dowdall, Moeykens, & Castillo, 1994).

Although segmenting drinking events into time-specific (pre-gaming), social (drinking games), or geospatial (bars) elements allows one to more easily study this behavior, such segmentation obscures an understanding of the systemic and complex nature of events (Miller & Page, 2007) and potentially results in ineffective policy solutions to alcohol-related problems (Wells, Graham, & Purcell, 2009). For instance, over the course of an individual's drinking event, pre-gaming can occur in a small private setting with a few friends, followed by drinking games in a larger party setting, and culminating in a public setting like a bar. Each activity and setting comes with its own dynamics, resulting in complexity and transitory risk as well as protection across an entire event (Fitzpatrick & Martinez, 2012; Clapp, Johnson, Shillington, Lange, & Voas, 2008a; Clapp et al., 2009). The segmentation approach to studying drinking events, however, may soon be changing.

Technology and Theory

Recent studies have begun to embrace mobile continuous monitoring of physiological measures such as heart rate as a means of monitoring drug and alcohol relapse triggers prior to having a solid theoretical understanding of the underlying relationship between these indicators and relapse triggers (Kennedy et al., 2015). New "smart" technologies have the potential to complement universal prevention efforts by targeting "leverage points" in events (Stokols, 2000). Technologies like GPS, Bluetooth networking, SMS-based ecological momentary assessments, and transdermal alcohol sensors may greatly increase both our understanding of drinking events and our ability to intervene in real time and in a tailored manner (Riley et al., 2011). For instance, SMS texting interventions are increasingly used in related behavior-change efforts such as tobacco cessation and management of depressive symptoms (Riley et al., 2011; Scott-Sheldon et al., 2016; Agyapong, McLoughlin, & Farren, 2013). Furthermore, smartphone applications are now being used to implement interventions for at-risk individuals with drug use issues or other addictions such as gambling (Zhang & Ho, 2016). For example, the application Triggr Health (https://triggrhealth.com) leverages real-time data to monitor individuals in recovery. The app administers support in the form of supportive text messages at points in time when it gathers the individual may be at risk of relapse based on the individual's behavior (determined based on SMS behaviors and proximity to bars based on the phone's geolocator). To better guide the use of these emergent technologies, it is critical to better understand the conceptualization of drinking events.

Riley et al. (2011) note the importance of developing "health behavior models that have dynamic, regulatory system components to guide rapid intervention adaptation based on the individual's current and past behavior and situational context" (54). Our work, detailed below, begins to fill this critical gap.

Collaborative Modeling of Drinking Events: Case Study Methods

This case study explores an ongoing collaboration between two teams of applied researchers coming from different fields—social work and engineering. The ongoing collaboration began in 2013 and this case study examines the entire collaboration period. In this section, we aim to describe

- how the collaboration came about;
- our team and respective backgrounds;
- the institutional environment in which the efforts have taken place;
- the overall collaborative modeling approach we used;
- how we communicated complex concepts using boundary objects (Star & Griesemer, 1989);
- early efforts and products;
- our model in its current state; and
- our plans for validation and future steps.

Data for this case study comes from field notes of the senior author, group discussions among the team members, review of simulations and models, and a review of the published papers and presentations related to the work (Clapp et al., 2018; Giraldo, Passino, & Clapp, 2017; Giraldo, Passino, Clapp, & Madden, 2016). The case study is presented sequentially and we conclude with a brief discussion section.

Beginning the Collaboration: Drunken Bees

Our modeling effort began serendipitously. Shortly after Dr. John Clapp—the senior social work member of the team—joined the faculty at The Ohio State University (OSU), he was introduced to Dr. Kevin Passino—the senior engineering member of the team—who was looking for collaborators in social work to help his students on a project related to homelessness. During the course of this initial meeting, Dr. Clapp shared his work related to studying drinking behavior with an eye towards preventing problems. In turn, Dr. Passino discussed his work modeling the system dynamics of bee swarms. Dr. Clapp related that his past studies on drinking events (Clapp, Min, Shillington, Reed, & Croff, 2008b; Clapp et al., 2009) left him with the feeling that he was looking at a low-resolution photo of something better suited for a high-definition video. After watching a short YouTube video of bee swarm behavior provided by Dr. Passino, Dr. Clapp pulled up a video of an alcohol-fueled riot at a college party. Dr. Passino, joking that the students looked like drunken bees, noted that the behavior appeared inherently complex and dynamic. One week later, Dr. Clapp, Dr. Passino, and their respective doctoral students met to begin the modeling process.

Our Team

As mentioned above, the team consists of Drs. Clapp and Passino and their respective doctoral students. Dr. Clapp is a professor of social work who has studied alcohol-related behavior for over two decades. Dr. Passino is a professor of engineering and his work focuses on modeling complex systems. Dr. Clapp's doctoral student, Danielle Madden, is interested in modeling drinking events and alcohol-related interventions. As of this writing, she is working on her dissertation. Dr. Passino's former student (now a faculty member), Dr. Luis Filipe Giraldo, worked on the project for the first two years of the collaboration. Dr. Giraldo is interested in modeling complex human systems. Dr. Passino's current student, Hugo Gonzalez Villasanti, joined the team after Dr. Giraldo's graduation and is also interested in modeling complex human systems.

Environmental Support

This effort began during a period in which OSU was heavily engaged in developing cross-disciplinary collaborations through many university-led initiatives. The team was encouraged to move forward by our respective deans and provided with start-up resources, ample meeting space, and access to a variety of software packages. In addition, Drs. Clapp and Passino both have long histories of interdisciplinary research collaboration and extramural funding. This experience enhanced official supports.

Our General Modeling Approach

Our general approach to developing a dynamics-driven framework for drinking events evolved into something consistent with Pentland's (2014) approach to social physics: "Just as the goal of traditional physics is to understand how the flow of energy translates into changes in motion, social physics seeks to understand how the flow of ideas and information translates into changes in behavior" (5).

Our ongoing aim is to understand how different social and environmental factors translate into changes in the dynamics of a drinking event while considering the impairment of drinking. While there is no standard approach to developing dynamical models, we followed an approach similar to others (Richardson & Pugh, 1981; Sterman, 2002) by engaging in the following steps to develop our model: (1) problem definition, (2) system conceptualization, (3) model formulation, (4) testing and simulation, and (5) model evaluation. We note that steps 2–5 follow an iterative process.

Communication and Boundary Objects

During the early stages of our work, both teams worked to better understand the conceptual and methodological approaches used by their respective partners. This was accomplished in several ways: each team read previous research conducted by the two chief researchers (Clapp and Passino); the engineering team read social science and alcohol research related to the modeling problem; the social work team read several introductory texts on system dynamics modeling; both teams read the extant literature on dynamic modeling of drinking behavior; and Dr. Clapp audited Dr. Passino's graduate simulation course.

Consistent with Star and Griesmer (1989), we focused on identifying and better understanding boundary objects related to the modeling problem. Boundary objects are the core elements in the model that, in the early stages of a collaborative effort, might have different meanings for different stakeholders. During this early stage, much of the boundary object tasks centered on developing a common language and means of communicating complex ideas without relying on either equations, for which the social work team was not fully trained, or arcane social science conceptualizations and terms unfamiliar to the engineering team. To bridge this early gap in common understanding (something that developed over the course of the collaboration), the team relied heavily on visual depictions of concepts. It is important to note that initial attempts at visualization did not cleanly employ standard dynamic-like modeling methods such as causal loop diagrams (CLD) or stock and flow models. Rather, many of the early efforts of visualizing concepts were drawn from control systems depictions or social science inspired path models. Other times, hybrid depictions were created.

One issue that came up fairly early was how to depict the basic elements of a drinking event. In the early phases of the collaboration, the social work partners presented alcohol research related to drinking events (Clapp et al., 2008b; Clapp et al., 2014; Wells, Mihic, Tremblay, Graham, & Demers, 2008; Thombs et al., 2010; Neighbors et al., 2011; Kuntsche, Otten, & Labhart, 2015). These presentations helped to define the problem by specifically identifying the key elements of the drinking event system. Examples related to the influence of variables at different levels of abstraction were discussed in depth. For instance, the relationship between a drinker's motivation and BAC at the individual level was discussed (see O'Grady, Cullum, Tennen, & Armeli, 2011; Neal & Carey, 2007; Wetherill & Fromme, 2009). Similarly, studies related to group influence on drinking (Cullum, O'Grady, Armeli, & Tennen, 2012; Wells et al., 2015; Reed, Clapp, Martell, & Hidalgo-Sotelo, 2013) and environmental influences on drinking (Clapp et al, 2008b; Clapp et al., 2009) were discussed. Additionally, the engineering team read key papers related to BAC metabolism (Wilkinson, 1980; Jones, 2010; Lundquist & Wolthers, 1958; Norberg, Jones, Hahn, & Gabrielsson, 2003).

Figures 1–3 illustrate the evolution of how we visualized drinking events. Figure 1 illustrates a social group of drinkers and how each member's drinking might shift and peak over the course of an event. A continuous line reflects sequential drinking, while a broken line indicates a break in drinking during the event. Thicker portions of the lines indicate a heavy drinking period (more drinks or stronger drinks). Figure 2 illustrates how drinking groups might shift locations and composition over time. Finally, figure 3—the most complex depiction of drinking events—illustrates peer influence (arrows), gender of group members (small circles or squares), intoxication (shading or color of shapes), and movement from environment to environment (large circles) by individuals or the group (i.e., shifts in group composition). A member of the engineering team eventually animated figure 3. The animation was especially useful and was used in numerous presentations to visualize how various elements of the model—individual drinkers and peer networks—move across environments through time.

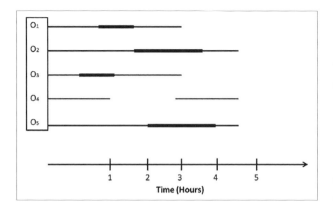

FIGURE 1. Relationship between time and group events. Note: Each O represents a different individual. Lines represent BAC with thicker lines representing increased intoxication. A continuous line reflects continuous consumption of alcohol, while a broken line indicates a break in drinking during the event.

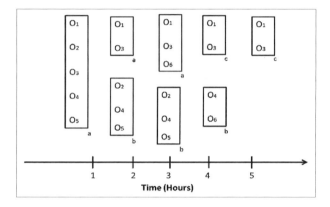

FIGURE 2. Shift of drinking groups over time. Note: Each O represents a different individual. Different locations are represented by a square and labeled *a*, *b*, or *c*.

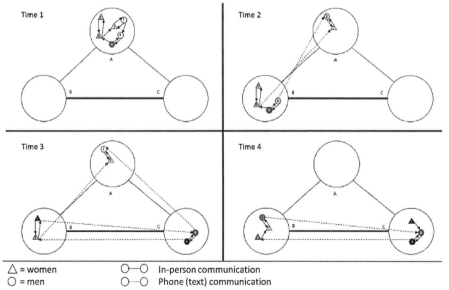

FIGURE 3. Change in composition of drinking groups over time.

Early Efforts and Products

The first actual modeling attempt was led by Dr. Giraldo. Working closely with Dr. Clapp and consulting frequently with Dr. Passino, Dr. Giraldo developed a series of computational models related to peer influence BAC. This work used field data from one of Dr. Clapp's earlier projects (Clapp et al., 2009) and it helped us refine some of the concepts presented below. It also allowed the team to collaboratively discuss actual simulations related to the bigger project. In addition, the use of Dr. Clapp's data helped the engineering team better understand the types of data future fieldwork might generate to validate our later work.

Similar to earlier phases, we used a variety of visualizations and animations to illustrate our concepts and communicate with each other. Often, the engineering doctoral students prepared these visualizations and presented them at our regular meetings. Figures 4a and 4b

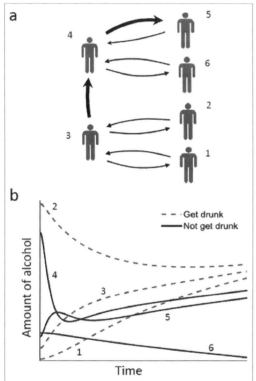

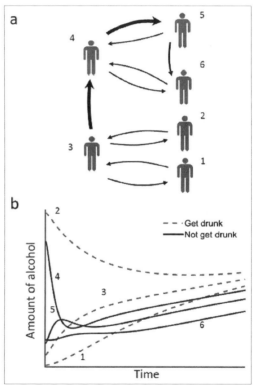

FIGURE 4A. Influence of group members on drinking behavior: Example 1. Note: Network that represents the influence between the group members (a). The thickness of the arrows denote the influence strength from one individual to another. Color is associated with personal preference. Behavior of the individuals in the group with respect to the consumption of alcohol (b).

FIGURE 4B. Influence of group members on drinking behavior: Example 2. Note: In this case, now there is an influence of individual 5 on individual 6 (a). Behavior of the individuals in the group with respect to the consumption of alcohol (b).

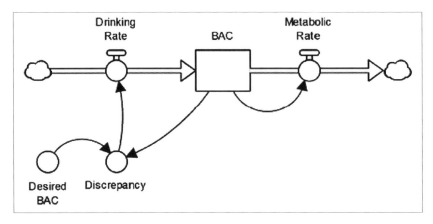

FIGURE 5. Stock and flow model for BAC.

provide examples of the visualizations of the influence of group members on drinking behavior. Dr. Giraldo and Dr. Clapp presented this work at two conferences, a modeling conference and a social work research conference. This work was then published in an engineering journal (Giraldo et al., 2017).

Although the modeling efforts were useful, they represented low-hanging fruit. The more difficult task of developing a dynamical model and mathematical proofs for a variable critical to the overall modeling effort—BAC—was the focus of the second phase of our work. Similarly critical to our efforts was developing an overall conceptual system dynamics model to tie together all the levels of abstraction represented in drinking events. To address these needs, the team divided tasks: the engineering group worked on the dynamical model of BAC and the social work group worked on the overall conceptual model.

The BAC model went through several iterations. The engineering team presented computational models and simulations that reflected the pharmacokinetics related to BAC relative to the drinker's decision-making process. Although others have modeled dynamics of BAC, we could find no other work attempting to link BAC dynamics to the dynamics of decision-making (Andr´easson & Jones, 1996; Lundquist & Wolthers, 1958; Norberg et al., 2003; Umulis, Gürmen, Singh, & Fogler, 2005; Plawecki, Han, Doerschuk, Ramchandani, & O'Connor, 2008; MIT, 1999). To facilitate understanding, the social work team developed CLDs and stock and flow models to visualize the quantitative work. Given that the BAC model included a second-order system, the entire team jointly developed several iterations of these graphical depictions. Several of the iterations resulted in "the math doesn't work" from the engineers or "the conceptual flow is wrong" from the social work team, until we landed on a depiction that reflects both the underlying math and the conceptual constructs in a clear manner (see figure 5).

Results: Our Model in Its Current State

Figure 6 represents an overall conceptual model of drinking events. The figure depicts individuals during a drinking event (filled-in small circles) who are situated in groups (enclosed

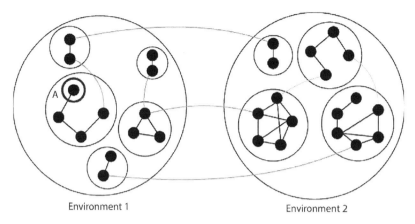

Environment 1   Environment 2

FIGURE 6. Conceptual model of drinking events.

in medium-sized circles) and drinking in specific environments (the largest circles). Lines between individuals represent communication between group members, across groups, or between people in different locations. To get to the current model, the social work team took the lead on developing a CLD and complete stock and flow model of the entire drinking event system. Similar to the BAC models discussed above, initial CLDs and stock and flow models were presented in our regular meetings and the group altered the visualizations until they reflected the concepts and computations clearly. Figures 7 and 8 present the CLD and full stock and flow model, respectively. During this phase of the work, the social work members familiarized themselves with Vensim software and took several online courses in system dynamics modeling offered by STELLA (Chichakly, 2016). Once the social work team was familiar with the software, Mr. Villasanti worked with the social work team members to run simulations of the entire model.

Our model focuses on the aspects of a drinking event for only one of these hypothetical drinkers (for example, the individual marked *A* in figure 6). Figure 7 presents the CLD for the drinking event system. Conceptually, our model includes four key stocks: (1) BAC, (2) desired state (of intoxication) or desired BAC, (3) group wetness, and (4) environmental wetness. From a social ecological framework, BAC and desired state are micro-level variables, group wetness is a mezzo-level variable, and environmental wetness is a macro-level variable. Together, these stocks represent the various levels of abstraction found in the literature examining drinking events in a highly aggregated model consistent with a 10,000-foot view of the system (Clapp et al., 2009; Reed et al., 2013; Jessor, 1982; Richmond, 2004).

Beginning from the bottom of the CLD (the micro level) in figure 7, there is a balancing causal feedback loop between the BAC stock and the drinking rate. Conceptually, this represents that drinkers, either implicitly or tacitly, attempt to obtain a desired state during a drinking event. As their BAC increases, their drinking rate decreases until equilibrium is achieved. A reinforcement loop is generated via the disinhibitory effects of alcohol on cognitive control, specifically on inhibitory control causing increased motivation to drink (Steele & Josephs, 1990; Field, Wiers, Christiansen, Fillmore, & Verster, 2010). A delay is introduced before the BAC stock, representing the transit of alcohol through the gastrointestinal tract before entering the blood by an

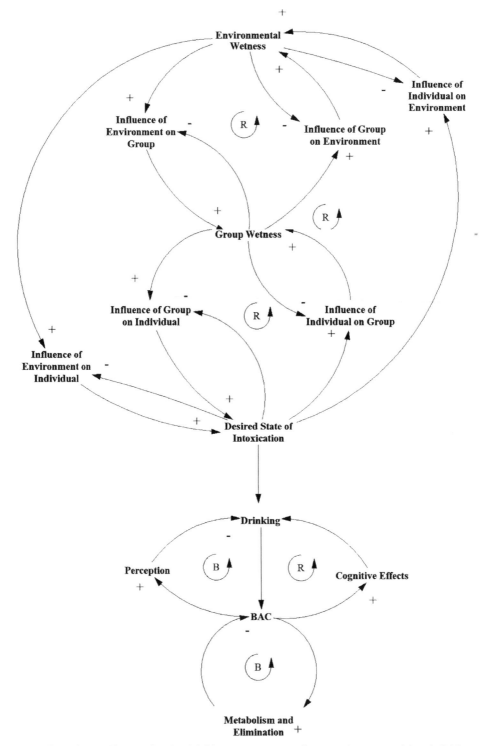

FIGURE 7. Causal loop diagram for the drinking event system. Four stocks are considered: BAC on individual and desired state of intoxication of individual (micro-level variables), group wetness (mezzo-level variable), and environmental wetness (macro-level variable).

Table 1. Description of elements in the model

	BAC	DESIRED BAC	GROUP WETNESS	ENVIRONMENTAL WETNESS
Ecological Level of Abstraction	Biological *Micro*	Psychological *Micro*	Social *Mezzo*	Social/Physical *Macro*
Definition	Represents the drinker's blood alcohol concentration.	The state of intoxication a drinker hopes to obtain at any given point during the drinking event.	Represents the mean BAC of the peer group over the event. Could also include mean of group's Desired State.	Represents the extent the environment promotes heavy drinking.
Parameters	Grams of ethanol/100 ML of blood. Values range from 0.0–0.03. (Bounded not to go below 0.0 or above 0.03 to reflect typical values) A standard drink = 0.02 (+) in BAC. Metabolism = −0.02 (−) in BAC per hour. (Dubowski, 1985)	Measured on Likert scale with values ranging from "drink but not get buzzed" to "drink to get very drunk." Can also measure *strength* of desire by Likert scale. (Clapp et al., 2009; Thombs et al., 2010)	Mean values ranging from 0.0– 0.03	Measured by an index of availability including: average dollar amount per standard drink; average time to obtain a drink; and the number of fixed and temporary servers. Could also include the social aspects of the environment such as the presence of many intoxicated people. (Clapp et al., 2009).
Assumptions	Influenced by: rate and volume of drinking. Influences desired state. Food delays metabolism. Delay drinking and ability to perceive BAC level.	May be conscious or subconscious. Can shift over the course of event. Initial strength of desire relates to likelihood of change. Influences and is influenced by Group Wetness. Some group members might have more influence than others.	Influences individual drinker's BAC and Desired State. Is influenced by individual drinker's BAC and desired state. Influences and is influenced by environmental wetness and selection.	Influences and is influenced by group wetness. Influences and is influenced by individual drinker BAC and Desired State. Is selected based on the weighted mean of a group's Desired State (giving more weight to influential group members).

absorption process; it could also be delayed further by food intake. Put in practical terms, decisions by drinkers about whether to have another drink to maintain or obtain a "buzz" are often based on a misperception of the amount of alcohol they have in their system (Richmond, 2004).

Continuing with figure 7 and moving up a level of abstraction, the drinker's desired BAC stock is also influenced by the group wetness stock in a reinforcing feedback structure. As described in table 1, group wetness is a form of social influence that includes the average BAC of a drinker's companions at the drinking event, the average desired BAC of the drinker's companions, and the relative influence of each member of the group on the drinker. In our earlier work (Giraldo et al., 2017), we model how peer influence varies in strength and interacts with a drinker's own desired state to alter drinking trajectories. Through a series of computer simulations, we show that a strong influence within a peer network pulls all but those with very strong desires toward a BAC trajectory similar to the peer exerting the influence. In turn, completing this reinforcing feedback loop as a member of the group, the drinker's BAC and desired BAC also influences the group wetness stock.

Finally, moving to the top of the CLD in figure 7 to the group and environmental levels, we posit a reinforcing feedback loop between group wetness and environmental wetness. Our earlier studies of drinking events (Clapp, Shillington, & Segars, 2000; Clapp et al., 2009) found that the presence of "many intoxicated people," whether observed by researchers or reported by survey respondents, consistently contribute to high BAC or self-reported heavy drinking. We also found that heavier drinkers seek out wetter environments, suggesting that influence flows in both directions (Trim, Clapp, Reed, Shillington, & Thombs, 2011). As group wetness increases, environmental wetness increases. In turn, environmental wetness, which represents the overall average BAC among bar patrons coupled with alcohol availability in the environment (Clapp et al., 2009), influences group wetness in a reinforcing way.

Table 1 describes each element in the model except for the GAC stock. This stock simply represents the aggregate amount of alcohol (for example, the unit of measure could be standard drinks) residing in the gastrointestinal tract. We refer to this stock as "GAC" to differentiate alcohol that remains in the gastrointestinal tract from the concentration of alcohol in the blood. We offer basic definitions of each element, theoretical parameters based on our mathematical models, how the elements might be or have been measured, and some assumptions about how each element operates in the system based on the literature and our previous research.

Figure 8 shows a series of our hypothesized reference behavior over time graphs for various BAC outcomes generated via simulation of the model. Although we are interested in conceptually understanding the entire drinking event system, understanding how different elements of the model affect the BAC is particularly important for guiding prevention efforts. The graphs shown in figure 8a portray the effect of metabolism on BAC. The plots in figure 8b shed light on the reinforcing cognitive effects on BAC while the plots in figure 8c show the effect of peer and environmental influence on individual's intoxication. In all cases, it is assumed that the drinking period lasts for three hours.

While the graphs in figures 8b and 8c only illustrate "peak" BAC and do not show the decline of BAC back to zero, figure 8a shows the entire BAC curve for a drinker who desired to get "very buzzed or drunk." As presented, the drinker reaches a peak BAC of over 0.1 by hour three of the event, before the BAC begins to decrease slowly. The fluctuations in the decreasing BAC are due to consumption of more alcohol after stopping drinking for a period. The steep growth of BAC in the early hours of the event is related to the rate of drinking. That is, to obtain the BAC shown, the rate of drinking would be fairly fast.

The graph shown in figure 8b illustrates the BAC curve for a drinker with the desire to "get slightly buzzed" (desired BAC = 0.03). In this graph, the drinker reaches an initial peak BAC of about 0.035 and decreases his intake rate towards his initial desired BAC. However, due to the disinhibitory effect which increases his desire to drink, the individual resumes drinking at a lower rate, which increases his BAC level.

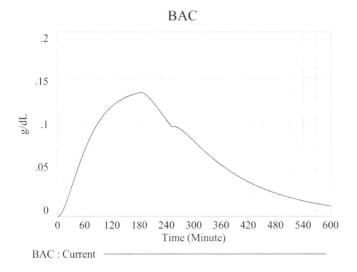

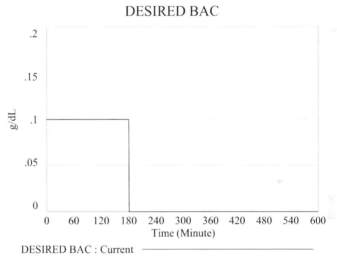

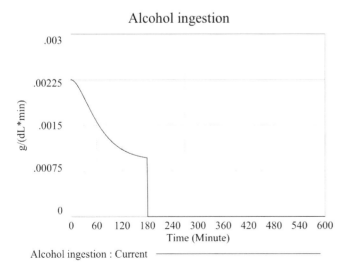

FIGURE 8A. Effect of metabolism on BAC.

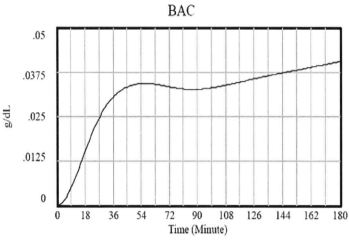

BAC : Current ————————————

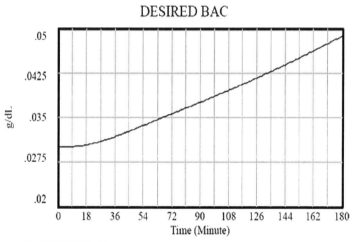

DESIRED BAC : Current ————————————

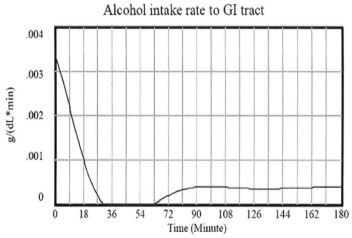

Alcohol intake rate to GI tract : Current ————————————

FIGURE 8B. Cognitive effects on BAC.

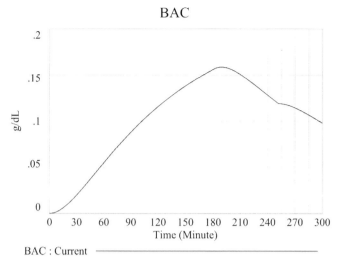

BAC : Current ―――――――――――――――――

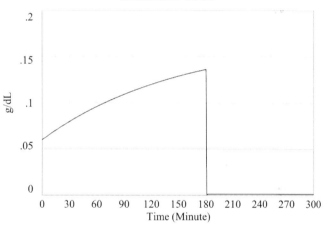

DESIRED BAC : Current ―――――――――――――――――

Alcohol ingestion : Current ―――――――――――――――――

FIGURE 8C. Effect of peer and environmental influences on individual's intoxication.

Table 2. Potential random variables and disturbances by level of abstraction

LEVEL	RANDOM VARIABLE	
Micro/Individual	• Taking medication • Level of hydration • Level of rest	• Drinking history (e.g., binge drinker) • Genetic markers • Tolerance
Mezzo/Group	• New group member(s) during event • Exiting group members during event	• Sexual attraction among group members • Social media or SMS connection among group members during event
Macro/Environment	• Moving locations during event • Fights or aggression at events	• Introduction of music or dancing during event • Influx or outflow of other groups during event

Note: This is not an exhaustive list.

The final graph in the series, figure 8c, illustrates a drinker who desires to "get buzzed" (desired BAC = 0.06), but is pulled off that trajectory later in the event. Conceptually, such "overshooting" is a function of group and/or environmental dynamics. Empirically, we found this to be fairly common during drinking events (Giraldo et al., 2017; Clapp et al., 2009; Trim et al., 2011). The mathematics underlying the dynamics of overshooting or undershooting desired intoxication levels is presented in our more technical work (Giraldo et al., 2017).

Finally, table 2 presents potential random variables (disturbances), at each level of abstraction, which theoretically may alter the dynamics in the model. The list is provided as both a means to set the exogenous boundaries of the model and to guide potential simulations in the future.

Validation and Future Plans

The modeling process is currently moving into a validation phase. Based on these efforts, we anticipate modifications to the model presented above. To facilitate this work, Dr. Clapp funded Mr. Villasanti and Mrs. Madden for an academic year. During this period, under the supervision of Dr. Clapp, Mrs. Madden is overseeing a field study that will capture data for each element in the CLD (figure 7): repeated BAC measures; ecological momentary assessments of drinking intentions and perceptions; group roles and influences; and drinking environments. Mr. Villasanti is currently running simulations and mathematical models to facilitate policy simulations. We have continued our regular modeling meetings to jointly conceptualize, test, and refine our models.

Discussion

The modeling effort described above is an ongoing endeavor. We view our current work to be the first phase in a much longer effort that will expand our collaboration with an eye towards preventing problem or high-risk drinking events. From a collaborative perspective, the modeling effort described can best be classified as "team science" (Stokols, 2000). From this perspective, our group has several of the characteristics associated with effective team science, including good environmental conditions and infrastructure, shared leadership and goal setting, organizational support, and collaborative readiness. As the project has progressed we have begun to formulate a common method for engaging and presenting work, our own terminology related to constructs, and a planned method for future stages of work. In short, we are in the process of evolving from an interdisciplinary approach to a transdisciplinary approach.

Drinking events remain an important area of study for alcohol researchers. Understanding drinking events and the complex dynamics that underlie them is important both conceptually and to help guide prevention efforts that use "smart" technologies in situ. Our previous work and model advance a conceptual approach, which we hope aids understanding of drinking behavior while guiding the development of prevention approaches (Giraldo et al., 2017; Giraldo et al., 2016).

By considering the underlying interactions among the biological, psychological, social, and environmental interactions related to drinking behavior as it occurs, the model presented here is one of the few attempts to address the inherent complexity of drinking events noted by Jessor (1982) and Harford & Gaines (1982a) over three decades ago. Our conceptual and mathematical results begin to illustrate the potential of dynamics at several levels that can result in heavy drinking or drinking more than was initially intended.

The modeling efforts and simulation results presented in figure 8 illustrate the importance of dynamics in drinking behavior. For instance, figure 8b shows a drinker's desired level of intoxication and its impact by BAC levels. The issue of how one's BAC curve impacts an overall drinking event was raised by Jessor (1982) over thirty years ago, yet little further work to date has focused on this issue.

Lessons Learned

Several lessons can be drawn from our experience. First, having administrative support was extremely useful. Although both senior researchers are tenured full professors, having university administrators within and outside their respective units supporting the collaborative efforts provided legitimacy to the work. Access to adequate space and software, pilot funding, and the ability to support doctoral students was critical. A conference room with a large whiteboard and a large projector and screen was very helpful for working through the iterations of the models and demonstrating simulations.

Second, building linkages among our doctoral students proved to be very useful and encouraging. Several times over the course of the collaboration, the students independently interacted with each other to work on aspects of the models or manuscripts. The social work doctoral student was included in modeling conferences and the engineering doctoral students were included in social work conferences. It is our hope that, by training these specific students to work across disciplinary lines, we will expand interest in collaborative modeling as our students move forward and engage their own students in future work.

Third, in presenting our work, we found that the "modeling audience" was highly supportive, the engineering audience was very receptive, the social work audience was generally supportive, and the alcohol research community was the least interested. Our experience with engineering journals has been fairly straightforward. The reviews have focused on the technical merit of our work. Our experience with the journals related to modeling has been routine, with our main struggle being our ability to find a standard way to present CLDs and stock and flow models that fit with the requirements of each journal. In contrast, the alcohol research–related journals we initially sent manuscripts to have often questioned the underlying assumptions of our models; that is, they seem to question whether a dynamical model is being done as opposed to more traditional statistical modeling. Editors of a few major alcohol and drug journals have also questioned the utility of the work for their readers.

Given that the reason we entered this collaboration was to ultimately move the research forward concerning alcohol-related problems at the event level, the response from the alcohol research community has been a bit concerning. To address this, we have begun presenting our work or integrating it into presentations aimed at alcohol prevention professionals. In addition, we hope to conduct a Delphi study in which alcohol researchers familiar with drinking events assess the theoretical validity of the model. Finally, we hope to conduct a similar study with young adult college student drinkers. These efforts, coupled with our current field studies meant to parameterize the model, will hopefully move this type of work into the mainstream alcohol research and practice community.

In summary, our modeling efforts have been a rewarding and fruitful collaboration. Coming together from two different applied fields to address a real-world problem has, in our estimation, increased our understanding of this complex behavior. Further, we have laid the groundwork to continue this work through publications, presentations, and expanding our collaborative network via students. It is our hope these efforts ultimately lead to real-time interventions that reduce harm in a sustainable manner.

REFERENCES

Agyapong, V. I. O., McLoughlin, D. M., & Farren, C. K. (2013). Six-month outcomes of a randomized trial of supportive text messaging for depression and comorbid alcohol use disorder. *Journal of Affective Disorders, 151*(1), 100–104.

Anderson, P. (2004). State of the world's alcohol policy. *Addiction, 99,* 1367–1369.

Anderson, P., & Baumberg, B. (2006). *Alcohol in Europe: A public health perspective.* Brussels: European Commission. http://ec.europa.eu/.

Andr´easson, R., & Jones, A. W. (1996). The life and work of Erik MP Widmark. *American Journal of Forensic Medicine and Pathology, 17*(3), 177–190.

Borsari, B., Boyle, K. E., Hustad, J. T. P., Barnett, N. P., O'Leary Tevyaw, T., & Kahler, C. W. (2007). Drinking before drinking: Pregaming and drinking games in mandated students. *Addictive Behaviors, 32*(11), 2694–2705.

Chichakly, K. (2016). *Introduction to Dynamic Modeling I* [PowerPoint slides]. http://www.iseesystems.com.

Clapp, J. D., Holmes, M. R., Reed, M. B., Shillington, A. M., Freisthler, B., & Lange, J. E. (2007). Measuring college students' alcohol consumption in natural drinking environments: Field methodologies for bars and parties. *Evaluation Review, 31*(5), 469–489.

Clapp, J. D., Johnson, M. B., Shillington, A. M., Lange, J. E., & Voas, R. B. (2008a). Breath alcohol concentrations of college students in field settings: seasonal, temporal, and contextual patterns. *Journal of Studies on Alcohol and Drugs, 69*(2), 323–331.

Clapp, J. D., Madden, D. R., Gonzalez Villasanti, H. J., Giraldo, L. F., Passino, K. M., Reed, M. B., & Fernandez, I. (2018). A System Dynamics Model of Drinking Events: Multi-level Ecological Approach. *Systems Research and Behavioral Science, 35*(6), 265–281. doi: 10.1002/sres.2478.

Clapp, J. D., Min, J. W., Shillington, A. M., Reed, M. B., & Croff, J. K. (2008b). Person and environment predictors of blood alcohol concentrations: A multi-level study of college parties. *Alcoholism: Clinical and Experimental Research, 32(1),* 100–107.

Clapp, J. D., Reed, M. B., Min, J. W., Shillington, A. M., Croff, J. M., Holmes, M. R., & Trim, R. S. (2009). Blood alcohol concentrations among bar patrons: A multi-level study of drinking behavior. *Drug and Alcohol Dependence, 102*(1–3), 41–48.

Clapp, J. D., Reed, M. B., & Ruderman, D. E. (2014). The relationship between drinking games and intentions to continue drinking, intentions to drive after drinking, and adverse consequences: Results of a field study. *American Journal of Drug and Alcohol Abuse, 40(5),* 374–379.

Clapp, J. D., Shillington, A. M., & Segars, L. (2000). Deconstructing contexts of binge drinking among college students. *American Journal of Drug and Alcohol Abuse, 26(1),* 139–154.

Covault, J., Tennen, H., Armeli, S., Conner, T. S., Herman, A. I., Cillessen, A. H., & Kranzler, H. R. (2007). Interactive effects of the serotonin transporter 5-HTTLPR polymorphism and stressful life events on college student drinking and drug use. *Biological Psychiatry, 61,* 609–616.

Cullum, J., O'Grady, M., Armeli, S., & Tennen, H. (2012). Change and stability in active and passive social influence dynamics during natural drinking events: A longitudinal measurement-burst study. *Journal of Social and Clinical Psychology, 31(1),* 51–80.

Denzin, N. K. (1987). *The alcoholic self.* Thousand Oaks: Sage Publications.

Dubowski, K. M. (1985). Absorption, distribution and elimination of alcohol: Highway safety aspects. *Journal of Studies on Alcohol, Supplement No. 10,* 98–108.

Field, M., Wiers, R. W., Christiansen, P., Fillmore, M. T., & Verster, J. C. (2010). Acute alcohol effects on inhibitory control and implicit cognition: Implications for loss of control over drinking. *Alcoholism: Clinical and Experimental Research, 34*(8), 1346–1352.

Fitzpatrick, B., & Martinez, J. (2012). Agent-based modeling of ecological niche theory and assortative drinking. *Journal of Artificial Societies and Social Simulation, 15*(2), 4–17.

Gacek, P., Conner, T. S., Tennen, H., Kranzler, H. R., & Covault, J. (2008). Tryptophan hydroxylase 2 gene and alcohol use among college students. *Addiction Biology, 13,* 440–448.

Giraldo, L. F., Passino, K. M., & Clapp, J. D. (2017). Modeling and analysis of group dynamics in alcohol-consumption environments. *IEEE Transactions on Cybernetics, 47*(1), 165–176.

Giraldo, L. F., Passino, K. M., Clapp, J. D., & Madden, D. (2016). Dynamics of metabolism and decision-making during alcohol consumption: Modeling and analysis. *IEEE Transactions on Cybernetics, 47*(11), 3955–3966. doi: 10.1109/TCYB.2016.2593009.

Gorman, D. M., Mezic, J., Mezic, I., & Gruenewald, P. J. (2006). Agent-based modeling of drinking behavior: A preliminary model and potential applications to theory and practice. *American Journal of Public Health, 96*(11), 2055–2060.

Gorman, D. M., Speer, P. W., Gruenewald, P. J., & Labouvie, E. W. (2001). Spatial dynamics of alcohol availability, neighborhood structure and violent crime. *Journal of Studies on Alcohol, 62*(5), 628–636.

Gruenewald, P. J. (2006). The spatial ecology of alcohol problems: Niche theory and assortative drinking. *Addiction, 102*(6), 870–878.

Gusfield, J. R. (1996). *Contested Meanings: The Construction of Alcohol Problems.* Madison: University of Wisconsin Press.

Harford, T. C., & Gaines, L. S. (1982a). Social drinking contexts: An introduction. In *Social Drinking Contexts: Proceedings of a Workshop, September 17–19, 1979, Washington, DC* (pp. 1–7). Rockville: National Institute of Alcohol Abuse and Alcoholism.

Harford, T. C., & Gaines, L. S. (Eds.). (1982b). *Social Drinking Contexts: Proceedings of a Workshop, September 17–19, 1979, Washington, DC.* Rockville: National Institute of Alcohol Abuse and Alcoholism.

Hingson, R., Zha, W., & Weitzman, E. R. (2009). Magnitudes of and trends in alcohol related mortality and morbidity among U.S. college students ages 18–24. *Journal of Studies on Alcohol and Drugs, Suppl. 16,* 12–20.

Holder, H. D. (2006). *Alcohol and the community: A systems approach to prevention.* Cambridge: Cambridge University Press.

Jessor, R. (1982). Some problematic aspects of research on drinking contexts. In T. C. Hardford & L. S. Gaines (Eds.), *Social Drinking Contexts: Proceedings of a Workshop, September 17–19, 1979, Washington, DC* (pp. 228–233). Rockville: National Institute of Alcohol Abuse and Alcoholism.

Johnston, L. D., O'Malley, P. M., Bachman, J. G., & Schulenberg, J. E. (2011). *Monitoring the future: National results on adolescent drug use: Overview of key findings 2011.* Washington, DC: National Institute on Drug Abuse. http://www.monitoringthefuture.org.

Johnston, L. D., O'Malley, P. M., Bachman, J. G., Schulenberg, J. E., & Patrick, M. E. (2013). *Monitoring the future: National survey results on drug use 1975–2012.* (Vol. 2, *College students and adults age 19–50.*) Ann Arbor: Institute for Social Research.

Jones, A. W. (2010). Evidence-based survey of the elimination rates of ethanol from blood with applications in forensic casework. *Forensic Science International, 200*(1), 1–20.

Kaufman, J., Yang, B. Z., Douglas-Palumberi, H., Crouse-Artus, M., Lipshitz, D., Krystal, J. H., & Gelernter, J. (2007). Genetic and environmental predictors of early alcohol use. *Biological Psychiatry, 61,* 1228–1234.

Kennedy, A. P., Epstein, D. H., Jobes, M. L., Agage, D., Tyburski, M., Phillips, K. A., . . . & Preston, K. L. (2015). Continuous in-the-field measurement of heart rate: Correlates of drug use, craving, stress, and mood in polydrug users. *Drug and Alcohol Dependence, 151,* 159–166.

Koenig, C. (2011, August 17). Rioting over wine led to 90 deaths. *Oxford Times.* http://www.oxfordtimes.co.uk.

Kuhn, A. (1974). *The logic of social systems: A unified deductive system based approach to social science.* San Francisco: Jossey-Bass.

Kuntsche, E., Dietze, P., & Jenkinson, R. (2014). Understanding alcohol and other drug use during the event. *Drug and Alcohol Review, 33*(4), 335–337.

Kuntsche, E., Otten, R., & Labhart, F. (2015). Identifying risky drinking patterns over the course of Saturday evenings: An event-level study. *Psychology of Addictive Behaviors, 39*(3), 744–752.

Lenk, K. M., Erickson, D. J., Nelson, T. F., Winters, K. C., & Toomey, T. L. (2012). Alcohol policies and practices among four-year colleges in the United States: Prevalence and patterns. *Journal of Studies on Alcohol and Drugs, 73*(3), 361–367.

Lewin, K. (1951). *Field theory in social science: Selected theoretical papers.* Oxford: Harper.

Lundquist, F., & Wolthers, H. (1958). The kinetics of alcohol elimination in man. *Acta Pharmacologica et Toxicologica, 14*(3), 265–289.

Massachusetts Institute of Technology. (1999). *Guided study program in system dynamics.* http://www.clexchange.org.

McCaig, L. F., & Burt, C. W. (2005). *National hospital ambulatory medical care survey: 2003 emergency department summary.* (Vol. 358, *Advance data from vital and health statistics.*) Hyattsville, Maryland: National Center for Health Statistics.

Miller, J. H., & Page, S. E. (2007). *Complex Adaptive Systems: An Introduction to Computational Models of Social Life.* Princeton: Princeton University Press.

Mundt, M. P., & Zakletskaia, L. I. (2012.) Prevention for college students who suffer alcohol-induced blackouts could deter high-cost emergency department visits. *Health Affairs, 31*(4), 863–870.

NIAAA [National Institute of Alcohol Abuse and Alcoholism]. (2004) NIAAA council approves definition of binge drinking. *NIAAA Newsletter, 3,* 3.

NIAAA [National Institute of Alcohol Abuse and Alcoholism. (2015). *college fact sheet.* http://pubs.niaaa.nih.gov.

NIDA [National Institute of Drug Abuse]. (2011). *Results from the 2010 national survey on drug use and health: Summary of national findings.* http://www.oas.samhsa.gov.

NIH [National Institute of Health]. (2000). *10th special report to the U.S. Congress on alcohol and health.* Washington, DC: U.S. Department of Health and Human Services.

Neal, D. J., & Carey, K. B. (2007). Association between alcohol intoxication and alcohol-related problems: An event-level analysis. *Psychology of Addictive Behaviors, 21*(2), 194–204.

Neighbors, C., Atkins, D. C., Lewis, M. A., Lee, C. M., Kaysen, D., Mittmann, A., . . . & Rodriguez, L. M. (2011). Event-specific drinking among college students. *Psychology of Addictive Behaviors, 25*(4), 702–707.

Norberg, A., Jones, A. W., Hahn, R. G., & Gabrielsson, J. L. (2003). Role of variability in explaining ethanol pharmacokinetics. *Clinical Pharmacokinetics, 42*(1), 1–31.

O'Grady, M. A., Cullum, J., Tennen, H., & Armeli, S. (2011). Daily relationship between event-specific drinking norms and alcohol use: A four-year longitudinal study. *Journal of Studies on Alcohol and Drugs, 72,* 633–641.

Pentland, A. (2014). *Social physics: How good ideas spread—the lessons from a new science.* New York: Penguin.

Perkins, H. W. (2002). Surveying the damage: A review of research on consequences of alcohol misuse in college populations. *Journal of Studies on Alcohol, Supplement, s14,* 91–100.

Plawecki, M. H., Han, J.-J., Doerschuk, P. C., Ramchandani, V. A., & O'Connor, S. J. (2008). Physiologically based pharmacokinetic (PBPK) models for ethanol. *IEEE Transactions on Biomedical Engineering, 55*(12), 2691–2700.

Reed, M. B., Clapp, J. D., Martell, B., & Hidalgo-Sotelo, A. (2013). The relationship between group size, intoxication and continuing to drink after bar attendance. *Drug and Alcohol Dependence, 133,* 198–203.

Reed, M. B., Clapp, J. D., Weber, M., Trim, R., Lange, J., & Shillington, A. M. (2011). Predictors of partying prior to bar attendance and subsequent BAC. *Addictive Behaviors, 36*(12), 1341–1343.

Rehm, J., Mathers, C., Popova, S., Thavorncharoensap, M., Teerawattananon, Y., & Patra, J. (2009).

Global burden of disease and injury and economic cost attributable to alcohol use and alcohol-use disorders. *Lancet, 373*(9682), 2223–2233.

Renna, F. (2007). The economic cost of teen drinking: Late graduation and lowered earnings. *HEC Health Economics, 16*(4), 407–419.

Richardson, G. P., & Pugh, A. L. (1981). *Introduction to system dynamics modeling with Dynamo.* Cambridge, MA: MIT Press.

Richmond, B. (2004). *An introduction to systems thinking with STELLA.* Lebanon, NH: ISEE Systems.

Riley, W. T., Rivera, D. E., Atienza, A. A., Nilsen, W., Allison, S. M., & Mermelstein, R. (2011). Health behavior models in the age of mobile interventions: Are our theories up to the task? *Translational Behavioral Medicine, 1*(1), 53–71.

Rosen, S. M., Miller, T. R., & Simon, M. (2008). The cost of alcohol in California. *Alcoholism: Clinical and Experimental Research, 32*(11), 1925–1936.

Saltz, R. F., Paschall, M. J., McGaffigan, R. P., & Nygaard, P. M. O. (2010). Alcohol risk management in college settings: The safer California universities randomized trial. *American Journal of Preventive Medicine, 39*(6), 491–499.

Scribner, R., Ackleh, A. S., Fitzpatrick, B. G., Jacquez, G., Thibodeaux, J. J., Rommel, R., & Simonsen, N. (2009). A systems approach to college drinking: Development of a deterministic model for testing alcohol control polices. *Journal of Studies on Alcohol and Drugs, 70*(5), 805–821.

Scott-Sheldon, L. A., Lantini, R., Jennings, E. G., Thind, H., Rosen, R. K., Salmoirago-Blotcher, E., & Bock, B. C. (2016). Text messaging-based interventions for smoking cessation: A systematic review and meta-analysis. *JMIR mHealth and uHealth, 4*(2), e49. doi:10.2196/mhealth.8946.

Star, S. L., & Griesemer, J. R. (1989). Institutional ecology, "translations" and boundary objects: Amateurs and professionals in Berkeley's Museum of Vertebrate Zoology, 1907–39. *Social Studies of Science, 19,* 387–420.

Steele, C. M., & Josephs, R. A. (1990). Alcohol myopia: Its prized and dangerous effects. *American Psychologist, 45*(8), 921–933.

Sterman, J. D. 2002. All models are wrong: Reflections on becoming a systems scientist. *System Dynamics Review, 18*(4): 501–531.

Stokols, D. (2000). Creating health-promotive environments: Implications for research and theory. In M. S. Jamner & D. Stokols (Eds.), *Promoting human wellness: New frontiers for research and practice* (pp. 135–162). Berkeley: University of California Press.

Teeters, J. B., Pickover, A. M., Dennhardt, A. A., Murphy, J. G., & Martens, M. P. (2014). Elevated alcohol demand is associated with driving after drinking among college student binge drinkers. *Alcoholism: Clinical and Experimental Research, 38*(7), 2066–2072.

Thombs, D. L., O'Mara, R. J., Tsukamoto, M., Rossheim, M., Weiler, R. M., Merves, M. L., & Goldberger, B. A. (2010). Event-level analyses of energy drink consumption and alcohol intoxication in bar patrons. *Addictive Behaviors, 35,* 325–330.

Thrul, J., & Kuntsche, E. (2015). The impact of friends on young adults' drinking over the course of the evening—an event-level analysis. *Addiction, 110,* 619–626.

Trim, R. S., Clapp, J. D., Reed, M. B., Shillington, A., & Thombs, D. (2011). Drinking plans and drinking outcomes: Examining young adults' weekend drinking behavior. *Journal of Drug Education, 41*(3), 253–270.

Umulis, D. M., Gürmen, N. M., Singh, P., & Fogler, H. S. (2005). A physiologically based model for ethanol and acetaldehyde metabolism in human beings. *Alcohol, 35*(1), 3–12.

Verster, J. C., Benjaminsen, J. M. E., van Lanen, J. H. M., van Stavel, N. M. D., & Olivier, B. (2015). Effects of mixing alcohol with energy drink on objective and subjective intoxication: Results from a Dutch on-premise study. *Psychopharmacology, 232,* 835–842.

Wechsler, H., Davenport, A., Dowdall, G., Moeykens, B., & Castillo, S. (1994). Health and behavioral consequences of binge drinking in college. *JAMA, 272*(21), 1672–1677.

Wechsler, H., Lee, J. E., Kuo, M., Seibring, M., Nelson, T. F., & Lee, H. P. (2002). Trends in college binge drinking during a period of increased prevention efforts: Findings from four Harvard School of Public Health study surveys, 1993–2001. *Journal of American College Health, 50*(5), 203–217.

Wells, S., Dumas, T. M., Bernards, S., Kuntsche, E., Labhart, F., & Graham, K. (2015). Predrinking, Alcohol use, and breath alcohol concentration: A study of young adult bargoers. *Psychology of Addictive Behaviors, 29*(3), 683–689.

Wells, S., Graham, K., & Purcell, J. (2009). Policy implications of the widespread practice of "pre-drinking" or "pre-gaming" before going to public drinking establishments—Are current prevention strategies backfiring? *Addiction, 104*(1), 4–9.

Wells, S., Mihic, L., Tremblay, P. F., Graham, K., & Demers, A. (2008). Where, with whom, and how much alcohol is consumed on drinking events involving aggression? Event-level associations in a Canadian national survey of university students. *Alcoholism: Clinical and Experimental Research, 32*(3), 522–533.

Wetherill, R. R., & Fromme, K. (2009). Subjective responses to alcohol prime event-specific alcohol consumption and predict blackouts and hangover. *Journal of Studies on Alcohol and Drugs, 70,* 593–600.

Wilkinson, P. (1980). Pharmacokinetics of ethanol: A review. *Alcoholism: Clinical and Experimental Research, 4(1),* 6–21.

Wolaver, A. M. (2002). Effects of heavy drinking in college on study effort, grade point average, and major choice. *Contemporary Economic Policy, 20(4),* 415–428.

Zhang, M. W. B., & Ho, R. C. M. (2016). Tapping onto the potential of smartphone applications for psycho-education and early intervention in addictions. *Frontiers in Psychiatry, 7,* 1–70.

Using Systems Thinking to Promote Wellness Program Planning and Implementation in Urban High Schools

David W. Lounsbury, Lynn Fredericks, Camille Jimenez, Sarah N. Martin, Jean Lim, Kelly Nimmer, Moonseong Heo, Ralph Levine, Michelle Bouchard, and Judith Wylie-Rosett

The National Health and Nutrition Examination Survey (NHANES) data from 2007–2008 indicate that almost half of children and adolescents in the United States are overweight or obese (Ogden, Carroll, Curtin, Lamb, & Flegal, 2010; Ogden et al., 2016). Because socioeconomic and biological factors contribute to obesity-related disparities, efforts to address obesity need to focus on systemic issues to help reduce racial and ethnic as well as geographic and economic obesity-related disparities using a multi-component approach (Kenney, Wang, & Iannotti, 2014; Krueger & Reither, 2015).

Schools are promising settings for engaging youth in obesity prevention programming (Honeycutt et al., 2015). Recent reports suggest that multi-component, high-quality school wellness programs that integrate physical activity with nutrition education can improve students' academic performance as well as their health outcomes (Basch, 2011; Basch, Basch, Ruggles, & Rajan, 2014; Lavelle, Mackay, & Pell, 2012; Michael, Merlo, Basch, Wentzel, & Wechsler, 2015; Mura, Vellante, Nardi, Machado, & Carta, 2015).

In the current chapter, we present "systems thinking" as a general approach for cultivating collaborative wellness programming in high school settings. System dynamics modeling, the methodology that underpins our approach to systems thinking, is derived from the premise that a systems approach can help key stakeholders in schools build a deeper, more critical understanding of how to achieve and sustain wellness programming aims (Trochim, Cabera, Milstein, Gallagher, & Leischow, 2006). Useful systems thinking projects can help wellness programmers identify potential barriers and facilitators affecting implementation in both the short and long term. School administrators, teachers, key staff (e.g., food service personnel), community-based service representatives (e.g., local farmers' associations), as well as students and their parents are all important stakeholders who, working collaboratively, can contribute to effective systems thinking for wellness program planning and implementation (Durán-Narucki, 2008; Freedman & Bess, 2011; Freedman, Blake, & Liese, 2013).

Below, we provide background on current national dietary standards for adolescents and how systems thinking can be used to inform behavior change interventions in complex settings like high schools. Next, we describe the project's partnership with FamilyCook Productions and its relationship with the network of high schools that participated in this work. The main product of the project, our Wellness Programming Toolkit—comprised of five components—is presented in detail. We then describe the collaborative process used to facilitate our partnership with HealthCorps and our school-based wellness champions. Finally, we discuss strategies for further dissemination of the toolkit, appreciating its limitations as well as its intended potential.

Using the Dietary Guidelines to Address Adolescent Obesity

Our systems thinking approach to wellness programming in high schools begins by reflecting upon the United States Department of Health and Human Services (HHS) and the United States Department of Agriculture (USDA) Dietary Guidelines (DGs) for Americans, which are published every five years and reflect the most current scientific evidence for government nutrition policies and programs (DeSalvo, Olson, & Casavale, 2016). The DGs inform guidance for all school districts participating in the National School Lunch Program (NSLP), which requires implementation of local wellness policies that promote changes to school systems and environments. Although recent studies show that meaningful improvements are being made in the nutritional content of meals served in public middle and high schools, schools need continued help with implementation and compliance monitoring in order to have the best opportunity to improve the nutrition environments for US students (Terry-McElrath, O'Malley, & Johnston, 2015).

Based on the DGs for adolescents, we identify six general behavioral goals, namely: (1) decreasing sugary beverage intake; (2) increasing frequency of breakfast; (3) increasing vegetable and fruit intake to 2.5 cups per day; (4) decreasing frequency of fast food; (5) increasing physical activity to one hour per day; and (6) reducing sedentary behavior time to less than two hours per day. Our approach to programming serves the essential premise that high school students who can adopt and regularly practice more of these behaviors every day will be more likely to achieve and sustain improved wellness, a healthy weight, and other academic, vocational, and social aspirations. Here, the DGs are disseminated as evidence-based concepts that, if adopted as personal behaviors, will help adolescents make healthier choices each day while they are at school and at home.

Further, our programming is designed to foster engaging ways of working with students such that they, as well as other school-based stakeholders, become a vibrant resource for achieving school-level wellness goals and objectives. We introduce collaborative capacity as a means for planning and implementing tools and exercises to foster students' skill-based learning of health-promotion strategies. Consistent with other organizational and community research, we define "collaborative capacity" as the ability for stakeholders to work together effectively and achieve common goals within their specific environment and available resources (Foster-Fishman, Berkowitz, Lounsbury, Jacobson, & Allen, 2001; Goodman et al., 1998). We define "skill-based learning" as educational activities that teach specific action steps that demonstrate a behavior that can be observed, emulated and shared with others (Kaphingst et al., 2012).

Systems Thinking and Behavior Change

Broadly, systems-oriented methods include a variety of approaches to foster better understanding of complex problems, with the common objective being to move away from framing problems in terms of risk factors and outcomes and towards looking at them as a system comprised of interacting parts with a particular goal (Maani & Cavana, 2000; Trochim et al., 2006). A key objective is to promote a more holistic way of examining a challenge or dilemma by deliberately questioning how key elements of a problem interact as parts of a system (Richardson & Pugh, 1981).

Approached in this way, systems thinking prompts an iterative process of theory building and testing. Systems thinking elicits stakeholders' "mental models," or personal conceptualizations about how things work (Forrester, 2016; Maani & Cavana, 2000; Wolstenholme, 1983). Rigorous systems thinking is akin to Einsteinian "thought experiments," where problems and solutions are explored through a structured process of intellectual deliberation in order to speculate about potential causal relationships (Nersessian, 1992; Richardson, 1991). Systems thinking can clarify communication about the nature of a problem and its potential solutions, which can increase confidence about what kinds of actions would be most likely to produce a desired future outcome.

Building upon tenets of theories of behavior change, a systems thinking approach can help guide planning, implementation, and analysis of behavioral interventions in dynamically complex settings like high schools. It is well documented that simply knowing what is healthy is not sufficient to support long-term healthy lifestyles and, moreover, that personal choices and habits are influenced by a variety of factors embedded in the social and built environment (IOM, 2005). In a recent paper about research on behavioral processes, Miller, Dannals, and Zlatev (2017) underscore the need to adopt a theory of change that explains how interventions impact individuals' psychological states as well as the associated activity or skill that is necessary to influence the targeted behavior.

The Theory of Triadic Influence (TTI) can be used to provide a comprehensive orientation for understanding health behavior change. TTI suggests behavioral choices and their development are influenced by a complex system of factors. These are expressed through three "streams of influence," namely (1) intra-personal/psychological, (2) interpersonal/social, and (3) sociocultural/attitudinal (Flay, Petraitis, & Hu, 1999; Petraitis, Flay, & Miller, 1995; Petraitis, Flay, Miller, Torpy, & Greiner, 1998). Given our focus on skill-based learning in high school students, TTI's interactive and dynamic theory of behavior change supports a multi-level systems thinking framework to guide development and evaluation of our toolkit.

Figure 1 shows how school-level collaborative capacity and student-level skill-based learning form a reinforcing process that mediates a relationship between policies, systems and environment (PSE) and TTI's "streams of influence," which ultimately impact behavior change. PSE effects include local school wellness policy mandates, programming (e.g., breakfast and lunch food service, fitness curricula), and environmental conditions (e.g., the quality, accessibility, and capacity of recreational facilities). Schools with PSE resources that are aligned with wellness initiatives may be more successful in their efforts to design, implement and sustain programming that supports health initiatives (Honeycutt et al., 2015).

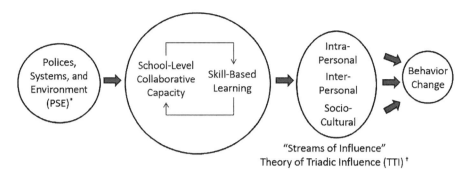

FIGURE 1. Conceptual framework of behavior change in high school students.

*Honeycutt et al. (2015). † Petraitis, Flay, and Miller (1995).

Awareness and knowledge about nutritional health may seem to be a logical primary goal of school-based nutrition education programs. However, teaching students skills they need to develop and implement to achieve behavioral goals can be easily overlooked (Kaphingst et al., 2012). Our previous program development and research of the *Teen Battle Chef* (TBC) program (Bukhari, Fredericks, & Wylie-Rosett, 2011), developed by FamilyCook Productions, a partner to the current project, demonstrated that changes in behavior are driven by enhanced skills related to food preparation for self and others. This is not surprising, since adolescents' social networks may strongly influence their behavior. Behavior-change programming for high school students may need to leverage the potential of multiple streams of influence to broaden exposure to and deepen engagement in skill-building activities.

Project Partnership

In 2013, the Albert Einstein College of Medicine was awarded funding by the National Institute of Diabetes and Digestive and Kidney Diseases (NIDDK) to conduct a four-year research project in partnership with HealthCorps and FamilyCook Productions (NIDDK, R01 DK097096). The purpose of the research was to jointly develop and test school-based activities that foster behavior change consistent with the DGs for adolescents. Focusing on activities that would help develop the school's collaborative capacity and its students' skill-based learning, the project's partners worked to design and pilot a multi-component toolkit for wellness programming in diverse high schools.

All high schools engaged in the project were recruited by HealthCorps, a nationwide nonprofit agency (501(c)(3); incorporated in New York in 2007) that offers a health curriculum grounded in nationally recognized, evidence-based guidelines that seek to reduce adolescent obesity. A recent evaluation of its curriculum in a sample of New York City high schools suggests that it significantly increases students' knowledge about nutrition, mental health, and physical activity (Heo et al., 2016). HealthCorps's main vehicle for achieving these aims is its core curriculum, which is implemented over the course of the school year and organized around three pillars: (1) nutrition (healthy eating), (2) physical exercise (healthy body), and (3) mental resilience (healthy mind and purposeful self-care). The HealthCorps core curriculum and a current student survey that served as HealthCorps' primary evaluation tool at the start of the project were the basis for applying our systems thinking approach to wellness programming.

All access to school staff and students and all programming and evaluation activities in the project were supervised by HealthCorps. HealthCorps also supervised full-time, school-based coordinators who were recent college graduates trained by HealthCorps to promote planning and implementation of the HealthCorps program. Overall organization and administration of HealthCorps resembles the U.S. PeaceCorps and AmeriCorps programs. In general, HealthCorps coordinators serve for two-year periods in designated high schools as liaisons among teachers, students, and administrators; they are trained to lead lessons inside the classroom as well as after school through clubs and other student activities (e.g., cooking, fitness, and youth empowerment).

Wellness Programming Toolkit

Our systems thinking toolkit for skill-based wellness programming in diverse high schools is comprised of five components: (1) wellness program–planning causal loop diagrams (CLDs); (2) the Healthy Me Snapshot; (3) the student SMART goal-setting lesson; (4) the student-led skill-based learning activities; and (5) the wellness champion development and assessment method. Table 1 provides an overview of the toolkit with reference to materials developed for each component and how each supports a two-level intervention: the student level (skill-based learning) and school level (collaborative capacity building).

The materials and procedures described are intended to be the basis of some skill-developing programing in participating high schools to generate measurable behavior change and evaluation metrics that can be compared from year to year. School districts, principals, and school wellness champions can use the data the tools yield to see change in students' habits and adherence to the dietary guidelines based on wellness campaign efforts from year to year and assess progress. For example, a year-long campaign to increase breakfast consumption among students can be measured for efficacy by comparing school breakfast consumption rates and student Healthy Me Snapshot aggregate reports from baseline to one year later and then cross-referencing students' SMART goal success with their Snapshot assessments.

Toolkit Component 1: Wellness Program Planning Causal Loop Diagrams (CLDs)

System dynamics modeling, the methodology that underpins our approach to systems thinking, uses CLDs to depict relationships among key concepts of interest to a given project. Specifically, CLDs reveal feedback structures that define how these concepts interact with each other over time (Forrester, 1971; Richardson & Pugh, 1981). In our toolkit, we use CLDs to represent an ongoing process, or narrative about how wellness programming in high schools can help high school students develop and sustain strong health behaviors through exposure to student-level skill-based learning and opportunities to build school-level collaborative capacity (see figure 2). Consistent with TTI, these causal loops involve intrapersonal, interpersonal, and behavioral influences. For students, the hypothesized behavior change involves their adoption of the DGS,

Table 1. Systems thinking toolkit to promote skill-based wellness programming in diverse high school settings

TOOLKIT COMPONENT	MATERIALS	STUDENT LEVEL (SKILL-BASED LEARNING)	SCHOOL LEVEL (COLLABORATIVE CAPACITY)
Wellness Program Planning Causal Loop Diagrams (CLDs)	Animated CLD slide set; Glossary of terms.	Used to engage stakeholders and to foster wellness program planning and evaluation.	Used to engage stakeholders and to foster wellness program planning and evaluation.
Healthy Me Snapshot Lesson	Classroom lesson guide; Student survey; Sample Snapshot reports (Individual and aggregate).	Personal feedback report generated for each student. Reflects self-reported adherence to DGs and other nutrition and physical activity behaviors.	Aggregate report used to support wellness planning and evaluation. Features descriptive statistics about students' self-reported adherence to DGs and other wellness behaviors.
Student SMART Goal-Setting Lesson	Classroom lesson guide; Student worksheet; SMART goal quality assessment; Student reflection exercise; Sample evaluation reports.	Health education classroom lessons on the DGs culminating in personal SMART goal setting and outcomes reflection exercise for each student.	Aggregate report used to describe students' SMART goal choices, quality and outcomes.
Student-Led Learning Activities	Activity guides, recipes, messaging; Activity evaluation and reporting form; Student participant feedback form; Sample evaluation report.	Students demonstrate to their peers ways of making healthier choices that support adherence to the DGs.	Wellness champions plan and conduct a series of activities to help reach and engage as many students as possible.
Wellness Champion Development and Assessment Method	Wellness Champion Nominee form; Collaborative capacity assessment survey; Sample assessment reports.	Provides an opportunity for students to be recognized as wellness champions and to help identify ways to improve collaboration for wellness programming in their school.	Documents a network of stakeholders who are willing and able to promote wellness programming in their school.

which are expected to lead to better personal health and wellness for students and a school environment that facilitates and supports awareness about and the capacity to make healthier choices, day by day, over time.

SKILL-BASED LEARNING PROCESS

Our students' skill-based learning CLD is represented by the feedback structure on the right side of figure 2 (see "Student Level"). Students' skill-based learning is shown as a collection of processes that explains how, over time, students' participation in wellness activities at school can help them learn new health-related skills to achieve targeted behavior outcomes. An example of this would be students watching easy-to-assemble, no-cook breakfast strategies presented as interactive cafeteria demos by their peers. A different breakfast recipe example might be presented at least once a month for a minimum of three months with an invitation for observing students to make their own samples. By trying such strategies out on their own (experimentation) and building confidence that they can do them (self-efficacy), students acquire and use new skills (making healthy choices). A sense of confidence is fostered that can build to a level of self-actualization at which values begin to shift about what is healthy and what should

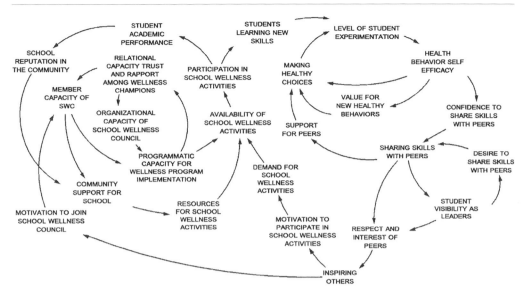

FIGURE 2. CLD of school-level collaborative capacity building and students' skill-based learning processes. Note: SWC = School Wellness Champion(s).

be consumed. At this point, students develop the motivation to maintain these new skills and shift to healthier food and fitness behaviors. Over time, they share their skills with their peers (marketing and sharing), which motivates others to start participating in wellness activities. In this way, many if not all students in the school can benefit from schools providing the most basic wellness activities as long as they lead to new, demonstrable skill-building. The positively reinforcing dynamics expressed in the CLD are constrained only by the availability of wellness activities, which is driven by demand among students. Where demand exceeds capacity, students face barriers to participation. One task presented to stakeholders is to consider other factors that inhibit or slow availability of wellness activities in a given school.

The skill-based learning loops in the CLD are based upon the proposition that skill-based learning is a key characteristic of effective wellness programming, drawing from tenets of TTI, which delineates the effects of multiple streams of influence (intra-personal/psychological, interpersonal/social, and sociocultural/attitudinal) driving students' success in adopting the DGS (Flay & Petraitis, 1991). For example, the loop that includes "student experimentation," "self-efficacy," "values shift," and "healthy choices" describes intrapersonal dynamics. The loop that includes "sharing with social networks" and "peer behavior influence" describes interpersonal and social dynamics. Finally, the loop that includes "visibility" and "enhanced demand for [wellness] activities" describes more of a socio-cultural effect on the student body and the school as a whole.

In addition, these skill-based learning loops are empirically supported by program evaluation outcomes for a culinary skill-based nutrition program, TBC, which has been implemented in over 150 schools and community sites in over thirty states since 2008 (Bukhari et al., 2011). TBC evaluation data were collected from fifteen HealthCorps high schools in New York City from 2011–2013 as well as from eight HealthCorps high schools in California in 2013. Results suggest outcomes of enhanced self-efficacy driving a number of positive dietary and leadership behavior changes. Analysis of qualitative data from TBC students provides insight into the "whys" of behavior change. For example, students were motivated to continue to prepare and consume new meals and snacks that they found to be flavorful or that included ingredients that they discovered they liked.

In addition, TBC students shared their new culinary skills and recipes with family and friends (Sliva, 2014). These effects are consistent with the TTI streams-of-influence CLD. The more confident students were in their public speaking abilities, the more motivated they were to share their cooking skills and new, healthy recipes with peers. The more students were recognized as leaders in their school and achievers in special food-related skills, the more demand for program participation grew. The more adventurous students became in broadening their palates and what they found acceptable to eat, the more they made positive, lasting changes to their daily food habits.

Collaborative Capacity Process. Our collaborative capacity CLD is represented by the feedback structure on the left side of figure 2 (see "School Level"). It shows how various stakeholders within a school can work together effectively to achieve common goals, given their unique environment and available resources. It illustrates how networks of individuals have the potential to create informal teams or, in some cases, formal working groups, committees, or councils—of "wellness champions" in a school. These teams or working groups may include students and teachers of any academic or vocational subject as well as support staff, including school nurses, administrators, school food staff, custodians, and counselors. Parents of students and community members from local agencies or clinics are also stakeholders who could contribute to collaborative capacity for wellness programming in a school.

Collaborative capacity is a multi-dimensional concept, as described in an extensive review of the literature on community-based coalition-building to improve public health (Foster-Fishman et al., 2001). In figure 2, we show how four distinct, critical types of capacity define the quality of collaboration among diverse stakeholders. These four critical capacities include: (1) organizational capacity, 2) relational capacity, (3) member capacity, and (4) programmatic capacity. Organizational capacity refers to the team's or the group's access to resources to help facilitate meetings and communications. An important aspect of organizational capacity is the designation of one or two members who take on the role of group facilitator. These individuals keep members in touch with each other, keep everyone aware of upcoming meetings, and help shape the group's general purpose and mission. Relational capacity is about the quality of rapport among group members. Trust, respect, and ability to communicate openly with each other are markers of high levels of relational capacity. Member capacity reflects the team's or group's collective knowledge, experience, expertise, and access to resources, which can include persons such the school principal, for example. Creativity is often served when the team's or group's members can offer different perspectives or experiences that can inform innovative programming. Finally, programmatic capacity is the ability of the group to design and implement activities and exercises, which in this case promote wellness by helping students learn how to try and sustain healthy choice-making.

These components make up the heart of our school-level CLD. Where collaborative capacity is developed, other positive outcomes are reinforced for the school. Hypothetically, if the availability of a new fitness program is planned and launched in a fall semester, some students would take advantage of it, driving up participation rates. More students being more physically active during the school week would boost those students' academic performance. In turn, these observed changes would reinforce or improve the school's reputation in the community. The community might then respond by increasing support for the school. The increased support could be manifested in the form of a community grant or simply more parent volunteering.

Note that the availability of wellness activities in school is driven by programmatic capacity. It is at this juncture that school-level collaborative capacity links to student-level skill-based learning. The two processes are hypothesized to help reinforce each other over time. It is this larger narrative that the CLD seeks to communicate to stakeholders, to help build commitment to planning and implementing wellness activities at their school.

Toolkit Component 2: The Healthy Me Snapshot

The Healthy Me Snapshot is both a student- and school-level tool. Students take the questionnaire and receive a personalized feedback report via email, usually within the same day. The Snapshot report provides a profile to the student about their DG adherence, itemizing what they performed well on and what needs attention. An algorithm is used to classify students' self-reported answers compared to the desired standard for each behavior (e.g., "eat a healthy breakfast 5 days each week"). The report is designed to be visually appealing and easy to understand (see Appendix [on-line] https://github.com/dlounsbu/HS_wellness_toolkit).

To identify patterns of adherence among students at the school level, data are reported in aggregate. Results can be reported for either a specific classroom and/or for all participating classrooms. Such information may be useful for identifying wellness programming priorities for the school or for specific subgroups of students. Aggregate results can be reported by gender and age and potentially with other school community characteristics of interest. Results may also prove useful for reporting on federally recommended school wellness policies and for the development of specific goals to help implement and sustain such policies.

Toolkit Component 3: Student SMART Goal-Setting

To initiate a process for students' healthy behavior change, we disseminated curriculum modules that teach students the skill of setting a SMART goal. SMART goals are set by individuals to achieve a particular behavior change that is specific (meaning, it has a selected skill-building activity aim or objective), measurable (students can track it to see progress), actionable (students have the ability to follow and achieve it), realistic (it is reasonable and can be worked toward independently without inhibiting barriers), and time bound (it can be completed within a specified timeframe).

In this project, SMART goals are introduced after students receive their personal Snapshot reports (see Appendix). A classroom lesson is dedicated to the skill of setting a SMART goal. The lesson plan addresses the purpose and evidence supporting each of the DGs and the potential benefits of adhering to each recommended behavior. The lesson is typically conducted as part of a health education course but could be integrated into any science, math, physical fitness, or current events curriculum. Students use their Healthy Me Snapshot feedback report to choose which of the DGs to focus on for their SMART goal. This is achieved by the SMART Goal Worksheet (see Appendix), which breaks down SMART goal setting into manageable steps and offers some "specific and actionable" examples of strategies to work on to help students along with the concept and process.

Over the course of the semester in the health or other class into which this goal setting is incorporated, students participate in periodic SMART goal reflection discussions to elicit their narratives about progress (or lack thereof) with their peers and, if necessary, revise and re-attempt their goal.

At semester end, the SMART Goal Reflection Exercise form documents students' efforts and their perceived levels of success (see Appendix). The form is organized into three parts. The first part captures the student's self-reported SMART goal focus, time expended in pursuing their SMART goal(s), and a self-reported assessment of their SMART goal level of achievement. All responses are structured. Students can document up to three SMART goals they have worked on over the course of the semester. The second part is semi-structured. It asks the respondent to reflect on how their SMART goal experience changed the way they think, feel, or look, or how they interact with peers, family members, and others in their community. The third part asks the student to record a new SMART goal, one that builds upon the prior experience and their current health behavior priorities.

Collectively, these three instruments create a practical, powerful dataset for program evaluation. If student identifiers are retained, these data can then be used to evaluate behavior outcomes by comparing self-reported current behaviors (Snapshot data) to their personal goals (SMART Goal Worksheet data) and to self-reported outcomes (SMART Goal Reflection Exercise data).

Lastly, facilitators can use our SMART Goal Lesson Assessment (see Appendix), which is intended to help code the quality of students' SMART Goal Worksheets. Each worksheet can be scored based on five indicators, one for each component of the SMART goal. Each indicator is evaluated as either sufficient (1 point) or insufficient (0 points). These results can be used to determine the effectiveness of the SMART goal lesson overall as well components (for example, specific, measurable), or categories (for example, goals related to physical activity, breakfast) that may require additional attention.

Toolkit Component 4: Student-Led Skill-Based Learning Activities

The purpose of the student-led skill-based activities is twofold: (1) to provide an opportunity for student wellness champions to gain leadership experience, ideally by assisting with all aspects the preparation, organization, delivery and evaluation of the event, and (2) to expose other students (peers) to novel ways of making healthy choices. These learning activities should impart "do-it-yourself" skills that participating students can quickly learn as well as share with friends and family members. They should be viewed as easy, fun, and novel enough that when watching their peers participate, most students would want to give them a try and test them out. The activities all correspond to one or more of the DGs.

In general, the five criteria defining an effective activity are as follows: (1) shares a demonstrable skill relevant to the guideline; (2) can be easily understood through visuals alone (cafeterias are loud, so it can be difficult to hear) by using signage and participatory engagement to make the "what" and "how" explicit; (3) can be easily recalled and recreated by youth (supported by distribution of recipe/instruction handouts); (4) can be easily shared with others (e.g., play the game with friends, recreate the breakfast or snack strategy with food at home); and (5) supports the SMART goal model as defined above (wherein student demo participants can use the skill to work toward achieving one or more personal SMART goals).

Resource materials for conducting these activities are available online and include suggested messaging ideas, recipe or game directions, and methods for modifying recipes, including substituting ingredients and altering recipes or procedures for local tastes, seasons, or other mediating factors (see Appendix). For each of the DGs, the resource map includes multiple suggested skill-based learning activities that can be easily conducted in a school venue such as a cafeteria or gym where many students can be invited to participate. Multiple activity options for each of the DGs have been developed. We recommend that no fewer than three activities be conducted within one semester, all focusing on one DG as part of a mini wellness campaign for the school. This creates the opportunity for greater exposure to and reinforcement of the desired behavioral skill. Which breakfast, hydration, or physical activity strategy in the toolkit is employed on a particular occasion should be left up to the student leaders so they can take ownership of the activity and do their best to make a real impression on their peers.

To evaluate the success of each activity, we designed a simple reporting form to be completed by a responsible organizer, or facilitator, at the school. Data collected build a structured archive and timeline of the student-led events. The archive includes items that document the targeted DGs, school settings, number of student leaders who conducted the activities, facilitators, and barriers to implementation, as well as the estimated number of student audience participants (i.e., the "reach").

In addition, to obtain the participating students' perspectives, a one-page feedback form is provided. All or a small sample of the student audience is asked to complete the form. Using a structured format, the form asks students to record the purpose or focus of the activity (i.e., the target DG), how much they "liked" the event, how likely they would be to try it out on their own at least once in the coming week, and how likely they would be to "share" the activity with friends and family at least once in the coming week. The feedback from students is anonymous but asks respondents to record their grade and gender (see Appendix). Although data were collected from a sample of convenience, we assert that summarized information is useful to the student leaders and for overall program evaluation needs.

Toolkit Component 5: Wellness Champion Development and Assessment Method

Working with the premise that the level and quality of wellness programming in any given school is a reflection of its collaborative capacity, this component of the toolkit emphasizes the need to help schools see who is contributing and how they work together. The assessment method is a two-step process that can be organized by an individual or a small group. The first task is to develop a list of individuals, which includes the organizing facilitator (likely a teacher or school support staff) who is actively assisting and committed to wellness programming at the school. When there are no such individuals, the immediate focus is to identify one or more potential wellness champions and expose them to our wellness program planning, described earlier.

However, if active wellness champions are identified, the Wellness Champion Nomination form and Wellness Champion survey can be used. Data collected can provide insights about how a local network of wellness champions currently work together to achieve common goals. Post-assessment review of results can be used to facilitate discussion about who to further develop or sustain collaborative capacity for wellness programming.

The Wellness Champion Nomination form is used to document the number of champions and the stakeholder groups they represent (e.g., the proportion who are students, teachers, or support staff) in a given school at a given time. Subsequently, the Wellness Champion survey can be completed by each nominated wellness champion. Items in the survey ask the wellness champion respondent to identify their peer wellness champions and reflect on the quality of their interactions with these individuals. Respondents are asked to record their current roles or positions at the school (e.g., student, teacher, administrator, parent, etc.). Next, respondents indicate the various ways that they have served to promote wellness at their school (e.g., "I planned or helped to plan one or more wellness activities"; "I taught or helped to teach a wellness lesson"; "I led or helped to lead a wellness activity"; "I participated in one more wellness activities").

Next, respondents are asked to consider a short list of all nominated wellness champions at the school and document how strongly they agree or disagree with a list of statements (N=34; e.g., "We work well together"; "We communicate with each other easily"; "We appreciate each other's point of view"; "We are good planners"; "We are good at getting things"). The full set of items allows assessment of the each of the four dimensions of collaborative capacity for the school's given number and composition of wellness champions. Results of the assessment provide insights about the current levels of collaborative capacity regarding which dimensions (relational, member, organizational, programmatic) are weak or strong and how the current composition of champions could be adjusted to facilitate greater growth. For example, in a school where no students are actively contributing to wellness programming, efforts to recruit and engage two or three would be prudent (member capacity). Alternatively, results might show that the number and composition of wellness champions is strong but they have challenges following through on planning and implementing activities (organizational capacity). The nomination form and survey instrument are included in the Appendix.

Wellness Programming Toolkit Development

Einstein and FamilyCook worked with staff at HealthCorps to adapt and implement educational strategies to disseminate the USDA DGs. In the first year of the project, HealthCorps linked Einstein and FamilyCook with two New York City high schools, one selected for its high academic and wellness programming performance and one for its comparatively low performance. Visits to these schools introduced the research team to each school's designated HealthCorps coordinator and other wellness champions.

During these initial visits, the research team introduced basic systems thinking concepts to the school wellness champions who were currently supporting program planning and evaluation. We emphasized that students, teachers, and other wellness champions can use this type of thinking to learn how to work together to make positive changes in systems. Additionally, we presented an initial prototype of our CLD for the project in a brief professional development session with participating HealthCorps coordinators. Our prototype CLD was created by our research team. It was based on several years of dissemination and evaluation of the TBC program in New York and California high schools, as well as on our synthesis of the academic literature on collaborative partnership development and behavior change theories in complex settings (TTI). Throughout this period, HealthCorps staff reviewed and helped clarify relationships in the CLD. Thereafter, we used it as a means to promote wellness programming in the school.

During this early stage of the project, we learned that the most popular wellness activities were those that could potentially engage a large number of students focused on a common goal. Coordinators and their champions discussed and demonstrated a variety of ongoing successful wellness activities at their school. One such activity was an initiative to get students to drink more water. A school-wide campaign to drink water and avoid sugary beverages was launched. Students and staff implemented the campaign with the support of the HealthCorps coordinator. Free water bottles were distributed which fostered a sense of school pride and collective identity.

We also learned that programming offering skill-based learning was consistently cited by students as a preferred activity. For example, HealthCorps students who participated in TBC described it as their favorite wellness activity. Although this program engaged a smaller number of students, they were cultivated as leaders to share their new (culinary) skills with friends at school and at home with family members. These examples support the connection to TTI's multiple streams of influence (Flay et al., 1994) and reinforce the utility of skill acquisition and sharing of new healthy behaviors (Sliva, 2014).

With these key observations, we worked with HealthCorps to develop skill-based learning activities that mapped onto a specific DG (e.g., eating breakfast each day). We also worked with coordinators to identify ways of cultivating student leadership via these skill-based learning activities, such that students could become increasingly effective resources to mount wellness activities in their schools.

During the second and third years of the project, we continued our collaborative efforts with HealthCorps, expanding our toolkit development efforts with a larger sample of high schools in New York City (N = 8). To obtain the voice and input of coordinators based as these schools, HealthCorps hosted monthly meetings to discuss the design of the toolkit components and their evaluation.

During the third year, we conducted small pilots of each component of the evolving toolkit. HealthCorps staff and coordinators played a central role in collecting and reviewing formative evaluation results, which were used to help finalize content and procedures. This phase of toolkit development culminated in a final round of site visits conducted by Einstein and FamilyCook, which re-emphasized how important understanding school ecology was, and how the diversity among school environments offers unique opportunities for and challenges to wellness programming initiatives. These visits included end-of-school-year key informant interviews with coordinators, who were asked to reflect on how the toolkit components preformed at their school. Specifically, we asked how a systems thinking approach was useful to planning with students and staff. With reference to the CLD in figure 2, coordinators reported the feedback structures representing skill-based learning and collaboration helped them show "how something feeds into something else" and that, for students, the loops helped to communicate that health can be fun and important and that simple efforts repeated by many students over time "build up and can take off."

The fourth and final year of our project was focused on dissemination of our final toolkit in a national sample of HealthCorps high schools. At this stage of the project, HealthCorps had active partnerships with $N = 23$ high schools for toolkit dissemination. Given requirements of local school IRBs and other authorities overseeing school-based research and program evaluation in our sample of high schools, procedures for either written active consent by a parent or guardian (i.e., opt-in), passive consent by a parent or guardian (i.e., opt-out), or exempt (informational flyer only, with oral consent) were developed and approved by Einstein's IRB. The Einstein protocol was presented to school principals and used to organize any further, necessary local review and approval. Six of $N = 22$ high schools asked to participate were not approved at the time of data analysis, yielding a final sample of $N = 16$ schools (see table 2). This sample of high schools represented three regions: Northeast ($n = 6$); Pacific West ($n = 5$); and Southwest Central ($n = 5$). They varied by size (small to very large) and by community (urban, suburban, and rural), as well as by demographics (enrollment, student/teacher ratio, eligibility for free and reduced lunch, and race/ethnicity mix).

Toolkit Instrument Data Collection

Data collected from participating HealthCorps high schools over the most recent academic year illustrate the utility of our toolkit (see Table 3). Sample sizes vary by toolkit instrument, reflecting the reality of working in high schools where there are multiple competing priorities and demands for HealthCorps Coordinators' limited time and resources.

Evaluation Data Management and Security

To facilitate data collection and processing across participating schools, we administered the Snapshot and other toolkit instruments electronically via a Research Electronic Data Capture (REDCap) portal maintained by the Albert Einstein College of Medicine. REDCap is a secure web application for building and managing online surveys and databases. All survey data is collected using unique identifiers to ensure confidentiality of student participants. HealthCorps coordinators did not maintain the survey data but they will maintain the list of unique identifiers which may be used to link other student curricular activities with their Healthy Me Snapshot. This database does not include student contact information. HealthCorps will not collect contact information on file for use after the data has been collected. Only data from those students whose parents provide a signed consent form are included in the evaluation.

Table 2. Profile of HealthCorps' participating pilot program high schools

COUNT	REGION	HIGH SCHOOL SIZE (US AVG. = 752)	COMMUNITY	STUDENT ENROLLMENT	CLASSROOM TEACHERS (FTE)	STUDENT-TEACHER RATIO	% FREE AND REDUCED LUNCH ELIGIBILITY	% BLACK	% HISPANIC	PARTICIPATION IN HEALTHCORPS CLASSROOM ACTIVITIES		
										GRADES SERVED	NUMBER OF STUDENTS	% OF SCHOOL ENROLLMENT
1	Northeast	Large	Suburban	1,279	106	12.1	83%	25%	68%	9–12	75	6%
2	Northeast	Medium	Suburban	701	53	13.4	63%	27%	21%	9–10	262	37%
3	Northeast	Large	Suburban	1,879	144	13.0	74%	1%	94%	9–12	132	7%
4	Northeast	Large	Urban	1,777	90	19.7	82%	36%	54%	9–12	195	11%
5	Northeast	Small	Urban	488	18	27.3	90%	30%	65%	9–12	126	26%
6	Northeast	Very large	Suburban	2,173	117	18.6	32%	49%	19%	9–12	165	8%
7	Pacific West	Very large	Urban	2,480	83	30.0	71%	0%	97%	9, 11, 12	605	24%
8	Pacific West	Medium	Small town	904	39	23.1	54%	1%	20%	9–12	186	21%
9	Pacific West	Large	Urban	1,985	76	26.0	80%	1%	90%	10–12	153	8%
10	Pacific West	Very large	Suburban	3,456	138	25.1	49%	9%	52%	9–12	97	3%
11	Pacific West	Medium	Small town	758	33	23.3	56%	1%	34%	9	65	9%
12	South West Central	Small	Small town	484	39	12.4	47%	5%	9%	10–12	137	28%
13	South West Central	Medium	Rural	789	45	17.6	80%	19%	14%	9–12	332	42%
14	South West Central	Small	Rural	318	26	12.2	52%	2%	5%	9–12	137	43%
15	South West Central	Small	Rural	220	15	14.4	34%	1%	5%	9, 11, 12	113	51%
16	South West Central	Small	Rural	271	25	10.9	58%	2%	3%	9–12	57	21%
Average				*1,293*	*66*	*19*	*64%*	*13%*	*42%*		*179*	*21%*

Source: National Center of Education Statistics (2016–2017) and HealthCorps (2016–2017).

Table 3. Toolkit pilot evaluation data sources

TOOLKIT INSTRUMENT	CONTRIBUTING SCHOOLS (*N*)	SAMPLE SIZE			
		TOTAL (*N*)	PER SCHOOL (*N*)		
			MEAN	MIN	MAX
Healthy Me Snapshot Survey*	16	2411	151	32	508
SMART Goal Worksheet[†]	9	551	61	21	111
SMART Goal Quality Assessment[†]	9	551	61	21	111
SMART Goal Reflection Exercise[†]	6	296	49	15	106
Student-led Learning Activity—Planning and Evaluation form[§]	13	39	3	2	5
Student-led Learning Activity—Participant Feedback Form[§]	11	795	72	36	197
Wellness Champion Nominee Form[‖]	8	48	6	2	15

Notes: *Supports Snapshot Lesson; † Supports Student SMART Goal-Setting Lesson; §Supports Student-Led Learning Activities; ‖Supports Wellness Champion Development and Assessment Method.

Healthy Me Snapshot

Healthy Me Snapshot data yielded the largest sample size, representing *N* = 2,309 students from *N* = 16 HealthCorps high schools. Snapshot data were collected at one time point either at the beginning of the fall semester (September or October) or the spring semester (January or February). Figure 3 illustrates the proportion of students who were not adherent ("need improvement") for each of the DGs and for HealthCorps's added guideline for mental resilience. Curbing consumption of junk food was reported to be the most challenging (96 percent indicated that most of the time they choose "less healthy" or "unhealthy" snacks such as chips, pizza, candy, and other sweets), followed by too much screen time (91 percent reported spending two or more hours per school day of time spent on electronics—phone, tablet, computer, TV, video game

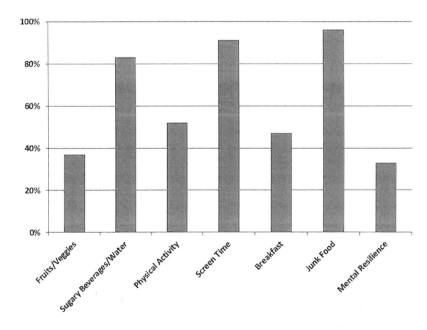

FIGURE 3. Healthy Me Snapshot by target behavior proportion of students not meeting guideline (*N* = 2,309).

devices), and drinking too many sugary beverages (83 percent reported having one or more sugary drinks—soda, Arizona sweetened iced tea, fruit punch—in a typical day).

Student SMART Goals

A matched sample of students who completed the SMART Goal Worksheet after completing the Snapshot was analyzed (N = 551), revealing a similar pattern of adherence to the DGs as in full sample, with the notable exception being consumption of fruits and vegetables (71 percent reported eating fruits and vegetables with only some meals, compared to 37 percent in the full sample, N = 2,309; see figure 4).

Regarding students' SMART goal choices, which are a product of the SMART goal lesson (Toolkit Component 3), the most commonly selected targets were increasing physical activity (25 percent) followed by eating breakfast (23 percent; see figure 5).

To demonstrate the use of the SMART Goal Quality Assessment, Einstein research staff coded students' SMART Goal Worksheets. Results show that the lesson was effective and that the large majority of students were able to record a viable personal SMART goal (see figure 6). Clarifying the time horizon during which they hoped to achieve their personal goal proved the most challenging (60 percent were not timebound), with other dimensions less problematic.

SMART Goal Reflection Exercises were obtained for N = 296 students from six HealthCorps high schools. Asked in retrospect about their personal experience in setting SMART goals, most (63 percent) reported that, in a time period of four to six weeks since completing their SMART Goal Worksheets, they had attempted no more than one goal, although 13 percent said they attempted three or more. They were asked to consider their primary, or most important, personal SMART goal of those they attempted and 25 percent said they achieved "most or all of it."

Student-Led Learning Activities

During the spring semester of 2017, HealthCorps coordinators were asked to pilot Toolkit Component 4, a series of events branded "Café-o-Yeas" (CoYs) by HealthCorps. Pilot activities started in mid-February and ended at the end of the school year, in mid-June. There were N = 13 participating schools, yielding a sample of N = 39 student-led events. Coordinators were instructed to attempt to mount no fewer than three such events. One school documented five events during this period. More than half of the activities (n = 23, 59 percent) focused on nutrition (NU; healthy eating), followed by mental resilience (MR; healthy mind and purposeful self-care; n = 12, 31 percent), then physical exercise (PE; healthy body; n = 4, 10 percent).

The most popular venue for holding student-led activities was an open area within the school building or schoolyard (n = 17, 45 percent), followed by the cafeteria (n = 15, 39 percent), the gym (n = 4; 10 percent), and the classroom (n = 3; 8 percent). PE activities were held in the gymnasium or outside, with NU and MR activities held most often in the cafeteria at the start of the school day or during lunch breaks.

HealthCorps coordinators reported that the choice of type of activity (CoY) was strongly linked to the interest levels of student leaders and support staff who volunteered to assist. The

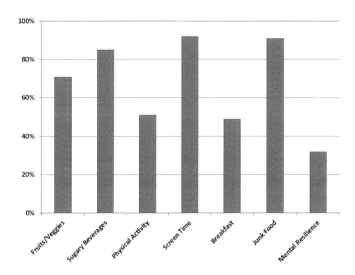

FIGURE 4. Healthy Me Snapshot by target behavior proportion of students not meeting guideline (Matched SMART Goal Sample; $N = 506$).

FIGURE 5. Students' SMART goal target (Matched Healthy Me Snapshot Sample; $N = 506$).

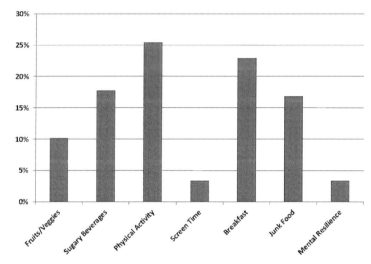

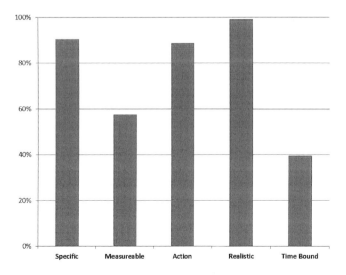

FIGURE 6. Coordinators' SMART goal quality assessment ($N = 506$).

Table 4. Peer-reported feedback for student-led learning activities

DIETARY GOAL	NO. STUDENT DEMOS	LIKE ($F = 5.7$, $df = 6$, $p < 0.001$)			TRY ($F = 6.8$, $df = 6$, $p < 0.001$)			SHARE ($F = 6.7$, $df = 6$, $p < 0.001$)		
		MEAN	SD	N	MEAN	SD	N	MEAN	SD	N
Eat breakfast	13	8.1	2.0	423	7.2	2.4	423	7.2	2.3	420
Avoid sugary beverages	3	7.9	2.5	36	6.3	2.7	36	6.8	2.7	35
Increase physical activity	4	7.9	2.0	29	6.7	2.0	29	8.6	1.4	29
Build mental resilience	12	7.9	2.3	124	6.9	2.5	124	6.7	2.3	124
Drink more water	2	7.9	2.2	76	7.3	2.1	76	7.0	2.2	76
Eat more fruits and veggies	4	6.7	3.0	97	5.5	3.4	96	6.0	3.0	97
Avoid junk food	1	6.6	2.3	8	5.1	2.1	8	4.9	2.4	8
Total	*39*	*7.9*	*2.3*	*793*	*6.9*	*2.6*	*792*	*6.9*	*2.5*	*789*

strong interest in MR activities reflected students' stated need for academic stress relief and support for a positive social climate within the school. Results of aggregated Snapshot reports were also noted to be an important part of choosing a specific CoY.

WHAT WORKED WELL? (STRENGTHS)

Coordinators reported that the commitment and enthusiasm of the students contributed to the overall success of a specific CoY event. Of the eight schools, three schools each stated that it being a student-led event, helpful staff and the interactive or engaging nature of the event was reason for its effectiveness. Two schools credited offering healthier food options and alternative meal preparation methods with creating more-successful events.

Some coordinators reported that student-led activities helped build relationships with and break down barriers to working with food service staff and other school support staff. Events also served to build awareness about health behaviors among students, make HealthCorps and its the role in the school more visible, which also led to new student and staff recruitment to assist in supporting wellness programming at the school.

WHAT WAS CHALLENGING? (WEAKNESS)

The logistics of the set-up and tear-down of the CoY events were a frequent challenge for Coordinators and their student leaders, as well as insufficient supplies or simply poor organization. Well-attended events were sometimes included too few student leaders. Being able to attract peers to the student-led events proved to be problematic at times, which was often due to competing activities at the school or too little awareness or marketing of the event ahead of time.

PEER-REPORTED STUDENT FEEDBACK

Table 4 indicates that students rated the student-led events highly. On a scale from 0 (did not like it) to 10 (loved it!), the average response was $M = 7.9$ ($N = 793$). Events targeting "eating breakfast" were most popular ($F = 5.7$, $df = 6$, $p < 0.001$), with similar results for likelihood of trying out the activity on their own ($M = 6.9$; 0 = will not try it; 10 = will definitely try it!) and for sharing the event with friends and family ($M = 6.9$; 0 = will not share it; 10 = will definitely share it!). We found that the majority of students correctly identified the purpose of the event

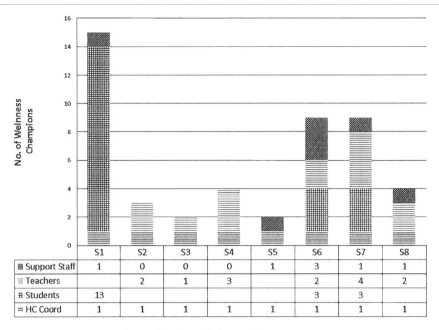

FIGURE 7. Nominated Wellness Champions (*N* = 8 Schools).

(78 percent), and that there was a positive association between knowing the purpose and liking the event (*p* < 0.01).

Students who actively led these events tended to be older (more likely eleventh and twelfth graders than eighth or ninth graders). On average, three students took an active role in planning, organizing and or conducting an event (*M* = 3.05 students, *sd* = 1.76). Including students and other staff, *M* = 4.8 stakeholders (*sd* = 3.12) assisted in mounting any given event. Teachers were the most commonly named staff assistance (72 percent of events), with food service, gym staff, and other community members assisting students 25 percent of the time. Notably, for this set of pilot activities, parents did not assist in any event (0 percent).

Wellness Champion Nominees

As described above, Toolkit Component 5 is a two-step method intended to, first, identify a network of stakeholders who are engaged or are potentially engaged in wellness programming at a given school and, second, characterize how they work with each other based on items that assess each dimension of collaborative capacity (organizational capacity, relational capacity, member capacity, and programmatic capacity).

Our pilot evaluation report is limited to examination of local networks of wellness champion nominees from *n* = 8 high schools. Figure 7 allows comparison of the number of identified wellness champions as reported by each school's HealthCorps coordinator at end of the school year. Note that each school's wellness champion profile includes the HealthCorps coordinator. The first wellness champion profile (S1) includes the most champions (*n* = 15) and the largest number of students (*n* = 13), with one teacher. The next three profiles (S2–S4) do not include student leaders, and feature one or two teachers who work with HealthCorps coordinator. The wellness champion profile for S5 includes not student leaders or teachers, but one school-based support staff. The last three champion profiles (S6–S8) are a mix of students, teachers and support staff who are working together with the HealthCorps Coordinator. Due to incomplete Wellness Champion survey data, further analyses of patterns of self-reported collaborative capacity are not presented here.

Discussion

Schools offer great potential for interventions seeking to engage children and adolescents in wellness programming (Gross & Cinelli, 2004). Yet, as our project demonstrates, schools are complex systems comprised of diverse stakeholders (students, teachers, support staff, others) with many competing priories and agendas. In recent years, public health interventions for nutrition and obesity in schools have emphasized PSE efforts over direct, skill-based education. These approaches use indices and checklists for compliance, but such measures do not reveal whether or not students make behavior changes. Our systems approach to behavior change attempts to move to new ground, building upon the notion that skill-building in adolescents to help them follow the evidence-based DGs is more likely to result in behavioral outcomes than knowledge transfer or policy changes alone. Our toolkit supports the essential premise that high school students who can adopt and regularly practice more of these behaviors every day are more likely to achieve and sustain improved wellness, healthy weights, and other academic, vocational, and social aspirations (Basch, 2011; Durán-Narucki, 2008; Langford et al., 2014; Martin, Saunders, Shenkin, & Sproule, 2014; Michael et al., 2015). They form a practical, adaptable set of materials that can be used by any school or school district to establish a student-driven approach to systemic school wellness.

Schools or school districts adopting this toolkit's systems perspective will note the emphasis on employing an iterative process among school stakeholders when adopting various toolkit components. Each component of the toolkit supports important dynamics that schools need to explore in their unique settings:

- facilitating skill-based learning (SMART goals, strategies to achieve the DGs) that fosters experimentation;
- inspiring students to share their new skills with their social networks;
- cultivating peer leaders and providing a public platform at school for peer-to-peer skill sharing; and
- mounting wellness campaigns aimed at a specific DGs to maximize resource utilization and prompt measurable behavior changes.

All of these components leave room for school stakeholders to adapt to their own school system and establish their school-specific best practices. In this way, more effective, sustainable wellness programming can reach more students, support student academic success, and build the school's reputation. Successful outcomes can attract external support and resources from the school community and district, which in turn further contributes to the sustainability of wellness programming.

With our project partner, HealthCorps, we built our own collaborative capacity over time to combine perspectives and priorities to design the toolkit and its evaluation components. HealthCorps afforded the project access to a sample of high schools that varied in many ways (large and small; urban, rural, and suburban; socioeconomically and racially diverse). Although systems thinking guided our planning and the implementation and analysis of the toolkit components in participating HealthCorps high schools, our study was not equipped to conduct an intensive participatory intervention with the school-based wellness champions themselves. Originally, when we were working exclusively with New York City high schools in project years one and two, we thought such an intervention might be possible. However, coordination across schools in multiple geographic locations with limited time and resources among the research team hampered our ability to do so. Notably, school-specific IRBs and other administrative and privacy concerns by school systems restricted our ability to work directly with participating schools. Hence, the participatory quality of our approach was shaped mainly through our regular, face-to-face meetings with HealthCorps program staff and their coordinators.

Periodically, through each phase of the project, HealthCorps coordinators needed to improvise when, for example, a new principal changed school policies that directly related to student-led activities (CoYs) in the cafeteria or forbade posters and other public announcements that drive attention to wellness campaigns. Schools differed in their successful development of student leaders as well. In some schools, students with strong culinary or athletic skills took their roles as leaders very seriously and really "owned" the CoYs and shared their knowledge with a great number of other students publicly. In other schools, coordinators struggled to find enough student leaders or to allow students take the lead in planning, executing, and really "owning" their demo. This was a learning curve but our results show that the strongest events were those where more students were driving the content and execution.

As for the Healthy Me Snapshot and SMART goal setting process, we attempted various combinations of electronic and paper-based survey taking and goal setting. By and large, students greatly preferred electronic interfaces. Yet many schools were not equipped with enough computers per student and some had internet connectivity challenges. These inconsistencies are especially common for an organization like HealthCorps that engages schools across the United States with different capacities. School districts contemplating our model and toolkit will likely face more similarities among school capabilities vis-á-vis technology or other implementation challenges.

Since the overarching aim of our toolkit is to help schools develop their capacity to expose as many students as possible to skill-based learning, understanding and anticipating the process and time needed to achieve this systemically and ongoing cannot be overemphasized. For example, as peer leaders share their new skills and behaviors and cycle through the loops of experimentation and peer sharing, the healthy behaviors they are demonstrating become normative within the school community and inspire new students to emerge as leaders and continue these dynamics. This supports the school system to generate more resources and support to further build momentum for wellness programming.

Limitations and Future Directions

Overall, our pilot results support the potential utility and flexibility of the materials currently included in our toolkit. However, there is much more to explore, such as effects related to demographics, likes gender, age, grade, and BMI can be pursued with our toolkit and its instruments. Similarly, associations regarding school characteristics, including school size, teacher-student ratio, and urban vs. rural or suburban settings, can be studied.

Appreciating that schools operate on an annual cycle is essential to effective application of our toolkit. Currently, we have featured dissemination data from a single year, presenting a matched sample of students' Snapshots, SMART Goal Worksheets, and SMART Goal Reflection Exercises. Use of these three instruments trace how the toolkit can be used to document students' learning and progress with personal goals for health behavior change.

Arguably the most challenging component of our toolkit to design and implement has to do with cultivating and sustaining wellness champions within a school. Although engaging students in skill-based learning fosters motivation to share with peers, leveraging such positive outcomes to enhance wellness programming can be difficult. Our preliminary evaluation results show that among $N = 8$ reporting schools, only three indicated a robust mix of eight or more engaged stakeholders (teachers, students, and support staff). Further, only one school reported a group of wellness champions predominantly comprised of students (thirteen of fifteen champions). As illustrated in our CLD (figure 2), student leaders are an important driver of wellness programming and schools that can cultivate more student leaders are likely to accelerate the dynamics of learning and sharing, which in turn raise school-level collaborative capacity for wellness programming.

Notably, our Wellness Champion Nominee form and its companion, the School Wellness Champion survey—which facilitates assessment of stakeholder engagement and collaborative capacity—were not introduced to participating schools until the spring semester of our dissemination year and they require active informed consent. The delayed introduction of these forms and the added administrative steps restricted their full application in our project's school sample. Nonetheless, the potential utility of these instruments was acknowledged by HealthCorps coordinators and staff as a way to document current needs and/or current success in stakeholder engagement at any juncture in a school's wellness programming initiative.

This point raises the matter of how to support school administrators and teaching staff with professional development to best use this toolkit. During the project, Einstein and FamilyCook Productions provided professional development to HealthCorps to co-develop and apply our wellness programming materials. However, professional development training is not included in the toolkit. Moving forward, HealthCorps University (HCU) has been established as one resource to meet this need (http://www.healthcorps.org). HCU is a "train the trainer" professional development program that certifies participants to bring HealthCorps's curriculum to their organization, whether it's a school system, community group, or corporation. HCU offers a short-course program training certificate that is designed to teach to HealthCorps's core curriculum, which includes most of the components in this toolkit. In addition, FamilyCook Productions (http://

www.FamilyCookProductions.com) disseminates an evidence-based nutritional skill-building curriculum as well as professional development designed to support this toolkit.

Lastly, evaluation data presented here are largely qualitative and descriptive and do not explicitly account for the nested nature of school interventions. We acknowledge that to more fully understand and appreciate the utility of our toolkit, additional, more sophisticated hierarchical statistical approaches, or, at minimum, purposeful comparison of different types of schools are needed. Similarly, our project experiences while developing the toolkit lend themselves to formal system dynamics simulation modeling (Forrester, 1992; 2016; Richardson & Pugh, 1981). To accomplish this, we will apply existing data and feedback obtained from our formative toolkit evaluation. These envisioned models will complement our existing materials as decision-making aides for application of this toolkit by schools.

REFERENCES

Basch, C. E. (2011). Healthier students are better learners: High-quality, strategically planned, and effectively coordinated school health programs must be a fundamental mission of schools to help close the achievement gap. *Journal of School Health, 81*(10), 650–662. doi:10.1111/j.1746-1561.2011.00640.x.

Basch, C. E., Basch, C. H., Ruggles, K. V., & Rajan, S. (2014). Prevalence of sleep duration on an average school night among four nationally representative successive samples of American high school students, 2007–2013. *Prev Chronic Dis, 11,* E216. doi:10.5888/pcd11.140383.

Bukhari, A., Fredericks, L., & Wylie-Rosett, J. (2011). Strategies to promote high school students' healthful food choices. *Journal of Nutrition Education and Behavior, 43*(5), 414–418. doi:10.1016/j.jneb.2011.01.008.

DeSalvo, K. B., Olson, R., & Casavale, K. O. (2016). Dietary guidelines for Americans. *JAMA, 315*(5), 457–458. doi:10.1001/jama.2015.18396.

Durán-Narucki, V. (2008). School building condition, school attendance, and academic achievement in New York City public schools: A mediation model. *Journal of Environmental Psychology, 28*(3), 278–286.

Flay, B. R., Hu, F. B., Siddiqui, O., Day, L. E., Hedeker, D., Petraitis, J., . . . & Sussman, S. (1994). Differential influence of parental smoking and friends' smoking on adolescent initiation and escalation of smoking. *Journal of Health and Social Behavior, 35*(3), 248–265.

Flay, B. R., & Petraitis, J. (1991). Methodological issues in drug use prevention research: Theoretical foundations. *NIDA Research Monograph, 107,* 81–109.

Flay, B. R., Petraitis, J., & Hu, F. B. (1999). Psychosocial risk and protective factors for adolescent tobacco use. *Nicotine and Tobacco Research, 1 Suppl 1,* S59–65.

Forrester, J. W. (1971). *Principles of systems* (2nd ed.). Cambridge: Wright-Allen Press.

Forrester, J. W. (1992). Policies, decisions, and information sources for modeling. *European Journal of Operational Research, 59*(1), 42–63.

Forrester, J. W. (2016). Learning through System dynamics as preparation for the 21st century. *System Dynamics Review, 32*(3–4), 187–203. doi:10.1002/sdr.1571.

Foster-Fishman, P. G., Berkowitz, S. L., Lounsbury, D. W., Jacobson, S., & Allen, N. A. (2001). Building collaborative capacity in community coalitions: A review and integrative framework. *American Journal of Community Psychology, 29*(2), 241–261. doi:10.1023/a:1010378613583.

Freedman, D. A., & Bess, K. D. (2011). Food systems change and the environment: Local and global connections. *American Journal of Community Psychology, 47*(3–4), 397–409. doi:10.1007/s10464-010-9392-z.

Freedman, D. A., Blake, C. E., & Liese, A. D. (2013). Developing a multicomponent model of nutritious food access and related implications for community and policy practice. *Journal of Community Practice, 21*(4), 379–409. doi:10.1080/10705422.2013.842197.

Goodman, R. M., Speers, M. A., McLeroy, K., Fawcett, S., Kegler, M., Parker, E., . . . & Wallerstein, N. (1998). Identifying and defining the dimensions of community capacity to provide a basis for measurement. *Health Education and Behavior, 25*(3), 258–278. doi:10.1177/109019819802500303.

Gross, S. M., & Cinelli, B. (2004). Coordinated school health program and dietetics professionals: Partners in promoting healthful eating. *Journal of the Academy of Nutrition and Dietetics, 104*(5), 793–798. doi:10.1016/j.jada.2004.02.024.

Heo, M., Irvin, E., Ostrovsky, N., Isasi, C., Blank, A. E., Lounsbury, D. W., . . . & Wylie-Rosett, J. (2016). Behaviors and knowledge of HealthCorps New York City high schoolsStudents: Nutrition, Mental health, and physical activity. *Journal of School Health, 86*(2), 84–95. doi:10.1111/josh.12355.

Honeycutt, S., Leeman, J., McCarthy, W. J., Bastani, R., Carter-Edwards, L., & Clark, H., . . . & Kegler, M. (2015). Evaluating policy, systems, and environmental change interventions: Lessons learned from CDC's prevention research centers. *Prevention of Chronic Disease, 12*(150281).

IOM [Institute of Medicine]. (2005). *Preventing childhood obesity: Health in the balance.* Washington, DC: National Academies Press.

Kaphingst, K. A., Kreuter, M. W., Casey, C., Leme, L., Thompson, T., Cheng, M. R., . . . Lapka, C. (2012). Health literacy index: Development, reliability, and validity of a new tool for evaluating the health literacy demands of health information materials. *Journal of Health Communication, 17 Suppl 3,* 203–221. doi:10.1080/10810730.2012.712612.

Kenney, M. K., Wang, J., & Iannotti, R. (2014). Residency and racial/ethnic differences in weight status and lifestyle behaviors among US youth. *Journal of Rural Health, 30*(1), 89–100. doi:10.1111/jrh.12034.

Krueger, P. M., & Reither, E. N. (2015). Mind the gap: Race/ethnic and socioeconomic disparities in obesity. *Current Diabetes Reports, 15*(11), 95. doi:10.1007/s11892-015-0666-6.

Langford, R., Bonell, C. P., Jones, H. E., Pouliou, T., Murphy, S. M., Waters, E., . . . Campbell, R. (2014). The WHO health-promoting school framework for improving the health and well-being of students and their academic achievement. *Cochrane Database of Systematic Reviews* (4), https://doi.org/10.1002/14651858.CD008958.pub2.

Lavelle, H. V., Mackay, D. F., & Pell, J. P. (2012). Systematic review and meta-analysis of school-based interventions to reduce body mass index. *Journal of Public Health (Oxf), 34*(3), 360–369. doi:10.1093/pubmed/fdr116.

Maani, K. E., & Cavana, R. Y. (2000). *Systems thinking and modeling: Understanding change and complexity.* Auckland, New Zealand: Pearson Education.

Martin, A., Saunders, D. H., Shenkin, S. D., & Sproule, J. (2014). Lifestyle intervention for improving school achievement in overweight or obese children and adolescents. *Cochrane Database Syst Rev*(3), Cd009728. doi:10.1002/14651858.CD009728.pub2.

Michael, S. L., Merlo, C. L., Basch, C. E., Wentzel, K. R., & Wechsler, H. (2015). Critical connections: Health and academics. *Jouranl of School Health, 85*(11), 740–758. doi:10.1111/josh.12309.

Miller, D. T., Dannals, J. E., & Zlatev, J. J. (2017). Behavioral Processes in long-lag intervention studies. *Perspectives on Psychological Science, 12*(3), 454–467. doi:10.1177/1745691616681645.

Mura, G., Vellante, M., Nardi, A. E., Machado, S., & Carta, M. G. (2015). Effects of school-based physical activity interventions on cognition and academic achievement: A Systematic review. *CNS Neurological Disorder Drug Targets, 14*(9), 1194–1208.

Nersessian, N. J. (1992). *In the theoretician's laboratory: Thought experimenting as mental modeling.* Paper presented at the Biennial Meeting of the Philosophy of Science Association, East Lansing, Michigan.

Ogden, C. L., Carroll, M. D., Curtin, L. R., Lamb, M. M., & Flegal, K. M. (2010). Prevalence of high body mass index in US children and adolescents, 2007–2008. *JAMA, 303*(3), 242–249. doi:10.1001/jama.2009.2012.

Ogden, C. L., Carroll, M. D., Lawman, H. G., Fryar, C. D., Kruszon-Moran, D., Kit, B. K., & Flegal, K. M. (2016). Trends in Obesity prevalence among children and adolescents in the United States, 1988–1994 through 2013–2014. *JAMA, 315*(21), 2292–2299. doi:10.1001/jama.2016.6361.

Petraitis, J., Flay, B. R., & Miller, T. Q. (1995). Reviewing theories of adolescent substance use: Organizing pieces in the puzzle. *Psycholical Bulletin, 117*(1), 67–86.

Petraitis, J., Flay, B. R., Miller, T. Q., Torpy, E. J., & Greiner, B. (1998). Illicit substance use among adolescents: a matrix of prospective predictors. *Substance Use and Misuse, 33*(13), 2561–2604.

Richardson, G. P. (1991). *Feedback thought in social science and systems theory.* Waltham, MA: Pegasus Communications.

Richardson, G. P., & Pugh, A. L., III. (1981). *Introduction to system dynamics modeling.* Portland: Productivity Press.

Sliva, N. (2014). *Using a knowledge and skills-based intervention to improve the cooking skills and self-efficacy in adolescents, and the influence on friends and family.* (Unpublished Master's thesis). Columbia University, New York.

Terry-McElrath, Y. M., O'Malley, P. M., & Johnston, L. D. (2015). Foods and beverages offered in US public secondary schools through the National School Lunch Program from 2011–2013: Early evidence of improved nutrition and reduced disparities. *PrevMED, 78,* 52–58. doi:10.1016/j.ypmed.2015.07.010.

Trochim, W. M., Cabera, D. A., Milstein, B., Gallagher, R. S., & Leischow, S. J. (2006). Practical challenges of systems thinking and modeling in public health. *American Journal of Public Health, 96*(3), 538–546.

Wolstenholme, E. F. (1983). System dynamics: A system methodology or a system modelling technique. *Dynamica, 9*(2), 84–90.

Participatory Modeling with Fuzzy Cognitive Maps: Studying Veterans' Perspectives on Access and Participation in Higher Education

Ronda J. Jenson, Alexis N. Petri, Antonie J. Jetter, Arden D. Day, and George S. Gotto

articipatory modeling approaches are gaining prominence in a variety of fields: human services and social sciences, business and product development, and environmental sciences, to name only a few. When needing to hypothesize solutions to complex systems issues, participatory modeling is an approach to identifying the critical components of the system and investigating the relationships between components through the perspectives of experts and stakeholders. Fuzzy cognitive mapping (FCM) is a participatory modeling technique that allows modelers to capture individual (and incomplete) views on a complex system in one-on-one interviews and mathematically integrate them into a collaborative model. Stakeholders can then interpret meaning from the model and use the model for decision-making.

Often, participatory modeling relies on group approaches such as facilitated modeling workshops. If the workshop attendees share similar roles or perspectives, there may be high levels of agreement on the types and values of the components identified as critical to the model, thus leading to cohesion and consistency in the resulting model. While often more convenient and leading to cleaner data and models, group approaches can be challenging for geographically dispersed respondents and results may be biased in favor of participants who are strongly committed to the topic of investigation, self-confident, outspoken, and well-connected in their communities.

The chapter describes the FCM approach followed by a case example of an integrated systems model constructed from individual interviews with sixty-nine participants in five locations across the United States. With funding from the National Science Foundation, the research study Veterans in STEM examined the critical factors affecting the success of military veterans with service-connected disabilities pursuing college-level STEM education toward STEM careers. The study's objective was the creation of a collaborative system model of veterans' learning, participation, persistence, and success in STEM education. The model was used to simulate the likely impact of various educational programs and structures on veterans' success in completing their STEM education and entering the STEM workforce.

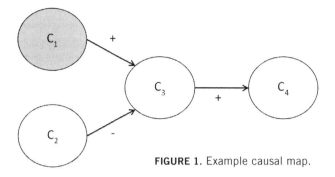

FIGURE 1. Example causal map.

Fuzzy Cognitive Mapping

FCM is a system modeling technique with roots in social science and artificial intelligence. Bart Kosko (1986) first proposed the method to make qualitative cognitive maps, which had originated in social science (see, e.g., Axelrod, 1976; Eden, 1988; Huff, 1990), computable. The starting point of any FCM is a causal map like the map depicted in figure 1. Concepts ("nodes" or "ovals") are linked through arrows that represent causality. Concepts are described verbally and can represent hard-to-quantify phenomena such as "well-being" and "success." A positive (negative) arrow between two concepts denotes that an increase (decrease) in the first concept causes the second concept to also increase (decrease).

Causal cognitive maps—the predecessors of FCM—are frequently used in social sciences. As a research tool, they capture the mental models of key decision makers, such as political leaders (e.g., Axelrod, 1976) and business managers (e.g., Huff, 1990) as well as stakeholders (e.g., Soetanto, Dainty, Goodier, & Austin, 2011; Tikkanen, Isokääntä, Pykäläinen, & Leskinen, 2006). This allows researchers to understand how decision-makers and stakeholders reason about a given subject and identify areas of agreement and disagreement, which in turn helps the researchers to anticipate their likely actions. When used as a method for participatory modeling, cognitive maps are used in group decision-making to promote learning about dynamic and complex issues (Axelrod, 1976; Eden & Ackermann, 2006; Langfield-Smith & Wirth, 1992; Gomez & Probst, 1989). Studies of this nature assemble groups of decision-makers and stakeholders to participate in the creation and analysis of a qualitative system model to help them exchange knowledge, understand the system and its inherent dynamic, and identify policy levers that can be used to improve the system to achieve the group objectives. Traditional causal cognitive maps, however, are difficult to analyze because limitations to human cognition make it impossible to keep track of cumulative direct and indirect effects (Sterman, 2000). Additionally, if a concept has the same number of in-going positive and negative arrows (e.g., C_3 in figure 1), it is undetermined if the concept increases, decreases, or remains the same (Axelrod, 1976).

FCM addresses these issues by applying principles of fuzzy set theory and neural networks to traditional cognitive maps. FCMs regard cognitive maps as a simple form of recurrent neural networks: concepts are equivalent to neurons that, if activated, transmit their activation to other neurons and subsequently change their state. However, while neurons in natural neural networks can only have states of either "on" (= 1) or "off" (= 0), the concepts in FCMs can take on states to varying degrees, resulting in "fuzziness." Fuzzy concepts are nonlinear functions that transform the path-weighted activations directed towards them (their "causes") into a value between [0, 1] or [−1, 1]. When a neuron "fires," (i.e., when a concept changes its state), it affects all concepts that are causally dependent upon it. This firing process and resulting change in state depends on the relationship between concepts shown as directionality and type of influence (positive or negative), the weight of the relationships between concepts (e.g., high, medium, low), and the threshold levels of the dependent concepts. As concepts are directly activated, connected concepts subsequently may change their states as well, thus activating further concepts within the network. Since activation spreads in a nonlinear fashion and allows for feedback loops, it is possible that the newly activated concepts influence concepts that have been previously activated. Thus, the activation spreads through the FCM network until the system reaches stability.

FCMs have several properties that make them attractive for participatory processes (Jetter & Schweinfort, 2011; Jetter, 2003; Jetter, 2005; Jetter, 2006; Kosko, 1988).

FCM knowledge acquisition is relatively easy: causal cognitive maps are intuitive and a variety of methods exist to uncover knowledge from written documents through interviews, mapping exercises, and group sessions. New knowledge, such as the views of additional stakeholders or experts, can be easily integrated into the models so that large knowledge bases that reflect the world views of multiple respondents can be created.

FCM can process fuzzy and qualitative data, which plays an important role in the analysis of social systems. In these systems, detailed quantitative studies that reflect conditions on a regional or local scale are frequently unavailable. Instead, researchers have to rely on qualitative inputs from stakeholders and local experts.

FCMs can answer "what-if" questions and allow planners to assess how stakeholders will likely respond to a chosen alternative and which changes to the alternative will increase or decrease stakeholder acceptance.

FCMs can provide a simulation environment for planners that allows them to experiment with and anticipate the consequences of different alternatives and different scenarios. This enables them to develop robust policies and avoid decisions with unintended consequences because indirect effects, feedback cycles, or fringe stakeholder needs were not sufficiently obvious.

Because of these properties, FCMs are increasingly popular across multiple domains and FCM-related publications have seen a tenfold increase between 2000 and 2010 (Papageorgiou, 2011). In environmental research, participatory FCM modeling has been used to investigate stakeholder opinions about large dam projects (Özesmi & Özesmi, 2004), water use (Kafetzis, McRoberts, & Mouratiadou, 2010), fishery management (Gray, Chan, Clark, & Jordan, 2012), tourism planning (Yuksel, Bramwell, & Yuksel, 1999), risks to marine environments (Kontogianni, Papageorgiou, Salomatina, Skourtos, & Zanou, 2012), and their own vulnerability to ecosystem changes (Murungweni, van Wijk, Andersson, Smaling, & Giller, 2011). In collaborative technology planning and adoption, FCMs have been used to investigate energy technologies, namely solar energy (Jetter & Schweinfort, 2011; Jetter & Sperry, 2013), wind energy (Amer, Jetter, & Daim, 2011), and hydrogen for low-carbon transportation (Kontogianni, Papageorgiou, & Tourkolias, 2012).

Despite great variation in practices, these collaborative FCM studies all include three basic steps, namely knowledge capture, FCM modeling and testing, and model-based simulation and interpretation of results (Jetter & Kok, 2014). The knowledge capture step leads to (weighted) causal cognitive maps about the knowledge domain that are provided by the study participants in one-on-one interviews or workshops. During FCM modeling, the causal cognitive maps are translated into an adjacency matrix and merged to create an aggregated FCM model. This frequently requires that the cognitive maps that are provided by the participant are modified: for example, researchers standardize the terms used for concepts with similar meaning, delete concepts that are outside of the scope of the project, and check for and adjust causal links with unsuitable timescales. Moreover, they set up and calibrate the FCM model so that it can be used as a quantitative simulation model that answers what-if questions. They define "squashing" functions for the causal relationships between concepts. They also determine the initial activation level (i.e., whether the concept is turned on or off) for each concept in the FCM in an "input vector." The vector represents a combination of the initial concept's states of interest, such as a particular policy (e.g., "funding is active," "public support is active," "legal barriers are inactive") or decision alternatives. The researchers follow the standard procedure for calculating FCM to determine whether and how the concepts in the system change their final states in response to the changes introduced by the input vector. Initially, these simulation "runs" are done to test and calibrate the FCM model so that it fully reflects the behavior of the system under study. For example, the researchers test whether the model results in an increase or decrease of the same concepts that they expect to increase or decrease as a result of the policy change or decision. Once the model is tested, it is used to answer what-if questions such as, "what if we change our policy?"; "what if we pick alternative *B*?"; "what if concept *A* continues to increase?" Results can be used to compare the effectiveness and desirability of different possible actions. The same overall process was applied in the case study below.

Case Example: Veterans in STEM

Veterans in STEM is a case example of using FCM to create a model of the critical factors supporting military veterans as they transition from the military to civilian education and careers. With funding provided by the National Science Foundation, Veterans in STEM focused on education and careers in science, technology, engineering, and mathematics. Using FCM, varying contexts and perspectives from veterans across the United States were compiled to form a comprehensive model of transition to higher education.

The purpose of the study was to address a single research question: What are the critical factors reported by veterans with invisible disabilities (conditions that may affect daily life but are not immediately apparent) influencing their decision to enroll and persist in STEM undergraduate education? Using FCM with data gathered across the United States, researchers identified the critical factors and built a model showing the relationships between factors from the collective perspectives of veterans. Researchers then shared and validated the model with stakeholders through a participatory process. The interview protocol, including the cognitive mapping process, was approved through the Institutional Review Boards at University of Missouri-Kansas City, University of Maryland–Baltimore County, and University of California–Riverside.

Numerous organizations and programs have taken an interest in supporting veteran transitions and issued reports listing many recommendations for quality services and programmatic features. While these reports are helpful, veteran services and higher education lack clarifying guidance for how to implement and manage the many recommendations. For example, as colleges and universities reach out to veterans, it is essential they understand veterans as adult learners with unique sets of prior experiences affecting their daily lives. This study was designed to investigate both veteran-specific and context-specific variables. For example, a veteran-specific variable might be Peer Supports (Veteran-Specific), which would include peer groups that specifically include other veterans but would not include other types of peer groups such as non-military classmates. By engaging service members in out-processing, or transitioning out of the military, and undergraduate veteran college students with disabilities majoring in STEM, this research study aims to clearly identify and describe in detail the learning challenges veterans experience and the implications for college-level supports and instruction.

Background and Context for Veterans in STEM

The Veterans in STEM study focused on the youngest cohort of veterans: post-9/11 veterans. As of 2014, there were 2.6 million post-9/11 veterans, a population expected to grow to 3.5 million by 2019 (U.S. Department of Veterans Affairs, 2016). Post-9/11 veterans are young, with 76 percent ages forty-five and under; racially diverse, with 30.1 percent non-white, non-Hispanic and 13.1 percent Hispanic; and more likely to have a service-connected disability, 32 percent compared to 17.4 percent of other veterans (U.S. Department of Veterans Affairs, 2016). For Iraq and Afghanistan veterans, their transition to civilian life is complicated by traumatic brain injury and post-traumatic stress disorder (PTSD), which have become signature injuries due to the length of the wars and exposure to improvised explosive devices and mortar attacks (U.S. Department of Defense, 2012). Studies suggest that 50 percent of post-9/11 veterans experience some form of mental health challenges, including PTSD (29.5 percent), acute stress disorder (6.6 percent), and anxiety, depression, and other mental health disorders (11.5 percent; Frayne, Chiu, et al, 2010; Nazarian, Kimerling, & Frayne, 2012). Additionally, Pew Research Center (2011) found that 37 percent of post-9/11 veterans said that, regardless of diagnosis, they believe they have suffered from PTSD, compared to just 16 percent of veterans from earlier eras. This percentage increases to nearly 50 percent among veterans who were in direct combat.

Large numbers of veterans are transitioning to civilian life and using the educational benefits they earned. Over 1 million veterans used their benefits in 2014 (U.S. Department of Veterans Affairs, 2016). However, disabilities related to military experiences can bring increased barriers to transition to higher education. These barriers may include awareness of and access to benefits and accommodations as well as misconceptions or lack of information about veterans' needs (Disabilities, Opportunities, Internetworking, and Technology, 2008; Elliott, Gonzalez, & Larsen, 2011; American Council on Education, 2010; Jenson & Petri, 2011; Shackelford, 2009). Student veterans with a diagnosis of PTSD were also found to experience a greater sense of alienation on campus (Norman et al., 2015; Elliott, Gonzalez & Larsen, 2011). Due to their trauma experiences, student veterans need structure, reasonable accommodations, and strategies for persisting

(Cook & Kim, 2009; American Council on Education, 2011; Burnett & Segoria, 2009; Shackelford, 2009). Clear guidance as to the specific strategies for addressing the challenges faced by student veterans is lacking (Vance & Miller, 2009).

In addition to barriers due to disabilities, college culture, which differs significantly from the highly structured military culture, can also present barriers (Cook & Kim, 2009). Some veterans may view academic culture as chaotic, due to colleges' and universities' lack of a discernable chain of command (Griffin & Gilbert, 2015; Glasser, Powers & Zywiak, 2009). Other veterans long for the camaraderie they experienced in the military and feel like outsiders on campus because most of their classmates are traditional ages (eighteen to twenty-two years old) and they sense faculty members do not understand them.

While there are challenges to transitioning to higher education, many colleges and universities also provide resources that are beneficial to student veterans. Student veterans commonly stress the importance of the following resources: connection with other veterans (American Council on Education, 2010; Burnett & Segoria, 2009; Do-It, 2008; Madaus, Miller, & Vance, 2009; Vance & Miller, 2009; American Council on Education, 2010), availability of sensitivity training to campus communities (American Council on Education, 2010; Burnett & Segoria, 2009; Cook & Kim, 2009; Do-It , 2008), and better coordination between the administrative offices and staff who work with veterans (Norman, et al., 2015). Most significant to overcoming the challenges for many student veterans is an individual within an institution with the authority to advocate for the student veterans (Griffin & Gilbert, 2015).

Increasing the number of student veterans earning degrees in STEM is of national importance. Engineering, in particular, is facing a critical shortage in the United States, with only 9 percent of high school SAT takers expressing an interest in an engineering career (Goldberg, Cooper, Milleville, Barry, & Schein, 2015). Veterans have the aptitude and prior skills to help bridge this gap. For example, in 2011, the Armed Services Vocational Aptitude Battery, which is used at enlistment to assess qualifications, showed that 72 percent of enlisted recruits performed above the median and showed an aptitude in STEM (Goldberg, Cooper, Milleville, Barry, & Schein, 2015; Office of the Under Secretary of Defense, Personnel and Readiness, 2011). Because the barriers to higher education completion increase for veterans with service-connected disabilities, access to STEM-career support programs is essential (Goldberg, Cooper, Milleville, Barry, & Schein, 2015; Jenson & Petri, 2011). Studies such as Veterans in STEM are poised to help colleges and universities understand which support programs help student veterans with disabilities complete STEM degrees.

Participants

Military veterans, as well as service men and women preparing to transition to civilian status, participated in the study by responding to interview questions and constructing mental model maps of the critical factors leading to or detracting from veteran success in STEM college education and STEM careers. A purposeful sampling approach was used to recruit participants from geographical locations across the United States and include participants who had already transitioned out of the military and were currently college students as well as those preparing to transition soon. College students were recruited from four colleges in Missouri, California, Maryland, and Hawaii. Active-duty participants were recruited at one Midwest Army installation and one East Coast Naval Base. Modeling methodologies, particularly FCM, assume and rely on expert knowledge for construction of a valid and viable model (Gray, Zanre, & Gray, 2014). Purposeful sampling is an approach to identifying the key attributes of "experts" and recruiting with the purpose of gathering the necessary varying perspectives essential for a cohesive and representative synthesis (Sandelowski, 2000; Patton, 1999). In the case of Veterans in STEM, researchers hypothesized variance in pre- and post-military transition veteran perspectives due to where the experiences were occurring and phase of decision-making regarding plans after the military, during college, and preparation for the workforce. A total of sixty-nine individuals participated. A third of the participants (33 percent) were active-duty status at the time of the interview and the rest were either civilian status or in the Reserve or National Guard. Participants reported experiencing a range of conditions that can be potentially disabling. These include psychological conditions, mobility impairments, health conditions, traumatic brain injury, sensory impairments, and learning challenges. While participants were interviewed in five locations, they reported home states across the country. Due to their military placements, the participants were often relocated. Fifteen states were identified as home states, representing the East and West Coasts, Hawaii, the Midwest, the South, and New England.

Data Collection

Individual participant cognitive maps were gathered through a two-step process of first interviewing the participants in order to prompt their perceptions and elicit deeper reflections and then engaging the participants in the creation of their personal cognitive maps. This section outlines the processes used for structuring the interview and the cognitive mapping.

Interviews

The researchers designed a standardized set of interview questions to help participants identify and explain critical factors leading to their success. The questions were informed by a national think-tank (Transition STEM) study conducted by the researchers in 2011 that, like this study, was also funded by the National Science Foundation (award #0929212). With a lens focused primarily on the education supports for success, the interview questions asked

1. What are your education and work plans?
2. What types of transition resources have been offered to you or did you receive when you were leaving the military? Which resources have been helpful and not helpful?
3. What would a veteran-supportive college look like?
4. What types of resources have been available to you in college? Which resources have been helpful and not helpful?
5. What are specific factors that you think lead to veteran success in STEM education and careers?

As the participants identified factors, they were instructed to write the factors on a sticky note. The interview was a fluid process of dialogue and writing critical factors on individual sticky notes. When the interview questions were complete, the participant was asked to review the collection of sticky notes, create additional notes, and add definitions to terms when necessary. The sticky notes were used to create the cognitive maps.

Cognitive mapping began by asking each participant to first write the words "Veteran Success" on a large piece of paper. With instructions that, for this project, we defined "success" as graduation from college leading to employment in a desired STEM field, each participant was asked to arrange the sticky notes on the paper and draw lines to show relationships between factors. Once connections were drawn, the participant indicated the directions of the relationships (leading to or away from) using directional arrows. Lastly, using a six-point scale (strong/ moderate/low positive connection or low/moderate/strong negative connection), the participant then assigned weight to each relationship between concepts.

From a qualitative research standpoint, retaining the participant's voice in the mapping process was important. Therefore, participants labeled the factors using terminology that was logical to their understanding and experiences. The interview prompted each participant to define their concept for the record and to inform the data-cleaning and analysis stages of the research. Through the interview and cognitive mapping process with individual participants, we gained a deeper understanding of their perceptions and experiences with supports available for transition from military to civilian life, higher education processes and systems, and the range of other contributing factors influencing their success in achieving a STEM education and degree.

Data Review and Cleaning

Data review and cleaning began with analyzing the factors (for analysis purposes, now referred to as "concepts") in terms of name, definition, and function within maps. Through the interview data, it was apparent that while different terminology was used across the nation, there were similar definitions and characteristics. Looking at the raw data across the sixty-nine cognitive maps, a total of 837 concepts were identified. The average number of concepts was 16.65 ± 4.13 concepts and the range was nine to thirty-one concepts per cognitive map. The maps had an average of 20.83 ± 6.35 connections that resulted in a low density value of 0.09 ± 0.04. Density is an index of connectivity and is calculated as the number of connections divided by the maximum number of possible connections; therefore, a maximum density would equal 1.0 (Özesmi & Özesmi, 2004). By reviewing the concepts, definitions, and contextual conversation collected through the interview notes and video recording (when permitted by the participant), researchers were able to find common terminology and definitions to more accurately depict the concepts across participants. Researchers used a consensus approach to arrive at a final working list of concepts and corresponding definitions. External reviewers, as required by the funder, also reviewed the terminology and verified it was representative of the data and a suitable working list. This process dramatically focused the resulting number of concepts and connections. Through this data-cleaning process, a final model of fifty-five concepts, with 518 connections and a density of 0.17, resulted. Additionally, to improve the ability to conceptualize the model components,

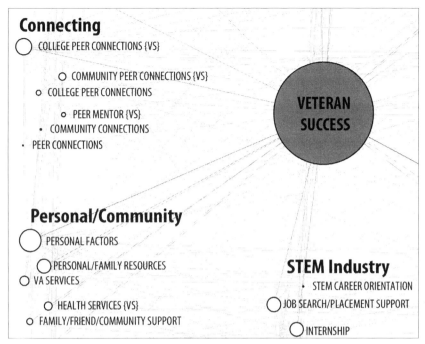

FIGURE 2. Excerpt of Veterans in STEM integrated full model, with clustering.

relationships, and functions, these fifty-five concepts were clustered into eight descriptive categories or themes. Table 1 displays the concepts by theme and figure 2 shows an excerpt of the overall model organized by clusters. (Also, see the description later in this chapter regarding the stakeholder workshop, because this was an opportunity for stakeholders to provide further clarification as to the concept terminology and definitions and suggest revisions.)

Presentation of the Model

The overall model tells a story of veteran success in STEM education toward STEM employment. The most important concepts in the cognitive maps can be determined by looking at centrality values (Özesmi & Özesmi, 2004). Centrality is computed as the sum of indegree and outdegree. High indegree indicates that the concept is affected very much by other concepts. High outdegree indicates that the concept greatly affects other concepts. Indegree and outdegree are calculated by averaging the absolute value of the weight of inputs and outputs. Table 2 lists the concepts in rank order from the largest degree of centrality to the smallest and shows the average indegree, outdegree, and centrality values. The varying shape sizes in figure 2 represent centrality.

Considering the values of indegree, outdegree, and centrality, a subset of concepts is critical to the model. Twenty-one concepts show centrality values above the computed average value across all concepts (> 0.36). Of these concepts, seventeen concepts have indegree values greater than average (> 0.23) and sixteen concepts have outdegree values greater than average (> 0.13). The following eleven concepts have greater-than-average values across all three measures. Their

Table 1. Concepts by cluster

CLUSTER	CONCEPT	CLUSTER	CONCEPT
Personal/community	Personal factors	Navigating College	Centralized college resources (VS)
	Personal/family resources		Clear academic path for veterans
	VA services		Convenient course options
	Health services (VS)*		Academic advisor (VS)
	Family/friend/community support		College orientation course (VS)
	Community resources		Course sections for veterans
	Assistance navigating resources (VS)		Convenient Campus Services
	Awareness of available resources (VS)		Unauthentic education opportunities
	Community connections	University Services	Comprehensive academic supports
	Time management skills		Learning supports (VS)
	Community service		Services for students with disabilities
Transition	Military provided transition training (TAP)†		Access to technology
	Military training transfer credits		Flexibility in courses/academic accommodations
	Military provided transition counseling	Attitudes Toward Veterans	Faculty/staff with military experience
	Military/college collaboration		Stigma (ageism)
	Veteran Benefits Advising		Employer values military experience
Connecting	College peer connections (VS)		Faculty attitude toward Veterans
	Community peer connections (VS)		Faculty attitude toward Veterans (barrier)
	College peer connections		College value veterans as students
	Peer mentor (VS)	STEM Industry	Job search/ placement support
	Positive community attitude toward veterans		Internship
	Community peer connections		Job preparation resources
Finances	Education funding (VS)		STEM job fairs
	Education benefits advising		STEM industry/college collaboration
	Financial stability		STEM industry mentor
	Funding options (nonmilitary)		Networking with STEM industry
			STEM career orientation

*VS denotes "veteran specific." †TAP denotes "Transition Assistance Program."

high importance to the overall model is due to veterans including these concepts in their maps and assigning strong values of connectedness to other concepts that lead to "Veteran Success."

- Education funding (veteran-specific)
- Personal factors
- Military-provided transition training (Transition Assistance Program)
- College peer connections (veteran-specific)
- Job search/placement support
- Personal/family resources
- Centralized college resources (veteran-specific)
- Internship
- Education benefits advising

Table 2. Rank order of concepts by centrality

CONCEPTS	INDEGREE	OUTDEGREE	CENTRALITY	CONCEPTS	INDEGREE	OUTDEGREE	CENTRALITY
Average	0.23	0.13	0.36	Average	0.23	0.13	0.36
Education funding (VS)	0.79	0.51	1.30	College orientation course (VS)	0.17	0.10	0.27
Personal factors	0.57	0.65	1.21	College peer connections	0.13	0.13	0.27
Military provided transition training (TAP)	0.90	0.21	1.11	Learning supports (VS)	0.13	0.14	0.27
College peer connections (VS)	0.53	0.36	0.89	Community resources	0.18	0.07	0.24
Job search/placement support	0.33	0.45	0.78	Services for Students with Disabilities	0.09	0.14	0.23
Personal/family resources	0.50	0.28	0.77	Peer mentor (VS)	0.14	0.09	0.23
Centralized college resources (VS)	0.57	0.18	0.75	Assistance navigating resources (VS)	0.15	0.07	0.22
Internship	0.42	0.33	0.75	Faculty attitude toward veterans	0.15	0.06	0.21
Faculty/staff with military experience	0.55	0.08	0.62	Awareness of available resources (VS)	0.12	0.06	0.18
Education benefits advising	0.37	0.16	0.53	STEM industry/college collaboration	0.13	0.05	0.18
Financial stability	0.27	0.25	0.52	Faculty attitude toward veterans (Barrier)	0.14	0.02	0.16
VA services	0.33	0.18	0.51	Positive community attitude toward veterans	0.08	0.07	0.15
Military training transfer credits	0.39	0.11	0.50	Access to technology	0.11	0.03	0.14
Stigma	0.42	0.04	0.47	Funding options (nonmilitary)	0.1	0.04	0.14
Clear academic path for veterans	0.17	0.29	0.46	STEM industry mentor	0.09	0.04	0.13
Employer values military experience	0.32	0.13	0.45	Networking with STEM industry	0.07	0.05	0.11
Military provided transition counseling	0.39	0.06	0.45	College value veterans as students	0.04	0.05	0.1
Health services (VS)	0.34	0.10	0.44	Community connections	0.08	0.00	0.09
Community peer connection (VS)	0.22	0.17	0.40	Course sections for veterans	0.05	0.04	0.09
Job preparation resources	0.22	0.16	0.39	Time management skills	0.02	0.05	0.08
Comprehensive academic supports	0.21	0.15	0.36	STEM career orientation	0.04	0.02	0.07
Family/friend/community support	0.22	0.11	0.34	Convenient campus services	0.05	0.01	0.06
Industry/military collaboration (VS)	0.23	0.11	0.34	Veteran benefits advising	0.06	0.00	0.06
Military/college collaboration	0.19	0.12	0.30	Peer connections	0.03	0.02	0.05
Convenient course options	0.21	0.08	0.29	Flexibility in Courses/ Academic Accommodations	0.02	0.02	0.04
STEM job fairs	0.13	0.14	0.28	Community service	0.03	0.01	0.04
Academic advisor (VS)	0.22	0.05	0.27	Unauthentic education opportunities	0.04	0.00	0.04

- Financial stability
- VA (Veterans Administration) services

Examining the concepts with above-average centrality but either below-average indegree or outdegree values is also interesting. There are four concepts with above-average centrality and below-average indegree—community peer connections (veteran-specific), clear academic path for veterans, comprehensive academic supports, and job preparation resources—indicating an importance to the overall model; however, few or lower-weighted connections were drawn to these concepts and greater-than-average connections were drawn leading from these concepts. The explanation for few or lower-weighted connections could be that veterans have limited prior experience with these services yet believe improved availability and quality would be highly beneficial. However, their role in leading to Veteran Success is highly connected.

In contrast, there were five concepts with above-average centrality and below-average out-degree—health services (veteran-specific), military training transfer credits, military provided transition counseling, faculty/staff with military experience, and stigma (ageism)—still indicating an importance to the overall model. However, more or greater-weighted connections were drawn to these concepts and lower-than-average connections were drawn leading from the concept. The explanation for few or lower-weighted connections leading from these concepts could be that veterans experiences with these services or supports were of low quality or lacking in significant effects that would lead to Veteran Success.

Verification and Validation of the Model

The FCM model resulting from this research is an "interpretive model," which explores uncertainties in a complex system so that consensus can be reached and actions can be taken (Pidd, 2003). Verification of such models occurs for each step of the transformation of individual-level interview data into an integrated FCM model, which are described above. For example, researchers make sure that the standardization of concept terminology remains true to the intentions and interpretations of the study participants, that information on assigned weights is carried over into the integrated model, and that the mathematical combination of individual FCM into the integrated map is done correctly. Verification, however, does not guarantee that the model adequately reflects the behavior of the real-world system under study nor does it ensure that it fulfills its interpretive function. Therefore, the model also needs to be validated. In interpretive models, validation is based on utility and the extent to which model components and function accurately portray current reality. The model is valid if it moves groups toward a shared understanding and action and helps the group gain insights that were previously hidden or unknown. While even "wrong" models can serve this function, researchers of course strive to present models that adequately represent what is known about the real-world system under study. Accordingly, study participants and subject matter experts have two important roles during validation: they review the model structure and behavior to ensure that it reflects their knowledge about the real world (validity as reality) and they use the model and assess its role in gaining insights and facilitating agreement (validity as utility).

In this study context, both functions were performed during a stakeholder workshop in which a group of stakeholders convened for the purpose of interpreting and refining the model, posing scenarios to examine how the model functions, and generating recommendations. The stakeholder group met in Kansas City and consisted of people from three groups: (1) student veteran participants in the study, (2) professionals from institutions of higher education, STEM fields, or veteran education services and supports, and (3) community members who provide resources and support to veterans. The overall purpose of the stakeholder workshop was, first, to show and explain the model, describe its basic functions, and confirm that the model indeed represented the study's contexts. Second, the stakeholders were provided opportunity to interact with the model by posing real-world examples and discussing the results shown in the model. The agenda for the two-day stakeholder meeting proceeded as follows:

1. Stakeholder group mission and purpose
2. Overview of the study and FCM methodology
3. Examination of the concept terminology and definitions
4. Review of model response to scenarios drawn from nationally and regionally published recommendations for higher education systems, resources, and supports for veterans
5. Discussion about insights resulting from model reactions to tested scenarios
6. Adjustments to terminology and clarity of definitions based on insights
7. Composition of best-case scenario based on insights and discussion of model reaction

The model behaved in expected ways and the stakeholders agreed the model is a valid decision-making tool. Additionally, an external audit of the researchers' interpretative processes was conducted. The role of the external audit was to check for researcher bias and examine the logic in the chain of reasoning leading to resulting model and researcher interpretations (Cutcliffe, & McKenna, 2004). As required by National Science Foundation (NSF) funding, an evaluation team completed the audit. After an orientation to the study purpose and methodology, the evaluation team reviewed study files and chain of reasoning and verified alignment between raw interview data and conclusions. In summary, the auditors reported the research processes were conducted with fidelity and the findings were credible and valid.

FCM Simulations and Stakeholder Engagement in the Model

Four nationally published and widely available reports addressing specific sets of recommendations affecting veteran student success in college and the path to non-military career were reviewed. For each report, the recommendations were aligned with concepts in the model to form a scenario. The following four sources were used for formulating scenarios for testing the model: (1) the Student Veterans of America (SVA) website (http://studentventerans.org), (2) Mitcham's (2013) report "Academic Recognition of Military Experience in STEM" from the American Council on Education (ACE) website, (3) the "Toolkit for Veteran-Friendly Institutions" from the ACE website (http://vetfriendlytoolkit.acenet.edu), and (4) the Council for Adult and Experiential Learning (CAEL) website's "Best Practices for Serving the Student Veteran" (http://www.cael.org).

In addition to these, the stakeholders generated a scenario during the stakeholder workshop, bringing the total number of scenarios tested to five.

Each report was written to address a specific aspect of a veteran's transition from the military to civilian employment. The ways the model reacts to these recommendation sets reflects this differing focus. The ways in which recommendations are articulated in the report directly affected the manner in which the corresponding concept was activated. For example, a policy or service recommendation may present a single only a few opportunities over the course of a student veteran's education, in contrast to a policy or service that may be more pervasive throughout the student veteran's education. Concepts representing policies or services intended to be ongoing or continuously accessed are "clamped," which causes the concept to reactivate throughout the computation cycles. Other concepts are only activated at the beginning of the computation. The following results offer suggestions for further refinement for how recommendations are posed. For example, recommendations reflecting an ongoing service or program for veterans yielded more impact on veteran success than single-occurrence events. Also, the number of concepts in a scenario does not correspond to a greater impact on veteran success. Rather, selected concepts tend to have more influence on veteran outcomes than others.

Table 3 shows the computed vector change from baseline based on the activation of selected concepts corresponding to each scenario. In the initial state column, the value is 1 if the concept is activated and B denotes baseline value. An asterisk beside a 1 indicates the concept was clamped throughout computation cycles. The final state column shows the values of each concept once the computation cycles have completed. As various scenarios were applied, researchers noticed the value of Veteran Success increasing toward 1.0 (as mentioned, the parameters of values between −1.0 and +1.0 were established during the cognitive mapping phase). The following summaries highlight the ways the model responded when each scenario was tested.

Student Veterans of America

Seven concepts emerged from the SVA recommendations for higher education and one of the concepts was treated as ongoing in the computations: college peer connections (veteran specific, vs). Given the focus of the SVA on connecting student veterans, it is logical that their recommendations feature ongoing, student veteran–to–student veteran connections. Other SVA recommendations applied to the model were two concepts aimed at assisting the process of getting a STEM job, two concepts forming student-to-community ties, improved faculty attitude toward veterans, and alternatives to military-provided education funding. The application of this set of concepts to the model results in a Veteran Success increase of 0.62. This recommendation set also had an impact on nearly half of the concepts (21) representing all eight clusters.

Academic Recognition of Military Experience in STEM Education (Mitcham)

The set of recommendations in the report "Academic Recognition of Military Experience in STEM Education" comes from ACE and its campaign to increase the acceptance of military credit at institutions of higher education. Review of the report found six concepts matching concepts in this study's model. In computations, two concepts were treated as ongoing services ("clear academic path for veterans" and "convenient course options") and the other four were regarded as single occurrences or events. The resulting impact on Veteran Success was 0.51. Eleven other concepts were affected by this set of recommendations; however, in comparison to other scenarios tested, the results showed lower impact across concepts. Also, connections with the community or STEM industry remained unchanged when this simulation was applied. This is likely due to the report's focus on the transition to higher education as opposed to transition to community or STEM careers.

Toolkit for Veteran Friendly Institutions (ACE)

The "Toolkit for Veteran Friendly Institutions" is an online resource developed by ACE. This toolkit contains a comprehensive set of suggestions for higher education to improve the education experience for veterans. Eighteen concepts were pulled from the toolkit recommendations and three of these were treated as ongoing. Table 3 identifies activated concepts and those that were treated as ongoing. Interestingly, this is the only set of recommendations to address veteran-specific education funding. In most cases, the availability of military-provided education funding is considered a constant and not mentioned in recommendations. The results show the greatest impact of all tested recommendations on Veteran Success (0.98). Due to the focus of this recommendation set, this is the only scenario to show impact on improving faculty attitude toward veterans. Additionally, due to the focus of this set of recommendations, the cluster of STEM industry was not represented in the list of activated concepts or the list of results.

Best Practices for Serving the Student Veteran (CAEL)

CAEL reviewed current literature to identify ways in which higher education can serve student military veterans. The recommendations in this report matched sixteen concepts. Similar to other scenarios, two concepts were considered ongoing during computations: "centralized college resources" and "convenient campus services." The resulting impact on Veteran Success was 0.70. Similar to other scenarios without a STEM focus, the activated set of concepts did not represent the STEM industry cluster; however, this cluster was still represented in the results, albeit with comparatively little change from baseline. It is also interesting to note the results show more of an impact on the concepts within university services, which represent services to support learning and potential learning challenges.

Veterans in STEM Research Study Stakeholders (VIS)

During the stakeholder meeting, the stakeholders were presented with the four reports and sets of recommendations and were then asked to formulate their own recommendations. Their recommendations are informed by the reports and results, but also by their own personal and professional experiences. From the list of concepts, they selected eight to activate and identified three as ongoing: flexibility in courses/academic accommodations, centralized college

Table 3. Initial state (IS) and final state (FS) vectors for baseline (B) and recommendations sets

	BASELINE		RECOMMENDATIONS									
			SVA		MITCHAM		ACE		CAEL		VIS	
Concepts	IS	FS	IS	FS	IS	FS	IS	FS	IS	FS	IS	FS
Academic advisor (VS)	1	4.4E-06	B	0.013	B	0.000	B	0.040	B	0.022	B	0.033
Access to technology	1	2.0E-06	B	0.011	B	0.000	B	0.030	B	0.030	B	0.039
Flexibility in courses/academic accommodations	1	2.4E-06	B	0.002	B	0.000	1	0.002	B	0.001	1*	0.003
Stigma	1	-5.3E-06	B	-0.003	B	-0.002	B	-0.005	B	-0.003	B	-0.005
Assistance navigating resources (VS)	1	8.1E-06	B	0.006	B	0.004	B	0.027	B	0.024	1	0.028
Awareness of available resources (VS)	1	4.1E-06	B	0.003	B	0.000	B	0.041	B	0.039	B	0.040
Centralized college resources (VS)	1	1.0E-05	B	0.037	B	0.001	1*	0.013	1*	0.008	1*	0.042
Clear academic path for veterans	1	2.2E-05	B	0.023	1*	0.051	1*	0.052	B	0.041	B	0.060
College orientation course (VS)	1	5.3E-06	B	0.033	B	0.000	1	0.007	1	0.005	1	0.036
College peer connections	1	5.8E-06	B	0.021	B	0.001	B	0.004	1	0.003	B	0.022
College peer connections (VS)	1	2.1E-05	1*	0.015	B	0.004	1	0.110	1	0.081	1*	0.073
College value veterans as students	1	1.9E-06	B	0.000	B	0.029	B	0.002	B	0.001	B	0.001
Positive community attitude toward veterans	1	1.1E-05	B	0.024	B	0.005	B	0.011	B	0.008	B	0.029
Community connections	1	4.1E-07	B	0.000	B	0.000	B	0.001	B	0.001	B	0.001
Community peer connection (VS)	1	1.3E-05	1	0.007	B	0.002	B	0.056	B	0.047	B	0.052
Community resources	1	3.3E-06	B	0.003	B	0.001	B	0.003	B	0.002	B	0.004
Community service	1	1.9E-07	1	0.000	B	0.001	B	0.001	B	0.000	B	0.000
Comprehensive academic supports	1	1.3E-05	B	0.029	B	0.042	1	0.051	B	0.047	B	0.072
Convenient course options	1	7.7E-06	B	0.005	1*	0.014	B	0.034	B	0.006	B	0.010
Convenient campus services	1	1.4E-06	B	0.000	B	0.000	B	0.010	1*	0.001	B	0.001
Course sections for veterans	1	2.0E-06	B	0.003	B	0.001	1	0.002	1	0.002	B	0.004
Services for students with disabilities	1	1.5E-05	B	0.055	B	0.004	B	0.053	B	0.031	B	0.080
Education benefits advising	1	1.3E-05	B	0.053	B	0.003	1	0.051	1	0.045	1	0.092
Education funding (VS)	1	3.7E-05	B	0.024	B	0.013	1*	0.105	B	0.081	B	0.100
Employer values military experience	1	8.4E-06	B	0.004	B	0.001	B	0.008	B	0.004	B	0.008
Faculty attitude toward veterans	1	3.3E-06	1	0.002	1	0.048	1	0.030	1	0.002	B	0.004
Faculty attitude toward veterans (Barrier)	1	-1.1E-06	B	-0.001	B	0.000	B	-0.001	B	0.000	B	-0.001

resources, and college peer connections (vs). The resulting impact on Veteran Success was 0.90. Additionally, there was notable impact on 16 other concepts representing all clusters except for the cluster of "attitudes toward veterans."

Across all scenarios, a few observations are made. First, the concepts within the category of personal/community have a critical role in the model. The issues of transitioning from military to civilian life are personal and often urgent for veterans. Even when concepts in this cluster are not activated (i.e., not mentioned in the sets of recommendations applied to the model), the application of the full array of other services and supports has an effect on the personal and community factors. Second, activating more concepts does not necessarily equate to higher impact across more concepts. When concepts are ongoing, the results show more impact on

| | | | RECOMMENDATIONS | | | | | | | | |
| | BASELINE | | SVA | | MITCHAM | | ACE | | CAEL | | VIS | |
Concepts	IS	FS	IS	FS	IS	FS	IS	FS	IS	FS	IS	FS
Faculty/staff with military experience	1	4.8E-06	B	0.030	B	0.001	B	0.006	1	0.003	B	0.030
Family/friend/community support	1	1.3E-05	B	0.024	B	0.004	B	0.018	B	0.009	B	0.031
Funding options (nonmilitary)	1	2.2E-06	1	0.000	B	0.000	1	0.004	1	0.004	B	0.004
Health services (VS)	1	1.1E-05	B	0.007	B	0.001	1	0.042	1	0.010	B	0.016
Industry/military collaboration (VS)	1	7.7E-06	B	0.005	B	0.001	B	0.065	B	0.062	B	0.064
Internship	1	2.7E-05	B	0.052	B	0.005	B	0.053	B	0.041	1	0.088
Job preparation resources	1	1.4E-05	1	0.026	B	0.004	1	0.062	1	0.047	B	0.068
Job search/placement support	1	3.6E-05	B	0.057	B	0.024	B	0.128	B	0.075	B	0.142
Learning supports (VS)	1	1.5E-05	B	0.009	B	0.016	B	0.017	B	0.012	B	0.019
Military provided transition counseling	1	5.2E-06	B	0.003	B	0.001	B	0.006	B	0.002	B	0.005
Military provided transition training (TAP)	1	1.9E-05	B	0.026	B	0.004	B	0.048	B	0.012	B	0.034
Military training transfer credits	1	6.5E-06	B	0.004	1	0.000	1	0.007	1	0.004	B	0.007
Military/college collaboration	1	9.2E-06	B	0.003	1	0.002	1	0.042	B	0.004	B	0.007
Personal factors	1	5.6E-05	B	0.091	B	0.104	B	0.147	B	0.100	B	0.162
Networking with STEM industry	1	4.7E-06	B	0.021	B	0.001	B	0.007	B	0.004	B	0.023
Peer connections	1	2.0E-06	B	0.020	B	0.000	B	0.003	B	0.002	B	0.020
Peer mentor (VS)	1	8.4E-06	B	0.068	B	0.001	1	0.032	1	0.026	B	0.088
Personal/family resources	1	2.8E-05	B	0.041	B	0.004	1	0.181	1	0.111	B	0.144
Financial stability	1	3.6E-05	B	0.015	B	0.006	B	0.193	B	0.046	B	0.057
STEM career orientation	1	2.3E-06	B	0.001	B	0.000	B	0.003	B	0.002	B	0.003
STEM industry mentor	1	2.5E-06	B	0.002	B	0.000	B	0.003	B	0.001	B	0.003
STEM industry/ college collaboration	1	5.3E-06	1	0.003	1	0.001	B	0.004	B	0.003	1	0.006
STEM job fairs	1	1.1E-05	B	0.006	B	0.002	B	0.034	B	0.029	B	0.034
Time-management skills	1	5.9E-06	B	0.004	B	0.012	B	0.006	B	0.004	B	0.007
Unauthentic education opportunities	1	0.0E+00	B	0.000	B	0.000	B	0.000	B	0.000	B	0.000
VA services	1	1.4E-05	B	0.036	B	0.022	1	0.080	B	0.057	B	0.088
Veteran benefits advising	1	0.0E+00	B	0.000	B	0.000	B	0.000	1	0.000	B	0.000
Veteran success	0	6.4E-04	B	0.618	B	0.509	B	0.980	B	0.696	B	0.896

*Denotes clamped concept. Sources: Student Veterans of America (SVA); Mitcham, 2013; American Council on Education (ACE) (2013); Council for Adult and Experiential Learning (CAEL) (2012); Veterans in STEM (VIS) Stakeholder Meeting (2015).

other concepts as well as Veteran Success overall. Single-occurrence events such as job fairs or orientation courses show lower impact than ongoing systems or services such as centralized college resources and college peer connections.

Lessons Learned and Future Work

Using the combined one-on-one interview with the cognitive mapping process had multiple benefits and challenges. As intended, the interviews were helpful to prime the participants' thinking (or mental models) in preparation for the cognitive mapping process. During the interview process, the researcher and participant noted key concepts and relationships between concepts. This initial assortment of key concepts and relationships were then used as starting points for the cognitive mapping. During the mapping process, and with the interviewer posing clarifying questions about defining concepts and relationships, the participants' descriptions of their experiences and the impact of their experiences on their success deepened. The mapping process prompted the participants to think more deeply about the nuances and considerations defining the concepts as well as the connections between concepts. As compared to a traditional qualitative interview approach, in which participants often share surface-level perspectives, the cognitive mapping component provided opportunity for participants to reflect more on their perspectives and provided a richer description from which to construct individual cognitive maps, which then lead to an overall integrated model.

Another benefit to the one-on-one interview and mapping process was the focus on individual perspectives without bias or persuasion that can occur in a group mapping process. In group mapping, a strong personality can dominate the process and the resulting model. With an individual approach, each voice had an opportunity to have equal weight in the overall model. Additionally, the participants spoke of feeling their perspectives were heard, valued, and accurately represented. The mapping process validated their viewpoints.

A challenge with the individual approach was the time required to conduct the combined interviews and mapping process. The full process for each interview required one to one and a half hours to complete. Within this time frame were introductions to the researchers, the project, and the mapping process. The mapping process was intuitive to some participants and abstract to others. To avoid imposing researcher opinions on individual maps, the researchers used a simple sample cognitive map to explain the process and, from there, the participants generalized to their own cognitive maps. Some participants required more instruction on the process than others and thus required more time to complete a thorough process. However, despite the amount of time needed to complete the process, only one participant did not complete due to confusion and fatigue.

The extended amount of time needed to complete the interview and mapping process also contributed to the challenges with data management and computations. First, the participants often revised what they meant by a particular concept during the interview when arranging concepts on their maps. More significantly, the interviews and mapping process resulted in a large number of concepts, since they emerged from the interviews as opposed to a process more structured around a pre-established base catalog of concepts. Using a pre-established catalog of concepts would have the given structure needed by some of the participants who seemingly struggled with the open-endedness. However, in early planning of the research design, researchers identified an overwhelming number of potential concepts and found it difficult to limit the scope of concepts without imposing researcher bias. Therefore, the decision was made to allow concepts to emerge from the interviews. The results yielded concepts that were not on the research team's original list (e.g., concepts within the personal factors domain), yet prominent in the resulting overall model. This open-ended approach produced a lengthy list of concepts, thus requiring substantial care and time to identify common terminology across the national sample of perspectives and necessitating thematic clustering in order to better facilitate communication about the model.

From a computational standpoint, the number of concepts, the varying perspectives as to presence, strength of presence, or absence in individual maps, and the process of averaging matrices to form an integrated matrix resulted in very small weights. The small weights were cumbersome for computations and for communicating about relationships and effects when scenarios were applied. Additionally, and as expected, managing this large dataset required substantial time from researchers in order to maintain accuracy of the data and reach valid interpretations.

This study focuses only on the veteran perspective and that is a limitation to constructing a model of the higher education system. While higher education and community stakeholders were involved in the stakeholder validation meeting, their perspectives were not captured within the model. A next step would be to replicate the process with higher education and related community service professionals and then to add their maps to the model begun with student veterans and transitioning service members. The resulting expanded model would depict a more comprehensive representation of the system.

During the stakeholder validation meeting, the stakeholders shared enthusiasm for the results and the potential for applying the model to decision-making in their own contexts. However, it is difficult for stakeholders to directly apply the study results without knowledge of FCM. To address this need, a user-friendly decision-making tool for applying the study results in unique contexts would be beneficial.

Another next step is to share the benefits of participatory modeling and FCM across the education field. As the study purpose and results have been shared with researchers and professionals, many questions and speculation about the approach have been posed. During the early recruitment conversations with selected sites, there were lengthy conversations explaining the process, risk for fatigue, and likelihood of yielding valid results. While some attention to FCM has been given in the education field, the application and benefits of the methodology deserve more description and validation in respected methodology sources often referenced within the field. When proposing participatory modeling with direct service professionals, a step-by-step outline and/or a video showing the process would provide helpful visuals for better understanding the process.

Conclusion

Participatory modeling is a viable approach for gathering and integrating perspectives from multiple stakeholders to form a visual and functional representation of the interplay between critical components of a system. This interplay can depict both positive and negative interactions between components, ultimately having an effect on a desired outcome. Veterans in STEM used individual interviews paired with FCM to answer the research question. This study design applied the standards of qualitative research in the interview protocol and the standards of FCM in the cognitive mapping and computational processes. The benefit of this process was authentic representation of individual perspectives through participant-led identification and definition of critical concepts. Additionally, the cognitive mapping process elicited more reflective and descriptive responses than are typical with traditional interviews. The challenge with this study design was the cumbersome management aspects: analyzing data for common terminology and definitions and then applying the common terminology and definitions to the model. Despite this challenge, since this method resulted in a more authentic model, researchers would replicate the process if given the opportunity to expand the collected viewpoints to include higher education and related community service professionals. Because the mapping and validation processes place a premium on stakeholder knowledge, we envision the use of FCM in applied, community-based research as an effective way to generate community-specific, testable hypotheses and questions.

ACKNOWLEDGMENTS

The National Science Foundation (NSF) under NSF Award #1246221 supported this research in full. While the study was solely funded by the mentioned NSF award, it was informed by a prior NSF award (#0929212) and reference is made accordingly in the chapter. Any opinions, findings, and conclusions or recommendations expressed in this material are those of the author(s) and do not necessarily reflect those of the NSF.

REFERENCES

Amer, M., Jetter, A., & Daim, T. (2011). Development of fuzzy cognitive map (FCM)-based scenarios for wind energy. *International Journal of Energy Sector Management, 5*(4), 564–584.

American Council on Education (2010). *Veterans success JAM: Ensuring success for returning veterans.* www.acenet.edu/links/military/ensuring_success.html.

American Council on Education (2011). *Accommodating student veterans with traumatic brain injury and post-traumatic stress disorder: Tips for campus faculty and staff.* http://www. acenet.edu/Content/NavigationMenu/ProgramsServices/MilitaryPrograms/serving/ AccommodatingStudentVeterans_06222011.pdf.

American Council on Education (2013). Toolkit for Veteran Friendly Institutions . https:// vetfriendlytoolkit.acenet.edu.

Axelrod, R. (1976). The analysis of cognitive maps. In R. Axelrod (Ed), *Structure of decision: The cognitive maps of political elites* (pp. 55–73). Princeton, NJ: Princeton University Press.

Burnett, S. E., & Segoria, J. (2009). Collaboration for military transition students from combat to college: It takes a community. *Journal of Postsecondary Education and Disability, 22*(1), 233–238.

Cook, B. J., & Kim, Y. (2009). *From soldier to student: Easing the transition of service members on campus.* Washington, DC: American Council on Education.

Council for Adult and Experiential Learning (2012). *Best practices for serving the student Veteran.* Chicago: Author. http://www.cael.org/pdfs/best-practices-handout-final.

Cutcliffe, J. R., & McKenna, H. P. (2004). Expert qualitative researchers and the use of audit trails. *Journal of Advanced Nursing, 45*(2), 126–133.

Do-It, Disabilities, Opportunities, Internetworking, and Technology (2008). *Think Tank: Serving Veterans with Disabilities.* http://www.washington.edu/doit/cbi/veterans/proceedings.html

Eden, C. (1988). Cognitive mapping. *European Journal of Operational Research, 36*(1), 1–13.

Eden, C., & Ackermann, F. (2006). Where next for problem structuring methods. *Journal of the Operational Research Society, 57*(7), 766–768.

Elliot, M., Gonzalez, C., & Larsen, B. (2011). U.S. military veterans transition to college: Combat, PTSD, and alienation on campus. *Journal of Student Affairs Research and Practice, 48*(3), 279–296.

Frayne, S. M., Chiu, V. Y., Iqbal, S., Berg, E. A., Laugani, K. J., Cronkite, R. C., Pavao, J., Kimerling, R. (2010). Medical care needs of returning veterans with PTSD: Their other burden. *Journal of General Internal Medicine*, 26(1), 33–39. doi: 10.1007/s11606-010-1497-4.

Glasser, I., Powers, J. T., & Zywiak, W. H. (2009). Military veterans at universities: A case of culture clash. *Anthropology News*, *50*(5), 33–33.

Goldberg, M., Cooper, R., Milleville, M., Barry, A., & Schein, M. L. (2015). Ensuring success for veterans with disabilities in STEM degree programs: Recommendations from a workshop and case study of an evidence-based transition program. *Journal of STEM Education: Innovations and Research*, *16*(1), 16.

Gomez, P., & Probst, G. (1989). Thinking in networks to avoid the pitfalls of managerial thinking. *Human Systems Management*, (8), 201–212.

Gray, S., Chan, A., Clark, D., & Jordan, R. (2012). Modeling the integration of stakeholder knowledge in social–ecological decision-making: Benefits and limitations to knowledge diversity. *Ecological Modelling, 229*, 88–96.

Gray, S. A., Zanre, E., & Gray, S. R. J. (2014). Fuzzy cognitive maps as representations of mental models and group beliefs. In E. Papageorgiou (Ed.), *Fuzzy cognitive maps for applied sciences and engineering* (pp. 29–48). Berlin: Springer .

Griffin, K. A., & Gilbert, C. K. (2015). Better transitions for troops: An application of Schlossberg's transition framework to analyses of barriers and institutional support structures for student veterans. *Journal of Higher Education*, *86*(1), 71–97.

Huff, A. S. (1990). *Mapping strategic thought*. Chichester: John Wiley & Sons.

Jenson, R. & Petri, A. (2011). *Transition STEM: A wounded warrior think tank summary*. Kansas City, MO: UMKC Institute for Human Development.

Jetter, A. (2003). Educating the guess: Strategies, concepts and tools for the fuzzy front end of product development. In Management of Engineering and Technology, 2003. PICMET'03. Technology Management for Reshaping the World. Portland International Conference on (pp. 261–273). Portland, OR: Institute of Electrical and Electronic Engineers. https://pdxscholar.library.pdx.edu/cgi/viewcontent.cgi?article=1031&context=etm_fac.

Jetter, A. (2005). *Product planning in fuzzy front end*. Wiesbaden: Deutscher Universitätsverlag.

Jetter, A. (2006). Fuzzy cognitive maps for engineering and technology management: What works in practice. *PICMET 2006 Proceedings*, Istanbul, Turkey: IEEE.

Jetter, A., & Kok, K. (2014). Fuzzy cognitive maps for future studies: A methodological assessment of concepts and methods. *Futures, 61*, 45–57.

Jetter, A., & Schweinfort, W. (2011). Building scenarios with fuzzy cognitive maps: An exploratory study of solar energy. *Futures, 43*, 52–66.

Jetter, A., & Sperry, R. C. (2013). Fuzzy cognitive maps for product planning: using stakeholder knowledge to achieve corporate responsibility. In System Sciences (HICSS), 2013 46th Hawaii International Conference on (pp. 925–934).

Kafetzis, A., McRoberts, N., & Mouratiadou, I. (2010). Using fuzzy cognitive maps to support the analysis of stakeholders' views of water resource use and water quality policy. In M. Glykas (Ed.) *Fuzzy cognitive maps: Advances in theory, methodologies, tools, and applications* (pp. 383–402). Berlin: Springer,.

Kontogianni, A., Papageorgiou, E., Salomatina, L., Skourtos, M., & Zanou, B. (2012). Risks for the Black Sea marine environment as perceived by Ukrainian stakeholders: A fuzzy cognitive mapping application. *Ocean & coastal management, 62*, 34–42.

Kontogianni, A. D., Papageorgiou, E. I., & Tourkolias, C. (2012). How do you perceive environmental change? Fuzzy cognitive mapping informing stakeholder analysis for environmental policy making and non-market valuation. *Applied Soft Computing, 12*(12), 3725–3735.

Kosko, B. (1986). Fuzzy cognitive maps. *International Journal of Man-Machine Studies, 24*, 65–75.

Kosko, B. (1988). Hidden patterns in combined and adaptive knowledge networks. *International Journal of Approximate Reasoning, 2*(4), 377–393.

Langfield-Smith, K., & Wirth, A. (1992). Measuring differences between cognitive maps. *Journal of the Operational Research Society, 43*(12), 1135–1150.

Madaus, J. W., Miller, W. K., & Vance, M. L. (2009). Veterans with disabilities in postsecondary education. *Journal of Postsecondary Education and Disability, 22*(1), 191–198.

Mitcham, M. (2013). *Academic recognition of military experience in STEM education.* Washington, DC: American Council on Education. http://www.acenet.edu/news-room/Documents/Academic-Recognition-of-Military-Experience-in-STEM-Education.pdf.

Murungweni, C., Van Wijk, M. T., Andersson, J. A., Smaling, E. M., & Giller, K. E. (2011). Application of fuzzy cognitive mapping in livelihood vulnerability analysis. *Ecology and Society, 16*(4), 8.

Nazarian, D., Kimerling, R., & Frayne, S.M. (2012). Posttraumatic stress disorder, substance use disorders, and medical comorbidity among returning U.S. veterans. *International Society for Traumatic Stress Studies*, 25, 220–225.

Norman S.B. Rosen, J., Himmerich, S., Myers, U.S., Davis, B., Browne, KC, and Piland, N. (2015). Student veteran perceptions of facilitators and barriers to achieving academic goals. *Journal of rehabilitation research and development, 52*(6), 701–12. doi: http://dx.doi.org/10.1682/JRRD.2015.01.0013.

Office of the Under Secretary of Defense, Personnel and Readiness. (2011). *Population representation in the military services.* Washington, DC: Author.

Özesmi, U., & Özesmi, S. L. (2004). Ecological models based on people's knowledge: a multi-step fuzzy cognitive mapping approach. *Ecological Modelling, 176*(1), 43–64.

Papageorgiou E. I. (2011). Review study on fuzzy cognitive maps and their applications during the last decade. *IEEE International Conference on Fuzzy Systems*, Taipei, Taiwan.

Patton, M. Q. (1999). Enhancing the quality and credibility of qualitative analysis. *Health Services Research, 34*(5. 2), 1189–1208.

Pew Research Center. (2011). *Military and civilian life: War and sacrifice in the post 9/11 era.* http://www.pewsocialtrends.org/2011/10/05/war-and-sacrifice-in-the-post-9-11-era.

Pidd, M. (2003). *Tools for thinking* (2nd ed.). Chichester: John Wiley & Sons.

Sandelowski, M. (2000). Combining qualitative and quantitative sampling, data collection, and analysis techniques in mixed-method studies. *Research in Nursing & Health, 23*(3), 246–255.

Shackelford, A. L. (2009). Documenting the needs of student veterans with disabilities: Intersection roadblocks, solutions, and legal realities. *Journal of Postsecondary Education and Disability, 22*(1),

217–223.

Soetanto, R., Dainty, A. R., Goodier, C. I., & Austin, S. A. (2011). Unravelling the complexity of collective mental models: A method for developing and analysing scenarios in multi-organisational contexts. *Futures, 43*(8), 890–907.

Sterman, J. D. (2000). *Business dynamics systems thinking and modeling for a complex world.* New York: McGraw-Hill.

Tikkanen, J., Isokääntä, T., Pykäläinen, J., & Leskinen, P. (2006). Applying cognitive mapping approach to explore the objective–structure of forest owners in a Northern Finnish case area. *Forest Policy and Economics, 9*(2), 139–152.

U.S. Department of Veterans Affairs, Office of Policy and Planning and National Center for Veterans Analysis and Statistics (2016). Profile of Post-9/11 Veterans: 2014. http://www.va.gov/vetdata/docs/SpecialReports/Post_911_ Veterans_Profile_2014.pdf.

U.S. Department of Defense. (2012). *DoD worldwide numbers for traumatic brain injury.* https://dvbic.dcoe.mil/dod-worldwide-numbers-tbi.

Vance, M. L., & Miller, W. K. (2009). Serving wounded warriors: Current practices in postsecondary education. *Journal of Postsecondary Education and Disability, 22*(1), 199–216.

Veterans in STEM Research Stakeholders. (2015, April 17–18). Research results presentation. UMKC Institute for Human Development, Kansas City, MO.

Yuksel, F., Bramwell, B., & Yuksel, A. (1999). Stakeholder interviews and tourism planning at Pamukkale, Turkey. *Tourism Management, 20*(3), 351–360.

Contributors

Michelle Bouchard brings thirty years of experience in public/private partnerships to her position as president of HealthCorps. She oversees the national nonprofit wellness educational program founded and chaired by Dr. Oz, which has impacted almost 2 million high school students since 2007 across nineteen states and Washington, DC. She has received citations for her work at HealthCorps from the California State Senate, the Clinton Global Initiative, the New York City Family Caregiver Coalition, the mayor of Oklahoma City, and the New York City Council. Bouchard graduated from Wellesley College (1984) with a BA in Political Science.

Victoria Breeze is a PhD candidate in the Department of Geography, Environment, and Spatial Sciences at Michigan State University. As part of her graduate certificate in Environmental and Social Systems Modeling, she has investigated applications of several model types (including agent-based modeling and system dynamics modeling) to linked agricultural and economic systems.

Nathan G. Brugnone is a doctoral student pursuing a dual PhD in community sustainability and in computational mathematics, science, and engineering at Michigan State University. His research develops and applies computational harmonic analysis, graph theory, and data science methods to complex social-ecological systems. His areas of interest include the development of computational tools to support agricultural sustainability and the development of theories of emergence in complex systems. Nathan earned an MS in agriculture from Washington State University.

Ian Burns has a BS in environmental studies from Oberlin College and is currently studying mechanical engineering at Cleveland State University. He has studied computational modeling applications in astronomy, environmental studies, and psychology. He has worked extensively with Nova since its inception and is currently developing and refining models for the Nova modeling library and for inclusion in modeling textbooks.

John D. Clapp, PhD, is a professor of social work and preventive medicine at the University of Southern California. Clapp's research has focused on the complex nature of drinking behavior for the past two decades. He has conducted numerous multi-level field studies to examine drinking behavior as it naturally occurs with the goal of better understanding event dynamics to identify leverage points that might be amenable to prevention efforts.

Nancy Darling is the William and Jeanette Smith Professor of Psychology at Oberlin College. She is a developmental psychologist whose work focuses on contextual variability in parent-adolescent relationships. For the past thirty years, she has examined how adolescents influence and are influenced by parents, peers, unrelated adults, and romantic partners. This work includes data from adolescents in Chile, Italy, Japan, the Philippines, Uganda, Sweden, and the United States. She has published almost sixty peer-reviewed papers and chapters and delivered well over one hundred conference presentations and is currently editor-in-chief for the *Journal of Adolescence*. In recent years, she has extended her interest in research methodology and statistics to computational modeling and is currently focusing on extending this methodology in developmental research.

Arden D. Day is a senior research associate at the Northern Arizona University Institute for Human Development. She has a BA and MA in psychology with a focus in quantitative methods and currently works with quantitative data and website design. She also helps coordinate projects focused on access to services. Her research areas include health disparities specifically related to youth and program evaluation.

Riva C. H. Denny is a research associate in the Department of Sociology at Michigan State University. Her research focuses on human decision-making in coupled human and natural systems, as well as food systems and food security. She has a PhD in sociology from Michigan State University and an MS in rural sociology from Auburn University. Her work has been published in *Rural Sociology* (2017 Best Paper Award winner), *Sociology of Development*, *Society and Natural Resources*, and *Environment Systems and Decisions*.

Eric Jing Du is an assistant professor in the Department of Construction Science at Texas A&M University (TAMU). He received his PhD in construction management from Michigan State University in 2012, along with an MBA and a civil engineering degree from Tianjin University in China. Before joining TAMU in 2015, he worked for a power plant builder for four years. Du investigates how decision-making processes and behaviors affect the quality, sustainability, and safety of complex civil engineering projects. To this end, he uses computer simulation (agent-based modeling, discrete event simulation, and system dynamics), statistical and mathematical modeling (scenario analysis and topological data analysis), and visualization techniques (BIM game engine, virtual reality, and augmented reality). He has published more than forty journal and conference articles on the theories, algorithms, and applications of a variety of simulation paradigms.

Lynn Fredericks is founder of FamilyCook Productions and an award-winning pioneer in obesity prevention and nutrition. She is the author of *Cooking Time Is Family Time* (1999) and *Get Your Family Eating Right!* (2013). Since 1995, the nutrition education efforts under her lead have reached over 300,000 parents and children. Fredericks's work in NYC public schools was awarded the 2002 Leadership Award from the New York City Council of School Administrators, among other awards. Building upon her successful development of the *Teen Battle Chef* program, Fredericks has designed and disseminated strategies that foster student leadership development, emphasizing skill building and peer sharing. Fredericks has served within the leadership of numerous professional societies.

Michel de Garine-Wichatitsky (PhD, MSc, DVM) is an ecologist and field epidemiologist who has been working for the past twenty-two years in Africa and the Pacific. He is a senior researcher for the French Center for Agricultural Research for Development and a research associate with the Department of Biological Sciences of the University of Zimbabwe. Since 2007, he has been the Coordinator of the research platform "Production and Conservation in Partnership," a research consortium associating research organizations from France, Zimbabwe and the SADC region. His current research interest focuses on understanding and managing wildlife-livestock-human interfaces, which he aims to address through an interdisciplinary approach associating biological, veterinary, and social sciences.

Luis Felipe Giraldo, PhD, is an assistant professor in the Department of Electrical and Electronic Engineering at the Universidad de los Andes. His current research interests include modeling and analysis of linear and nonlinear dynamical systems, pattern recognition, and signal processing.

Madeline Goldkamp has a diverse work and research background in landscape architecture and engineering. As a De Pietro Fellow in Civil Engineering at Harvey Mudd College, she studied aging dam infrastructure and helped to develop performance-based testing and analysis techniques. While completing her MLA at the University of Minnesota she was part of the collaborative GeoDesign research group, where she analyzed multifunctional agricultural landscape system designs and developed strategies for preserving and promoting green and blue infrastructure for Esri's green infrastructure initiative. She currently works as a landscape designer for Stantec, a multidisciplinary engineering and design firm. Her design approach creates functional and sustainable solutions for urban and rural design challenges through visioning, design iteration, and modeling. Through her work, she aims to create impactful outdoor places that foster community engagement with the landscape.

George S. Gotto is the interim director of the University of Missouri-Kansas City Institute for Human Development. He works throughout the state of Missouri to conduct applied research and training projects related to health and wellness for people with intellectual and developmental disabilities. He employs cognitive mapping techniques to identify community-based solutions to the health disparities experienced by people with disabilities. George is a founding member of the Missouri Self-Determination Association. He is trained as an applied medical anthropologist with an emphasis in community-based research and cross-cultural perspectives on health and disability.

Steven Gray is an assistant professor in the Department of Community Sustainability at Michigan State University. His research focuses on understanding how individuals and groups make decisions about complex social-ecological systems and addresses questions about how values, attitudes, beliefs or local conditions influence human behavior toward the environment. This effort has recently led to a focus on understanding how collaborative modeling software tools help communities, resource managers, and other decision-makers understand and adapt to the social impacts of climate and other environmental changes through iterative learning. He is the lead editor of the book *Environmental Modeling with Stakeholders: Methods, Theories and Applications* (2016). His research has been funded domestically by the National Science Foundation, the Socio-Environmental Synthesis Center, and federal resource management agencies including the National Oceanic and Atmospheric Administration, the United States Department of Agriculture, and the United States Geological Survey. Internationally, his research has been supported by the Leibniz-Institute, the Australian Academy of Sciences, and the Belmont Forum.

Marcus Grubbs is a strategic planning and stakeholder engagement professional with experience working and consulting in the public, academic, and not-for-profit sectors. He is passionate about empowering customers and partners to fulfill their missions and achieve measurable environmental, financial, and social outcomes. He does this by creating strategies with stakeholders to align financial and human resources. Marcus holds a MURP from the University of Minnesota and is a member of the American Institute of Certified Planners. Marcus is currently the enterprise sustainability planner in the Department of Administration for the State of Minnesota, developing sustainability action plans for the operations of the State in the areas of energy, water, procurement, solid waste, fleet, and greenhouse gases and assisting agencies in developing their sustainability plans. Marcus was the coordinator for the New Agricultural Bioeconomy Project at the University of Minnesota from October 2014 to September 2016.

Alexander Heid is a designer, researcher, and maker thinking about future social-ecological systems. He is fascinated by the complexity and uncertainty inherent in social-ecological relationships and works to pick apart their components in order to reassemble them into communities ready to adapt to rapid environmental change. His research centers on the connections among people, knowledge, and place across multiple system scales. He has an MLA from the University of Minnesota; a graduate certificate in natural resource management from James Cook University, Australia; and a BA from Carleton College. He is cofounder and partner of Landbase Ventures, a mission-driven design research consultancy.

Moonseong Heo is professor of epidemiology and population health at the Albert Einstein College of Medicine. Before joining the faculty at Einstein, he worked as a biostatistician at two NIH-funded research centers: the New York Obesity Research Center, affiliated with the Columbia

University College of Physicians and Surgeons, and the Advanced Center for Interventions and Services Research, affiliated with the Cornell Institute of Geriatric Mood Disorders at the Weill Medical College of Cornell University. At Einstein, he serves as the senior biostatistician for the Einstein-Rockefeller-CUNY Center for AIDS Research and a consulting statistician for the Clinical and Translational Research Institute. In addition, he is actively involved in numerous NIH-funded studies, one of which is the school-based HealthCorps trial. Much of his work focuses on design of longitudinal studies, including clinical trials and observational studies, and epidemiologic studies of pediatric and adult obesity.

Charles Hoch taught urban planning at the University of Illinois at Chicago for thirty-six years. He studied how professional planners and others make spatial plans and the kind of work plans do. Hoch has focused on the history, theory, organization, and practice of urban planning. His publications include the planning theory book *Pragmatic Spatial Planning* (2019).

Ronda J. Jenson is an associate professor and the director of research at the Northern Arizona University Institute for Human Development. She directs research, evaluation, and technical assistance projects focused on improving access to education and community services and supports the implementation of research methodologies throughout the institute. Jenson was the principal investigator for two projects funded by the National Science Foundation focused on veterans. Her research areas are access to education and community services, implementation science, and data visualization for data-driven problem-solving. Jenson holds a PhD in special education (2004) with an emphasis on research and access from the University of Kansas.

Antonie J. Jetter is an associate professor of engineering and technology management at Portland State University. She teaches courses on new product development, entrepreneurship, and technology marketing to graduate students in engineering. Her research is focused on new product development, managerial cognition, and decision-making and leads to insights and methods for managing the early stages of product innovation. In her dissertation, Antonie pioneers the use of the fuzzy cognitive map as a product-planning tool. Ongoing research uses fuzzy cognitive maps to model community risk perceptions, drivers of technology acceptance among elderly patients and their caregivers, and differences in the mental models of product development engineers and product users. Antonie holds an MBA (1998) and a PhD in Technology and Innovation Management (2006) from RWTH Aachen University, Germany, and has seven years of industry experience in a large technology firm and a tech start-up.

Camille Jimenez is a research program manager in the Department of Epidemiology and Population Health at the Albert Einstein College of Medicine in the Division of Health Promotion and Nutrition Research. She has experience working as a community advocate and mental health worker. Her research interests take a multi-disciplinary approach toward understanding health disparities and the impact of the home environment and psychosocial stressors on disease and health. Currently, she oversees the development and implementation of this participatory research intervention in the eight New York City high schools, analyzes data, and generates both aggregate and individual-level feedback reports of students' self-reported health behaviors. Camille has an MPH in epidemiology from Columbia University.

Nicholas Jordan is a professor of agronomy and plant genetics at the University of Minnesota. His research program in agricultural ecology addresses use of biological diversity to improve on-farm productivity and resource efficiency, while reducing harmful environmental effects of agroecosystems. Research, instruction, and many service and outreach activities are integrated in this theme.

Len Kne is the associate director of U-Spatial at the University of Minnesota, where he leads day-to-day operations to advance spatial research. His work includes infrastructure support, education, and creative activities that support research across traditional disciplinary and college boundaries. Len has particular expertise in internet web mapping and database management. He has an MGIS degree from the University of Minnesota.

Christophe Le Page is a modelling scientist from the French Center for Agricultural Research for Development and a member of the Green Research Unit. With a background in fish population dynamics, he has progressively specialized in building agent-based models to simulate the interplay between ecological and social dynamics. In the last twenty years, he has co-designed and used simple simulation tools with local stakeholders in various contexts to share representations and to foster dialogue, promoting the ComMod companion modeling approach as a method to study the resilience of socioecological systems. He is participating in the development of the CORMAS platform, with a special interest on spatial aspects and computer-assisted role-playing games.

Ralph Levine is professor emeritus in the Departments of Psychology and Community Sustainability at Michigan State University. He uses system dynamics models as a tool for developing and evaluating problem-based programs and policies. He includes social processes in system dynamics models to help stakeholders gain better understanding of the causes and solutions to their problems. He has modeled burnout in the workplace, family dynamics, community response to plant closings, the team dynamics, and tobacco dependence and treatment in primary care. He helped develop epidemiological models that include social processes in the dynamics of the HIV/AIDS and the pneumonic plague. Recently, he modeled the community's responses to extreme heat events and changing children's dental habits and behaviors.

Arika Ligmann-Zielinska is an associate professor of geography and environmental science and policy at Michigan State University. She graduated from a joint doctoral program in geography at San Diego State University and University of California, Santa Barbara in 2008. Her research activities encompass spatial modeling approaches that capture the dynamic relationships within coupled human and natural systems, with a special focus on agent-based modeling. She has pioneered a spatiotemporal sensitivity analysis of model output, which partitions model outcome variability such that the underlying causes of the simulated macro phenomena can be identified and adequately addressed. Ligmann-Zielinska has published in GIS and modeling journals. She has also been a principal investigator on a number of research projects funded by federal and local agencies.

Jean Lim is the research scientist at HealthCorps, where she oversees nationwide program evaluation and manages special research projects. She has served HealthCorps for the past three years and has been promoted from data clerk to research assistant to her current position while working directly under the programs director. She graduated from the University of Pennsylvania with a BA in biology in 2014.

Saweda Liverpool-Tasie is an assistant professor in the Department of Agricultural, Food, and Resource Economics at Michigan State University. Her research focusses on emergent issues related to smallholder productivity and welfare within rapidly changing environments with often poorly functioning markets. Her work has looked at issues of poverty dynamics, technology adoption, and food security in Sub-Saharan Africa. In addition to evaluating the heterogeneous effects of poverty reduction strategies on rural household behavior and livelihood, she has a keen interest in understanding input use and input markets as well as evaluating input policies. She was a Norman Borlaug Fellow in 2007 and has a PhD in agricultural economics from the University of Illinois, Urbana-Champaign.

David W. Lounsbury is an assistant professor of epidemiology and population health at the Albert Einstein College of Medicine of Yeshiva University. A community psychologist (PhD, Michigan State University, 2002) and psycho-oncologist (post-doctoral fellow, Memorial Sloan-Kettering Cancer Center, 2005), his academic work is health services research in prevention and control of chronic illnesses. He applies ecologically grounded social science methodologies, such as participatory action research and system dynamics modeling, to explore and assess complex, multi-level problems in primary care and public health. Current modeling projects address breast cancer survivorship; school-based wellness programming; HIV care for women of color; tobacco dependence and treatment in primary care; and cancer prevention health literacy in low- and middle-income countries (Nigeria). He currently serves as co-chair of the System Dynamics Society's Psychology Special Interest group and the Society for Community Research and Action's Community Health Interest group.

Leilah Lyons holds a dual appointment as an associate research professor of computer science and the learning sciences at the University of Illinois at Chicago and as the director of Digital Learning Research at the New York Hall of Science, a children's science museum. Lyons conducts research at the intersection of human-computer interaction and the learning sciences, partnering with domain specialists and informal educators to discover how new human-computer interaction techniques can be exploited to gently introduce learners to otherwise challenging STEM topics. Much of her work involves the design and study of digital museum exhibits specialized in studying collaborative user interfaces and how interaction design can support novices as they learn from complex systems simulations. Lyons earned her PhD in computer science at the University of Michigan and is a graduate of the University of Michigan Museum Studies Program.

Danielle R. Madden, PhD, is an assistant research professor in the School of Social Work at the University of Southern California. Madden has experience measuring drinking events in natural settings and is currently studying potential leverage points amenable to prevention interventions in drinking events.

Sandy Marquart-Pyatt is an associate professor of sociology and environmental science and policy at Michigan State University. Her research examines interrelations among environmental issues, outlooks and concerns, and sustainability and includes both macro-comparative and micro-level work. Marquart-Pyatt is also a quantitative modeler with expertise in techniques including structural equation modeling and hierarchical linear modeling. Marquart-Pyatt helped develop the new Environmental Science and Policy Program on Modeling Environmental and Social Systems (MESS). The MESS certificate program introduces students to cutting-edge modeling methodologies to build a thorough foundation of the theory of models and complex systems, and provide hands-on experience with model design, development, and evaluation geared toward specific research topics. In addition to regularly teaching graduate quantitative modeling courses at MSU, she also teaches at the InterUniversity Consortium for Political and Social Research's (ICPSR) Summer Program in Quantitative Methods at the University of Michigan.

Sarah N. Martin is a research program manager in the Department of Epidemiology and Population Health at the Albert Einstein College of Medicine in the Division of Health Promotion and Nutrition Research. She earned a BS in biomedical engineering from the University of Southern California and an MPH in community and international health from New York University. Sarah has extensive experience managing both clinical research for the pharmaceutical industry as well as academic research focusing on health behavior and decision-making. Currently, she oversees monitoring and evaluation activities for a health intervention in over twenty low-income high schools across the United States.

Dean Massey is a research specialist with the Institute for Environmental Science and Policy at the University of Illinois at Chicago (UIC). In this position, he has worked on projects developing agent-based models of integrated land-use and hydrologic processes, transportation, and collective decision-making. He obtained a MUPP at UIC. Before transitioning to urban planning and academia, he worked for the state legislature of Connecticut.

Alexander Metzger earned his PhD in environmental science at the University of Massachusetts, Boston as part of the National Science Foundation Integrated Graduate Education and Research Traineeship. His interests lie in the resilience of social-ecological systems and using dynamics system models and collaborative processes to better inform decision-making. His research focused on creating tools and techniques for flood managers in Boston, Massachusetts to better inform extreme flood event response and climate-change adaptation. This research involved using participatory fuzzy cognitive mapping to encourage shared learning and collaboration in flood management decision-making. He also contributed to a stakeholder-led integrated landscape management project for the Global Resilience Challenge, funded by USAID, the

Rockefeller Institute, and the Swedish International Development Cooperation Agency. His goal is to develop science-driven, participatory approaches that are transferrable to challenges in diverse social-ecological systems.

Daniel Milz holds a dual appointment as an assistant professor in the Department of Urban and Regional Planning and in the Matsunaga Institute for Peace and Conflict Resolution at the University of Hawai'i at Mānoa. He completed his doctoral research in urban planning and policy at the University of Illinois at Chicago in 2015. Milz's research focuses on the judgments that inform collaborative environmental planning. He uses methods adapted from the learning sciences to tease apart the judgments groups make as they compose plans for common pool resources, like water resource systems. He draws practical examples from extended case studies to show planners how to improve and enhance the plan-making judgments of groups and individuals in order to overcome obstacles like cognitive biases, spatial scale mismatches, and political conflict. Milz teaches courses in environmental planning, facilitation, community engagement, land use planning, negotiation and dispute resolution, and environmental equity.

David Mulla is a professor of soil, water and climate at the University of Minnesota. His research emphasizes the measurement, modeling, and management of uncertainty and risk for non-point source pollution of surface and groundwater; the characterization and estimation of field-scale variability for precision farming; the evaluation of alternative farm management strategies for improved soil quality and sustainability; and evaluation of policies for soil and water resources.

Kelly Nimmer is currently the program director of HealthCorps' Education Programs and the chair of the Partnership for a Healthy Ventura County. Kelly has a strong background in managing public health programs and educational interventions collaboratively across sectors. She obtained an MPH from the University of Southern California. Previously, she was the Ventura County based Program Coordinator for the California Department of Public Health's Training and Resource Center supporting five public health departments with their nutrition education obesity prevention programs. Kelly also has worked and lived abroad in South America and India, where she coordinated Operation Smile India's surgical quality assurance and nutrition programs. Kelly is a passionate advocate for engaging communities and young people in improving health outcomes and creating healthier ecosystems.

Elpiniki Papageorgiou is an associate professor at the Department of Electrical Engineering, University of Thessaly, Larisa, Hellas. Her main expertise in the development of novel algorithms and cognitive models for intelligent decision support systems focused on fuzzy cognitive maps. She also specializes in developing and applying artificial intelligent models and algorithms to decision support problems for modeling, prediction, strategic decisions, scenario analysis, and data mining, and solving important existing and/or emerging problems arising in engineering, business, medicine, agriculture, and environment. Papageorgiou has worked for over sixteen years as principal investigator, project manager, and senior researcher in several European Union–funded and national research projects; authored than 202 publications in journals, conference papers, and book chapters; and is the editor of *"Fuzzy Cognitive Maps for Applied Sciences and Engineering: From Fundamentals to Extensions and Learning Algorithms.* Papageorgiou was also the main organizer of special sessions and workshops on fuzzy cognitive mapping; organizer of the First Summer School for Fuzzy Cognitive Maps in July 2016 in Volos, Greece; and guest editor for the special issue on fuzzy cognitive maps in *Applied Soft Computing.* Her research interests include intelligent systems, fuzzy cognitive maps, soft computing methods, decision support systems, cognitive systems, data mining, and machine learning.

Kevin M. Passino, PhD, is a professor in the Department of Electrical and Computer Engineering at the Ohio State University. Passino's current research focuses on dynamical modeling of complex human systems.

Rajiv Paudel is a PhD student in geography and the Environmental Science and Policy Program (ESPP) at Michigan State University. He finished his masters' degrees from the UK in ecology/environment management and in geographical information systems (GIS). He has worked for a number of years in Nepal using his expertise in GIS to analyze issues in species conservation, environmental protection, and rural food security. His research interests are in GIS and modeling, rural food security, and biodiversity conservation. He is currently an ESPP fellow at MSU working with Ligmann-Zielinska on the NSF-funded research "Participatory Ensemble Modeling to Study the Multiscale Social and Behavioral Dynamics of Food Security in Dryland West Africa."

Arthur Perrotton is a system scientist from the French Center for Agricultural Research for Development and a member of the AGIRs research unit. For the past five years, he has studied the relationships between conservation areas and their peripheries in Zimbabwe. He recently joined the ComMod companion modeling group and implemented the ComMod principles in a dissertation that studies and simulates cattle-herding strategies at the edge of a protected area in Zimbabwe. Interdisciplinarity is at the heart of his approach, which brings together anthropology, political ecology, environmental sciences, and agent-based modeling.

Alexis N. Petri is an associate research professor at the University of Missouri-Kansas City College of Arts and Sciences, Department of Psychology, where she directs the Propel Program and researches access to higher education. Throughout her career, she has taken leadership roles in university-wide, high-impact learning programs and the campus-community partnerships that are their foundation. Alexis is principal investigator on a U.S. Department of Education grant to include college students with intellectual disabilities at the university. She leads the writing of UMKC's Higher Learning Commission reaffirmation of accreditation assurance argument. She has an EdD in higher education administration and public policy and a BA and MA in English. Her research areas are access to postsecondary education, urban education, service learning, data visualization, and cities.

Joshua Radinsky is an associate professor of curriculum studies and the learning sciences at the University of Illinois at Chicago. His research applies sociocultural frameworks to the study of teaching and learning with data visualizations, with a focus on historical inquiry, spatial reasoning, and narrations of data. His work includes studies of teaching and learning with geographic information systems, in middle school, high school, and college classrooms; studies of policymakers and stakeholders engaging in planning and policy debates with geospatial data; design-based research; and professional development focused on data visualization tools for teaching and learning.

Robert B. Richardson is an ecological economist and professor in the Department of Community Sustainability at Michigan State University. His research program focuses primarily on sustainable development and he uses a variety of methods from the behavioral and social sciences to study decision-making related to the use of natural resources and the protection of ecosystem services. His research has included assessments of the role of natural resources in poverty alleviation and food security, agricultural-environmental linkages, vulnerability to climate change, and tradeoffs in decision making about environmental management.

Louie Rivers III is an assistant professor at North Carolina State University in the Department of Forestry and Environmental Resources. His research focuses on the examination of risk and judgment and decision processes in minority and marginalized communities, particularly in regard to the natural environment. Methodologically, he is interested in qualitative modeling techniques. Specifically, his work examines the refinement and advancement of mental modeling (a qualitative modeling technique developed in the cognitive sciences) to include an explicit focus on individual decision-making processes. He has done past mental model work in the context of criminal opportunity structures in carbon markets and the global carbon market, examining climate induced migration and law enforcement interventions to counter the effects of open-air drug markets.

Bryan C. Runck is a geocomputing scientist in the GEMS Agroinformatics Initiative at the University of Minnesota. His work unpacks socio-environmental systems using environmental and agronomic modeling in geographic information systems combined with stakeholder engagement process development. In 2014, he received an MS in applied plant science from the Department of Agronomy and Plant Genetics at the University of Minnesota, and he holds a PhD in geography from the University of Minnesota.

Richard Salter is a professor of computer science at Oberlin College. During the past ten years, his research has focused on the development of Nova and the use of modeling software to support STEM pedagogy. His recent work has involved researching new ways advances in computer technology can be used across disciplines, particularly finding innovative uses for the extraordinary (by yesterday's standards) power of even the most common of today's laptop computers. He has over thirty years of experience as a researcher in programming languages, which includes creating high-impact, interactive software for use both as research tools and in the classroom. Among the applications he has built are visual tools used for (1) teaching and demonstrating the alignment algorithms used in DNA sequencing, (2) creating multilevel digital circuits, and (3) providing an environment for solving classical cryptographic problems. He has served as PI on grants totaling over $2 million from the National Science Foundation, Office of Naval Research, and other funding agencies and has published over forty peer-reviewed journal and conference papers in addition to the software he has developed. During a single sabbatical year at the MITRE Corporation, the applications he developed were honored with Director's Distinguished Accomplishment and Special Recognition awards.

Udita Sanga is pursuing a PhD in environment science and policy in the Department of Community Sustainability at Michigan State University. She has an MA in ecology from Utah State University and a BSE in biotechnology from the Birla Institute of Technology in Mesra, India. Currently, Udita is working with Schmitt Olabisi on the NSF-funded project "Participatory Ensemble Modeling to Study the Multiscale Social and Behavioral Dynamics of Food Security in Dryland West Africa." Her research interests are in understanding the differential vulnerability and capacity of rural farmers to adapt to climatic shocks and their mental models of climatic risk perception and decision making. She is interested in using system dynamics and agent-based modeling approaches to explore the social, environmental, economic, and behavioral and cognitive aspects of the response of farmers to climate change.

Carissa Schively Slotterback is an associate professor of urban and regional planning at the University of Minnesota and teaches courses in environmental planning, public engagement, and sustainability planning. Her research focuses on stakeholder involvement and decision-making related to environmental, land-use, and transportation planning. She has a particular interest in how stakeholders perceive impacts and use information to make decisions, focusing on impact assessment, collaborative decision-making, and sustainability planning approaches. She also serves as Director of Research Engagement in the Office of the Vice President for Research.

Laura Schmitt Olabisi is an assistant professor at Michigan State University, jointly appointed in the Environmental Science and Policy Program and the Department of Community Sustainability. She uses system dynamics modeling and scenario visioning to investigate the future of complex socioecological systems, often working directly with stakeholders by applying participatory research methods. Schmitt Olabisi's research addresses soil erosion, climate change, water sustainability, energy use, sustainable agriculture, and food security. She has led modeling and scenario exercises with stakeholders in the United States, the Philippines, Nigeria, Zambia, Malawi, and Burkina Faso, and has published her work in *Environmental Science & Technology*, *Ecology and Society*, and *Society & Natural Resources*, among other outlets. Schmitt Olabisi holds a BS in environmental science from Brown University and a PhD in systems ecology from the State University of New York College of Environmental Science and Forestry.

Joey T. R. Shelley earned a doctoral degree in computer science from the University of Illinois at Chicago, focusing on human-computer interaction research centered on the emerging area of compromise. Shelley now works as the lead user experience researcher for Common Sensing, a medical device seeking to improve quality of life for individuals who use disposable pen injectors.

Bernard C. Patten is Emeritus Regents' Professor of Ecology at the University of Georgia. He is a systems ecologist and ecological modeler interested in the application of mathematical system theory to ecosystems. He and his colleagues have formulated a system theory of environment called "environ" theory and analysis that pioneers the use of network mathematics to represent and analyze ecosystem networks such as food webs and biogeochemical cycles. His research publications include almost two hundred papers on a variety of ecological topics spanning marine, freshwater and wetland ecosystems. From 1975 to 1986, Patten was principal investigator of an National Science Foundation–sponsored ecosystem study of Georgia's Okefenokee Swamp. His edited works include the four-volume book series Systems Analysis and Simulation in Ecology (1972–1976).

David Pitt is a professor of landscape architecture at the University of Minnesota. With several University of Minnesota colleagues, Pitt is developing a systemic approach to GeoDesign, which integrates spatiotemporal modeling of landscape performance and facilitates its application to collaborative design of multifunctional landscapes in the Minnesota River valley. His work on the GeoDesign decision lab examines how the presentation of information, group dynamics, and social and individual learning affect outcomes of landscape planning decision-making.

Naomi Sakana is an agriculture specialist with international research interests spanning the rural development nexus. Her research seeks to understand the paradox of low adoption of sustainable agricultural technologies and practices and what can be done to nudge adoption and hence to increase agricultural productivity, as well as food security and nutrition in sub-Saharan Africa. Her interests are related to farming systems, seed systems, and evaluating technologies to inform agricultural development policies. She has held previous positions with the World Bank Group, the Center for International Forestry Research, and the International Food Policy and Research Institute.

Marjan van den Belt is an ecological economist, holding a PhD in marine estuarine environmental science from the University of Maryland and an MBE from Erasmus University in Rotterdam, Netherlands. She is the convenor of ReGenSEA, a collaborative to foster the co-creation of a regenerative seaweed sector. She is also a strategic partner with Terra Moana Ltd. Previously, she was the assistant vice chancellor (sustainability) at Victoria University of Wellington, New Zealand. Upon arrival in New Zealand, she was associate professor and director of Ecological Economics Research New Zealand at Massey University, where she was a science leader on nationally funded programs, using stakeholder participatory processes guided by model building and scenario development, often applying an ecosystem services approach. She is the author of *Mediated Modeling: A System Dynamics Approach to Environmental Consensus Building*, published in 2004. Current appointments include a membership of the New Zealand Tax Working Group and the Sustainable Business Council Advisory Board. She arrived in New Zealand in 2009 from Vermont, where she ran an independent consulting business to bring together diverse stakeholders for systemic solutions. During this time, she also taught at the University of Vermont and cofounded a cohousing ecovillage (Champlain Valley Cohousing). In the 1990s, she spent five years in Stockholm, Sweden, working on waste reduction and systemic challenges with businesses and NGOs. She is native to the Netherlands.

Hugo J. Gonzalez Villasanti, PhD, is a postdoctoral researcher at the Crane Center for Early Childhood Research and Policy at the College of Education and Human Ecology at the Ohio State University.

Kurt B. Waldman is an assistant professor in the Department of Geography at Indiana University. His research applies behavioral economics and decision science to socio-environmental problems. His areas of interest include perceptions, judgment and decision-making related to environmental change, and agricultural sustainability. Kurt earned an MS in applied economics from Cornell University and a PhD in food and agricultural policy from Michigan State University.

Stuart J. Whipple is an adjunct assistant professor at the University of Georgia. He is a systems ecologist and ecological modeler. He has created models of aquatic ecosystems of Georgia's Okefenokee Swamp, the pelagic zone of Lake Ontario, Canada, and the northwest Atlantic continental shelf fish community. He was a member of a National Science Foundation Biocomplexity grant to Skidaway Institute of Oceanography from 2001 to 2008, where he co-developed a planktonic ecosystem model of a fjord mesocosm system in Norway. He was a co-principal investigator on a United States Department of Energy Biotechnological Investigations Ocean Margin Program grant investigating marine nitrogen and carbon biogeochemistry using simulation modeling. He co-developed methodology to extend network environ analysis to allow for the comparative analysis of time-series of ecosystem flow-storage models. He has co-designed and taught a marine ecosystem modeling class and a doctoral class in ecological thought past to present using literature review at the University of Georgia.

Peter Wiringa is a student in the MGIS program at the University of Minnesota, where he works as a graduate research assistant for U-Spatial. Before entering the program, he worked as an IT professional in the public sector for over a decade, working in web development, offering technology training, providing application support, and more. He holds a BA in mathematics from Macalester College and received his MGIS in 2018.

Alexa L. Wood is a PhD candidate in forestry and environmental resources at North Carolina State University. Her research focuses on how women subsistence farmers in West Africa perceive climate change and its impacts on their roles in food provisioning. This work is within her broader interests of food security, environmental justice, and environmental feminism. At present, she is under the supervision of Louie Rivers III on the National Science Foundation–-funded research "Participatory Ensemble Modeling to Study the Multiscale Social and Behavioral Dynamics of Food Security in Dryland West Africa."

Judith Wylie-Rosett is professor and division head for health promotion and nutrition research in the Department of Epidemiology at the Albert Einstein College of Medicine where she holds the Atran Foundation Chair in Social Medicine. Wylie-Rosett is associate editor of the journal *Diabetes Care* and serves on the board for the *Journal of the Academy of Nutrition and Dietetics*. Her research focuses on preventing obesity and reducing associated cardio-metabolic risks. She has been an investigator in multi-center trials, including the Diabetes Control and Complications Trial, the Women's Health Initiative, and the Diabetes Prevention Program. Her current investigator-initiated research includes a family-based weight control trial, a diabetes prevention trial for Chinese immigrants, and a school-based wellness program to facilitate achieving dietary guidelines. She has over two hundred peer-reviewed publications.

Yiqun Xie is a PhD candidate in the Department of Computer Science and Engineering at the University of Minnesota. His research focuses on geospatial data science, including spatial optimization, spatial pattern mining, and object detection using remote sensing data. Agricultural landscape design is an important application domain of his spatial optimization work. Unlike traditional optimization, his work enforces spatial contiguity constraints during optimization for practicality. Specifically, each patch of land use or land cover in a solution must satisfy a minimum area constraint to allow efficient operations of large farm equipment. The problem has been proved to be computationally challenging. The goal of his research is to design efficient algorithms to approach optimal land allocation schemes on the Pareto frontier.

Moira Zellner joined the Department of Urban Planning and Policy and the Institute for Environmental Science and Policy at the University of Illinois at Chicago (UIC) after pursuing graduate studies in planning and complex systems at the University of Michigan. Before becoming an academic, Zellner worked as a professional environmental consultant in Argentina and the United States. At UIC, Zellner has served as investigator in interdisciplinary projects studying how specific policy, technological, and behavioral changes can effectively address a range of complex environmental problems where interaction effects make responsibilities and burdens unclear. Her research also examines the value of complexity-based modeling for participatory policy exploration and social learning with stakeholders and policy makers. Zellner teaches a variety of classes and workshops on complexity-based modeling of socioecological systems for both scientists and decision-makers.

Index